FUNDAMENTALISM

FUNDAMENTALISM

by
James Barr

THE WESTMINSTER PRESS
Philadelphia

© James Barr 1977, 1978

Published by The Westminster Press ®
Philadelphia, Pennsylvania

PRINTED IN THE UNITED STATES OF AMERICA

9 8 7 6 5 4 3 2 1

Library of Congress Cataloging in Publication Data

Barr, James.
    Fundamentalism.

    Bibliography: p.
    Includes indexes.
    1. Fundamentalism — Controversial literature.
I. Title.
BT82.2.B37   230   77-14512
ISBN 0-664-24191-3

For Jane

Contents

Foreword to the American Edition   iii

Preface   ix

1 What is Fundamentalism?   1

2 The Religious Basis of Fundamentalism   11

3 The Bible – First Stage   40
  1. Being literal   40
  2. Harmonization   55
  3. How do we know that the Bible is inerrant?   72
  4. Maximal conservatism   85

4 Fundamentalism and Society   90
  1. Science and secularism   90
  2. 'Culture fundamentalism'   103
  3. Roman Catholicism   105
  4. Social and political ethics   108
  5. The Jews and Zionism   118

5 Conservative Biblical Scholarship   120
  1. General   120
  2. Study in the environing fields   128
  3. Some issues in biblical scholarship   132
  4. The presupposition question   145
  5. The influence of W. F. Albright and others   150
  6. Conclusion   152

6 Fundamentalism and Theology   160

7 Variations and Conflicts   187
  1. Calvinism and Arminianism   188
  2. Millennialism   190
  3. Pentecostalism and the like   207
  4. Modern translations of the Bible   209

5. Neo-orthodoxy, biblical theology and the new   213
   conservatives

8 Miracles and the Supernatural   234

9 Doctrine; Philosophy; Textual Variation   260
   1. Doctrine   260
   2. Philosophy   270
   3. Textual variation   279
   4. Jewish conservatism   284
   5. Verbal inspiration   286
   6. Semantics   299
   7. Conclusion   302

10 Mainly Personal Attitudes   304
   1. Conservative literature again   304
   2. Objectivity   310
   3. People and attitudes   317
   4. Ecumenicity   328
   5. The conservatism of moderates   331

11 Conclusion   338

   Notes   345

   Bibliography   363

   Index of Subjects   369

   Index of Names   375

   Index of Biblical References   379

Foreword
to the American Edition

It is a great pleasure to contribute an additional foreword to the American edition. Though I thought it easier to write the book in British terms in the first place and with British vocabulary, in my thinking I referred constantly to the American scene. I could hardly fail to do so, in view of my extensive personal experience of teaching biblical and theological subjects in North America, first in Canada (1953-5), then for four years at Princeton Theological Seminary (1961-5), plus periods as visiting professor at Princeton University (1962-3), at Union Theological Seminary, New York (1963), and most recently at the University of Chicago (1975), to which must be added occasional lecturing in a wide variety of other centres. One milestone in the development of my own thinking was the series of Currie Lectures I gave at the Presbyterian Theological Seminary in Austin, Texas, in 1964, later published as *Old and New in Interpretation* (New York: Harper & Row, 1966). In it (pp. 201-6) I included a short note in which I began to revise the diagnosis of fundamentalism that had been customary during the "biblical theology" movement of the post-war decades. This note was widely felt to be rather favourable towards fundamentalism. It formed the embryonic stage of the much more elaborate study published in this book.

Fundamentalism has been a transatlantic common enterprise; it is in many ways a striking common achievement of the Anglo-Saxon peoples, and builds upon their cultural and philosophical heritage. The greatest creativity has been on the American side. In the eighteenth century the names of the great revivalists came from both sides of the Atlantic: Wesley, Whitefield, Jonathan Edwards. But from the nineteenth century onwards the major names were American: Finney,

Torrey, Moody, Barnhouse, Billy Graham. From the United States came also the most powerful systematic statement of a rigid conservatism, which the intellectual leadership of fundamentalism adopted: the Princeton theology of the Hodges and Warfield. But the Princeton theologians drew their philosophical position largely from British antecedents: the Scottish philosophy of common sense influenced them notably. And Darby, who initiated the main stream of dispensational and premillennial interpretation of the Bible, which was to become very powerful in America as in Britain, was from Ireland. Interaction between the two sides of the Atlantic was always intense.

One main difference may be mentioned. In the United States, fundamentalism, and theological conservatism generally, has been much more a denominational matter than in Great Britain. As I explain in the book, no major denomination in Britain is fundamentalist, and fundamentalism has taken a nondenominational shape, working through informal and inter-denominational organizations, and yet nevertheless strongly institutionalized. Thus fundamentalism has not been the occasion of major denominational splits in Britain. British churches are much less confessional than American Protestant churches commonly are: their functioning is much less tied to written confessional standards. I have made this difference plain in the book, but it deserves to be re-emphasized here.

American Christianity, creative in the origins of fundamentalism, may also be creative in the discovery of ways for escaping from it. If I had been writing primarily for the American public, I would have made more reference to the extensive stirrings among evangelicals in the last decade or so, the remarkable change in their social outlooks and their active readiness to debate the problems of their position. Among recent American writings, I have learned much from Richard Quebedeaux (most recently his report, "The Evangelicals: New Trends and New Tensions," *Christianity and Crisis,* September 20, 1976, pp. 197-201). A work indicating an openness to new trends among evangelicals is the attractive *Confessions of a Conservative Evangelical* by Jack Rogers (Philadelphia: The Westminster Press, 1974); and an interesting expression of a search for an evangelical tradition different from the dominant fundamentalist one is the work of Donald W. Dayton, *Discovering an Evangelical Heritage*

(New York: Harper & Row, 1976), along with various articles. See also the valuable group of articles in *Union Seminary
Quarterly Review* 32:2 (Winter, 1977), especially that by
Dayton on social and political conservatism and that by Shep-
pard on biblical hermeneutics. Considerable freshness of
approach among evangelicals can be seen in Great Britain
also; cf. the documents of a recent congress at Nottingham
(*The Nottingham Statement;* London: Falcon Books, 1977).
But the American discussion is much more lively. In my
research for the present book I noted several times how American writers, even those holding very conservative positions,
could yet be free and vocal in their criticism of the prevailing
conservative tradition in a way little found in Britain. I remarked this especially of E. J. Carnell; but there are many
other instances that I did not cite, such as D. A. Hubbard's
article on "the Pentateuch" in *The New Bible Dictionary*
(pp. 957-64). If a generalization may be risked, it seems to
me that the intensity and the public character of the disagreement between complete fundamentalists and moderates in the
United States has been helpful in forcing a clearer statement
of the issues. In Britain the more moderate, while claiming
credit for difference from a completely fundamentalist line,
often continue their support to fundamentalist organizations,
write in terms that can be interpreted in a fundamentalist
sense, and refrain from public statements that might be dis-
turbing to fundamentalists.

In any case these shifts in evangelicalism and these upsurges
of new questioning do not alter the analysis of fundamentalism
which I present; on the contrary, they fit in excellently with it.
My thesis throughout is that evangelicalism is not necessarily
fundamentalism; rather, fundamentalism distorts and betrays
the basic true religious concerns of evangelical Christianity,
and its does this especially through its intellectual apologetic.
Evangelicals must resist the insistence that no one is truly
evangelical unless he accepts the fundamentalist position. It is
a matter for rejoicing that more and more evangelicals are
dissociating themselves from the fundamentalist tradition.

There is, however, good reason for caution. The recent
shifts of opinion have often been concerned with two things.
One is personal life-style: where the older evangelical forbade
drinking and dancing, the new-style sophisticated evangelical
discusses the relative merits of dry and medium sherry, before

dining and going to the theatre. Secondly, the strong political conservatism of the older fundamentalist movement is widely being replaced by a commitment to politics and social action; see, for example, the Chicago Declaration of 1973 and the style of a new periodical such as *Sojourners*. Both of these are remarkable changes of emphasis, and within limits they are welcome. But they may be evidence that evangelicalism is particularly susceptible to social pressures, whether in one direction or in the other. A single social movement such as modern feminism, once it attained to serious influence, seems to have done more to alter conservative evangelicalism than all the work of scholars and theologians. But my analysis has emphasized that neither personal life-style nor social conservatism forms the essence of fundamentalism. Both of these may alter without an abandonment of the basic structure of fundamentalist belief. The deeper questions are the relation of the evangelical to non-evangelical Christians, and his relation to non-conservative biblical scholarship. Fundamentalism has not been really abandoned until clear new positions are taken up on these two questions.

The fact that many evangelicals are moving towards a new and more open position does not in itself alter the fact or the character of fundamentalism. Fundamentalism has always been quick and ready to repudiate those evangelicals who do not hold to a fully conservative line. There is no reason to doubt that this may happen again. It is not surprising that, in a time of unusual ferment and fresh openness among evangelicals, there should appear a book like Harold Lindsell's *The Battle for the Bible* (Grand Rapids: Zondervan, 1976), insisting on a hard position of total inerrancy of the Bible. As some people may move away from the traditional fundamentalist position, others will begin to say that these people are no longer "sound," and a more strictly fundamentalist society will begin to close its ranks behind them. There is thus no reason to suppose that the active change and modernization of evangelical thinking will alter the character of fundamentalism.

This is reinforced by another question: Has evangelicalism succeeded in developing a conceptual framework recognizable, distinct from the fundamentalist one? If evangelicals, in departing from a strict fundamentalist position, continue to take that position as the base line for their thinking, and fail to construct a theology governed on quite other principles, fundamentalism will continue to be the governing force in their minds. Some of the disputes between total inerrancy and almost total inerrancy seem to be no more than minor territorial disputes within the total fundamentalist conceptuality, which is still presupposed by both parties (cf. Stephen T. Davis, *The Debate About the Bible;* Philadelphia: The Westminster Press, 1977). It is not clear that modernized and up-dated evangelicalism has yet attained to any conceptual framework that is intrinsically different from the fundamentalist one, or that it has even tried. Until this is done, the tried, stable, and powerful fundamentalist ideology will always be likely to regain the upper hand, and the very variety and mobility of newer evangelicalism will make solid conservatism seem a safer haven.

Nevertheless the vitality of the American debate is a sign of hope, and I shall be happy if this book contributes something to the discussion. Our support and understanding are due for all those who, emerging from a background in fundamentalism and conservatism, are seeking to relate themselves in a new way to the main stream of church life, of theology, and of biblical study.

J.B.

Oxford
August 1977

Preface

No more need be said in preface than that this is the fruit of a
long-lasting attempt to analyse and understand a problem that is
familiar to anyone who has taught a subject like Old Testament in a
variety of theological faculties. In part it is a continuation of
reflections mentioned in my earlier books. I have read preparatory
papers in a number of places and have benefited from the ensuing
discussion: I think especially of occasions in the University of Hull
and in Knox College, University of Otago, New Zealand. The Revd
Arthur Nelson helped me with discussion and with the loan of a
book. I am grateful to SCM Press, which obtained for me a great
deal of material for my research, without which it would scarcely
have been possible to complete the work.

My dear wife has worked with me through all the later stages of
preparation of the material and our many conversations about the
subject have been a source of much happiness.

J.B.

1 · What is Fundamentalism?

Is there really such a thing as fundamentalism, and what exactly is it? Readers like to begin with a clear and simple definition of the subject, but such a clear and simple definition cannot always be given. Complex social and religious movements cannot be defined in a few words: what has to be offered is not a definition, but an extended description. Thus the answer to our question, 'What is fundamentalism?', will not be found on this page or on any other one page of this book; rather, it will be provided by the book as a whole. The customary 'plain man's' definition, that a fundamentalist is a person who takes the Bible literally, is far from exact, as we shall soon see. Rather than begin from a clear definition and use it as a basis for argument, we have to begin with a rather vague recognition of something and then work slowly towards an understanding of what that something is.

The recognition from which we begin is this: there is something which many or most Christians perceive as or classify as fundamentalism. It is a group of characteristics which most Christians do not approve of or like, but which they feel to be shared in considerable measure by those whom they class together as fundamentalists. The most pronounced characteristics are the following:

(a) a very strong emphasis on the inerrancy of the Bible, the absence from it of any sort of error;

(b) a strong hostility to modern theology and to the methods, results and implications of modern critical study of the Bible;

(c) an assurance that those who do not share their religious viewpoint are not really 'true Christians' at all.

These are not all the characteristics that attach to the generally-held picture of the fundamentalist, and even these will require to be expanded and developed before we can say that they have been rightly stated; but at least they will serve to give a start to our discussion.

Now fundamentalism is a bad word: the people to whom it is applied do not like to be so called. It is often felt to be a hostile and opprobrious term, suggesting narrowness, bigotry, obscurantism and sectarianism. The people whom others call fundamentalists would generally wish to be known by another term altogether. To talk about fundamentalism therefore is not the same as discussing an opinion under the term by which its own advocates would choose to express it: it involves discussing underlying attitudes and our attitude to these attitudes.

A brief historical note: the word fundamentalism appears to have been derived from a series of booklets entitled *The Fundamentals*, which were published in America during 1910–15. In them the term 'the fundamentals' was used for elements of traditional doctrine – the inspiration and authority of scripture, the deity of Jesus Christ, the virgin birth and others – which are dear also to the fundamentalist of today. Sometimes it is suggested that the people called fundamentalists today should not be so called because their position is much broader, more sophisticated and more learned, less crude and combative, than that of the writers of *The Fundamentals* and their immediate successors. A reading of the literature must leave this claim unconceded: modern fundamentalism in many respects falls below the level of *The Fundamentals*, rather than rising above it. In any case, the teaching of *The Fundamentals* comes quite close to what is beloved and supported by the fundamentalist of today. But the historical origin of our term is not very important for the understanding of its usage in the present day.

By what term would 'fundamentalists' prefer to be called? The term favoured at present, at least in Great Britain, is 'conservative evangelical'. Indeed, some say that the word 'conservative' is strictly unnecessary, and that one cannot be a consistent evangelical without also being conservative; however, for the sake of clarity they are willing to use the fuller term 'conservative evangelical'. How far should people in their speech, and we in writing this book, accept this shift of terminology?

That 'conservative evangelical' is a non-opprobrious term is of course an advantage for polite discussion; but this does not mean that it is entirely adequate for our purpose. First, it has remained a somewhat technical and esoteric designation, and has scarcely established itself in general usage. We are talking about a problem which is felt by almost all persons who are at all, even marginally, concerned with religion; and of such persons there are fifty who know and use the term 'fundamentalism' for every one who has any idea what is meant by 'conservative evangelicalism'. Perhaps it would be agreeable if everyone suddenly stopped speaking about 'fundamentalism' and began to say 'conservative evangelicalism' instead, but it would be foolish to suppose that this is likely to happen except among a few. The fact is that 'fundamentalism' is the normal designation in common English for the phenomenon which we propose to discuss. In any case, is 'fundamentalist' really more pejorative than 'conservative'? Is it not even more unfitting to imply that conservatism is the final criterion of truth?

Secondly, and more important, 'fundamentalism' and 'conservative evangelicalism' seem not to say the same thing: they differ not only in that one of them has a pejorative connotation lacking to the other, but also in that their frames of reference are different. 'Fundamentalist' may seem opprobrious, but at least it also states basic personal and existential attitudes. 'Conservative evangelical' is a classification much more related to the politics of church parties, as when one says, for instance, 'the conservative evangelicals in the Church of England'. This identifies one part functioning among a number of other parts; it does not of itself identify a mental and theological make-up of highly distinctive type. The people who are fundamentalists are commonly also conservative evangelicals; but this does not mean that the two designations specify exactly the same features. In this sense the preference for a term like 'conservative evangelical' may well be an evasion of the issue. The question simply remains: how far do those who, within one frame of reference, are conservative evangelicals, and who prefer to be so termed, in fact show the characteristics which within another frame of reference are commonly taken to constitute fundamentalism?

For, thirdly, while the word 'fundamentalist' does carry the suggestion of narrowness, bigotry, obscurantism and sectarianism, it remains an open question whether this suggestion, though unpleasant, is not a true and just one. The dislike for the term 'fundamentalist' is itself a sign that people are sensitive to these suggestions, and when they prefer another term like 'conservative evangelical' they are making something of an effort to project a more favourable image. The image that comes through, however, is still very much the unwanted 'fundamentalist' image. The conservative evangelical argues that this is unjust and unfair, and he may be right. We on the other hand are entitled to ask whether the ideas and practice of many conservative evangelicals are in fact so different from those suggested by the word 'fundamentalism'. The question is not whether they dissociate themselves from the term, but whether they in their religious practice and biblical interpretation show substantial difference from the characteristics suggested by it. The difference should be one of substance before a difference of terms can be considered useful: if conservative evangelicals actively disagree with something in what is normally called 'fundamentalism' – for instance, if they consider themselves to be less extreme – then they have to show clearly in what respect they disagree and in what degree. If this cannot be done, then, though the term 'fundamentalism' may be felt as an irritation, there is no reason in substance to dissociate oneself from it.

The case of the word 'Methodist' is sometimes mentioned as a possible parallel. In early times this term was widely used with a very derogatory set of implications. This is true, but the comparison works in the opposite direction. The early Methodists, far from repudiating the designation which had fallen upon them and seeking to be called by some other name, accepted it. Through the impression that the Methodist movement made upon people the derogatory connotations gradually disappeared from the term. If people in fact hold the set of views that are generally designated as 'fundamentalism' – and it is not to be doubted that many do so – there is no reason why they should be so sensitive about the term: they could equally well accept it as a matter-of-fact statement of their position, and seek to let their position itself make a good impression upon people. It is with this matter-of-fact use of the term that my own statements in this book work: if in fact persons and organizations hold the views which are considered to be 'fundamentalist', then this term may as well be used, especially since there is no other term in normal currency which can equally well be used.

There is, however, another and a deeper reason for the difficulty over the terminology, and this will be only touched on at this point, since it depends on the exposition to be given in the next chapter. The people whom others call 'fundamentalists' think of themselves as, and would like to call themselves, just 'Christians' or 'true Christians': this is their real perception of themselves. For this reason they are dissatisfied with *any* more restricted designation. They want to think of their own position as *the* or *the only* Christian position: there is, for them, no other truly 'Christian' position that can be contrasted with their own. As so often, a highly partisan minority position aspires to use for itself the term that belongs to the whole. They would like to use terms in such a way as to suggest that all criticism of their partisan position is direct criticism of Christianity itself, and among themselves they often speak in this way. They

therefore do not feel at home with any designation which suggests
that they form only one part in the totality of Christian life and faith.
Ironically, this aspect of their self-understanding, their thinking of
themselves as the 'true' Christians, is exactly the reason why they
are generally called not 'Christians' but 'fundamentalists'.

As a practical course of procedure within this book, I shall therefore continue to use the term 'fundamentalism' for a certain basic
personal religious and existential attitude, which will be described.
This attitude I consider to be a pathological condition of Christianity, and one which, when it appears, commonly appears within, and
overlaps with, the ecclesiastical grouping known as 'conservative
evangelical'. I do not say therefore that all conservative evangelicals
are also fundamentalists; but the overlap is very great. Persons,
organizations, books and articles will be referred to as 'conservative
evangelical' unless there is special reason to do otherwise. It is no
part of my purpose to stick the label of 'fundamentalist' upon any
individual; but it is quite ingenuous to argue that fundamentalists
just do not exist and that the term has no basis in reality, as one
would imagine from a reading of some conservative apologetic
works.

A little more should be said about the word 'conservative' itself.
This is used in a wide variety of contexts to indicate an approach that
accepts older views, that seeks to preserve rather than to rebuild. In
this book it will sometimes be used of theologies and theological
positions, sometimes of social and political views, but mostly of
biblical scholarship. There are many literary and historical issues
within biblical studies on which it is possible to take a 'conservative'
position on grounds that are quite historical (or linguistic,
archaeological, etc.), just as a more 'radical' or 'critical' position can
be taken on the same sort of grounds. Such questions might be, for
example: whether there were real people Abraham, Isaac and
Jacob, who did the things they are said to have done in Genesis;
whether Jesus spoke in substance the sayings ascribed to him in the
gospels; whether letters like Ephesians and Colossians were written
by St Paul; whether Acts presents a historically accurate account of
the period described. On many such matters there may be, and
usually is, a 'conservative' position, conceived and argued on historical grounds, which does not itself logically depend on any 'conservative evangelical' or 'fundamentalist' theological position. It is
therefore important to distinguish this historical or at any rate
non-theological conservatism from the theological conservatism of
fundamentalists and others. Conservative evangelicals and fun-

damentalists will almost always espouse a conservative solution to such questions, and they do this out of a religious compulsion, which is not necessarily connected with the historical reasoning by which the conservative position within biblical scholarship is sustained. It is enough at the moment if we indicate the difference in principle: later we shall study in depth the paradoxical relations between conservative biblical scholarship and the religious attitudes which seek to support themselves through it.

Two or three further notes about terms may be added here:

First, there is a difficulty, in that American and British terms seem not to agree precisely. I am not sure where the American distinction between Evangelicals and Fundamentalists, as it is found in recent usage, lies in relation to my own following description. My impression is that both of these terms are used in America to indicate a position more conservative or more extreme than is the common usage in Great Britain, so that fundamentalism as depicted here might fall into the more extreme segment of Evangelicalism and the less extreme of Fundamentalism, as the terms are used in the United States.[1]

Secondly, there are still some other terms that might be used, for example 'biblicism'. This word is not used very widely in English. Some writers seem to use it for a very extreme position.[2] I myself would use it for a position less extreme than fundamentalism in my sense. For instance, someone might maintain that all problems of faith, life and theology were to be solved simply by use and exegesis of the Bible, and conversely that no other consideration need be taken into account than the knowledge furnished by the Bible. He might maintain this without maintaining the characteristic fundamentalist tenet that the Bible is without error of any kind; he would simply be arguing that, though the Bible contained errors of various sorts, mainly no doubt historical inaccuracies, it remained in fact the sole guide for theology and all theological effort should be devoted solely to the interpretation of it. Such a position I would call biblicistic, but it would also be clearly distinct from fundamentalism as the latter normally presents itself. But the term is not much used in this book or in the discussion which it seeks to interpret.

Enough now has been said to explain and justify the terms which I shall be using: but, as has been indicated, these terms will require to be filled up with much more extensive description before their senses will be fully clear. This will be done in the ensuing chapters. Before we go on, however, we should say something more to define the scope and the purpose of the discussion.

Our main subject is fundamentalism, and conservative attitudes to the Bible, *within Christianity*. It is true that somewhat similar views exist within the bosom of some other religions. Some kinds of Judaism, for instance, are very conservative about the Bible, and these currents have often repudiated modern biblical criticism with almost as much fervour as that with which Christian conservatives have repudiated it. Nevertheless, there are many differences in the total religious setting, and one cannot handle conservatism about the Bible within Judaism as if it was of one piece with the phenomenon within Christianity. Islam also can be said to be 'fundamentalistic': Muslims believe that the Qur'an was verbally revealed to the Prophet in its Arabic words, and that the exact form of the text was divinely inspired; its purity cannot be questioned. Similar attitudes can possibly be found in yet other religions, wherever there is a given holy text, scripture or similar authority. Some of these points will be mentioned again below. But the method of this discussion will be to take the phenomenon within Christianity as the framework, for within Christianity the conflict between biblical conservatism and biblical criticism has been particularly acute; within this framework references to other religions, and even to secular ideologies, will be added where appropriate.

Equally, our study takes departure from conservative tendencies *within Protestantism*; Protestantism, for this purpose, includes Anglicanism. Certain features of Protestant conservatism and fundamentalism can be found to be shared also by other forms of Christianity: for instance, in official Roman Catholic documents one can find declarations about biblical inspiration and biblical criticism that are very similar to the views of Protestant conservatives. Yet, though particular views may be quite closely shared, the setting is considerably different. Thus, though many cross-references to Roman Catholic doctrine will be made, it is from the Protestant phenomenon, to which alone the term 'fundamentalism' in its primary sense is normally applied, that we shall begin. To treat the two as one entity would invite confusion.

Thirdly, we shall base ourselves upon what may be called a fairly *central and orthodox* current of Protestant conservatism. Fundamentalist attitudes to the Bible are shared by a wide variety of groups and religious currents, which may be primarily interested in faith healing, in speaking with tongues, or in forecasting the end of the world. Fundamentalism in the approach to holy writings may be found in groups with such diverse doctrines as the Jehovah's Witnesses, the Seventh Day Adventists and the Christadelphians. In this book it is not these groups, but the more orthodox fundamentalism more closely related to the mainstream churches and their doctrine, that is taken as the basis for exposition. The existence of these many more 'deviating' groups is far from irrelevant, however. On the one hand, their influence in relation to that of 'orthodox' conservative evangelicalism appears to be increasing, so that in the end they might become more important than the latter. On the other hand, their mere existence constitutes a challenge to the latter, in that one can argue, from the proliferation of such contradictory tendencies, all of them holding a fundamentalist approach to their scripture, that the conservative attitude to the Bible is incoherent and *must* lead to chaos, or at any rate that it fails to provide any secure authority in religion which would suffice to prevent the growth of numerous and violent contradictions. I shall not at this point take up any position about these questions. I merely observe that there is a central and 'orthodox' sort of conservative evangelicalism, which aspires to hold itself close to the traditional positions of the mainstream churches, considering that these traditional positions would have remained totally satisfactory if they had not been spoiled by deviation into 'modern' theology and biblical criticism. It is this 'orthodox' fundamentalism that is taken as the typical pattern in this book, and the 'non-orthodox' types will not be involved except where they are specifically mentioned. It would be unfair to orthodox fundamentalism to make it bear responsibility for positions and religious types of which it in fact disapproves. We should not forget on the other hand that the non-orthodox religious types may from their own inner structure have better reason to hold to a fundamentalism about scripture than the 'orthodox' fundamentalists have. Moreover, they have at least one thing in common with modern theology and biblical criticism, namely that they too have to suffer from 'orthodox' fundamentalists endless attacks upon their lack of orthodoxy.

It remains to say something about the purpose of this book. It is written with the goal of *understanding*. It will be clear to readers that I do not agree with fundamentalism. The form of religion out of which it arises is, or may be, a tolerable variation within the total body of Christianity. Its doctrinal position, however, especially in regard to the place of the Bible, and its entire intellectual apologetic, seem to me to be completely wrong. It is true that fundamentalism has often been misunderstood and that some of the arguments directed against it have themselves been faulty; and the clearing up of these misunderstandings is another of my aims. Yet, even when this has been done, and after the very thorough review of fundamentalist literature, mainly in its doctrinal aspects and in its interpretation of scripture, which I have carried out, I do not find any of its intellectual arguments to have validity except in very minor respects. But this book is not written for the sake of controversy with fundamentalists. I did not write in order to produce arguments that will make them feel they are wrong or cause them to change their minds. I am interested, not so much in altering their opinions, as in understanding an intellectual structure that will probably be little affected by these arguments anyway. My purpose is thus to understand fundamentalism as a religious and intellectual system and to see why it functions as it does. My main task, therefore, has been to attempt a theological analysis of fundamentalist beliefs and practices. The research will, I hope, have value not only on the level of theology but also on that of the history of religions: what is the phenomenon of fundamentalism, as a fact of world religion, and how does it operate? For, as readers will soon see, the actual mode of operation of fundamentalism is in many ways different, not only from the views of it held by non-fundamentalist Christians, but also from the picture of it drawn by fundamentalist apologists themselves.

There is, however, also a second reason for the writing of this work. Fundamentalism has an effect on theology and biblical study, not only through the positive pressure towards conservative positions that it exercises, but also negatively, through the decisions people take in the effort to avoid a fundamentalist position. Among scholars, indeed, this latter has been much more influential than the former. A fresh description of the phenomenon of fundamentalism may assist theologians and biblical scholars to recognize more correctly what the issues are, and thereby to avoid both over-reactions and reactions in a mistaken direction.

In other words, this book is not addressed primarily to a fundamentalist readership. It is addressed to the church as a whole, to theology, and to biblical studies. It is they who have the task of understanding fundamentalism, of coping with it and deciding what can be done with it. My argument therefore assumes that the reader has some knowledge – not a technical knowledge, but some understanding – of how modern theology operates and of what modern biblical study is like. I have not tried, therefore, to explain in detail why we should think, let us say, that the Book of Isaiah was written by a variety of authors over a period of some centuries; nor have I tried to assemble a battery of arguments intended to convince a sceptic that this approach to the prophet (or prophets) in question is right. This book is therefore not an arsenal of arguments over the authorship of books or their dating; that sort of information can be found in any critical introduction. Nor have I attempted, except for sketchy indications at various points, to state a doctrine of biblical authority such as I would consider viable for the present day; to do this would be to reiterate what I have written elsewhere, especially in my *The Bible in the Modern World* (SCM Press 1973).

Although I have assumed some general background in the subject, I think and hope that the book will be read by many who have no detailed or technical knowledge, and for this reason I have inserted a number of notes explaining unusual words and giving information about various persons, the time when they lived and the importance of their historical contribution. Chapter and verse numbers in biblical references are to the numbering of the English versions of the Bible.

There is a further purpose I have in mind. Quite apart from those who have committed themselves to a fundamentalist position, there are very many who have their minds still open and uncertain, who have their life in the church as a whole and have some knowledge of its theology and of the academic biblical studies that inform it, but who nevertheless are under much pressure from the arguments of fundamentalists and are deeply impressed by the seeming attractiveness of their position. Many students of the Bible and of theology are in just this position. They are not fundamentalists, but fundamentalism has a powerful effect upon them. I hope that the analysis of the phenomenon provided in this book will help them to make an intelligent and deliberate decision in their uncertainty.

Finally, readers will observe that I have at many points outrun the sphere of my own technical expertise. The study of the subject has carried me into such diverse fields as American church history, the history of doctrine and its relation to philosophy, and various questions of social studies, about which my competence might well be questioned. Nevertheless the task had to be attempted and I hope that my inexpert judgments in certain matters have not vitiated the whole.

2 · The Religious Basis of Fundamentalism

Contrary to general belief, the core of fundamentalism resides not in the Bible but in a particular kind of religion. Fundamentalists indeed suppose that this kind of religion is theirs because it follows as a necessary consequence from the acceptance of biblical authority. But here we have to disagree and say that the reverse is true: a particular type of religious experience, which indeed in the past was believed to arise from the Bible, has come to be itself dominant. This religious tradition on the one hand controls the interpretation of the Bible within fundamentalist circles; on the other hand it entails, not as its source but as its symbol and as an apparently necessary condition of its own self-preservation, the fundamentalist doctrine of the Bible. In other words, fundamentalism is based on a particular kind of religious tradition, and uses the form, rather than the reality, of biblical authority to provide a shield for this tradition. This analysis will be basic to the argument of this book. It is the powerful hold of this religion on the soul that supplies the dynamic for the zeal and the cohesive force of the fundamentalist movement, and that also forges the bonds that make it difficult for fundamentalists either to change their theological position or to talk with other Christians on even terms.

What, then, is this religious tradition? There are, indeed, several streams of tradition that have gone into the making of modern fundamentalism; but the basic and dominant one is the religious experience of the Evangelical Revivals.[1] The characteristic experience of the Revivals was the sense of a church that was cold and dead, but where the introduction of a warm, living and biblical gospel brought about for many a personal conversion to a living faith, such as they had not known before. The conclusion that seemed irresistibly to follow was this: that personal salvation came not simply through belonging to the church, but through the hearing and acceptance of a particular kind of message or gospel which was not necessarily or universally preached in the churches. Salvation, which sinful men so profoundly need, is not to be found in just belonging to the church or going to the church. Rather, the characteristic experience is that of the man brought up as a member of the church, who nevertheless comes to realize that his previous Christianity has been merely 'nominal' – either a life of hypocrisy and insincerity or, more commonly, an attempt to build one's salvation upon the basis of one's own goodness. This last, though widely taken to be obvious natural ethics, was seen and felt in the experience of the Revivals to be the very worst of sins: it builds up man's pride in himself and increases his self-satisfaction, and it therefore leads him to reject the help of divine grace, to ignore our dependence upon it, and thereby it comes near to making salvation impossible. This sense that the man *within the church* may by his own religiosity and his own goodness, both actually encouraged and abetted by the church, become alienated from God and thus be ripe for a total conversion through the hearing of the gospel, is one of the deepest characteristic insights of evangelicalism. Its message, indeed, has gone not only to those within the church who, though good people, were yet only 'nominal' Christians, but also to the gross sinners – the scoffers at God, the drunkards, the blasphemers. But, in the experience of evangelicals, the two belong together: it is the message which calls the apparently righteous to conversion and repentance that can also reach the obviously alienated. It can reach them because it sees and emphasizes the deep sinfulness of *all* men and their need of conversion, and it thus breaks down the barriers which the 'good people' with their very goodness, like the Pharisees of the gospels, had raised against the supposed 'sinners' of society. Thus a church which evangelizes within will also evangelize without; one which encourages the complacency of those within can have nothing to say to those without. Experience of the churches in the time of the Revivals, and since then, appeared to confirm all this.

Now, why does this unhappy situation prevail in the church? How is it that church membership and church attendance can not only fail to bring a person into a living and saving faith, but can even encourage him in a belief in his own goodness which can only prevent his entry into such a faith? The answer of conservative evangelicals is, that the true gospel is not preached: false, 'liberal' or 'modernist', ideas have taken its place. If people had not lost sight of the traditional Christian message based squarely on the Bible, all this would not have happened. Theoretically it might be admitted that, even if the true gospel was preached, some 'nominal Christianity' might still be found, such is the hardness of men's hearts. Nevertheless, the blame for the enormous incidence of nominal Christianity in the churches lies in false teaching. This false teaching, far from calling men from darkness into light and from sin into faith, actually encourages the natural man in his self-assurance, and instead of making clear to him his sinful state gives him an impression of being well set in the ways of good. Rather than directing man to his one hope of salvation, namely cleansing in the blood of Christ as received through personal faith in him, it is unhappily vague about the uniqueness, indeed about the need, of any such salvation. Finally, rather than basing itself squarely upon the Bible, it is wishy-washy about the authority of the Bible, uses it only vaguely and intermittently, and holds itself free to look elsewhere for its sources of authority. Not only is such false teaching factually present: more, it is something to be expected, for in all ages men have been tempted to water down the essential gospel and dilute it into something that is easier for themselves and more comforting to their environment.

Now to hold the opinions that have just been outlined is not in itself to be a fundamentalist. These ideas, though shared by most or all fundamentalists, are common property to a much wider circle also: one might say that they are in a wide sense the ideas of evangelicals. All sorts of Christians – and this could include the 'Catholic' wing of the church as well as the evangelical – have been shocked by the formalism, the externality and the hypocrisy of church life and become convinced that this is not the true Christian life. But this point, which many Christians would affirm in some way and to some degree, is taken by fundamentalists and made by them into the cornerstone of all Christian experience, into the design which comes to dominate the shape of the Christian soul. The contrast between the 'nominal Christian' and the 'true Christian' is a distinction basic to all fundamentalist thought and action. On the one hand the distrust of the existing church is carried to the point of cynicism. On the other hand the failures of the church are diagnosed univocally as failure to preserve something that had been there all the time, a gospel or a message that was given by the Bible and understood in the Revivals, the effectiveness of which was undimmed and undiminished, which was yet gratuitously thrown away because clergy and theologians wanted to say something more modern, more up-to-date, more in tune with the spirit of their age.

This same distrust of the existing church, applied in another way, produces in fundamentalism an acute anxiety about the guarantees of pure doctrine. Everywhere there is conspiracy against the truth and the purity of the gospel, and one cannot trust what is said and taught in the church unless it conforms very closely to a norm. This conformity to the norm is absolutely vital, because it is closely linked with the distinction between 'nominal' and 'true' Christian faith. On the one hand, the teaching and preaching accepted within fundamentalism continually reiterates and reinforces the picture of the 'nominal' and the 'true' Christian, and the difference between them is commonly set through the non-acceptance or acceptance respectively of conservative evangelical doctrine. Conversely, on the other hand, the fact that this picture dominates the fundamentalist's understanding of himself as a Christian is a main reason for his doctrinal exclusiveness. If one wants to understand fundamentalism, one must see that this set of connections is built into the absolute centre of the fundamentalist consciousness. Central to fundamentalism is the correlation between two pairs of contrasts: on the one side the contrast between the true Christian and the nominal Christian, on the other side the contrast between the more conservative theological opinions and the more 'liberal'. The 'true' Christian is normally the person who also holds the more conservative opinions. In theory there might be exceptions; but in fact things work very much as I have said. One who makes the proper evangelical noises, who professes to believe in the virgin birth and the inspiration of the Bible, is likely to be accepted as a true Christian without too much further scrutiny; one who utters 'liberal' opinions is likely to be deemed a non-Christian without too much consideration of other factors which might counterbalance his doctrinal failings. Thus, though the contrast between 'true' and 'nominal' Christians began as a contrast on the level of personal faith and commitment, worked out in seriousness of Christian life, in fundamentalism it very quickly comes to be moved to the level of doctrine and opinions.

But is this not simply an unforgiveable narrowness and lack of charity? However strongly one holds one's convictions, can one not admit that there have always been various kinds of Christians, whose different opinions and different forms of service have all alike been pleasing to God? The question is something of an embarrassment to conservatives, who do not want to appear simply and gratuitously uncharitable. For the most part, I think, they deal with the question by the simple means of not thinking about it very much: pressed by non-fundamentalists, they will give the matter some consideration; left to themselves, they will not trouble much about it. Basically they cannot deal with the question because there is nothing in their equipment, nothing in their experience of themselves as Christians, that provides them with the means of recognizing and understanding as 'true Christians' those who are not also conservative evangelicals. The more open-minded will admit that God is able to make himself known to people through more ways than one and that his mercy is not tied without exception to the acceptance of conservative evangelical doctrine; but this remains an 'uncovenanted mercy', an act of the mysterious wisdom of God which lies beyond our comprehension. It is something that we can perhaps recognize but that, even if recognized, cannot be made into the rule; there would be great danger that even in recognizing it we might obscure the unique and God-given way by which men must come to God. There is no value in talking of manifold ways of coming to God or knowing him when he himself has made known to us the way by which he intends us to know him. This way is the way set forth authoritatively in the Bible, and since none but conservative evangelicals fully recognize the authority of the Bible, they have no alternative but to set forth that way as the only one by which man may be saved. Thus fundamentalists, however much they may recognize in theory that non-evangelicals may conceivably be true Christians and accepted by God, have no theological means of making anything positive out of this recognition; it does not alter their position as a whole.

In this the fundamentalist is affected both by his concentration upon doctrinal conformity and by his non-historical understanding of Christianity. He experiences a non-fundamentalist as an anti-evangelical, an opponent of true doctrine and therefore of the gospel itself. Can such a person have lived by the true faith of Jesus Christ and under the true grace of God, as set out in scripture, when so many of his own sayings have been in direct contradiction to scriptural teaching? It is possible – for with God all things are possible – but the likelihood is not very great.

Moreover, one will not make a great impression on a convinced fundamentalist by pointing to the noble life, the good deeds, the saintly character of this or that non-evangelical Christian. True, the argument may have something in it, and the fundamentalist recognizes the duty to acknowledge goodness wherever it is to be seen or found. But he is also warned that we are saved by grace through faith, and not by the goodness of any human works or achievements. Whatever the validity of the argument from the goodness and saintliness of Christians of other persuasions, on the fundamentalist its main effect will be to drive him back to reiterate the more convincedly the position from which he began. Moreover, he will say, consider where that argument, if logically pursued, will take us: it will lead us not only to acknowledge that great non-evangelicals are true Christians, but also to acknowledge that great non-Christians are true Christians also! The fact that striking qualities of goodness and saintliness are to be found outside evangelical Christianity is thus by no means a proof that the possessors of them are true Christians, living by the grace of God through faith in Jesus Christ and his atoning blood.

But what of the time when there were no conservative evangelicals, when this type of Christian thinking and piety just did not exist? Did God, let us say in the Middle Ages, not have any true Christians to worship him? The answer of the fundamentalist is that there was no such time. The faith and practice of conservative evangelicals today is, apart from some non-essentials, identical with the faith and practice of the church of New Testament times, and throughout all history there have been those who, though often submerged in numbers, kept alive the essentials of this faith and practice. Though names like 'fundamentalist' and 'conservative evangelical' may be modern, and though the present forms of this faith may well have been inherited primarily from the Evangelical Revivals, the thing itself is not new: it is the dominant faith of the Reformation as well as of the earliest church, and it has always had its witnesses in being. Historical change therefore does not cast any doubt upon the validity of the conception of the 'true Christian'.

It is the same if we start with the names of individuals from ancient or mediaeval times. Judged by the criteria which modern fundamentalists apply, was Athanasius – to whom, after all, they owe the Trinitarian orthodoxy by which they set so much store – a true Christian? Was St Francis of Assisi? The fundamentalist is not much troubled by the question. He does not know much about these people; and late antiquity and the Middle Ages are not a period of great interest to him. He does not really have to take a position about it. What does come into his awareness is the conflict of a more modern period in which, as he believes, the increasing degree of scientific and historical knowledge has led to a large-scale dilution of the gospel through 'liberal' theology and negative biblical criticism. He may indeed have no more factually exact knowledge of this more modern period than he has about the Middle Ages; but he feels it more, for this is what has entered into his consciousness. It is in this more modern situation that he feels at home, in it that his terminology of the true and the nominal Christian, correlated with the difference between conservative and liberal types of doctrine, seems to him to fit. Whatever was the case in the fourth century or the twelfth, he feels, in the modern context it is clear that liberal or modernist theology and biblical criticism are enemies of the true gospel; and is one likely to be a true Christian while at the same time (as he sees it) denying the biblical truths by which alone a man may become a true Christian?

One who wishes to understand fundamentalism must realize that this idea of the true Christian is not accessory but essential: it is not an unpleasant accretion to a position which would be quite satisfactory once the accretion were removed, but a central and fundamental element, the absence of which would alter the structure of the whole. One often hears well-meaning appeals to the fundamentalist to be more tolerant and more charitable: if only he would recognize that other ways besides his own are also valid, if he would only, without abandoning his own convictions, be willing to work alongside those of other convictions and in co-operation with them! If only he would abandon this negative aspect of his faith, this de-Christianizing of those who adopt other approaches, then the fine positive elements in his own viewpoint would come all the more clearly to view and receive all the more hearty recognition!

Such well-intentioned appeals are naive, for they do not recognize that the fundamentalist's position about true and nominal Christianity is intrinsic to his faith: to ask him to modify it is to ask him for something that he cannot perform. To abandon this element is for him not only to abandon an unnecessarily uncharitable judgment about others, but to abandon the very process of perception by which he understands himself as one grasped and held by God. In this perception the fact of conversion plays so central a part that it is almost impossible not to extend it universally and make it apply to all men, whether already active members of churches or not, even if this can be done only at the cost of supposing many or most such members to be only nominally Christian. Thus the fundamentalist is caught in a trap formed by his own innermost convictions and experiences.

It is often said against fundamentalist religion that its emphasis on conversion means a morbid interest in the emotional experience of conversion and, more generally, that fundamentalism is essentially an emotionally-based form of Christianity. This is true, however, only of some kinds of fundamentalist religion, and it is a mistake to generalize it and make it into a universal criticism. Indeed, while there are aspects of fundamentalist practice which are markedly emotional – the tense atmosphere of the revival meeting, the fervid use of music, the pressure for 'decisions', and the content of many personal 'testimonies' – it is equally true that other aspects of fundamentalism can be validly criticized for their cold intellectualism; and the importance of this latter will be seen when we look at the doctrinal side, and also at the relations between the religion and conservative scholarship. It would be more true to say that fundamentalism displays a peculiar balance between emotional and intellectual elements than to say that it is dominantly emotional. Thus while a morbid dwelling upon the emotional aspects of conversion can certainly be found within fundamentalism, it is not a necessary characteristic of it: many accept that a variety of emotional experiences may accompany conversion, and many do not insist that one must keep alive the emotions of one's conversion or even remember it at all. What is structurally essential for fundamentalist religion is rather this: the differentiation between true and nominal Christians, which is stressed by almost any kind of conversion experience, is allowed to become the paramount governing element in all judgments about the churches and their members; and it is assumed that the conversion which makes a man into a true Christian will coincide with an opinion change under which he will come to hold the views held by conservative evangelicals.

This emphasis on the holding of the right views, and the related anxiety about the domination of the churches by false teaching, is very important, for it explains why fundamentalism can be, and often is, at the same time non-denominational and unco-operative. Having introduced fundamentalist religion with an exposé of what I hold to be its basic convictions, we should now look briefly at its external and organizational manifestations. Characteristic at least of the British religious scene is the fact that most fundamentalists belong to denominations which are not as a whole fundamentalistic. Uniformly conservative denominations do exist – the clearest example is the Free Church of Scotland, a small, traditionally Calvinist denomination – but they form a very small element in the whole. Among the major denominations of British Christianity there is not one that could be counted as really fundamentalist, and thus most fundamentalists live within a denomination – Anglican, Methodist, Baptist and so on – within which they do not constitute a majority. As we shall later see, this is not the case in all parts of the world: there do exist areas of what might be called 'cultural fundamentalism', where fundamentalist religion is the majority faith and where the main stratum of society embraces fundamentalist views. For this book, however, the British type of situation will be taken as typical.

There is one Christian group that is something of an exception to the above, namely the Brethren movement, sometimes called the Plymouth Brethren. Uniformly conservative evangelical to a degree that none of the more mainstream churches are, this group has in institutional form some other characteristics which reflect tendencies visible within much of conservative evangelicalism in general: no ordained ministry, no formal theological education, extreme informality about the sacraments, and the tendency, in avoiding the use of the word 'church' for any visible or organized group, to suggest that there exists only the 'true' church of all true believers, wherever they may be (though more of them in proportion, one may suspect, are believed to be found among the Brethren than anywhere else!). No one with experience will deny that, in relation to their numbers, members of the Brethren have had very great influence in the maintenance of the entire conservative evangelical movement.

There is an important qualification to be added to what has been said about the denominations. A person belongs not only to a denomination, but also to his local congregation or parish. Though major denominations are not conservative evangelical, many important parishes and congregations are; and arrangements often exist whereby such communities can be kept as fairly 'pure' conservative areas over a long time, sometimes many generations. Denominational authorities, bishops and so on may either lack authority to modify this state of affairs or may feel that they should not try to do so. But it is a clear fact, as a result of this, that within a great church like the Church of England, which prides itself justly on its comprehensiveness and catholicity, strata exist where only the conservative evangelical viewpoint is to be heard, and people may live all their lives within such a stratum. The existence of such a stratum is, moreover, institutionalized through the existence of institutions like theological colleges which are exclusively conservative evangelical in their teaching. Thus, even when the great denominations are not conservative evangelical, substantial areas of church life exist which are such.

The issues that have caused divisions among the churches in the past and led to the formation of denominations are often regarded by fundamentalists with some tolerance. The official cause of many divisions has been a question of church polity (episcopal, presbyterian, congregational), which fundamentalists often regard as an *adiaphoron*, a matter of choice which is not dictated by the true gospel. Other divisions are over sacraments, or over relations with the state, and these may be regarded in the same way. Indeed, the tolerance of the average fundamentalist in these matters should not be set too high: many of them in the course of time develop characteristic denominational prejudices in addition to their conservative evangelical position, but at least it can be said that the latter does not necessarily support and generate denominational feeling. Thus fundamentalists can be and often are loyal Presbyterians, Episcopalians or Baptists; but to them the issues which have produced the major historical divisions of Christendom (apart from the division from Rome) are less important in principle than the distinction between the true gospel and false liberal or modernist doctrine. There is a deeper trust between people of different denominations who share a conservative evangelical faith than between any of them and people of their own denomination who do not share that faith. That fundamentalism cuts across denominational boundaries is one of its most obvious characteristics; and in this at least it has something in common with modern theology as a whole, for it is characteristic of much modern theology that its main lines of division do not coincide with ecclesiastical boundaries. Evangelicals feel that they belong together. They have a sort of 'ecumenical' feeling towards one another; and this makes them feel hurt when they are regarded as anti-ecumenical by supporters of the ecumenical movement.

Is it not remarkable, however, when one considers the way in which Christianity has split into denominations in the last four hundred years, that fundamentalism – commonly regarded as a divisive movement – has not much more been the cause of the origin of new denominations? In a sense, as conservative evangelicals see it, it has been. As they understand it, many of the denominations at the time of their origin stood for the true gospel. The Protestant Reformation, as they picture it, was a manifestation of just the same religious position which conservative evangelicals now maintain; Methodism was another; the Baptists represented yet another. But few or none of these churches succeeded in keeping themselves pure; in the course of time their original evangelical certainty was deeply subverted. Rather than try yet again to create a new church which would be purely and perfectly conservative evangelical, the fundamentalist is willing to work within the framework of the existing churches. In doing this he is often assisted and comforted by the official doctrinal documents which go back to the beginnings of the various denominations: greatly as the Presbyterians have degenerated, do they not still have the Westminster Confession, and do not the Thirty-Nine Articles have some status within Anglicanism? And do not these demonstrate that the classical, official and historical position of these churches is close to the conservative evangelical one? In general, the more a church has a strongly confessionalist character – as is to be seen, for instance, much more strongly in American Presbyterianism than in the Scottish church – the more fundamentalism has expressed itself through an emphasis upon a confessional document, usually of the Reformation period. Thus the appeal to a past and classical orthodoxy within his church is one of the things that enables the fundamentalist to remain within it; and this is one of the ways in which he shows his conservatism.

But while fundamentalism in Britain is not represented by major denominations in the traditional ecclesiastical sense, it has nevertheless produced its own special forms of organization, and these are of the greatest importance in any attempt to understand fundamentalism as a phenomenon. Characteristic such organizations are those which work among children, among young people and students, and certain overseas missionary societies. These organizations are not churches, and those who work in them will be Anglicans, Methodists or whatever it may be; they do not have a ministry of their own and do not celebrate the sacraments. But, though undenominational in this sense, they are commonly very exclusive and non-co-operative towards non-conservative-evangelical organizations which work in parallel with them. The classic case, and certainly the best known, is the organization working among students. In Britain this was long known as The Inter-Varsity Fellowship, but has recently (I understand) changed its name to The Universities and Colleges Christian Fellowship; the groups in individual universities and colleges are commonly called Christian Unions, formerly also often Evangelical Unions. Since this organization is not only in itself important but also publishes a substantial amount of literature, it has provided an excellent point of reference for the research done for this book, and its publications have been thoroughly consulted throughout. Students, or other persons belonging to analogous organizations, will also attend a normal local church and worship and perhaps work in it; their preference will be, of course, for a church of strongly conservative evangelical tradition, though sometimes they will remain, perhaps out of family loyalty, within the congregation of a non-evangelical church. But they will also be active within the conservative evangelical organization to which they belong or are attached.

Thus, though conservative evangelicals do not form a church or a denomination, they do have an organizational base which in some ways comes close to being a conservative evangelical denomination, though one of a peculiar kind. These organizations form a training ground, a publishing centre, and a remarkably stable ideological centre and point of reference. The main reason for this is their insistence on doctrinal homogeneity and purity. These organizations exist in order to provide a setting and a milieu in which the true gospel, and nothing else, will be preached; and in this purpose they are successful in a way that would not be possible within any of the traditional denominations.

Once again we see why it is naive to suggest that the conservative evangelical organizations should be more tolerant or should co-operate more with their non-evangelical counterparts. The fact must be faced: it is precisely in order not to co-operate with 'liberalism' and 'modernism' and other false gospels, precisely in order to be exclusive as against these views and against the modern biblical criticism associated with them, that organizations of this kind exist. The assurance that at least on this platform no false doctrine will be preached is a major reason for the moral hold of the conservative evangelical organization upon its members, for the liveliness, loyalty, zeal and assurance of its fellowship, and for its effectiveness as an evangelizing agency. When this is so, it is no easy thing for the conservative evangelical to envisage the loosening of the boundaries, the existence of which seems to him to form the real basis for life within his movement.

But does this emphasis on correct doctrine not make the conservative evangelical organization into a denomination after all? Does it not mean that it is taking over at least part of the function that should belong to the churches? This criticism is sometimes made, and it is true that such organizations, though they have no ministry or sacraments of their own, do in their insistence on true doctrine come nearer than in other things to usurping the function that belongs to the church. But this criticism cannot be carried too far, and is likely to prove a sterile one in debate. As seen from within, the conservative evangelical organization is by no means arrogating to itself the right to declare or define doctrine beyond what has already been declared or defined by the churches; rather, it is merely insisting on the application of historical standards already set up by the churches. As conservative evangelicals see it, there is nothing in their doctrine that is not stated or implied in the historic creeds and in the confessional documents of major churches like the

Presbyterian. In this of course they may be wrong; but a further investigation will be needed before we can say whether they are wrong or not. As they see the matter, if the churches have relaxed their own original stringency, this does not mean that those who wish to keep the old stringency unrelaxed are thereby taking over for themselves the functions that belong to the churches.

How then in practice does this insistence on true doctrine work out? It works out, I would suggest, in three main ways. The first is the selection of speakers for meetings, a matter of paramount importance in a conservative evangelical organization. One of the main strengths and appeals of such an organization, let us recall, is the assurance that those whom it invites to speak will be 'sound'. False gospels and false teachings can be heard all around us, but here is one place where one can rely on that which is said. Apart, therefore, from very limited exceptions, only speakers of known conservative evangelical views, or in sympathy with them, will be invited. Varieties of viewpoint within conservative evangelical belief are, of course, generally tolerated (this will be discussed later), but little or nothing is said in favour of obtaining speakers of really deviating viewpoint in order to 'hear the other side'. No one will ever be invited to give a sympathetic exposition of trends in modern theology or biblical criticism. In part this is straightforward narrowness and intolerance, the view that darkness does not illuminate light. But in order to understand it more fully one has to discern the underlying way in which conservative evangelicals perceive the world. They suppose that the 'other side' is already pretty well known, being (they think) the daily fare of preaching and the normal run of opinion in the majority of churches; this being so, it is *their* special calling to present their own distinctive witness, and not to confuse this through the reiteration of contradictory opinions which are in any case well known. Moreover, extreme importance is attached to what is said by an officially-invited speaker. What he says must adequately represent the movement in its essence. The invitation to the speaker indicates the sanction of the leaders of the community; his speaking is a message to the full gathering of the community; and, since all meetings are in principle evangelistic in character, he speaks also to the unconverted, and for their sake (for who knows if they will come back another time?) he must present the true and full gospel. Thus the insistence on purity of doctrine cannot be explained as *mere* intolerance: more deeply, it belongs to the general idea of what a meeting and a speaker are intended to perform.

Organizations may have a brief doctrinal statement, commonly called an 'Aims and Basis' or a 'Doctrinal Basis'.[2] This will commonly list certain points considered to be among the fundamental truths of Christianity, such as: the Trinity; the divine inspiration and infallibility of holy scripture and its supreme authority in matters of faith and conduct; universal sin and guilt; redemption from sin and guilt only through the atoning death of Jesus Christ; and so on. Speakers at important meetings will commonly be expected to be in substantial agreement with this statement. Full agreement with it, very rigorously tested through many conversations, will be expected of the actual staff employed by a conservative evangelical organization, who will thus display the highest degree of doctrinal purity that can be found on earth.

If the selection of speakers is the first way in which the insistence on correct doctrine is put into effect, the second is the choice of office-bearers. Where, as in student organizations, there is a rapid change of membership, the office-bearers provide continuity; and they may be expected to have fully sound views, and perhaps even required to sign the doctrinal statement, if there is one. It is by no means held that this degree of conformity is necessary for all members: among student organizations, for example, a simple declaration of faith, perhaps 'in Jesus Christ as my Saviour, my Lord and my God', may be sufficient to admit to membership. But greater assurance of conformity is held to be necessary for those who are responsible for planning and decisions, for the choice of speakers and for setting the tone of the movement as a whole.

Thirdly, however, the insistence on true doctrine works out in a more informal but more profound way, through a whole tradition of ways of speaking and doing things. The hearing of speakers, the discussion of difficulties, meetings for prayer and Bible study groups, evangelistic activity towards the non-believer and the informal fellowship of the group all build up together a powerful and sensitive consciousness of what is 'sound' doctrine and real Christianity. Very often it is this informal tradition, exercised by the life of the group, rather than the external guarantees of true doctrine, that brings new converts gradually into an increasing conformity. Indeed, this informal process is commonly so effective that comparatively little formal pressure towards conformity through doctrinal statements or the like is ever needed, except in cases of unusual conflict.

But we have said enough for the moment about the conservative evangelical organizations. As has been said, not all who are fundamentalists, or who hold conservative evangelical views, belong or have belonged to such organizations, and many such people have lived their lives in churches in which their viewpoint is that of a minority. Nevertheless these organizations are of primary importance, for the reasons that have been stated. Their evangelistic impact makes them major recruiting agencies for the conservative evangelical cause, and the solidity of their witness makes a deep impression, such as could scarcely be made by a conservative evangelical minority within a large denomination. Where major conservative evangelical denominations are lacking, these organizations present perhaps the clearest and most identifiable form of the religion.

We now return, then, to a further exploration of the character of that religion. The two main elements which have thus far been mentioned are (*a*) the distinction between the nominal Christian and the true Christian, and (*b*) the insistence on the maintenance of right doctrine, or of the true gospel, as against all sorts of modern teaching which seek to water it down. Let us now go on to say more about the lineaments of the true gospel as conservative evangelicals understand it.

The true gospel is a message, which in its simplest form announces salvation from sin through the blood of Christ and through personal faith in him. We can discuss various elements in this view of the gospel and in the religious practice that is associated with it.

For conservative evangelicals sin is a fearful horror, ever-present and all-embracing, which only the blood of Christ can dissipate. It does not by any means consist in individual evil deeds of recognizably sinful form; rather, it envelops the entire life of persons not yet brought into a saving relationship with Christ. Particular evil deeds are only the fruit of an underlying sinful disposition, which cannot be radically cured or overcome except through a saving act of God which deals with sin as a totality. So there is no greater error than the idea that one who has avoided the grosser moral evils and has lived by the accepted moral standards is therefore any the less a sinner in need of grace. On the contrary, the morality of the unsaved person is likely to be both hypocritical and prideful: at most, it is lightened by occasional rays of light communicated by conscience and the like, but these partial forms of light only make darker and more blameworthy the darkness that generally prevails. The sinfulness of people is thus by no means to be established through looking at demonstrable evil actions: one of the functions of the gospel is that it tells people of their sin, and in general the realization of one's sinfulness and the acceptance of Christ as saviour are correlative and belong together. One of the most common complaints against non-evangelical doctrine is that it fails to lay sufficient emphasis on human sinfulness.

It thus seems to me wrong to say, at least as far as concerns the basic theological principles, that the stress is laid on particular kinds of evil, especially on sexual faults or on social practices like smoking and drinking. Perhaps we have to draw a distinction between different kinds of fundamentalism in this respect. So many competent persons make this remark about fundamentalism that I feel I have to take it with respect. Marty quotes a source as saying that 'The Fundamentalist catalogue of "sins" is small and specific: commercial movies, dancing, gambling, card-playing, drinking beer or wine or liquor, and smoking'; the source (Carl Henry, who ought to know) goes on to speak of the 'never-ending tirade' against these things.[3] It is very doubtful if this is true of the sort of fundamentalism described in this book. It would be expected that an active Christian would be too busy in his work of witness, and too anxious to give a good example, to become seriously involved in dancing or card-playing; but there would not be 'tirades' against these practices, because the ethos of the group would make such tirades unnecessary in any case. While some of these activities, and gambling (surely rightly) most of all, would be regarded with disapproval, it is quite wrong to think that these would be thought of as constituting the basic depths of sin. At most one might say that the consciousness of particular faults, a consciousness socially conditioned, plays a significant part in the sense of guilt, and the fundamentalist preaching of human sinfulness appeals to this sense of guilt. But in any fairly educated context, say in a student situation, even extreme fundamentalist doctrine would lay the emphasis not on any list of detailed sins but on the universal and almost metaphysical character of sin.

An additional reason for our stressing this point is that the emphasis on certain particular social habits, like the use of alcohol, tends, unless I am mistaken, in the British tradition to be associated with *liberal* evangelicalism rather than with conservative.[4] In Methodism, for instance, a rather 'liberal' but still evangelical position has long been associated with a very strict position about alcoholic drinks; and this can probably be paralleled in other churches. The result is, paradoxically, that people have sometimes turned to a fundamentalist gospel precisely because, rather than stressing a list of individual dos and don'ts, it has emphasized sin as a total personal problem of deep profundity. This, if correct, is the opposite of many diagnoses, such as the one cited above.

Thus, at least for the sort of fundamentalism here taken as typical, sin is universal and almost metaphysical: it belongs to the 'nature' of fallen man. Though created good and in fellowship with God, man rebelled against him, and his continuing sin is a continuation of that rebellion. Through it he is deprived of fellowship with God; he lives for himself rather than for his creator. Moreover, the effect of sin is such that man cannot by his own efforts return to God; the barrier has to be crossed from God's side. The message of the gospel is that this has been done in Jesus Christ. We shall later notice, however, that though this radical and all-embracing view of sin is held in principle and is theologically essential, because it provides both the background for the message of salvation and the motivation for acceptance of that salvation, actual life in conservative evangelical circles can show a quite different assessment of sin, whether taking it rather lightly as a problem or, as appears to be the case in some areas, reverting quickly to the censorious condemnation of particular forms of social nonconformism. But for the moment this can be left aside.

Salvation is thus primarily the removal of that barrier which sin has set between God and man; it is the renewal of that relation of fellowship, righteousness and obedience which had been destroyed by sin. In this salvation the essential step is something that has already been accomplished by the work of Christ: it is not a step forward which has to be achieved by our human effort. On the cross Christ effected a once-for-all atonement, in which the power of sin was broken and the divine judgment due upon man for his sin was endured by God himself in his love.

Many conservative evangelicals may well have no consciously formulated understanding of the mode of this atonement. But where the matter is defined with some care the characteristic emphasis is on a *substitutionary* atonement, i.e. on the view that on the cross Christ took our place and endured the divine judgment due to men for their sins. When men were condemned to death for their sin, he who was sinless took their place and by suffering death for them in perfect obedience and submission overcame the power of sin and death; sin was thus cancelled or wiped away. The emphasis is also *sacrificial* in character: the death of Christ was a sacrifice for the removal of sin, seen on the pattern of the sacrificial atonement rituals of the Old Testament. Moreover, it is believed that in the events of the death of Christ God's anger against sin is operative; in this sense there is a *penal* character in the atonement.

The average conservative evangelical, however, is not concerned so much to argue about theories or explanations of the atonement, but rather to oppose any theologies in which the atonement itself seems less central. They bitterly oppose any trends which would concentrate on the teaching of Jesus, as an ethical guidance to be followed, while depending less upon his death upon the cross. It is totally wrong to suppose that by following his teaching or his example we might be able to do something to overcome sin. The teaching and the life of Jesus are subsidiary to his death and make sense only when seen as leading up to it.

Thus the concentration upon the cross in conservative evangelical religion is very marked. It supplies the key imagery ('the blood of Christ'), the haunting hymns ('When I survey the wondrous cross'), and the centre from which lines radiate to every aspect of religious practice – to the call for conversion, to the dedication for service and sacrifice, to the command to evangelize the world. In contrast, there is rather less emphasis upon the resurrection: it is very strongly affirmed that the event took place in bodily form, but its theological significance is certainly not as heavily stressed as that of the cross, of which atoning event it is seen as the completion.

Who, then, is the Jesus Christ who is the central figure in all this? Conservative evangelical faith asserts, with traditional orthodoxy, that Christ was both God and Man; but the actual emphasis is heavily on his being God. It is because he is Son of God that his suffering makes atonement: the love of God is expressed in the fact that he gave up his own son for our sakes. The story of the virgin birth shows that Jesus was more than merely human; and a Jesus who was merely human, however sublime and noble a man, could not have functioned in atonement as conservative evangelicals understand it. He is the Messiah or Christ of Israel, prophesied beforehand in the Old Testament. He is never merely teacher or leader or perfect man: if he is seen as any of these, it is only as part of the greater conception that he is the Son of God incarnate. Conservatives are nervous about any tendency which would understate the divine character of Christ; they are not equally sensitive about any tendency which would understate his humanity. 'Liberalism' and 'modernism', as they imagine them, tend towards a human Jesus, and they in opposition tend towards a being who not only comes from God but *is* God, is divine.[5]

Christ, then, has made atonement for us; the great act for the removal of sin has been accomplished. It remains, however, for the individual to appropriate the effects of that which was then done. God's gift, which is grace, has to have the response of faith: faith is the acceptance of God's grace. When faith is born, when a person accepts Jesus Christ as personal Lord and Saviour, then God's atoning love in Christ becomes effective for him and in him. He is justified, he is forgiven; he is adopted as a child of God; he is born again and becomes a new creature; he receives the gift of the Holy Spirit within him as his sanctifier. The beginning point of this saving faith may or may not be marked as a conversion experience, but in any case this faith continues, and the Christian lives by it and is continually built up in it.

Faith, then, by grasping the benefits of Christ's atoning work sets the believer in a new relationship with God. This new relationship, however, does not continue automatically, but has to be maintained in the Christian life through a growth in grace, a continual resistance against the renewed attacks of sin and temptation, a continual dying to self and rising again to obedience to the will of God. In traditional terminology, if justification gives the believer a new standing or position before God, sanctification is the production of a corresponding actual state or condition of holiness within him. Man has to work to make his calling sure: the study of the Bible and personal prayer are his instruments in this work. This task can also be described as a fight or struggle: the believer is assailed by temptation and by the devil, for although justified he still has the root of sinfulness in him. Yet temptation is not entirely a misfortune, for through it the believer learns to rely on God; he knows that the fact of temptation is one of the signs of the love of God towards him and one of the modes through which God purifies him.

The active force in the Christian life, in the right hearing of the gospel, in the acceptance of Christ as Saviour, and in the process of sanctification, is the Holy Spirit, God in person indwelling the believer and the church. As Christ is God, so also is the Holy Spirit God; and experience of the work of the Holy Spirit is one of the marks of the true Christian.

Concerning the view of the church held by conservative evangelicals, something on the more negative side has already been said. Positively stated, the church is one, holy and universal; it is a body of which Christ is the head, and it is constituted by the totality of true believers. Concerning certain other aspects of the doctrine of the church, however, no very clear view is to be found. What, for instance, is the relation between the one true and universal church constituted by the totality of true believers and the empirically existing organizations such as the Church of England, the Church of Scotland, the Congregationalists or the Methodists? Conservative evangelicals hardly suppose, and certainly no fundamentalist supposes, that these bodies are conterminous with the community of true believers.

An extreme and consistent fundamentalist position, holding that many members of the empirically existing churches are only nominally Christians and that much false doctrine is preached in these churches, might hold that there is really no relation between these bodies and the true church, and that these are connected with the true church only in so far as some of their members are true Christians. The doings of a body like the Church of England would then have no intrinsic connection with real Christianity at all. Such a position, logically pursued, would lead either to withdrawal into a group regarded as being all of them true Christians, in other words a sect solution, or to a conception of the true church as wholly invisible, having no definable empirical locus to which one should attach oneself. This extreme position, however, though occasionally met with, and supported by the deep influence which groups of the Brethren type exercise within evangelicalism, should not be taken as typical of conservative evangelical opinion. The more average conservative evangelical, though profoundly sceptical of the faith and doctrine of the average church, generally holds that the churches and their ministries, deeply defective as they may be, somehow reflect their institution by God. Even if the true gospel is not preached in its fullness, the scriptures are publicly read, the true God is worshipped and Jesus Christ is confessed; the hymns sung often reflect genuine evangelical piety, and the doctrine implied by the prayers and liturgy and stated in creeds and confessional documents comes close to acceptability. In spite, therefore, of the poor doctrine and consequent spiritual deadness of many churches it is still a worthwhile act to attend church and support the activities of a church. The presence of true and active Christians within the churches may perhaps at some time in the providence of God be the means of their return to their original purity of doctrine and the stimulus to a revival of true faith within them.

About such matters as the ordained ministry, conservative evangelicals on the whole do not have much to say: in general, their views are of the type commonly characterized as 'low'. The task of 'preaching' the true gospel does not belong uniquely to the ordained ministry: on the contrary, it can be done and must be done by every believer. Thus the idea of the priesthood of all believers is present in a fairly extreme form. The basic needs for the presentation of the true gospel are not either scholarly training or ministerial ordination, but personal faith in Jesus Christ, personal experience of the Holy Spirit, and a good knowledge of the Bible coupled with a full acceptance of its authority. Scholarship and the special experience of the professional minister are not necessarily despised; but they count for little if they come into conflict with the evangelical gospel or the authority of the Bible. Nevertheless, it is recognized that the professional ordained ministry provides a unique opportunity for Christian witness, and it is well known that vocations to the ministry from within conservative evangelical circles are frequent.

On sacraments there is even less distinctive doctrine among conservative evangelicals as a whole. So far as it is possible, these are considered to be like matters of church polity, that is, difference of opinion is permitted, and evangelicals will in general follow the patterns of their membership as Anglicans, Baptists or whatever it may be. This is especially true of the interdenominational conservative evangelical organizations. These are aware that the question of sacramental doctrine is a potentially explosive and disruptive force, and they seek to damp down excessive discussion of it, lest it should damage the unity of evangelicals in essential matters. The sacramental practice which occasions the most severe questioning is, of course, the baptism of infants, for on conservative evangelical logic it would seem most natural that baptism should take place in adult years and after a personal confession of faith – in other words, the traditional Baptist position. The fact remains that a very large number of conservative evangelicals, probably a considerable majority, continue to adhere to the churches which practise infant baptism. In any case all would agree that the church is constituted through faith rather than by sacrament, and they feel it important to make clear that no one becomes a true or full Christian merely through participation in a sacramental action.

In the life of Christians as understood by conservative evangelicals the importance of the sacraments is overshadowed by that of personal prayer. The emphasis does not lie upon the regular liturgical prayer of church worship. Fundamentalists are not necessarily contemptuous of this, but it is not the major element in their conception of prayer. At worst, it may be no more than a vain repetition of set formulas, a quasi-heathen practice against which the Lord himself warned. Moreover, God expects and seeks the personal prayer of each Christian, and not only the prayers conducted by a clergyman. Prayer at its best should be a personal expression of praise, of thanks, of needs and of seeking the further-ance of the will of God; it should include a strong element of self-examination, self-searching and confession, and seek the power of God for victory over sin. In this type of religion there is therefore, in addition to normal church worship, a heavy emphasis on (*a*) the time of private prayer of the individual and (*b*) the 'prayer meeting', in which Christians join to pray together, each presenting prayers in turn, while the others silently will their support of the prayers being uttered. The presence of the Holy Spirit in each Christian makes them able and ready to pray, and in the meeting where two or three are gathered together there Christ is in the midst of them.

Prayer thus occupies a place of importance correlative with that of the gospel itself. It is certain that the gospel will be effective, but it is equally sure that the preaching of it will be effective only in response to prayer. We cannot expect that even the purest of doctrine will overcome the hardness of human hearts unless the ground has already been prepared by prayer. It is by prayer that the Christian has communion with God and learns to submit to his will, by prayer that he comes to be more like Christ, by prayer that he receives a fuller measure of the Holy Spirit. Prayer is effectual: it changes things. It includes indeed such other elements as worship and praise, thanksgiving and self-submission. But a very strong emphasis is laid upon the efficacy of intercessory prayer: it is through prayer that people are 'brought to Christ', and through it difficult personal decisions are rightly concluded; through it money is made available for the needs of the church, and through it the sick are healed and dangers and temptations averted. The importunity and fervency of prayer are much emphasized: one must ask again and again, not wearying. Prayer should be intensely personal: the mention of particular persons and particular needs is right and proper. In both of these respects the prayers of a fundamentalist group differ greatly from the prayers of the average church.

Conservative evangelicals are not unaware of the difficult prob-lems inherent in the practice of prayer, and especially intercessory prayer; yet to them the biblical sanction, and indeed encourage-ment and command, of prayers that ask God to do things and to change things far outweigh the more philosophical objections and difficulties. They know that one may ask selfishly for one's own desires, and they tend to be piously anxious that one should pray not for what one wants but for what God wants. They know that prayers may be answered, but answered in a way quite different from that which was in the mind of the asker. They know that God inscrutably may withhold that which is most passionately asked for, whether it is the survival of a sick child or the conversion of a dear friend. These qualifications do not alter the centrality of prayer for the religion; they only add to its complexity. Prayer is not only the making known of our needs to God: it is also the whole milieu in which Christians live, the field in which they do battle with Satan the tempter, in which they learn their own way of obedience and submit themselves to divine guidance. Even the Bible is not read rightly or understood rightly except with prayer: even in all its infallibility, it is only when it is read prayerfully and with the presence of the Holy Spirit that it acts upon the heart.

The emphasis on prayer is matched by the emphasis on evangelism. Knowing that the hearing of the message has been the source of his own salvation, the believer must go on to pass that same message on to others. It is not conceivable that so great a salvation should have been received at all, if it did not also inspire a burning desire to tell others of the same opportunity. In fundamentalism this missionary impulse is acutely personal. The task of mission, of spreading the good news of the gospel, belongs to every individual Christian and not only to the official or ordained ministry. The non-Christian is all the more likely to listen with sympathy to a message that comes not from a professional clergyman but from a straightforward individual like himself. This centrality of lay evangelical witness is supported by, and in turn reinforces, the essential simplicity of the gospel as conservative evangelicals understand it. There is only one source that has to be mastered, namely the Bible; the complicated concepts even of orthodox theology, though doubtless justified in their own place, are not necessary or even valuable for the immediate task of witnessing to Christ, while the questionings and hesitations of non-evangelical theologies and philosophies are not only useless but actually constitute part of the opposition that has to be overcome.

Evangelism is personal also in that it sees the close relationships of kinship and friendship as an opportunity and a responsibility for witness. The believer has a special task of caring for those near to him, those with whom he works; he should pray continually for their conversion, seek to 'witness' to them and try to bring them to church or to evangelistic meetings. The motive for all this should lie in love, concerned for the need and the deprivation of the non-Christian, and in the joy of one's own faith, which cannot help expressing itself and seeking to share itself. But beyond this there lies also the graver motive of responsibility: did not the prophet Ezekiel make it clear that, if the wicked perishes, and the prophet has neglected to warn him, the responsibility falls upon the prophet while, if the prophet has duly warned him, then the responsibility is his own?

In making witness in this way the Christian expects, and receives, some hard knocks, but the motives just mentioned help him to overcome them. Did not people mock at the prophets and scorn them, and did not Christ himself warn his followers that those who loved him would be scorned and hated by the world? The question 'Will it work?' is not one to be taken too seriously. It is God's Word, and God has promised that it will be effective. One does not know how soon or in what way it will be effective, but this is all the more reason for persistence. Doubt about the effectiveness of this kind of communication is itself a cardinal failure in faith, a surrender to temptation. If the gospel is faithfully preached, God will 'honour' it: one may have to wait for the seed to germinate, but, so long as it is the true seed, it will certainly have power.

One thus sees how the very structure of ideas about evangelism encourages persistence within the same patterns and discourages the alteration of them in order to suit newer circumstances.

If the emphasis on evangelism has a closely personal character, its other side is the emphasis on the world-wide mission, what used to be called, and perhaps is still sometimes called, 'the foreign mission field'. The time during which modern conservative evangelicalism has been shaped, the period since the Evangelical Revivals, has also been the time during which the great expansion of Protestant missionary work throughout the world has taken place. The religious consciousness of fundamentalism is strongly missionary-minded. The gospel has to be preached into all the world; every true Christian has to support this expansion with his personal interest, his money and his prayers. There should lie heavy on his heart the sense of responsibility for the lands of deep darkness, where perhaps millions have never heard the name of Christ. The individual Christian has therefore to consider carefully whether he himself is not called to work overseas, even if it means the sacrifice of a comfortable life, an intended marriage or a promising career. Though the situation of the churches at home is bad, the need for overseas mission is paramount: in spite of the failings of the Western churches, at least the name of Christ is made known and people have the opportunity to find out about him, while in other parts of the world no word of the gospel is accessible or ever has been.

Enthusiasm for the overseas mission fits in with numerous characteristics of the fundamentalist viewpoint. The situation abroad well
accentuates the element of lay preaching and witness, for doctors,
nurses and agricultural instructors find they have little or no professional clerical ministry at hand and are accustomed to doing much of
the preaching work for themselves. This in turn appears to support
the need for, and the appeal of, a simple and clear theology, based
on a single well-known source, the Bible. The shilly-shallyings of
more sophisticated theology are out of place, being luxuries that
cannot be afforded outside of Western Christendom. Moreover, the
gospel has to be clear and must be affirmed without doubt or
qualification, since hesitations will be quickly noticed by hearers
from a non-Christian background and taken as evidence that the
Christians do not know what they are talking about, even in matters
of their own religion.

Moreover, experience abroad often provides triumphant evidence for the evangelical stress on a complete and radical conversion, while the communities thus formed are a shining example of
living Christianity as it should be. Foreign missionary experience, it
is supposed, thus reproduces in the modern world something that
Western Christendom has sorely lacked, a re-enactment of the story
of the Acts of the Apostles.

The enthusiasm for overseas missionary work is connected with
another outstanding feature of fundamentalist religion, namely its
eschatology.[6] Fundamentalists commonly have a vivid sense of an
impending end to the existing order of things. Their preaching is
often criticized as 'hell-fire preaching' and as holding out hopes of a
heavenly bliss after death, and no doubt this can be evidenced from
the practice of some preachers. Certainly for the fundamentalist
heaven and hell, eternity and possible damnation, are realities
clearly affirmed in the Bible, which therefore cannot be denied.
Nevertheless I think that the main emphasis in conservative
evangelical religion, and even in quite extreme fundamentalism, is
not on heaven and hell as the destiny of the individual after death,
but on the second coming of Jesus Christ in personal and physical
form, carrying with it the termination of the present stage of God's
dealings with the world and the transition to a new and different
stage. The second coming, most believe, may take place at any time,
and the Bible repeatedly warns us to be ready for it.

The second coming has a vital connection with the emphasis on
missionary preaching. Only until the second coming, according to
fundamentalist belief, is there an opportunity to hear the gospel, to

be converted to a saving faith. The task of witness is therefore one of extreme urgency, for the time is short. Moreover, though one could not say that it was universally held doctrine, it is certainly an influential opinion, that the carrying out of the world mission to its completion in a full geographical sense will soon be followed by the second coming, or, conversely, that the delay in the second coming has its purpose and meaning in the provision of opportunity for world mission. 'This gospel of the kingdom shall be preached in all the world for a witness to all nations; and then shall the end come' (Matt. 24.14 AV).

Finally, the Bible itself. For fundamentalists the Bible is more than the source of verity for their religion, more than the essential source or textbook. It is part of the religion itself, indeed it is practically the centre of the religion, the essential nuclear point from which lines of light radiate into every particular aspect. In the fundamentalist mind the Bible functions as a sort of correlate of Christ. Christ is the personal Lord and Saviour, who illuminates everything and enters into all relationships; the Bible is a verbalized, 'inscripturated' entity, the given form of words in which God has made himself known, and thus the Bible equally enters into all relations, its words cannot be quoted too often, its terms, cadences and lineaments are all to be held dear. While Christ is the divine Lord and Saviour, the Bible is the supreme religious symbol that is tangible, articulate, possessable, accessible to men on earth. Christ and the Bible can thus be said to play complementary roles. Christ is more important because he is the true Saviour: even fundamentalists do not believe that the Bible is the Saviour and Lord. From this point of view it is wrong to say, as is sometimes said, that they put the Bible in the place of Christ. But from another point of view the Bible is really more important: it is the Bible, because it is the accessible and articulate reality, available empirically for checking and verification, that provides the lines that run through the religion and determine its shape and character.

The Bible is thus the supreme tangible sacred reality. If you possess a Bible, you have the earthly essence of the church. Though all other forms of Christianity also have the Bible, its symbolic function within fundamentalism is different. The Bible in fundamentalism is comparable to the virgin Mary in Roman Catholicism: it is the human visible symbol involved in salvation: as she through the immaculate conception is free from the contagion of human imperfection, so it has a kind of perfection and sublimity that makes it sacrilegious for us to analyse and criticize its seamless fabric.[7] Or, if we were to make a comparison with high-church Anglicanism, the symbolic function of the Bible within fundamentalism is like that of the eucharist rather than that of scripture. Thus to compare the function of the Bible within other forms of Christianity with its function within fundamentalism is to make an inadequate comparison. The true comparison is with whatever, other than Christ himself, is the supreme symbol of the religious pattern. It is this function of the Bible as supreme religious symbol that justifies us in seeing fundamentalism as a quite separate religious form. Although much of the religious substructure is shared by fundamentalists with evangelicals generally, once the symbolic elevation of the Bible goes beyond a certain point it begins to alter the shape and character of evangelical religion altogether. Certain kinds of biblical criticism and theology are felt to threaten the status of the Bible as absolute and perfect symbol of the religion; and in order to protect that symbolic status of the Bible the religion itself has to be adjusted or distorted. We shall see many cases of this in the exposition that follows. Thus we have a reciprocal relation between the Bible and the religious tradition. On the one hand the religious tradition is an ultimate value for fundamentalists. They do not use the Bible to question and re-check this tradition, they just accept that this tradition is the true interpretation of the Bible. The fundamentalist position about the infallibility and inerrancy of the Bible is an attempt to prevent this tradition from being damaged through modes of interpretation that might make the Bible mean something else. But, this being so, fundamentalism has not been able to leave it at that point. Especially in its intellectual and apologetic work, in which it seeks to protect the Bible against other modes of interpretation, it finds that it gradually has to alter and even abandon essential elements in the very religious tradition from which it started out. When this happens it is valid to say that the Bible as symbol, rather than the Christ who speaks through the Bible, has become the supreme controlling factor.

This symbolic function of the Bible has a deep effect on personal behaviour. It lies behind such well-known (and trying) phenomena as the endless reiteration of biblical phrases, the love for the exact wording of the Bible (now becoming more muted as the Authorized Version begins to lose its hold even in conservative circles), the whole incantational use of scripture. In a religion lacking in ritual, the citation of scripture has often functioned as a practically ritualistic procedure. The Bible is a form of poetry, a myth that coheres with, undergirds and harmonizes with the fundamentalist tradition of religion. It is a matter of course that preaching will use biblical texts, celebrate the centrality and infallibility of the Bible, and quote it frequently. It is by no means, however, a matter of course that it will make a careful exegetical examination of the meaning of the passages. Most fundamentalist preaching merely reiterates the traditional evangelical point of view, quoting the accepted proof texts but not really asking openly after the meaning. Indeed, the symbolic function of the Bible, coupled with the high views of its authority, can mean that the fundamentalist view of the Bible is effectively transmitted and communicated without any substantial use of the Bible at all. It is not uncommon that people who are deeply convinced of the infallibility, centrality and inerrancy of the Bible have a poor knowledge of it and indeed have hardly even read it. The tendency in this direction is, I believe, increasing. It remains true that the traditional fundamentalist has often been a serious Bible-reader with an excellent knowledge at least of the verbal form of the text, and his devotion to it is often based on deep personal experience of help, encouragement and inspiration gained from certain parts of it. Nevertheless, the non-conservative Christian should not let himself be intimidated by fundamentalist arguments with their endless citation of texts and passages: the ability to produce these does not necessarily betoken any real or profound knowledge of the Bible at all.

Thus, to sum up, the position of the Bible within fundamentalist religion stands high above the particular formulations that seek to grasp it and the various arguments that are used to defend it. The religion is an entirety, in which the supreme position of the Bible is central: faith in Christ and the experience of salvation, as fundamentalists see it, are not separable from this position of the Bible. Therefore, just as a personal conversion is normal as an entry into fundamentalist religion, something not far short of another conversion may be needed before one can get out of it. And, because the Bible in fundamentalism is the central symbol of a personal and existential commitment, arguments about the Bible between fundamentalists and non-conservatives are commonly found to be frustrating on both sides. Nevertheless one should not despair of the importance of these arguments: they may touch upon the deep lines of stress that run through the solidest-seeming religious commitment, and, often only after long and wearisome repetition, they can suddenly have an effect – in either direction. But in general the simple and superficial arguments which arise in discussion with fundamentalists are bound to remain frustrating; their true importance and purport can be understood only when a much deeper investigation of the background has been carried out. The rest of this book will seek to provide some understanding of this background.

3 · The Bible – First Stage

1. *Being literal*

What is the point at which the fundamentalist use of the Bible conflicts with the use of it by other people? The 'plain man', asked this question, will commonly say that a fundamentalist is a person who 'takes the Bible literally'.[1] This, however, is far from being a correct or exact description. The point of conflict between fundamentalists and others is not over *literality* but over *inerrancy*. Even if fundamentalists sometimes say that they take the Bible literally, the facts of fundamentalist interpretation show that this is not so. What fundamentalists insist is not that the Bible must be taken literally but that it must be so interpreted as to avoid any admission that it contains any kind of *error*. In order to avoid imputing error to the Bible, fundamentalists twist and turn back and forward between literal and non-literal interpretation. The dominant fundamentalist assertions about the Bible, namely that it is divinely inspired and infallible, do not mean that it must be taken literally, and are not so interpreted in the conservative evangelical literature; what they mean, and are constantly interpreted as meaning, is that the Bible contains no error of any kind – not only theological error, but error in any sort of historical, geographical or scientific fact, is completely absent from the Bible. In order to expound the Bible as thus inerrant, the fundamentalist interpreter varies back and forward between literal and non-literal understandings, indeed he has to do so in order to obtain a Bible that is error-free.

To take a well-known instance, most conservative evangelical opinion today does not pursue a literal interpretation of the creation story in Genesis. A literal interpretation would hold that the world was created in six days, these days being the first of the series which we still experience as days and nights. Not at all, according to conservative evangelical sources; on the contrary, they are full of warnings about the dangers and difficulties involved for those who take the word *day* literally. In *The New Bible Commentary* (Inter-Varsity Press, 2nd ed. 1954, p. 77), E. F. Kevan tells us that there are 'serious difficulties' in taking them as ordinary days, i.e. taking 'day' literally. 'Others' conceive of these days as 'days of dramatic vision, the story being presented to Moses in a series of revelations spread over six days'; this 'immensely interesting suggestion' cannot be regarded as more than a conjecture, but is clearly not ruled out by the commentator as impossible. 'Many' maintain that each day represents not a twenty-four-hour period 'but a geological age'. In favour of these thoughts is advanced that hoary instance of Ps. 90.4, 'a thousand years in thy sight are like yesterday', which is supposed to show that 'in other parts of Scripture the word "day" is employed figuratively of a time of undefined length'. This thoroughly non-literal interpretation has, indeed, a 'difficulty', namely that each 'day' is represented as having an 'evening' and a 'morning', which might suggest very much the sort of day we are still having. But, says Kevan, 'this may perhaps be but a *purely figurative* way of saying that the creation was characterized by clearly defined epochs' (my italics). This last seems, then, to be the approved interpretation. But all of those surveyed by Kevan adopt not literal, but symbolic, interpretations of the seven-day structure of Gen. 1.

If we pass to *The New Bible Commentary Revised* (Inter-Varsity Press 1970), the interpretation of Genesis has been taken over by Meredith G. Kline, but there is no return to a literal interpretation. 'Exegesis indicates that the scheme of the creation week itself is a poetic figure and that the several pictures of creation history are set within the six work-day frames not chronologically but topically' (p.82a). Thus the story gives a 'normative disclosure' of the divine act of absolute creation *ex nihilo* and of a 'specific, terminated creation era' (p.81). It tells us that God created the world out of nothing and that he did this in a specific period which came to an end. But the scheme of the six-day sequence is poetic figure, which means that it does not correspond to any actual sequences in the process of creation. We move to yet another venerated conservative publication, *The New Bible Dictionary* (Inter-Varsity Press 1962), and J. A. Thompson there tells us (pp.271f.): 'Gn. i has an artificial literary structure and is not concerned to provide a picture of chronological sequence but only to assert the fact that God made everything.' *Only* that God made everything! How are the mighty fallen! and how ridiculous a mouse has the mountain of fundamentalist interpretation brought forth! What radical 'liberal' or wild 'modernist' did not believe 'only' that God had made everything?

We see, then, that a symbolic and non-literal interpretation of Gen. 1 is preferred, and it is now only very extreme fundamentalists who assert that a literal interpretation of the six days of creation is obligatory, or even desirable. The reason for the preference is plain. It has nothing to do with a softening of the fundamentalist rejection of the critical approach to the Bible; on the contrary, that rejection remains unaltered. What has happened is that the scientific evidence for the long duration of the beginnings of the world has become too strong to withstand. A literal interpretation would mean pitting the Bible against scientific truths which fundamentalist intellectuals now themselves accept; this would in turn force the admission that the Bible in this respect had been wrong. In order to avoid this, the conservative interpreter moves over into a non-literal exegesis; only this will save the inerrancy of the Bible. A hundred years ago, probably less, most fundamentalists would have insisted on a literal interpretation; if science said that this was impossible, they would just have damned science, or asserted that its claims had not been proved, that they were no more than unfounded speculations and hypotheses. As the scientific approach came to have more and more assent from fundamentalists themselves, they shifted their interpretation of the Bible passage from literal to non-literal in order to save that which for them was always paramount, namely the inerrancy of the Bible.

In fact the only natural exegesis is a literal one, in the sense that this is what the author meant. As we know from other parts of Genesis, he was deeply interested in chronology and calendar, and he depicted the story of creation in a carefully and deliberately arranged scheme of one week, As Kevan, cited above, rightly sees, the 'evening' and 'morning' phraseology clearly indicates that he thought of a day such as we understand a day to be; but that is only one of the multitudinous details of the story which show that the seven-day scheme is essential to his way of describing the creation. About the actual processes of the origin of the world as we know them he knew, of course, nothing, and set against our knowledge of these processes his account is certainly 'wrong'. Since, on the other hand, the processes and sequences which are known to us through modern science were certainly totally unknown to him, this 'wrongness' is quite irrelevant in our understanding the story. But for the fundamentalist any kind or degree of wrongness in the Bible would be catastrophic. In order to avoid this consequence he has tried every possible direction of interpretation other than the literal.[2]

Let us take another example: the genealogical lists which survey the generations from Adam to Noah (Gen. 5) and from Noah's son Shem to Abraham (Gen. 11.10–32). The reader of a list like Gen. 5 would gain the impression that Adam, the first man, had a son Seth, and he had a son Enosh, he a son Kenan, and so on, down to Noah. He would also learn that these people lived a remarkably long time, Adam for instance being 930 years old at the time of his death, Methuselah 969, the longest of all. He would also observe that, since Adam was the first man, Seth was born in the year 130 from the creation, Enosh in the year 235, and so on, leading up to the birth of Noah in the year 1056; and this in turn fixes the beginning of the flood, in the 600th year of Noah, in the year 1656 from the creation. In other words, the genealogical materials have the purpose, among others, of providing an absolute chronology from the beginning of the world down to events of major importance like the flood, the Exodus and so on; and the importance of this can be traced not only in the Bible but in post-biblical works like the Book of Jubilees, which has different figures but clearly works on a chronological scheme reaching from the creation of the world down to the taking possession of the land of Canaan.[3]

That is to say, the Book of Genesis presents us with a genealogical and chronological framework which is clearly a matter of the greatest interest to the writers, and which forms a more or less closed system within their world of thought, but which equally clearly has nothing to do with the antiquity of mankind or of the world as we know it. Not at all, say many conservative evangelical interpreters. The list, they tell us, does not mean that Adam was the actual father of Seth, or Seth of Enosh, so that there were only a mere ten or so generations from Adam down to the flood. All it means is that Seth was a descendant of Adam, as Enosh was of Seth, and Noah of Lamech, and so on. The story gives us no information at all about the number of generations, or the number of years, from Adam down to Noah, Here, in other words, we have the great 'gap' theory, which is one of the ingenious devices of fundamentalist hermeneutics, and which in this case enables the genealogy to be stretched so as to accommodate a more or less unlimited time span from the creation of the world down to Noah's flood.

Here once again fundamentalist interpretation abandons literality in view of overwhelming scientific evidence. An older generation of fundamentalists would not have done this: they would have stuck to the literal biblical chronology, which would have given them a clear date for the creation of the world, in the fifth millennium BC.

Fossils, geology, and science generally would simply have been damned if they had contradicted this. A modern fundamentalist goes the other way. The Bible cannot be wrong, and this means that it must square with the scientific evidence; this means in turn that the text cannot and must not be taken literally.

Does this mean that fundamentalist interpretation accepts that the picture of the beginnings of the world, as given in the Genesis texts, is a sort of legend or myth? Not at all. That is not what is meant. It would be most improper to suppose, just because of the schematic character of the genealogies, or because of their relation to Oriental genealogies which give even higher ages, often going beyond 20,000 years for an individual, or because of the high figures for the ages of persons like Adam and Methuselah, that these persons and figures belong to legend. There really were people of these names, and they lived in the sequence given by the biblical text, though there were many other generations in between each of them. There is no reason to suppose that, because they exist in so peculiar a genealogical list, they are not historical figures. But what of their ages, 930 for Adam, 969 for Methuselah at their deaths? Some interpreters say that they are 'puzzling'; but 'whatever one may make of the large figures' the names are not to be considered unhistorical.[4] Others find it quite clear that the numbers are to be taken literally, that is, that these persons actually lived these numbers of years. E. F. Kevan sternly rebukes attempts to explain them away. Suggestions that figures like Methuselah were tribes and not individuals, that the years were shorter, that the figures were mystical, are 'attempts to avoid the plain meaning of the passage'. In fact, it seems, 'the fathers of the human race were endowed with longevity, and this may have been according to divine purpose in His providential government of the race'. So also Kline in the revised edition: 'Mesopotamian traditions reflect the race's memory of remarkable longevity, especially in pre-diluvian times. Whatever the physiological explanation, a providential purpose was the preservation of mankind, still few in number, young in technology, and obliged to cope with a fractious environment.' There is no hint here that the longevity might be legendary. Similarly, *The New Bible Dictionary* seems to treat these figures solemnly as straight biographical data. Of Methuselah, for instance, it simply says that he lived to the great age of 969 years; it adds that he was not the same person as the Methushael of Gen. 4.18.[5]

Thus, all in all, the interpretation provides a mixture of literal and non-literal. The genealogy is not to be taken literally as an account of succeeding generations; the persons mentioned, however, are to be taken literally; as for the ages to which they lived, we have the choice of taking them literally or leaving the whole matter vague and 'puzzling'.

The gap theory, as here illustrated, means that what is written in the biblical text can be stretched out to cover almost limitless additional periods of time or other additional events. According to the Scofield Reference Bible, perhaps the most important single document in all fundamentalist literature,[6] the phrase 'And God said, Let there be light: and there was light' (Gen. 1.3) and similarly the passage about the making of 'lights' in the firmament to rule the day and the night (1.14–18) do not refer to the creation of light or of the sun, moon and other stars. Why not? Because the creation of the heaven and the earth in Gen. 1.1 included the sun and the moon. They were created 'in the beginning'. The 'light' of 1.3 'of course came from the sun, but the vapour diffused the light. Later the sun appeared in an unclouded sky.' The point is this. Scofield inserts after 1.1 a huge gap: 'the first creative act refers to the dateless past, and gives scope for all the geologic ages'. The time span of Gen. 1 is thus stretched out to almost infinity in order to make room for geological fact; the effect of this is that it becomes consequentially necessary to follow a non-literal interpretation of the wording about the making of the light and the sun and moon.[7]

One other instance may be mentioned briefly at this point, since it will come in later also in another connection. Ex. 6.16ff. appears to give us a short genealogy: Levi had certain sons, one of whom was Kohath; Kohath had sons, one of whom was Amram. Then (v. 20) 'Amram took to wife Jochebed his father's sister and she bore him Aaron and Moses.' One might suppose from this that Amram and Jochebed were the father and mother of Moses and Aaron. Not at all, according to Kitchen. The statement 'does not prove immediate descent'; and the passage is not a full genealogy, but only gives the tribe (Levi), the clan (Kohath), and the family group (Amram by Jochebed) to which Moses and Aaron belonged, not their actual parents, who in Ex. 2 are also anonymous.[8] The importance of the interpretation is that it stretches out the distance between Levi and Moses to something adequate to allow for the descent into Egypt, and in particular for the 430 years of Ex. 12.40, the period that the children of Israel are supposed to have dwelt in Egypt. This latter figure is accepted as the more or less correct one, i.e. as corresponding to real historical facts. This, incidentally, in the opinion of many conservative scholars gives us a satisfactory date for the historical

Exodus, say about 1290–60 BC. But then is it not unfortunate that
I Kings 6.1 expressly says that Solomon began the building of the
temple in the 480th year after the exodus of Israel from Egypt? Not
at all, for this date is not to be taken seriously or taken as exact.
Kitchen tells us that oriental parallels show that temporal calcula-
tions might be somehow telescoped; LaSor tells us that this figure,
which would put the Exodus about 1447 BC, cannot be right, and
'there are indications that this verse may be a late gloss in the text'.[9]
Whichever way one goes, it is clear: some figures in the biblical text,
and some relations stated in genealogical form, are to be taken
literally, that is, as corresponding more or less precisely to historical
reality as it was; others are to be interpreted as being only loosely
related to that reality.

Thus, to sum up, these introductory examples already make it
clear that fundamentalist interpretation does not take the Bible
literally, but varies between taking it literally and taking it non-
literally. This variation is made necessary by the real guiding principle of fundamentalist interpretation, namely that one must ensure
that the Bible is inerrant, without error. Inerrancy is maintained
only by constantly altering the mode of interpretation, and in particular by abandoning the literal sense as soon as it would be an
embarrassment to the view of inerrancy held.

There is another very good reason, not commonly observed, why
fundamentalist interpretation is often not literal: biblical source
criticism, the operation which in the pentateuch detected sources
like, J, E, D and P, the very critical method that fundamentalists so
detest, is also the result of 'taking the Bible literally'.[10] It was just
because they took the texts literally that the critics were able to
break through the screen of ancient or more recent harmonizing
and apologetic interpretations and were led to reconstruct different
sources behind the biblical books. For example, it would at least
occur to an even mildly critical mind that, if one passage gives (or
even, if it *may* give) a mere three generations from Levi to Moses,
while another puts the period at 430 years, it might be considered
possible that there were two different sources, which had different
traditions about the same set of historical relations. The critical
solution takes departure from this possibility, and this follows the
literal sense of the passages. Because this possibility is absolutely
ruled out by fundamentalist interpretation, it has to have recourse
to non-literal interpretation.

Take another example: if one takes the Genesis story literally,
Ishmael was a small child when Hagar was driven into the

wilderness; Abraham 'put him on her shoulder' (21.14) and later, when she was exhausted, she 'threw' the child under a bush (21.15). But Gen. 17.25 says that Ishmael was already thirteen years old before Isaac was born. If one takes the texts literally, a critical separation of sources becomes very natural: this means that the genealogical material of ch. 17 (P?) was written independently of the personal story about Hagar and does not fit with it. Observation of hundreds of such discrepancies, patiently pieced together over a long period, and valued as evidence precisely because scholars did not allow defensive and harmonizing interpretations to push aside the literal sense of the text, led to the critical reconstruction. In order to avoid this critical reconstruction, which they rule out in principle, conservative evangelicals produce an apologetic explanation, the purpose of which is to make the two narrative passages agree into one harmonious story by avoiding the consequences of the literal sense. In a case of this kind we should distinguish between what the average conservative reader, even the average fundamentalist reader, and the scholarly conservative apologist, sees. The former, I am sure, reads the passage without ever doubting that the sense is of a small child. Only scholarly apologetic, anxious to avoid anything that could give a pretext for a separation of sources, notices the relation to the statement of 17.25. Thus *The New Bible Commentary*, p. 93: 'There is no need to suppose any inconsistency here with the other parts of Genesis, or to imagine this boy of seventeen being carried by his mother like an infant in arms . . . the growing youth would collapse . . . sooner than the physique of the mother who had become accustomed to the desert life . . . Hagar did her best to support him, but at last could hold him up no longer.' There cannot be any doubt that this sort of explanation is less *literal* than the source-critical one. It is only in part, therefore, that literal interpretation is a fundamentalist characteristic: it is in fact much more an element in critical scholarship.

Fundamentalists, then, are not literalists, or not consistent literalists; one could say that a main problem confronting a fundamentalist exegete is that of deciding which passages, or which elements in passages, he will take literally and which he will not. Of course, people are not without reason when they say that fundamentalist interpretation 'takes the Bible literally'. It does this – but only *sometimes*: in fact, it does it at those points at which the structure of fundamentalist religion requires that it should do so. This happens with the statement of certain events: the story of the virgin birth means that Jesus 'literally', i.e. in this case physically, was

born of a virgin mother; the prediction of his coming means that he
will physically appear, and so on. In cases like this, there not only is
an event to which the passage refers, but the correspondence between the biblical description and the actual event is absolutely
exact, or at least is as close as it can possibly be made to be. Similarly
entities and beings mentioned in the Bible are really existing things:
angels, devils, heaven and hell in some sense really exist. But,
contrary to the general impression, fundamentalism leaves a certain
amount of vagueness about the level on which the biblical descrip-
tions are related to the actual entities. For instance, if a person
believes in hell as a really existing topographically extended place,
full of flames and smoke and so on, that would be regarded as
'taking hell literally' and thus as a fundamentalist position; but one
can move this to a different level and consider that hell does not
exist on the topographical or geographical level, and is a state or
condition of separation from God, with pain and punishment, and
one may still be a fundamentalist. So long as one considers that hell
is some really and objectively existing reality, though it may not be
literal, it will still count as valid for fundamentalism. It is said that
Billy Graham grew up believing that heaven was spatially extended,
being a cube 1600 miles on each side; hell burned with a physical
fire;[11] it is often this kind of corporeal conception of theological
realities that people have in mind when they say that an opinion is
'literal'. But Graham's move out of this conception and into one on
a different level does not necessarily make a difference to his
fundamentalism. The difference of levels in this respect is normal
within fundamentalism itself. The same is true if we think of, say,
the ascension of Jesus to heaven: Acts 1.9 as it stands suggests a
vertical spatial ascension, which invites the sceptical questions, how
fast he went upwards, how far up is heaven, and how long did he
take to get there; but fundamentalism is not at all tied to so crass a
literalism. It is fully acceptable to say that this was a passage from
the normal earthly state to a quite different state, and that this
passage was not really a spatial bodily movement, though it was so
depicted in the text of Acts.[12]

The same is the case if we think of the contrast between 'literal'
and parabolic uses of language. It is certainly not true that for
conservative evangelicals the literal is the only kind of truth. Even
extreme fundamentalists, after all, do not generally take explicit
parables and similes as if they were literal historical narrations: even
they do not insist that there was a real Good Samaritan, a real
wedding with ten virgins, or a real steward who was entrusted

with a million pounds or so, wrapped up in a napkin. The category of the parabolic and the symbolic is familiar to them, indeed we have already shown how essential it is to them for their interpretative methods.

It is thus certainly wrong to say, as has often been said, that for fundamentalists the literal is the only sense of truth.[13] Conservative apologists are right in repudiating this allegation.[14] Unfortunately, the truth is much worse than the allegation that they rightly reject. Literality, though it might well be deserving of criticism, would at least be a somewhat consistent interpretative principle, and the carrying out of it would deserve some attention as a significant achievement. What fundamentalists do pursue is a completely unprincipled – in the strict sense unprincipled, because guided by no principle of interpretation – approach, in which the only guiding criterion is that the Bible should, by the sorts of truth that fundamentalists respect and follow, be true and not in any sort of error.

What, then, is the sort of truth that is important for the fundamentalist? The answer seems to be: correspondence to external reality. This is particularly clear where a biblical passage refers to an external event in space and time. For fundamentalist interpretation this means: not only is there an event to which the passage refers, but the event is extremely like the description of it given in the Bible. The correspondence between the actual event and the biblical description is absolutely exact, or at least is as close as it can possibly be made to be. Not only so, but the correspondence between the biblical account and the actual event or entity is the supremely important thing about the Bible. A biblical account of some event is approached and evaluated primarily not in terms of significance but in terms of correspondence with external actuality. Veracity as correspondence with empirical actuality has precedence over veracity as significance. There is variation in the degree of directness with which biblical passages describe external events or realities, but there is always, or almost always, an actual external event or reality which corresponds to the description. Sometimes the description is taken as very direct: the reports of the resurrection of Jesus correspond to the fact that he became alive again in his physical body and emerged from the grave. Sometimes they are less direct: the ascension of Jesus was not, as the surface text of Acts might suggest, a vertical movement upwards; nevertheless it was a real event in the sense that the physical body of the risen Jesus was removed from the presence of the disciples into the presence of God. Sometimes they are still less direct: there is no real wedding with ten virgins, but this is a parabolic representation of a real event, the coming of the Lord, which will be an event in space and time, and one in which the characteristics described in the parable – foolishness, unreadiness, trying to get in when it is too late – will have quite precise correspondences in the behaviour of actual people. Though the degree of correspondence is allowed to vary, and in this sense, as we have just seen, fundamentalist interpretation is not literal, correspondence with external reality must be affirmed as an inalienable and essential property of the biblical texts, and especially so when they narrate events that seem on the surface to be events in space and time.

We can best illustrate this by putting it negatively: for fundamentalists it is usually wrong to interpret a biblical passage as if it were a myth, or a legend, or the product of theological reflection, unless it itself represents itself as a piece of theological reflection. If you ask the question, why does the story or passage have this form and not some other, the answer is: because that form was generated and dictated by the actual course of events, by the structure of external reality. Perhaps, if one is dealing with a theological passage in the letters of St Paul, it may be acceptable to treat it as St Paul's theological reflections; but if it is a story, in which Jesus is represented as healing someone and uttering certain sayings, then it is quite wrong to treat that as the result of theological reflection, still worse to treat it as legend or myth: the story has this form because Jesus did this healing in this way and uttered these sayings as they are reported. Slight variations in form (as between different narrations in different gospels) are probably admitted, and so, as we have shown, are different degrees in the directness of description: but passage over into an interpretation which would suggest that the story was actually generated by theological needs, or by influence of myth and legend, is generally entirely forbidden.

Viewing the question, then, as we are now doing, as a matter of hermeneutics, of interpretative method, we can go on to state the following. Firstly, the question comes back to words and their meanings, or, more correctly, to the meanings of literary structures. Can the word 'day', as it is used within the type of structure we find in Gen. 1, mean anything other than a day in the normal sense of the term, the same kind of day as every Monday or Tuesday? Can the statement that Jochebed 'bore to Amram' Aaron and Moses mean anything other than that they were the actual parents of the children – and by 'actual' I mean here, of course, actual from the point of view of this literary unit, this particular passage; whether they were the actual parents from the historical point of view is quite another matter.

But, secondly, this brings us to the point where we can state the fundamentalist position in terms of hermeneutic procedure. In fundamentalism the truth of the Bible, its inerrancy, understood principally as correspondence with external reality and events, is fed into the interpretative process at its very beginning. That is to say, one does not first interpret the passage on the basis of linguistic and literary structure, and then raise the question whether this is true as a matter of correspondence to external reality or to historical events. On the contrary, though linguistic and literary structure are respected as guides, and indeed conservative literature contains a good deal of boasting about the command of these disciplines by conservative interpreters, the principle of the inerrancy of scripture has an overriding function. It dominates the interpretative process entirely. The questions: Might the linguistic and literary form suggest that the passage is a myth or legend? Might it be mistaken in matters of historical fact? Might it be something generated not by external events which occurred in this sequence, but by problems in the inner experience of the early church? – such questions are therefore eliminated from the interpretative process from the beginning. The fundamentalist interpreter may consider them, but only in so far as they are forced upon him by the arguments of critical scholars. They do not form part of his own interpretative procedure at all. This means, however, that though linguistic and literary form are respected as guides, they operate as guides only under the overriding control of the principle of inerrancy. The question is, therefore, which of the various interpretations is supported by the linguistic and literary evidence, under the overriding assumption that the passage is inerrant as a description of external events and realities? The passage is inerrant: the only question is, which is the correct path to the necessarily inerrant meaning?

This helps us to understand two important points. First of all, inerrancy is the constant factor in all fundamentalist interpretation. Literalness is not a constant factor, but may vary up and down. To others there seems to be a serious inconsistency here: some things are literal, others are not. The persons from Adam to Noah are real persons with these names, and the figures of the duration of their lives are also correct; but the total effect of the passage is not to be taken literally; on the contrary the key to it is to be found precisely in that which it does not say, in the supposition that there were dozens or hundreds of extra generations, all totally unmentioned in the passage. The 430 years of Ex. 12.40 is taken literally, that is, it is historically correct, with at the most slight variation, but the 480 years of I Kings 6.1 has in some way to be eliminated as an exact statement. Does it not seem wholly inconsistent that one can be literal at one point and non-literal at another? Not at all. As seen from the fundamentalist's point of view, there is nothing wrong in this. On one hand, he ties himself not to the 'literal' meaning, which would be methodologically controllable, but rather to the 'plain' meaning, the meaning which is clearly the right one. But since the principle of inerrancy is the overriding one in all interpretation, no meanings turn out to be 'plain' if they disagree with the inerrancy of the Bible. The 'plain' meaning is the one selected, from among those which might be in conformity with the inerrancy of the Bible, by various exegetical considerations.

Thus the fundamentalist interpreter is not at all insincere in his oscillation back and forward between literal and non-literal interpretations. Given his principle of inerrancy, fed in as the architectonic control in his approach to the Bible, it is obvious that the meanings he discovers are to him indeed the 'plain' meanings. Since the world and man has existed far longer than the genealogy of Gen. 5 can allow for, it is transparently obvious that the passage does not give a complete genealogy, but one with gaps. Meanings of this kind are quite 'plain'. And since they are plain, the linguistic and literary structures are examined, but only in a way subsidiary to the perception of this plain meaning. The language and literary structure is perceived in a way subservient to the meaning dictated by the principle of inerrancy. This is not to say that there is no freedom of choice or manoeuvre in fundamentalist interpretation: there is, because there may often be several interpretations all of which in some way satisfy the principle of inerrancy, and then the linguistic and literary evidence may be used to evaluate each of these. But the fact that the meanings perceived by fundamentalist interpretation are commonly quite plain and obvious to fundamentalists is one of the main reasons for the difficulty of communication between them and critical interpreters.

Does not this oscillation between literal and non-literal approaches nevertheless bring about in the end a deep tension and sense of contradiction within fundamentalism? No, and for two reasons, both of which lie in the character of fundamentalist religion. First of all, the prominence and the functions assigned to passages are related to the structure of the religion: for instance, the virgin birth is taken literally because its physical reality is supposed to be essential for the religion; but the law that the seventh day should be observed as a day of rest is not taken literally, since Sunday is taken as the day of rest, and this is because the structure of the religion has accepted that, among the Old Testament commandments, many or most are either not observed at all, or are observed only in an altered sense, within Christianity. Seventh Day Adventism, by contrast, also fundamentalist, insists on the literality of the seventh-day commandment because its religious structure has adopted that particular point as a vital one.

Secondly, many of the points of interpretation that have been taken as illustrations in this section are points that might easily be by-passed within fundamentalist religion itself. Even as a fundamentalist one can live a long time without thinking much about the age of Methuselah or the number of actual generations covered by Gen. 5. For the direct functioning of the religion these matters are not very important. They become important, not within the primary level, the actual functioning of the religion, but within the secondary levels, namely the apologetic and the scholarly exposition. Here they become important: these passages have to be given their interpretation, based upon the principle of inerrancy, not so much because the passages themselves are vital for the religion, but because the interpretation of them acts as a defence which is necessary for the protection of the general principle of biblical inerrancy. As we saw above, the same is true of a story like that of the expulsion of Hagar: the religion of the average fundamentalist is fully satisfied with Ishmael as a small child, indeed religiously this is a much more natural and more pathetic picture; only scholarly apologetics, with the need to avoid a source-critical solution, passes over to a non-literal understanding.

We thus see an important point: the inerrancy of the Bible, the entire Bible including its details, is indeed the constant principle of rationality within fundamentalism. Seen from outside, it distorts and deranges all sorts of relations which to the student of the Bible seem quite obvious; but, seen from within, it is a constant and dependable principle which applies equally at every point. The ramifications of this will have to be examined in due course.

We have argued sufficiently that fundamentalist interpretation is not tied to a principle of literality, and no more illustrations need be added here, because evidence for this will accumulate throughout this book. It is interesting to reflect, however, that moderates have almost always classed the fundamentalists as literalists and criticized them on this ground: and there was some ground for this, since fundamentalists can be annoyingly literalistic on one point or on another. Basically, however, the criticism was a misunderstanding and a wrong conceptualization of the issue, and this for another reason which we have not yet mentioned: this criticism, though intended to damage the fundamentalist position, usually granted too much to it. People tended to say, yes, the Bible is of course right, but not in the literal sense in which the fundamentalists take it; that is, people held to the rightness of what the Bible says, but tried to take it in a more indirect sense, to make it apply in a more vague and general way. Sometimes, indeed, this approach may be justified. But at many points the reverse must be said: the text should indeed be understood 'literally', in that the literal sense was the one intended by the author, but this must mean that, in passing from the sense of the text to the statement of what happened, or to a statement of the real theological entities involved, one must make a critical reconstruction which does not follow the exact lines of the text: in other words one must take a line that for the fundamentalist means that the text is 'wrong'. The common criticism of fundamentalism for being 'literal' has too often been a plea for a vaguer understanding of scripture, when what was needed was a critical approach to scripture.

Perhaps, however, it is in the doctrinal portions of the Bible that we come nearest to what people feel to be a literalism in fundamentalist interpretation. Not all doctrinal passages are taken literally, and some are skated over very lightly indeed; but, when one is taken seriously, the biblical wording is taken, within the religion itself and not only in the secondary scholarship and apologetic, as an exact and direct reflection or transcript of God's intention. The wording itself is then a final and fully expressive transcript of God's mind.

In concluding this section we may make two general points about the inerrancy of the Bible. First of all, conservative apologists will sometimes say that they are not bound to the absolute inerrancy of the Bible. As we shall later see,[15] there have been those who maintained that there could not be a single error anywhere in the Bible, because the smallest error, if a real error, would totally destroy the inspiration of the whole. Others, unwilling to commit themselves to this drastic doctrine, pretend to allow a slight flexibility here. 'We are delivered from the paralysing fear that if one single discrepancy should be found in Scripture we should have to abandon all belief in its authority.'[16] This argument of Green's is not against the theme of this section, that inerrancy is basic to the conservative evangelical approach to the Bible. Inerrancy is their approach even if they allow very occasional theoretical exceptions. It is the principle of inerrancy, and nothing else, that motivates the conservative position in all the instances surveyed in this section. The flexibility of the 'possible occasional minor error' is to be understood as a convenient escape route: no actual instance of error is admitted. In all actual cases, therefore, the Bible is interpreted in such a way as to avoid the possibility of error; the flexibility, as Green himself well shows, has no effect other than to avoid the psychological consequences entailed if complete inerrancy was affirmed as an absolute doctrine.[17]

The second point is this. In talking about errors and inerrancy we are to a considerable degree accommodating ourselves to the fundamentalist way of perceiving the matter. It should not be supposed that critical scholarship is exercised to discover 'errors' in the Bible or that the critical reconstruction of biblical literature is built upon the detection of such 'errors'. Readers of critical introductions and commentaries will not find much about 'errors' in them at all. Indeed one could take the opposite position and say that the critical approach to biblical literature is the one in which it becomes (for the first time!) possible to understand the literature without having to use the category of 'error'. It is only within the fundamentalist world-view that it seems as if critical scholars are primarily concerned with the imputation of 'error' to scripture. It is the fundamentalist doctrine, and not any other, that insists on pressing the category of error to the forefront of the discussion. In giving to the idea of inerrancy the space and attention we are doing, we are to some extent accepting the proportions and perspectives in which fundamentalists see our question. As seen from within critical scholarship the proportions are quite different. Although discrepancies and 'errors' can be important as indications of source differences and the like, and thus of the way in which the traditions have grown up historically, they are in themselves a matter of comparatively little interest to scholarship and other elements of the critical operation are much more important.

2. *Harmonization*

The inerrancy of the Bible means that its statements correspond to sequences of actual events, or to relations between actual existing realities, and that they correspond very closely, if not perfectly. It follows that, just as any single biblical passage corresponds to relations or events in external reality, where there are two or more passages which refer to the same events or realities, these passages must correspond with one another. If this is not so, then one or both of them will be 'wrong' and the whole fabric of inerrancy will be destroyed. The harmonizing of biblical passages which appear to refer to the same realities but to say something different about them is thus one of the most essential elements in conservative evangelical interpretation.

Some of the explanations we considered above in our discussion of literalism can be considered also as instances of harmonizing. If Hagar's child, as he is in Gen. 21.14, suddenly grows into a strapping adolescent, this is a harmonizing explanation, to bring the passage into agreement with 17.25, and thus to avoid the suggestion (*a*) that one of the two passages was 'wrong' about the facts of Ishmael's age, and (*b*) that the two passages came from different sources, which had different ideas, traditions or information about Hagar and Ishmael. If the passage describing the descent of Moses and Aaron is stretched to include numerous generations who are totally unmentioned, this is in order to harmonize it with the figure of 430 years for the sojourn of the children of Israel in Egypt.

But the practice of harmonization is even more familiar when applied to documents closer to the majority of Christians, like the gospels. If two passages in the gospels describe in different terms what seems to be the same incident, they are harmonized in the conservative literature. The most common way to do this is to add the two together, so that what one says complements what the other says. Certainly it is admitted that one evangelist has seen things or described things rather differently from another, just as two persons who witness the same road accident will describe it differently. But they cannot be in real contradiction, they cannot be saying really different things that cannot be reconciled. The most striking example is the famous incident of the cleansing of the Temple by Jesus. In the synoptic gospels this is narrated at the very end of the ministry of Jesus, at the beginning of passion week (Matt. 21.10–17; Mark 11.15–19; Luke 19.45–48), while John has it right at the beginning of the ministry (John 2.13–17). *The New Bible Commentary Revised* (on Mark, C. E. Graham Swift, p. 875b) gives us the simple but ludicrous harmonization: 'By far the most satisfactory solution is that Jesus cleansed the Temple twice.' Why not? By the same account, why should the ascension of Jesus to heaven not have taken place twice? This would successfully harmonize the facts that, according to Luke 24.51, the ascension appears to have taken place on the same day as the resurrection, while Acts 1 expressly makes it about forty days later. Jesus was carried up to heaven, but later returned, appeared and spoke with his disciples for forty days, and then finally ascended again. Why not? I have actually heard this explanation offered in all seriousness by a prominent conservative scholar. I do not suggest that it circulates widely; nevertheless it is a perfectly logical application of the harmonization techniques normal in conservative apologetic, and conveys their atmosphere very well. The difficulty is felt by *The New Bible Commentary Revised* (I. H. Marshall, p. 925): 'If the account is taken literally, it would imply that the resurrection and ascension both occurred on Easter Sunday.' Quite so. The commentator then, typically of conservative interpretation, abandons the literal sense as soon as it would imply error or disagreement in the Bible; he achieves harmonization by taking the Acts account literally in this respect (i.e. in respect of the time of the events) and holding that the Luke account is telescoped or otherwise imprecise. Multiple ascensions form a different method of harmonization: in this case one has the advantage that both narratives, that in Luke and that in Acts, can be taken literally in this respect. In either case, what never enters the head of the conservative interpreter is that there was no certain knowledge of the temporal sequence, or that quite contradictory accounts existed, or that some source represented the events in such and such a way not because that was the way it happened but because that was important for the theological message of that particular source.

Harmonization through the production of multiple events is the most thoroughly laughable of all devices of interpretation. It is not new, but goes back at least to the Reformation. As Roland Bainton tells us, 'The simplest way to achieve a reconciliation between contradictory accounts of the same event is to have the event occur in as many forms and on as many occasions as may be needful to validate all the versions.'[18] Andreas Osiander in his *Harmonia Evangelica* (Paris 1545) maintained that 'Christ must have twice been crowned with thorns and clad in purple, and that Peter must have warmed himself four times.' Against this Castellio argued that 'since there are four accounts of Peter's denial and four accounts of the prediction of the denial and since the fulfilment must be assumed to have corresponded perfectly to the prediction, therefore to account for all the verbal differences one would have to assume eight denials.' This amusing situation certainly goes beyond what can be found among modern fundamentalists: the case of the double cleansing of the temple is the nearest one comes to it.[19] But, if modern fundamentalists do not follow Osiander in his repeated positing of multiple events, it is not to be supposed that they are the more ready to accept and tolerate errors in the biblical accounts. There is nothing in their principles that entitles them to do that. But they approach the matter in a different way.

Everyone knows the story of the person who came to Jesus and asked him what he should do in order to inherit eternal life, or words coming more or less to this (Mark 10.17f.; Matt. 19.16ff.; Luke 18.18ff.). According to Mark and Luke, Jesus answered: 'Why do you call me good? There is no one good except one, namely God.' Matthew says the same thing according to a common, but less good, text. The best text of Matthew, as is probably universally agreed, says something different. According to it Jesus said: 'Why do you ask me concerning the good? One alone is good.'

What, then, did Jesus in fact say on this occasion? Did he say, 'Why do you call me good? There is no one good except one, namely God,' or did he say 'Why do you ask me concerning the good? One alone is good'? We could of course follow Osiander and say that the incident took place twice, Jesus answering one way the first time and the other the second. But modern conservatives do not seem to like this solution. But then, if the incident happened only once, it must mean that either Mark and Luke, or Matthew, correctly reports what Jesus said. One of them must be wrong. Or, worse, both of them may be wrong, and Jesus said something quite different altogether. The Bible then seems to be quite unreliable. No so fast, says a rigid conservative like E. J. Young. This depends on what the evangelists were trying to do. Young agrees that it is a matter of the utmost importance that we should ascertain precisely what the words spoken by Jesus were; we cannot dismiss the matter by saying that it is all roughly the same thing; no, it is vital that we should know, and the quest for the actual words of Jesus is fully justified. But there are two reasons why we should not suppose that there is any error or discrepancy here. Firstly, we do not know that the intention of the writers was to give a verbatim report of all the words of the questioner and of Jesus. Secondly, the original conversation took place in Aramaic, while the gospel text is in Greek, that is, a translation from the original.

Young is thus taking refuge in vagueness. The writers perhaps did not want to give a verbatim report; they only put in what was germane to their own purpose. It was no 'slavish imitation' but 'variety of a useful and instructive kind'. Young thus, making a virtue out of necessity, tells us that the 'minor contradictions and errors' actually increase our confidence in the whole. This is typical of what happens when several eye-witnesses in real life see the same incident: none of them tell it exactly as any other tells it. 'The minor divergencies, therefore, are a sign of genuineness.'[20] This argument is in fact widely used by conservative polemicists in discussion of the New Testament.

But Young, by introducing the intention of the author, is pulling wool over the eyes of his readers. He has in fact now changed his ground. He has abandoned the position that the Bible actually tells you what Jesus said. It doesn't. It tells you what Matthew or Mark, who were not reporting verbatim, intended the reader to understand. In so far as this is a 'sign of genuineness', it can only be a sign that the Bible genuinely goes back to the intention of Matthew or Mark. But the intention of Matthew, Mark or Luke, according to the argument itself, is not to reproduce the words that Jesus spoke. All words in the Bible are expressions of their author's intentions: that tells us nothing, for their intentions could have been to invent a likely story, to embellish a legend, or anything. The mention of an Aramaic original is also entirely irrelevant. All this could mean would be that Jesus spoke a sentence in Aramaic, and that either Matthew, or Mark and Luke, or all three, misunderstood its meaning, and therefore stated it wrongly in Greek. But this also means that the words of Jesus were wrongly reported by one or more of the gospels. If inspiration did not guide them correctly in understanding the meaning of the Aramaic sentences of Jesus, then of course any of the teaching ascribed to Jesus in the gospels may be totally wrong, the gospel writers having misunderstood the meaning when they translated it into Greek. Young is in fact in a cleft stick. If the biblical text reports the words of Jesus, then one or more of the gospels is wrong. Therefore the text reports not the words actually spoken, but the words as the evangelist intended us to hear them. Here Young is going off in a liberal direction: what the biblical text tells us is not what took place, but what the writers intended. But by confusing the argument he leaves the reader with the impression of having salvaged the 'genuineness' of the report.

This is the characteristic vague approach to these matters, which runs through much of the conservative evangelical literature. In the commentaries the writers often make no attempt to tell the reader which of the varying versions states the actual words spoken by Jesus, or the things he precisely did. In many cases the scholarly writers probably know that this cannot be done. But their readers will read on, supposing that all the versions give a transcript of what was actually said and done.

It is interesting to consider the question, why conservative evangelical commentators at some points remain satisfied with this vague and soft treatment of the variations, while at others they go over to more acute and drastic methods of harmonization, such as the supposition that Jesus cleansed the temple twice. I would surmise that the difference is connected with the potential for the raising of *critical* suggestions. In the synoptic gospels there always were three texts, and it was always known that they varied. To admit a variation as between Matthew and Mark, or Luke and Mark, was nothing very revolutionary. Moreover, the number of variations between these gospels was so very high that an enormous apparatus of harmonizations would be necessary, as we have seen, to bring it about that all of them perfectly related the detailed historical facts. The cleansing of the temple in John is a different matter. This is a single and isolated incident, where a drastic harmonization can do a lot of good. Moreover, the variation of John from the synoptics is a more serious matter for the fundamentalist than the numerous variations of the synoptics against one another, for it might be used to suggest that John is not reporting the actual words of Jesus but, in Young's own term, telling a story according to his own intention. This could be very dangerous, because it might suggest that John was not intending to give a historical account of Jesus's words or deeds; and this would be most unwelcome to conservatives, because John is one of their major sources for Jesus' 'claims' to be God.

In general, then, modern conservative evangelical publications alternate their methods: sometimes they use explicit harmonizations of events, sometimes they leave differing accounts in vague juxtaposition. The former has the advantage that it enables one to suppose that the Bible gives a quite correct report of the incident each time it occurred. In the latter case there is probably a tacit abandonment of the notion that the exact words as spoken, or the exact sequence of the incident, can be read straight out of the biblical text. Yet this is a large shift of emphasis. An infallible account of what Jesus said is one thing; an infallible account of what Matthew intended to convey in reporting Jesus is quite another thing. The difference, however, has not much troubled conservative opinion. Conservative writers, and their readers, are not looking for variations, they are looking for ways to minimize them or discount them. If harmonization is one way, vagueness is another. Detail, as we have seen, is on the side of critical scholarship and not of conservatism. In any case, apart from the deliberate harmonization of detailed speeches and narratives, conservative interpretation depends on an extensive harmonization in a wider sense. There has to be doctrinal harmonization as well as harmonization in details of narratives. Harmonization in a general sense pervades the conservative approach.

The amount of harmonization that is necessary in order to sustain a consistent and detailed fundamentalist understanding of the Bible is very great, and it is probable that very few fundamentalists, apart from scholarly apologists, are aware of the amount involved. This is just as well for the fundamentalist movement, for there is no element in the entire fundamentalist approach to the Bible that is more likely to draw upon itself ridicule and derision from without and a deep sense of absurdity from even within the ranks of the faithful. Here once again we have an element that is not particularly necessary for the active religious use of scripture, which is primarily important to the average fundamentalist, but becomes increasingly essential as the attempt is made to shore up and complete the defences of the total fundamentalist position on the more scholarly level. In order to understand this we may go back to the religious principles from which the need for harmonization on the scholarly level is generated.

There often seems to be an absurd lack of proportion between the things that are religiously important to fundamentalists and the arguments about scripture by which they seek to guarantee them. In what way would the form of religious life, outlined in the previous chapter, be imperilled, if it were to be believed that the book named after the prophet Isaiah were written by a series of other prophets, or if Deuteronomy were known to have been written not by Moses but many centuries after his death, or if it was thought that the Epistle to Titus were not written by St Paul? Not in the slightest! There is absolutely nothing in the characteristic evangelical religious pattern that would necessarily be imperilled if these elementary concepts of biblical criticism were to be accepted. This, incidentally, is exactly the reason why not all evangelicals are conservative evangelicals, and why we must thoroughly reject the claim that, in order to be a consistent evangelical, one must also be a conservative evangelical. On the contrary, as we shall see in due course, the only way of maintaining a consistently evangelical position is if one carefully avoids the non-evangelical modes of thinking which are essential to the conservative evangelical position. It is in fact perfectly easy to preach and practise the entire evangelical scheme of religion while accepting that Deuteronomy came from many centuries after Moses and that Titus was not written by St Paul. Only comparatively small adjustments in one's thinking are necessary in order to adopt these critical concepts within an evangelical view of the Bible; and most evangelicals do in fact succeed in making these adjustments. Why should a matter like the authorship of books be so important?

According to the fundamentalist understanding, the whole Bible hangs together; all parts are related to all others. Any defect, any criticism attaching to any part, however small, is therefore a wound which injures the entirety. To say that Deuteronomy came from a writer many centuries after Moses, or that Titus was not written by St Paul, is thus to make a jagged tear that runs through and spoils the total seamless garment of scripture.

Here again subtle distinctions have to be made, for it is important to understand what is meant. It is often said that fundamentalists ascribe equal authority and importance to every word and every passage anywhere in the Bible. Even if fundamentalists occasionally say this, it is not to be taken very seriously. The actual situation is much more complex. On the one hand fundamentalists hold that all segments or portions of the Bible are the Word of God and that any such segment or portion, or at least any intelligible unit within it, can at least in principle be used as a text for exposition in preaching and can be taken as relevant for the establishment of doctrine. This does not mean in fact that everything is taken on the same level, and the wiser statements of conservative evangelicals accept this. No one really supposes that Esther or Ecclesiastes draws the same interest or plays the same role within fundamentalist Christianity as the letters of St Paul or the gospel of St John. Though these books are read and pondered as holy books they are seldom preached on and little or no doctrinal construction is based upon them. If Esther or Ecclesiastes were to be accorded equal attention with St John's gospel, this would only come about if a preacher or someone else were to read the entire content of the gospel, or of the New Testament generally, into the Old Testament book, by some sort of allegorical process; this has at times been done, especially with books like the Song of Songs for which a strong tradition of allegorical exposition exists. But though such exposition can be found amply evidenced in older Protestant preaching, say in the eighteenth century, I doubt if it is much to be found in modern fundamentalism. It is a perfectly sensible statement of the situation when *Evangelical Belief* tells us (p. 18) that 'The more homely advice of Proverbs, relating to the conduct of life, differs considerably from the majestic presentations of the character of Christ . . . in

John's gospel . . . Both are necessary if men are to apprehend more fully the mind of God.'

In spite of these differences, scripture can be seen as a whole, in that the will of the one God is discerned through all or any part of it, and in that each part contributes something distinctive to the total impression of the whole, just as in a picture every detail contributes something to its total effect as a work of art. This view, though not unquestionable, is in itself a perfectly reasonable position, and one that could well be affirmed by a fully critical scholar or theologian. In this, as often, conservative evangelicals are simply mistaken in supposing that their positive insights are such that critical scholarship and modern theology cannot also affirm them.

There are, then, for conservative evangelicals as for others, distinctions in function, and therefore implicitly in value and centrality, within the biblical books. These distinctions are dictated on the one hand by the content of the books themselves, and on the other by the total religious structure within which they are used. For instance, the fact that the religion is Christian evangelicalism necessarily generates a certain priority of the New Testament as against parts at least of the Old. It is probably a fair judgment if one says that active fundamentalist groups give more attention to the Pauline letters than to any other single body of biblical material;[21] this is because these give the strongest concentration of teaching that can be understood as doctrine, and we shall see that this is an important ingredient in the total fundamentalist outlook on the Bible.

But, though distinctions within the scripture, however great, that are dictated by content or by the situation of whole books (for example, within the Old Testament rather than the New) are validated and absorbed by the religious structure of fundamentalism, it is quite a different matter with distinctions that are created by *critical* examination. These may be quite minute in their effects: as we have seen, practically no imaginable difference could be made to evangelical doctrine or practice if Deuteronomy were substantially later than Moses, or if Titus were not by St Paul; no change other than a small adjustment in the view of scripture would be required. But even such small changes in the assessment of relations between books, when made on critical grounds, are felt as a deep and dangerous threat to the unity, authority and effectiveness of scripture. Such suggestions are treated with the utmost suspicion and every possible argument is marshalled against them. Why is this? The basic evangelical religious impulse could and would continue quite unchanged, even if it were believed that there were two sources in Genesis, one of which treated Ishmael as a small child while the other reckoned him as a teenager; why then must these suggestions be repudiated?

One way of understanding the answer is this: the fundamentalist is asking himself the question, what can be the motives of those who make such suggestions in the first place? What can be their purposes, and what would be the implications of these suggestions if they were to be accepted? What reason can one have for thinking that Deuteronomy comes from a time long after Moses, but that one perceives a break, a cleft, between Deuteronomy and what is otherwise said about Moses? It implies that harmonizing will no longer work, that differences are not merely apparent: on the contrary, they are real. It means that there is a crack in the total body of scripture other than those that have already been allowed for in the evangelical religious structure and other than the fact that there is a variety of books from various times and authors.

This implies, as the fundamentalist sees it, that the reader or scholar is willing to set his own critical judgment against the intrinsic God-given harmony of the Bible and its doctrines. He has the incredible impertinence to suppose that, because he cannot see how varying elements hang together in harmony, this means that they actually disagree. It is a fundamental principle that the Christian, faced with difficulties in his reading of the Bible, should persevere in studying the variety of texts on the subject, 'comparing scripture with scripture' as the saying goes, so that in the end the fullness of truth as willed by God will become apparent to him. All this, it seems, would be gone if the reader, on finding a passage that seemed to differ from another, straightaway concluded that they came from different sources. The many-faceted harmony of the one scripture would have been changed into a variety of separate heaps.

Actually this argument has little validity, even on conservative terms. It requires very little flexibility of mind to see that a critical reader of the Bible, who may also be an evangelical, can still and does still carry on the same process of 'comparing scripture with scripture' as the fundamentalist does, except that he does it on a somewhat different level. He can, let us say, compare Galatians (by Paul) with Ephesians (let us suppose, by someone else), or the J source in Genesis with the P source, with exactly the same object in view: by exposing himself to the Word of God as mediated by two different biblical writers, he seeks to find the fullness of truth as willed by God. This is what happens in fact in theological biblical study informed by critical approaches. There is in principle no difference between reading and comparing two documents which have been distinguished by source criticism, like the J and P sources in Genesis, and two documents from different authors which were printed as separate books in the Bible itself, like Acts and Galatians. But even this very slight flexibility is looked on with severe suspicion by the fundamentalist mind.

Why is this? Fundamentalist ideas grew up in, or go back to, a time when the real author of the Bible was God. God revealed what he pleased of himself by giving such and such information to each of the human writers; but the whole hangs together because it all comes straight from him. It pleased him to channel all this knowledge through a variety of human writers, but the knowledge is all equally valid because it comes from him. Certain God-given differences were there from the beginning, and it is our task to overcome them and appreciate the harmony of the totality of his truth. It is quite another thing to create distinctions which were not there in the beginning: this is to proceed in the wrong direction. Though more and more attention is necessarily being given, even by fundamentalists, to the part and the contribution of the human authors of the Bible, the conception that God himself is the source, and therefore the guarantor of the unity, of the whole, continues to act as an obstacle blocking all arguments that proceed from diversity of viewpoint to the recognition of different sources.

Another aspect is as follows. Fundamentalists, though many of them may not admit it, accept in practice a certain grading of the biblical materials, so that, to repeat our example, St John's gospel has a much more central function than Ecclesiastes. They do not willingly concede that a similar grading can be carried out by others. Why not? Because they think that, among non-fundamentalists, this grading would be motivated by a will to demote some portions of scripture from their status of authority. Perhaps one could put it in this way: to them all of scripture has absolute authority, being the inspired Word of God, but some parts of it can be upgraded to a specially high status or function. If non-fundamentalists are allowed to perform a grading process, they think, it will be a downgrading process: some parts of the Bible will remain as Word of God, some of it will be reduced to a lower status. Thus it is acceptable to say that St John's gospel has higher status or a more important function than Ecclesiastes or Esther; but if you say that Esther or Ecclesiastes is not on the same level as the rest of the Bible, or as the New Testament, that is a very suspicious and dangerous statement, for you may well be setting out to deprive them of their status as absolute Word of God. All this is, indeed, pure theory and principle, engendered by the suspicion which is the normal fundamentalist attitude to other Christians, and probably has no relation to practice: there is no reason to believe that Esther or Ecclesiastes receive any more attention or interpretation within active fundamentalism than they received from those 'liberal' clergy who doubted whether they should really be within the canon of scripture. But it is of the way fundamentalists *think* that we are talking.

If this is so with actual biblical books, such as Esther or Ecclesiastes, so much the worse with sources like J and P, which were unknown until identified by critical methods. First of all, the identification of such a source may involve, and commonly does involve, a judgment about the theology of the source now discovered. The P source thinks about God in a way different from the J source. This means that there is some sort of conflict of theologies within the biblical material, and that the differing theology of this or that source is being used to form a picture of the mind and personality of the tradition that lies behind it. But, secondly, and a good deal worse, scholars may find that they prefer the theological outlook of the J source to that of the P source. The critical operation in such cases, as fundamentalists see it, may be motivated by the desire to elevate to a higher status the theological outlook that is congenial to the scholar, or to a school of scholars. No doubt the case of this sort that has most deeply burned itself into the mind of fundamentalists was the preference commonly expressed in the liberalism of the beginning of this century, for Mark and the early gospel source Q, as against St Paul and the gospel of St John, plus the later material in the synoptic gospels.[22] Fundamentalists picture this as a process by which scholars, armed with their own preconceived theology, have simply imposed it upon the texts. This is of course no very original criticism, since most theologies have said the same of other theologies for centuries; and certainly fundamentalism is in no good position to use that criticism, since it is in fact a uniquely effective device for doing just this, for imposing upon the Bible the fundamentalist religious pattern and preventing anyone from getting anything else out of it. But, justified or unjustified, this is how the fundamentalist is likely to see the matter.

Another aspect is the following. There are certain books which, taken just as books, are not so central in their functioning within fundamentalism as others, but which contain within themselves particular passages or formulations which are peculiarly important for fundamentalist doctrine. The obvious instance is the doctrine of the divine inspiration of scripture itself. Perhaps the two most-cited individual texts are II Tim. 3.16, the only place where the term 'inspired by God' occurs in the Bible, and II Peter 1.19–21. *Evangelical Belief*, a source of impeccable conservatism, says (p. 18) that these two are the only general statements about the actual process of inspiration in the Bible. But both II Timothy and II Peter can probably be considered somewhat marginal books, and are probably treated so in practice even by fundamentalist circles. But this immediately raises the spectre of a possibility that the doctrine of inspiration and the like, as enunciated in these passages, belongs to a secondary stratum of the thought of the New Testament and does not belong to its first line. Why, after all, did St Paul not include a strong statement on divine inspiration in his letters to the Romans and the Galatians, as a modern fundamentalist Paul would certainly have done? And this spectre is in fact made even more unpleasant by the critics, who allege exactly this, that Paul did not write Timothy and Titus, and that Peter did not write II Peter. Fundamentalists cannot possibly allow these two basic texts to slip out of their grasp. For exactly this sort of purpose they have to insist: (*a*) that any passage from anywhere within the Bible may be sufficient to express and prove a basic doctrine, and this is especially so if the passage in question is one in doctrinal form; (*b*) that the letters in question, II Timothy and II Peter, come in fact substantially or verbatim from Saints Paul and Peter, this being itself validated by their names at the beginning of the letters; and these names, being themselves part of inspired scripture, give an infallible assurance of their authorship. The authorship makes an important difference. If the letters are not in fact written by these apostles, this moves them more towards the margin of the New Testament; if they are really written by them, it brings them back more towards the centre. Thus, though no difference would be made to the fabric of active fundamentalist religion if Paul was not the author of Titus (or of I and II Timothy, for the three are necessarily grouped together for purposes of study), the fundamentalist doctrine of scripture must, because of the way it looks at things, take the question very seriously.

The instance which we have just studied displays a number of the essential facets of fundamentalism; it well illustrates in particular how, although fundamentalism allows and indeed requires a certain grading and ordering of the biblical material, it nevertheless combines this with the insistence that each and every part, anywhere in the Bible, is fully divinely inspired and able to bear the weight of validation of doctrine. It also illustrates how these theological necessities greatly increase the pressure upon the literary question, who was the actual author of this or that book?

Another reason is as follows. Conservative evangelicalism is much affected by the principle that, if you give them an inch, they will take a mile. Criticism, it is believed, will very quickly go to extremes, dissecting the simplest document into a multitude of fragments. The way to prevent this unhappy extreme from taking place is to prevent the process from beginning at all. If you allow a man to say that Deuteronomy is from a long time after Moses, then next he will be saying that Jesus never said the things he is reported in the gospels to have said, and from this it is but a short step to saying that Jesus never existed, or that the patriarchs were moon-gods, or that St Paul totally misunderstood the actual message and place of Jesus. All these things work by the same essential logic, and if you are to oppose the extreme developments you must already have opposed the smallest beginnings. Once the camel gets his nose into the tent he soon comes to occupy the whole space within.

This argument is, seen from another point of view, not one peculiar to Protestant fundamentalism. Rather, it is a general old-fashioned conservative position. Christian faith is the assent to an enormous corpus of beliefs, the 'Christian system' as it was sometimes called, and the alteration of any smallest part of the corpus threatens the destruction of everything. A touching and delightful passage was written by Guillaume Meignan, later to be Cardinal Archbishop of Tours, in 1856; it starts from worries about Balaam's ass and its speech to Balaam:

> If the words of the ass and the apparition of the angel are fiction or a dream, even though Sacred Scripture relates them as fact, why wouldn't the whole story of Balaam be fictitious and a dream, why then wouldn't the whole Bible be a mixture of truth and fiction? The door is open to arbitrary decisions. The Sacred Scriptures will be despoiled of their sacred character; their authority will vanish; the Bible, having become the most unreliable of histories, will no longer be the Bible.[23]

In fact it seems that Meignan gradually moved towards a more liberal position, later holding that scripture was free from error only 'in essential facts, dogma and morals'. But he is only one instance among thousands who have at some stage felt that any slightest deviation in matters of faith would inevitably bring the entire structure to the ground. Though not the slightest of the sort has happened, fundamentalist apologists are still using the same argument as if it had some originality in it.

Seen from this point of view, of course, everything is of equal potential importance. For modern fundamentalists, as no doubt for Meignan in 1856, St John's gospel has a more important function than the Book of Numbers, and they do not in fact build a great deal of their living faith upon the talking powers of Balaam's ass, of which they probably do not think more than once in ten years. But the moment someone questions the story of Balaam's ass everything is different. Any doubt about this, and the entire edifice of Christianity may tumble to the ground. In this negative sense anything and everything that could somehow suggest some sort of error or imperfection in the Bible, however small, can be fatal to all Christian faith and life. In fundamentalism this position is a necessary result of the way in which the doctrinal structure of the authority and inspiration of scripture is organized and of the way in which it is tied by chains of necessity to literary and historical questions. All this we shall gradually unravel in the course of this book. But we have already shown how the harmonization procedure is one of the most essential linkages in the total system of the fundamentalist outlook.

This section may be concluded with the following consideration. It is very striking that the main points of conflict between fundamentalists and critical scholarship are historical matters: who wrote this book, whether Jesus said these sayings, how many sources there are in the pentateuch? For the most part they are not real theological points, such as: whether the covenant is the centre of Old Testament theology, or what is the significance of 'Son of Man' in the New Testament, or how far the world of biblical thinking is distinctive as against the thought of the Canaanites, the Assyrians or the Greeks. On questions like these last, in so far as conservative evangelicals give attention to them, their opinions tend to run along lines that have already been marked out by critical scholars who are also strongly theologically interested. Conservative scholars who interest themselves in these questions do not generally initiate any answer that is peculiarly conservative; rather they fit into the patterns that have been already marked out by non-conservative scholars. If there are conflicts, they come down on the side of one party among the non-conservative scholars, but they do not offer a strictly conservative answer. Considering the extremely partisan character of conservative evangelical opinion on other matters, this failure to form a partisan position on matters of biblical theology calls for comment.

One way of explaining it would be to say that, for the fundamentalist, the casting of doubt upon the Bible in historical regards opens the way to the casting of doubt upon it in theological regards also. This might mean, for instance, that if one could claim that Deuteronomy did not come from the time of Moses, one would then probably go on to relativize the theological assertions of that book, saying that they represent the theological trends of one particular time, which were inserted in the book because they seemed to answer the problems of that time. Going far enough along this line, the scholar might come to doubt whether the Ten Commandments represented a precise transcript of the will of God for man of all ages. In order to prevent these disastrous theological consequences, fundamentalism stops the entire process at its first point: Moses, it insists, did write the book, or nearly all of it goes back to him, which is supposed to be just as good; and since this is so none of the further consequences can rightly follow. The same would be true of comparable assertions about sayings of Jesus narrated in the gospels. The person who begins to think that St John's gospel is not written by the disciple, John the son of Zebedee, on the basis of his actual personal eye-witness of the events, may be found also to doubt whether the historical Jesus uttered such phrases as 'before Abraham was, I am' (John 8.58); such a person might then go on to doubt whether Jesus could really have had eternal pre-existence as the Son of God, and so on. Since there are no limits to what such a person might think, the only course is to cut off his train of thought at the beginning, by insisting that the gospel in question was in fact written by John the son of Zebedee, on the basis of his personal eye-witness experiences. Either of these cases would suggest that theological correctness was the main thing: the insistence on biblical accuracy in historical matters could then be taken (to borrow Jewish terminology) as a 'fence around the Torah' of theological correctness.[24]

Though it is possible to interpret the situation in the way outlined above, it is more probable, in my opinion, that it should be read in the other way. Fundamentalists put historical or literary information and theological assertions all on the same level, indeed in a sense the historical and literary information is the more important. In any case both elements are alike appreciated in the same way, as correct information. For most other Christians, theological claims are personal address and not straight communicated information. Moreover, this is true also of fundamentalism as an active religion: even for it the 'claims of Christ' are personal address seeking a personal response, while information like (say) the number of years Paul spent in Arabia or the authorship of Titus, while useful ancillary information, is not personal address challenging to faith. But for fundamentalist doctrine and biblical scholarship historical and literary data and theological claims work in exactly the same way. Indeed, though for religion in itself the theological assertions are doubtless more important, for the controversy with non-conservatives the historical information is actually more important, because it is subject to empirically-grounded disputation. Theological claims may be believed or not believed. One may or may not believe that God is love, or that justification is by faith, or that salvation is by the blood of Christ; but whether one believes them or not, they are scarcely a matter for proof from empirical evidence. Historical and literary information, however, may be disputed on human and empirical grounds. Fundamentalists do not like, of course, a person who disagrees with an important theological belief, but they feel they can cope with him, for this is a plain case of unbelief. If someone says that God is not love, or that salvation is not and cannot be by the blood of Christ, that, though very wrong, is a simple matter, for it simply means that the person who says these things is denying Christian belief, is setting himself against the gospel of Christ. A person who says, on literary and historical grounds, that the Bible contains numerous factual discrepancies is really a more serious threat to the fundamentalist mentality. Such a person is alleging evidences which have to be considered on an empirical plane. These evidences, whether strong or weak, force the fundamentalist to argue on an empirical plane, to reason on a basis of factual evidence. He will have to reply that reasoning from the factual evidence forces one to conclude that the Bible is in fact inerrant, and this is of course what fundamentalist apologetic is doing all the time. This type of argument is in fact the main stream of fundamentalist argument, and so it is only natural to suppose that this is what is for them most important. Very likely they will also take another course: that is, they will argue that opponents, in arguing from empirical evidence, are in fact not motivated by a zeal for the empirical evidence but by a theological hostility to the true gospel. Fundamentalist argument usually takes both courses, but the former is beyond doubt the more important.

Thus if it can be shown that the historical and literary information of the Bible, even where it is in itself theologically marginal, is extremely accurate, the way seems clear for a claim that the entire body of scripture is perfectly accurate in all regards. The amazing accuracy of the Bible in the smallest detail of ancient history, of names of people and their ages, and so on cannot but support the idea that a divine impartation of truth lies behind it, and that must mean that the doctrinal teaching of the Bible, what it says about God and his ways, must be even more astoundingly perfect. This chain of argument is probably the reason why historical and literary matters, like the authorship of certain books or the identification of sources within them, though to others they seem theologically marginal and without effect on the religious structure, are for many fundamentalists of primary importance, and especially so on their controversial side, that is, in dispute with non-conservatives.

3. *How do we know that the Bible is inerrant?*

We have just been comparing the respective roles of the theological inerrancy of the Bible and its historical inerrancy. One may either ascend from the historical to the theological or descend from the theological to the historical. Fundamentalist apologetic literature seems to imply that the process works in both directions. On the ascending side, the historical accuracy of the Bible is so great that it guarantees for us the theological assertions also. This is done through guaranteeing the identity of the person who made these assertions. We can be sure that the words spoken or written came in fact from the persons from whom they are said to have come, from Jesus or from Moses or from Paul: the fact that they were historically uttered or written by that sacred person is itself a sufficient reason why we should and must believe them. On the descending side, the theological content of the Bible is so marvellous and so convincing that one can be sure that the book that contains it has no imperfection of any sort. If it is trustworthy in saying that God is love or that Christ died for our sins, then it must be accurate in saying that Deuteronomy was written by Moses or that II Peter was written by Peter. But, in addition to this general argument, there is a more specific argument which we have not as yet examined; and, since it is perhaps the weapon most incessantly used in all the conservative arsenal, some detailed attention must now be given to it.

The argument is easily stated: the Bible is authoritative, inspired, infallible and inerrant because it itself says so. The Bible 'claims' to be without error. Or, breaking it down into greater detail: Jesus says that the Bible is without error, Paul says so, Peter says so, and generally all biblical writers who are in a position to say anything about the matter say so. The Bible is inerrant because the Bible says it is inerrant, or because Jesus, Paul and Peter, as represented in the Bible, say that it is inerrant, which is the same thing.

Now, if this were a statement of the authoritative position exercised by the Old Testament in the minds of Jesus and the early church, the argument would be right but also for critical scholars would be unnecessary. They know perfectly well the vital and central status that the Old Testament held in the minds of Jews of the time, as of early Christians, and the fundamentalist appeal to an inerrant Bible as a guarantee of this is quite unnecessary, since the facts would be granted without any such appeal. What is more important is the use of the same argument to guarantee the historical inerrancy of the Old Testament. Fundamentalist polemicists seem really to think that, because the Jesus of Matt. 12.40 used the comparison 'as Jonah was three days and three nights in the belly of the whale', this means that Jesus is placing all his personal and spiritual authority in support of the thesis that there was a historical Jonah who was factually within the whale or fish and went through the different vicissitudes described in the book of Jonah. They really think that, because the Jesus of Mark 12.35 said that 'David himself, by the Holy Spirit said, The Lord said unto my Lord etc. (quoting Psalm 110)', this means that Jesus is personally guaranteeing that the Psalm was historically written by the original David. They really think that, when in Matt. 24.15 Jesus is represented as speaking of 'the abomination of desolation spoken of by the prophet Daniel', the historical Jesus is staking his whole authority and credibility as a teacher upon the assertion that the passage referred to (Dan. 12.11 etc.) was actually spoken by a historical Daniel, who lived in the times and circumstances in which Daniel is depicted as living in the book of that name. All these arguments are used again and again; they form an essential element in the structure of the fundamentalist arguments for the authority and inerrancy of the Bible, and they also constitute the principal or overriding arguments for the acceptance of the traditional attributions of books to Jonah, to David, to Daniel and so on.[25]

Thus the full theological status of Jesus Christ and the apostles is deployed as a power that will enforce the traditional authorship and historicity of these various documents. Jesus said this, and this is final; to question this is to say that he was wrong, and if he was wrong in this, then he may perfectly well have been wrong in everything. Worse than this, it is not only a matter of saying that Jesus might anywhere have been wrong in matters of fact and of theology, it means that as a person he has ceased to be trustworthy:

'If He (Jesus) could be mistaken on matters which He regarded as of the strictest relevance to His own person and ministry, it is difficult to see exactly how or why He either can or should be trusted anywhere else.'[26] The authority of Christ settles the literary and historical questions: of Psalm 110, C. E. Graham Swift writes, 'our Lord's attribution of the Psalm to David must foreclose the question of authorship for all who accept his authority.'[27] In his teaching Jesus mentioned Psalm 110 as if it was by David and the journey of Jonah in the belly of the fish as if it had really taken place; therefore the Psalm was composed by David, and the underwater journey of Jonah did in fact take place. If these things are not true, then no reliance can be placed on anything that he said about anything; he has become totally untrustworthy.

This endlessly repeated argument seeks to use the personal loyalty of Christians towards Jesus as a lever to force them into fundamentalist positions on historical and literary matters. There is no part of the fundamentalist world view that should inspire so much distaste in the mind of other Christians. Its distortion of the proper proportions of the Christian faith is extreme.

For Christians generally it is probably not necessary to offer this grotesque argument the dignity of a refutation. Nevertheless, certain useful understandings of the working of the fundamentalist mind can be gained from the further analysis of the argument. On the general approach to the argument I cannot do better than cite a well-written passage by Huxtable:

> If . . . an absent-minded professor tells me that the train for Penzance leaves Waterloo at noon and I find that in fact it leaves Paddington half an hour before, I do not conclude that my informant is a liar, nor that he is ill-disposed towards me, nor that his reputation as a scholar rests on a fraud. I take him for what he is, and do not suppose that being a great authority on Homer makes him a reliable substitute for a timetable . . . Jesus Christ came into the world to be its Saviour, not an authority on biblical criticism.[28]

Quite so; or, formally speaking, the fundamentalist argument can be described as a simple literary function-mistake. The entirety of utterances ascribed to Jesus is treated as 'teaching'; and no adequate distinction is drawn between that which Jesus seeks to teach, the message which he seeks to communicate, and any or all of the elements which are found in his utterance. For instance, if we take the passage Mark 12.35–7, Jesus asks the question, how the scribes say that the Christ is the son of David. He points out that in the Psalm 'David' calls him Lord; he then puts the further question, how then is he his son? The passage is 'teaching' only in the broad sense, that Jesus is communicating orally with his hearers; but what he says cannot be strictly regarded as 'teaching', i.e. as stating any true facts or realities about the son of David. Jesus is rather asking a question; we are not directly told what the answer is. When, in the course of this interrogative conversation, he includes the preamble to the Psalm quotation, 'David himself by the Holy Spirit said', there are no grounds for saying that Jesus is 'teaching' anything about the question who in fact wrote this Psalm. This is one of the many cases where for fundamentalist apologetic the question of significance is ignored in interpretation, and this may be considered as another kind of 'literalism': the existence of the *words* that David by the Holy Spirit said this in itself constitutes and fully guarantees the proof that this is what Jesus is 'teaching'.

Now the full ramifications of this mode of looking at biblical questions will not be studied at this point, for we shall come back to them in our later chapter on doctrine.[29] We shall look here only at certain ways in which it casts light on the fundamentalist use of the Bible.

Firstly, the strongest defence that can be used in extenuation of this argument would be, paradoxically, to say that fundamentalists themselves do not depend upon it. It is highly improbable that the fundamentalist himself within his religious context believes in the authority and inerrancy of the Bible on the grounds that various passages within the Bible appear to him to assert that it is true. For him, on the contrary, things work the other way: he believes the Bible implicitly in any case, and all that these passages do is to formulate for him suitably that belief in the Bible that he already has. He does not really believe that David wrote Psalm 110, or that Jonah really travelled inside the whale, or that Daniel in the sixth century foresaw the abomination of desolation, on the grounds that Jesus says these things about these passages. On the contrary, he believes all these things already, and he similarly believes hundreds of other things, just as difficult or as subject to question, on which he has no word from Jesus or from any New Testament writer to fall back upon. For it must be remembered that, in spite of the numerous references in the New Testament to incidents and passages of the Old, the vast majority of peculiarities and difficulties in the Old find no comment or reference whatever in the New. The fundamentalist believes all these things in any case, because believing in them fits into the total character of his religion. His belief in the truth of biblical passages is broad-based: it runs through all aspects of his experience of religion, and it would be more true to say that he believes in the truth of the entire Bible because every portion of it in his experience seems to speak to him of God and to bring to him a living experience of God in Jesus Christ. This is how he really works, and this is why the argument we are discussing is not a travesty only of non-conservative Christian faith, but a travesty of the faith of fundamentalists also. Here then, as so often, the arguments used in controversy and apologetic are very badly integrated with the way in which even fundamentalists, as men of faith, themselves think.

Secondly, however, one cannot go too far with this point, for the argument reveals an element that is very deeply embedded in all fundamentalist faith and practice, namely the didactic emphasis. Biblical texts are thought of as containing teaching, nay, of *being* teaching. No one, I think, can study the conservative evangelical literature without noticing its very heavy didactic bias, and a recent book like J. W. Wenham's *Christ and the Bible* (Tyndale Press 1972) has examples on almost every page. 'Some sort of verbal inspiration' is 'taught' by Christ (p. 27); he 'taught the divine authorship of the Old Testament scriptures' and he 'taught the entire truth of his own teaching' (p. 109). This highly didactic approach to the study of the Bible fits in with the history of the fundamentalist movement, with its leadership during much of the nineteenth century being held, with exceptions, by men who would have been considered not theologians but 'Bible teachers'.[30] Now according to this approach Jesus becomes a little like a 'Bible teacher' himself: the same sort of terminology is used of him as of any other person whose real activity and office was didactic. Jesus 'held' a 'view' about this or that subject; his 'views' were of course infallible, being identical with those held by God himself, but he is like any other teacher in that you approach the task of understanding him by getting at his 'view'. Wenham's entire thesis (p. 7) is that 'Christ's view of Scripture can and should still be the Christian's view of Scripture'. Correspondingly, such matters as the conflicts between Jesus and the Pharisees or Sadducees are seen as conflicts of one 'view' with another. This approach to things does not belong purely to the apologetic scholarly literature of fundamentalism, but is deeply rooted in the folk-perceptions of the movement; and, of course, if one starts from this way of perceiving things one can easily arrive at the idea that Jesus 'held the view' that David was the author of Psalm 110, and so on.

Now this general didactic emphasis reveals yet another deep contradiction in fundamentalism and in the way in which it sees its own relations with opposing theological currents. In taking this distinctively didactic approach to Jesus and the New Testament, fundamentalism is aligning itself with, rather than against, the 'liberal' sort of theology which it so detests. As we have already seen, the attempt of liberals to approach Jesus essentially through his teaching was violently opposed by the conservatives, who insisted that the reality of Christ's work for our salvation lay in his atoning death, in an event or events rather than in verbal teaching. But the conservative evangelical understanding of scripture was not derived from events, such as the death of Christ: for this they turned to his teaching. The understanding of scripture is not based upon a theological evaluation of the total effects of the work of Christ; it is based upon those individual texts in which, as fundamentalists see it, his 'view' of the subject is stated. Thus we have the curious situation that mainstream church thinking works theologically from the events and their total effect, while fundamentalism is aligned with one kind of liberalism in working from the teaching. One could perhaps say, to use terms that were fashionable until recently, that mainstream theology works kerygmatically and fundamentalism didactically:[31] the latter in its doctrinal thinking shows little understanding of what kerygma is or can be and treats it as if it were the teaching of divinely authorized 'views'.

The nearest one comes to a kerygmatic element in the fundamentalist approach to these matters is the much used word 'claim'. A 'claim' is not much different from a 'view', but is a view presented in a more peremptory and challenging fashion, and commonly about oneself. Conservative evangelicals often depict the New Testament situation as if Jesus made 'claims' about himself: he 'claimed' to be the Messiah, he 'claimed' to be God, he 'claimed' that his teaching had absolute truth. On the one hand, this picture completely ignores the complex and indirect character of Jesus' self-presentation in the gospels; on the other, it is possible only on fundamentalist assumptions, since the making of 'claims' of this sort is exactly what Jesus does not do except in limited and often marginal texts, and these can be made central only through the fundamentalist procedures which make them historically early, literarily authentic and theologically overriding. In any case, the fundamentalist preaching of Jesus often consists of a reassertion of these 'claims', to which people have then to assent or to dissent. It is as if Jesus simply in a rather roundabout way stated: I am God, I am the Messiah, do you accept these statements or not? And this brings us back to the matter of Jesus as being untrustworthy or even a liar, which was mentioned just above, for this is in fact standard procedure in the popular presentation of the gospel in fundamentalism: he made these claims, and since he made them he is either God, or mad, or a liar. Which is he? From this aspect the suggestion that Jesus made 'claims', e.g. that David wrote Psalm 110, and that if this is not so he must have been a liar, is well grounded in the popular parlance of the fundamentalist church.

But, according to conservative arguments, it is not only Jesus who made 'claims'; the Bible made 'claims' about itself. The Book of Daniel 'claims' to have been written by a historical Daniel some time in the sixth century BC; the Book of Deuteronomy 'claims' to have been written by Moses; and, more important still, the Bible as a whole 'claims' to be divinely inspired. All this is nonsense. There is no 'the Bible' that 'claims' to be divinely inspired, there is no 'it' that has a 'view of itself'.[32] There is only this or that source, like II Timothy or II Peter, which make statements about certain other writings, these rather undefined. There is no such thing as 'the Bible's view of itself' from which a fully authoritative answer to these questions can be obtained.[33] This whole side of the traditional conservative apologetic, though loudly vociferated, just does not exist; there is no case to answer. The most one can say is that one can see how, if one was in fact a fundamentalist, it could appear that there was ground for an argument along this line. It is only if one begins by looking at the Bible unhistorically, as if it was a variegated but in principle unitary system of thoughts and facts, all of which alike had come straight from God, that any talk about its 'claims' or its 'view of itself' could even appear to have any standing.

The most obvious difficulty is the absence from the New Testament of clear and unambiguous 'claims' about the infallibility and inerrancy of the total New Testament as we have it today. What Jesus said about scripture referred, of course, to the Old Testament, and this is true also of many or most of the passages in the New Testament: when they talk about 'scriptures' or 'as it is written' and the like, they are talking about the Old Testament. Whether 'scripture' in II Timothy 3.16 or 'prophecy of scripture' in II Peter 1.20 refer only to Old Testament writings, or whether they also include some New Testament material, I leave to New Testament scholars to decide. What does seem clear is that it is impossible to show that these passages refer expressly and uniquely to exactly the group of books which now constitute our New Testament canon, or our total biblical canon. But, even if they do, it does not matter much, for these books, belonging as they do to the margin and the late strata of the New Testament, or at least quite probably so, may very well express not the 'claims' of the total New Testament about itself. They may express only the position taken by limited trends of opinion at a time when the main core and growth of the New Testament was already well past. Notice that I do not in the slightest deny what is affirmed by these passages: I merely point out that what they say cannot be considered as the New Testament's 'view of itself'.

We should notice again the point made above about the canon. Some of us can perhaps take the canon fairly lightly, but the fundamentalist cannot. For him the canon is the precise and absolute boundary of divine inspiration. Every word that falls within the canonical books is divinely inspired, but no word that falls within non-canonical books is inspired. The fundamentalist use of key texts like II Timothy 3.16 and II Peter 1.20 goes back to a time when a traditional boundary for 'scripture' was simply assumed, that is, it was understood that a reference to the word 'scripture' would mean precisely the books of the present-day canon, no more and no less. But there is now no reason to assume this. Very likely the writer of II Timothy did not know some of the books of the present New Testament or, worse, knew them but considered them unauthentic, and perhaps he included within 'scripture' a few documents that now count as post-biblical or apocryphal. Conservative evangelical apologists will of course resist these suggestions, but they have absolutely no way of knowing other than wishful thinking. There are thus no 'claims' about the New Testament to be considered that can lead in the direction in which conservative evangelical argumentation would have to lead.

The lack of evidence for conservative evangelical claims about the New Testament is interestingly demonstrated by Wenham himself. Having established to his own satisfaction that Jesus (*a*) taught the divine authorship of the Old Testament and (*b*) taught the entire truth of his own teaching, we come to the third conclusion, namely, 'that Jesus in principle authenticated the New Testament'.[34] Why so? 'Once we have accepted as facts of revelation that God was incarnate in Jesus and that God is the author of the Old Testament, it is straining at a gnat to swallow the Old Testament *in toto*, while doubting even the substantial truth of the only documents left to us by Providence for an understanding of the central act of revelation. We shall therefore take the New Testament records as they stand.' That is to say, nobody who has become persuaded that God is the author of the Old Testament will find it difficult to accept the New as well (leaving Jews out of the argument, of course).[35] This strategy is a proper recognition of two things: firstly, that it is the Old Testament, and not the present New Testament books, that can be authenticated along fundamentalist lines through the teaching of Jesus; secondly, that for many people the Old Testament is the tougher nut to crack. This brings us therefore to look at the Old Testament's role in the structure of this argument.

Fundamentalist religion is in itself very much a New Testament religion: salvation, faith, the blood of Christ, the deity of Christ, the virgin birth – all these are New Testament themes rather than Old Testament themes. But when we come to the messy business of arguing out the details, as so often, we find ourselves in the Old Testament, for it is here that the generalizations about scripture, so confidently established on the basis of New Testament materials, come home to roost in the form of genealogies, numbers of years, the authenticity of Jonah and Daniel and so on. But, great as the complexity of these matters is, fundamentalists use among others the argument that Jesus showed a total acceptance of the inspiration and inerrancy of the Old Testament, and we have already surveyed some of the effects that follow from this argument.

Conservative argument is probably confused here through seeing two different problems as if they were one. The first problem comes into the experience of fundamentalists as an evangelistic problem. It is common experience to them that they meet people who are interested in the Christian message, as evangelicals present it, and who are deeply aware of the values attaching to a personal faith in Jesus Christ and to New Testament Christianity. But these people feel the Old Testament, or parts of it, as an obstacle; and the more conservative the Christianity with which they are in touch, the more it ties the acceptance of Christ to the acceptance of the Bible, and the more they feel troubled by their uncertainties about the Old Testament. Is not the God of the Old Testament a person of quite different type from the Father of whom Jesus spoke? Can the ceremonial and ritual laws of the pentateuch be relevant for modern Christians? Does not the Old Testament contain quite unspiritual love-songs like the Song of Songs and quite unworthily sceptical literature like Ecclesiastes? Does it not include imprecatory Psalms which are quite unworthy of the spirit of Christ?

Well, fundamentalists respond to all these questions, partly by trying to show the continuing values that all these Old Testament books and elements have within Christianity, but much more by the appeal to authority: Jesus himself considered all these books to be

inspired and inerrant, so did the apostles and everyone of importance in the early church. Whether this is an adequate argument,
and whether it in itself proves very much, can be left aside: to me it
seems possible that the beginner in evangelical religion comes to
accept the Old Testament not through the actual effect of all these
arguments, but through the personal and moral pressure of a community in which all the Bible counts as authoritative. But, in any
case, conservative evangelicals do here face a problem that is real
enough for many people entering the serious practice of Christianity, and they at least try to do something about it.

The confusion arises because they think that these arguments,
which have at least some relevance to persons entering active Christianity from the environing culture, are also the arguments with
which to establish the authority, not only of the Old Testament, but
of the Bible as a whole, as against critical scholarship and non-
conservative theological currents. In spite of the fundamentalist
conviction that non-conservative theology is in servitude to the
environing paganism, the problems are different in the latter case.
There are indeed some currents in modern theology that will feel
about the Old Testament just the same sort of questions as the
novice evangelical was putting two paragraphs back, but it would be
folly (though a sort of folly well instanced in fundamentalist literature) to suppose that this is true of all non-conservative theology.
The high status that the Old Testament holds in the minds of Jesus
and the early Christians will be granted by the most critical as a
matter of historical fact, and therefore the fundamentalist efforts to
prove this are of no importance. On the other hand, the fundamentalist attempts to argue that these sayings of Jesus and the New
Testament writers about Jonah, Daniel, Moses and other persons
and events prove the historical accuracy of the Old Testament are
futile, because they make no attempt to show that Jesus or the early
Christians were interested in such questions as the authorship of
books, the presence of sources, or the historical accuracy of data
and figures. Thus in general the attempt of fundamentalist
apologists to demonstrate the authority of the Old Testament and
its inerrancy from New Testament texts about it simply makes no
contact with the positions held in modern theology and biblical
criticism; as I suggest, the explanation may be that the attempt is
really an attempt to deal with a different situation, and this at least
partly explains why so irrelevant a series of arguments is deployed.

There is one further issue about the use of the Old Testament in
the conservative argument for biblical inspiration and inerrancy. As

all would agree, the Old Testament enjoyed a very high status in the minds of Jesus and the early Christians, being understood as the Word of God and the authoritative expression of his will. But is there not at the same time a critical element in their use of the Old Testament? Conservative writers find themselves forced to minimize this, to argue that Jesus and the early church, in their relations to the Old Testament, merely recognized its complete authority and never in any way exercised any sort of theological critique or critical selection in their approach to it. What about the famous 'antitheses' of the Sermon on the Mount, 'You have heard that it was said . . . but I say unto you'? Conservative evangelical apologists like Packer and Wenham interpret these as being a protest against current interpretation of the Old Testament passages:[36] they are in no sense an indication that the Old Testament text in itself came in any way short of finality, in no sense an indication that Jesus, though fully respecting the authority of the Old Testament, had something to say of his own that went beyond it. 'He never opposed His personal authority to that of the Old Testament. He never qualified the Jewish belief in its absolute authority in the slightest degree. The fact we have to face is that Jesus Christ, the Son of God Incarnate, who claimed divine authority for all that He did and taught, both confirmed the absolute authority of the Old Testament for others and submitted to it unreservedly Himself.'[37] But if there is nothing more to it than this, this can be considered as a judgment that Jesus himself was a straight biblicist, who did nothing but draw out his message from the existing inspired and inerrant sources; it makes Jesus into a 'Bible teacher' in the fundamentalist tradition: Jesus, in his relation to the Old Testament, was just the same sort of person as Packer would like us all to be, one who simply submitted himself to scripture and who used no sort of innovative, creative or critical approach towards it.

Here again, as in so many things, it is probable that the living religious instinct of fundamentalists is to see things differently from their scholarly apologists. In their actual faith and religious life the message of Jesus, though in manifold ways validated by the Old Testament and depending upon it, is a novel and creative message, far more important than the Old Testament texts to which it from time to time refers. It is in the defensive apologetic situation, where opposition to critical scholarship becomes the one supreme goal, that conservative writers find themselves forced to deny the critical character of Jesus' use of the Old Testament, in order to make the

Old Testament, and through it the New Testament also, absolutely and unqualifiably authoritative in all respects for the church.

As a footnote to this discussion we should note how great the effects of conservative viewpoints upon exegesis are likely to be. Clearly, any scholar who takes the point of view just cited from Packer and Wenham will, in interpreting the Sermon on the Mount, minimize any trace of a critical use of the Old Testament by Jesus, and this will then have manifold effects throughout the total interpretation of the New Testament. The principle of harmonization, to which we have already devoted so much attention, will strengthen this; passages which appear to suggest a more critical use of the Old Testament will be harmonized to agree with passages like Matt. 5.17–20, which emphasizes the eternal validity of the Old Testament law. To take another example, the eschatological expectation of an imminent end to the world represents a problem to conservative interpreters. Many would suppose, from a first reading of the New Testament, that such an expectation was then very lively and that Jesus himself taught that the end was at hand. 'Truly, I say to you, this generation will not pass away till all these things take place' (Mark 13.30, parallels Matt. 24.34, Luke 21.32), and numerous other similar remarks. Not at all, say at least some representative conservative evangelical interpreters. If Jesus had said that the end was imminent, we would have the difficulty that the world would in fact have ended in the first century AD; however, it did not end, and if Jesus had said that it would end he would have been wrong, and this would mean that his teaching had misled the church. In order to avoid this a variety of exegetical devices is used, primarily the taking of terms in a non-literal sense. For instance, where Matt. 24.29 tells us that 'immediately' after the tribulation of those days the sun and moon will be darkened, and the coming of the Son of Man will be discerned, Wenham assures us that 'immediately' is often used with 'very little force': any time from AD 70 up to the end, which in 1977 is still to come, will fit suitably under this term.[38] The blowing of the trumpet and the sending out of the angels, which might naturally be taken as an event of the end of the world, is the sending out of the messengers to proclaim the gospel.[39] All in all, Wenham concludes, it is a 'modern myth' to suppose that it was believed that the Lord would return at any moment to bring in the kingdom. 'There is no indication that the Christians lived at first in momentary expectation of his coming and that in course of time the hope gradually faded.'[40] The effect of such a conviction upon the interpretation of New Testament passages can readily be imagined. I do not suggest that all conservative evangelicals follow this line, only that it is a typical illustration of the way in which their general convictions can affect the exegesis of passages in detail. Here again the influence of the overriding device of harmonization is clear: there are certain New Testament passages which seek to make it clear that the time of the end is unknown, implying that it may be distant (Acts 1.7 is the most prominent), and other passages are harmonized as far as possible in order to fit with these. There is no idea of a doctrinal shift, conflict or development within the New Testament. Many critical scholars might argue that the first Christians had a belief in an imminent end, and that a different (or a later) school of opinion gradually modified the texts that had come down from that earlier stage and added others that diminished the emphasis on an early end. This would mean, ironically, that the New Testament writers were already engaged in the kind of reinterpretation that is still being practised by conservative evangelical scholars as quoted above. But this kind of approach to the New Testament, as if it contained within itself some doctrinal and exegetical development and conflict, is hateful to conservative interpreters: the New Testament for them was, and must have been, a unified body of teaching all of which was always right, and still is.

In concluding this section we shall simply reiterate the most important single point made. Conservative evangelical argumentation, as surveyed here, might be deemed to have made some sort of a case for the authority and even for the inspiration of the Bible. Far from being a stronger case, it is a much weaker case than that made by many other sorts of theology: but at least it is some sort of a case. But in no way at all has it even attempted to make a case for the *inerrancy* of the Bible. Whether one cites the customary New Testament texts about inspiration (II Timothy 3.16; II Peter 1.20–1) or Jesus' teaching about the Old Testament and his occasional references to Jonah, to Daniel, to Moses and so on, conservative evangelical apologists make no attempt to show exegetically that any of these passages were concerned with *inerrancy* in the sense in which they themselves as conservative evangelicals understand the term. They cannot show, and they do not even make a pretence of showing, by exegesis of the passages cited that these passages intended to make judgments about the dates and authorship of books, the presence or absence of sources, the accuracy of figures and the like. The link between authority or inspiration on the one side and inerrancy on the other rests on one basis only: supposition. Here conservative evangelicals go over to a purely philosophical and non-biblical argument: if it was inspired by God, then how could there be error of any kind in it? This is in fact the core of their argument. But, since this link has no rootage in the Bible and belongs to purely philosophical assumption, the entire attempt of conservative evangelicals to derive their position from 'the Bible's view of itself' is a waste of time. But we shall examine this again in our chapter on doctrine.

4. *Maximal conservatism*

A few pages ago we referred to the authorship of Psalm 110.[41] Critical scholars, or some of them, say that this Psalm was not written by David and came not from his time but from long afterwards. Now the fundamentalist can take two different attitudes to this.

The first we can call the dogmatic one. The Psalm, or at least its superscription, calls itself 'A Psalm of David': therefore it was composed by David or at least came from his time and environment. Again, Jesus quotes words from it as words of David, therefore again it was written or spoken by David. This ends the argument: there is no more to be said. Infallible words, guaranteed by the doctrine of authority, inspiration and inerrancy of the Bible, have settled the matter.

But there is another possible approach. Since a variety of scholarly approaches exist, preference among them is to be given to that which sets the Psalm in the time nearest to David. A critic who set the Psalm in the Maccabaean age would be shocking in his extremism; one who set it in the period of the Babylonian Exile would still be very bad, but would be better; a critic who set it in the time of Isaiah or soon after the disruption of the united kingdom would be still better, and the more he used terms like 'very old' or 'quite primitive' the better he would be. Or, with Deuteronomy, a critic who squarely put the whole book in the seventh century would be a much worse thing than one who, while holding that it came from, perhaps, the eighth or seventh, also thought that many elements are 'much older material' or 'come from Mosaic tradition' or, best of all, 'in some sense go back to Moses'. Similarly, in the gospels, a view that (say) fifty per cent of the sayings ascribed to Jesus came from a reliable chain of tradition going back to AD 60 would be better than a view that eighty per cent of them derived from church tradition during the sixties and seventies; still better would be the opinion that eighty per cent of them went back to the original eye-witnesses or their associates; and still better again would be the position that 'nearly all' went back 'practically' to Jesus himself.

This latter approach is what I call the 'maximal-conservative' approach. It is clear that it seeks to validate credence in practically the same beliefs as are validated through the dogmatic approach. This is especially so because the stress, the direction and tendency of the argument is heavily towards the earliest dating, maximal authenticity of authorship, and so on. When it is said that 'nearly all' in a document goes back to Moses, to Jesus, or whoever it may be, the interest is being directed towards the authenticity. In other words, the argument is negative: its purpose is not to interest the reader in identifying those elements that are really late, but to assure him that there are practically no such elements. If positive stress were laid upon the existence of any elements that really were late or secondary, then that would invite the question, why should not one or two other elements be late also? Moreover, the fundamentalist mind is not interested in exceptions to the general rule of authenticity of documents and inerrancy of attributions to authors, unless it is very strongly insisted that he must abandon these convictions. Unless it can be 'proved' that Deuteronomy is not written by Moses, the exceptions conceded by a phrase like 'practically all' will not interest him; to say that 'practically all' of Deuteronomy in some sense comes from Moses will be to him a licence to ignore the entire critical question. Thus the maximal-conservative approach strives to validate results that are as close as makes no matter to those achieved by the dogmatic approach. Psalm 110 comes from David after all, or as near so as makes no matter.

But though the two kinds of argument are similar in the sort of positions that they effectively support, in their real nature the two are quite different. One is dogmatic and quite precise: it is satisfied only and exclusively if David wrote or composed the Psalm. The other, however vehemently affirmed, can only be probabilistic or approximative in character. The former works dogmatically: the statements of scripture itself, when scripture is known to be infallible, settle the matter. The other works exegetically: it tries to show from the content of the text, taken in relation to other evidences within or even without the Bible, that it must be very old, much older than critical scholars have supposed.

The linkage between the two forms of argument is interesting. The dogmatic argument probably provides for many people the motivation that underlies the maximal-conservative argument.

Fundamentalists really believe (or have believed, or would like to believe) the validity of the dogmatic argument and its pre-suppositions; their will to believe it leads them into a maxi-mally-conservative position on all possible biblical questions. The smaller the deviation from the dogmatically required position the better. And the maximal-conservative argument is needed for another reason; there are a host of questions in the dating and origin of biblical documents on which there is simply no guidance to be obtained from the dogmatic argument, however zealously it is pressed. The two arguments thus work in sympathy.

On the other hand the maximal-conservative argument thoroughly contradicts the dogmatic argument. If the Word of God expressly and inerrantly teaches us that Psalm 110 was written or composed by David, then it is of no use to argue that, far from being a work of Maccabaean origin, it was very old, going back perhaps to the year 900 BC, written therefore quite soon after David, perhaps even by one of his personal friends. This does not satisfy the dogma-tic argument at all; on the contrary, by the arguments that have been described only a few pages ago, this would show the Bible to be utterly unreliable and prove Jesus himself to have been untrustwor-thy. The dogmatic argument has to work exactly, or it does not work at all. A conservative critic who attributes Psalm 110 to someone writing about 900 BC is, by normal fundamentalist logic, totally rejecting the witness of Jesus, who expressly says that it came from David. He is thus completely denying the veracity of Jesus's teach-ing on the matter and thereby implying that all of Jesus's teaching on any subject is untrustworthy. Or, to put the same thing in the opposite way, if it is satisfactory to attribute Psalm 110 to someone writing fifty years or so after David, then why not ascribe Timothy and Titus to a younger disciple of Paul, writing fifty years after his master's *floruit*? In other words, the maximal-conservative approach, by being approximative and not exact, leaves a gap quite large enough for the critic to get through. Or, yet another develop-ment of the same analysis, if the dogmatic argument cannot be precisely satisfied, then it does not provide the slightest reason why a document should be 'very old' or 'much earlier than the critics think': if Psalm 110 is not actually by David himself, and no other person, or if the Book of Daniel is not by the historical Daniel himself, then there is not the slightest reason, as far as the dogmatic argument goes, why they should be 'early' or 'very old'; they might as well belong to the Maccabaean age as to any other.

There is every reason to believe that within conservative

evangelical literature on the Bible the dogmatic argument is increasingly being replaced by the maximal-conservative one.[42] The dogmatic one still stands in the background, for it fixes the norms to which the maximal-conservative seeks to approximate. But this means that a great number of arguments levelled in the past against critical opinions are being tacitly and doubtless unconsciously abandoned. This means that much of the argument for the inerrancy of the Bible, as surveyed in the last section, is in effect being abandoned by conservative interpretation, although this is never admitted and the old dogmatic arguments continue to be rehearsed. Instead of concentrating the argument for Davidic authorship of Psalm 110 upon the testimony of Jesus himself, which is the traditional dogmatic argument, attempts are made to show by ancient near-eastern evidence, by linguistic data and so on, that the Psalm cannot be late and must be 'very early'. Yet the dogmatic argument, or its ghost, still remains present for there is no substantial reason for the conservative to press for an early date for the Psalm except for the quotation by Jesus. But the two arguments cannot be used to supplement one another, for the logic of one contradicts the logic of the other. Conservatives who are now using, as most are, the maximal-conservative argument owe at least an apology to all the critical scholars whose work they and their predecessors have mercilessly attacked because of its failure to satisfy the demands of the dogmatic argument.

The increasing use of the maximal-conservative argument is one of the signs of change within fundamentalism, and it may also betoken or introduce strains within the ranks of conservative people. It is consonant with the fact, to which we shall shortly be turning our attention, that fundamentalism is increasingly seeking to make its voice known through scholarship rather than through purely dogmatic assertion. In modern conservative scholarship questions are often not simply foreclosed through the use of the dogmatic argument. Contact is often made with non-conservative scholarship and the various options are laid out; among these scholarly options the most conservative available is adopted, or the most conservative is then pushed in a direction even more conservative.

But before we suppose that this change is bringing about an improvement, we should consider the other side of the coin. The dogmatic argument could be and often was a plain and honest one. If it seemed to a man that the Bible said a Psalm was written by David, and if the Bible was exactly infallible and inerrant in all matters and if its infallibility and inerrancy worked as fundamentalists have supposed them to work, what more could he do than submit? Such a man might see perfectly well a host of arguments from style and historical circumstances which would indicate a later date and would find these arguments extremely convincing; but his religious convictions would force him, even against his other convictions, to accept the dating and authorship which seemed to him to be dictated by scripture. This was very likely the position that many scholarly Christians took in the days when criticism was beginning.[43] The position, being honestly dogmatic, does not need to conceal the fact that the evidence draws in the other direction. In comparison with this the maximal-conservative argument is less honest and more prejudiced. The commentator may well conceal the norms to which he seeks to approximate. He works by the consideration of the evidence, but all evidence is slanted in favour of maximum approximation to the norm.[44] The fact that this mode of argumentation effectively cancels out the norm by which the interpreter is led is carefully or carelessly concealed. It is by no means clear that the shift is an improvement. But in any case it greatly affects the light in which we see the arguments for the inerrancy of the Bible that have been surveyed above.

Before we go farther into the analysis of conservative attitudes to the Bible we should fill out the picture with some other aspects; this chapter has, however, introduced some of the most characteristic elements.

4 · Fundamentalism and Society

1. *Science and secularism*

People sometimes suppose that fundamentalism is a product of a prescientific society and that it will in due course die away with the advance of scientific knowledge and the increasing secularization of life. This may sound good in theory but experience would seem to show that the reverse is true in practice. Our first purpose in this chapter will be to consider why it is that the increasingly secular society seems to be a soil in which fundamentalism flourishes perfectly well.

Only a professional sociologist could give a scientific judgment; but my impression from personal experience is that fundamentalism is quite evenly spread through the different social and professional classes. It is certainly not a preserve of the uneducated; on the contrary, anyone with personal experience will have noticed, I believe, the number of doctors, lawyers, experimental scientists and the like who are fundamentalists. Within the sciences one may guess that the physical more than the biological, and the biological more than the social, go with fundamentalism: perhaps one could say, the older sciences more than the newer.[1] To this should be added the strong representation of fundamentalism among university students.[2] There is certainly no reason to suppose that advanced education forms a barrier to fundamentalism.

The prominent American theologian H. Richard Niebuhr gave an interpretation of fundamentalism in social terms. It seems that he had in mind particularly the specific 'Fundamentalist Controversy' of the twenties and thirties in the United States, centred in the Tennessee evolution trial and the crises in various denominations as fundamentalists sought (and generally failed) to gain control. Niebuhr thought that fundamentalism had its roots in the older

rural culture, while the opposing liberalism belonged to the rising
industrialized urban culture.

> The opposing religious movement, modernism, was identified ... with
> bourgeois culture, having its strength in the cities and in the churches
> supported by the urban middle classes ... Fundamentalism in its
> aggressive forms was most prevalent in those isolated communities in
> which the traditions of pioneer society had been most effectively pre-
> served and which were least subject to the influence of modern science
> and industrial civilization.[3]

He connected this with a 'distrust of reason and emphasis on emotion' in fundamentalism.

There is good reason, however, to think that this diagnosis of
Niebuhr's, though attractive, is very largely wrong, or at most
applies to a limited period of manifestations of fundamentalism
such as the controversy over evolution. Sandeen argues, to me
convincingly, that the fundamentalist leadership came from exactly
the same social groups as the liberal leadership came from.[4] I shall
not pursue the question as a matter of specifically American history.
For the type of British fundamentalism which is taken as typical
here,[5] it seems to me that Sandeen is certainly right and that no gross
differentiation of social and educational background can be used to
provide a rationale for the phenomenon of fundamentalism. At
least among intellectuals, it seems rather that, of two people with
very similar background and education, one may opt for fundamentalism while the other will opt for a critical solution to the same set
of problems. The difference would seem to lie rather in the type of
intellectual exposure, the theological currents experienced, the
influence of particular churches attended and personal contacts
made.

We return therefore to the question of how science and fundamentalism co-exist. It may be true that a thorough and consistent
scientific attitude would be inimical to fundamentalism. But many
people whose work is in some sense scientific are concerned not
with science as a whole, or science as a total intellectual way of life,
but with their own particular function within it. The practice of
science, whatever the theory, makes a person competent and expert
in his own branch of knowledge, but on the condition that he
acknowledges his purely amateur status in the other branches. Thus
perfectly good performance within a scientific calling is quite compatible with fully non-scientific attitudes in those other spheres
which lie beyond one's own responsibility. On the other hand a
scientific education and career may involve a long and very heavy

concentration on natural facts and practical techniques, and it is possible that a strong and personal religious commitment, having its basis quite outside the scientific routine, may be a kind of revenge of human nature in its spiritual aspects, a sort of throw-back to an earlier age. Again, many aspects even of fundamentalist faith appear not to conflict blatantly with a scientific occupation as it is in fact carried out. For example, a doctor may feel he sees all sorts of remarkable cures which his professional knowledge cannot explain: and, if he believes that prayer may be efficacious in bringing about the healing of the sick, there is probably nothing in professional experience that makes this impossible, since belief in this power of prayer is not deterministic, that is, it is not believed that by praying for a person's cure one will necessarily bring about that cure.

Moreover, the older overt conflict between fundamentalism and science has greatly decreased. The matter of evolution, which was a major centre of the earlier fundamentalist controversy, has receded from the scene.[6] Though this is not admitted, the central current of conservative evangelical opinion has surrendered on this point. Thirty years or so ago typical conservative publishing houses were still issuing thunderings against the idea of evolution. Today we hear practically nothing about it. In the late forties, when I was a student, friends studying medicine were often in acute distress because of their inability to provide an answer to evolution, which they took to be in conflict with their biblical faith. Today *The New Bible Dictionary* tells us (p. 296): 'The biblical doctrine of creation . . . must not be confused or identified with any scientific theory of origins. The purpose of the biblical doctrine, in contrast to that of scientific investigation, is ethical and religious' (J. A. Thompson). But this is exactly the position that 'liberals' always took! If this had been said at the beginning, how much pain and trouble would have been saved! Yet not a word of regret is expressed for all the attacks that were made on non-conservatives over many decades for saying exactly the same thing. Bernard Ramm, a highly conservative writer, fences evolution round with many restrictions and qualifications, but for the practical person the upshot will be that one can go ahead and accept it: 'If it is a secondary law of biology, and not the metaphysics of creation, but viewed as part of the divine creation, an element in providence, then evolution is as harmless as, say, the relativity theory.'[7] As we have seen above, the idea that the six days of Genesis 1 might represent 'six geological ages' is also an attempt, not to impose the Genesis picture upon science, but to assimilate the understanding of Genesis to something like what is accepted as scientific fact.[8] Thus, at least in what concerns the origins of the world and of man, the conflict between fundamentalism and science has been very greatly reduced, and it is fundamentalism that has given way all along the line. As some far-seeing fundamentalist leaders no doubt perceived, this has in fact greatly strengthened fundamentalism as a faith for the latter part of the twentieth century. Admittedly, this still leaves a goodish area where fundamentalist faith seems to conflict with truths generally supposed to be scientific: what about the virgin birth of Jesus, for instance, or the resurrection? Of these and of other miraculous incidents more will be said later. But our general observation, that the overt conflict between fundamentalism and science, concentrated as it was on questions of cosmology and evolution, has greatly decreased, is hardly to be disputed.

Indeed, as a number of theologians have noted,[9] we may have to reverse the older way of looking at the conflict between fundamentalist and non-conservative forms of Christian faith. One of the main accusations made by conservatives against 'liberal' theology was that it accepted the standards and the results of natural science and diluted the Christian faith in order to suit them. It is now increasingly being said that the reverse is the case, and that it is the conservative evangelicals who are accepting from natural science their understanding of the nature of truth and insisting that the truth of the Bible must be this kind of truth. As we have seen, in the case of apparently 'historical' narratives, assuming that these are taken literally by fundamentalists, the stress in their interpretation falls entirely on the question whether this event took place materially and physically. This is the kind of truth that matters for them. Questions of significance can be looked at, if at all, only after this has been agreed. Non-conservative theology begins much more with the question about significance: what does it mean that this is narrated in this form? It is a reasonable comment, therefore, to say that the fundamentalist conception of truth is dominated by a materialistic view, derived from a scientific age. This stress on the accuracy of the Bible in its *material-physical* reporting separates modern fundamentalism entirely from that older theology, such as the theology of Luther and Calvin, which it ill-informedly claims as its own forebear. It is possible to argue further that the chief doctrinal stream accepted in fundamentalism, the Princeton theology of the Hodges and Warfield, took its method expressly from the analogy of natural science, and that natural science as seen in a traditional Newtonian mould.[10] This would suggest that fundamentalism, in its relations to science, might properly be criticized for attachment to an obsolete scientific model, perpetuated not through science itself but through its effect on the philosophical basis of doctrine as accepted by fundamentalists. This might well be a fruitful line of enquiry but I do not propose to press it very far. It does illuminate the situation but I doubt whether fundamentalism will be very much affected by what is said along this line.

A more telling judgment will be reached if we consider the role of natural science in relation to characteristic conservative evangelical treatments of problems in the Bible itself. Examples may be drawn from Bernard Ramm's *The Christian View of Science and Scripture*, a thoroughly and totally conservative work, which should be read by all evangelicals, since no more convincing advertisement for the critical approach to the Bible could be written. Ramm is an intelligent scholar who has done a prodigious amount of reading, and has looked into numerous detailed aspects of the Bible from the point of view of its relation to natural science. He totally ignores and rejects all critical approaches, so that it never enters his head that a story such as Noah's flood might be legend or myth. He is also totally devoid of humour. Now let us look at his discussion of the problem of the flood. The problem is whether the flood covered the whole earth or, as many conservative interpreters now maintain, was a local Mesopotamian flood. If it was a local flood, its effects would have been less catastrophic: the task of finding evidences of it would be less difficult, and the task of explaining the difficulties of the event less serious. The flood is, of course, a real event; following the 'gap' treatment of the biblical genealogies, it took place not around the third millennium BC (Archbishop Ussher's date was 2349 BC) since this is 'archaeologically fantastic', i.e. it does not fit with archaeological evidence, and the flood must have been much earlier.[11]

The question then is, whether the flood was a universal flood, covering the whole earth or, as many conservative interpreters hold, a local Mesopotamian flood. The latter is Ramm's own opinion. Many powerful arguments support this case. The highest mountain in the Mesopotamian area was Ararat, about 17,000 feet. But the Himalayas rise to 29,000 feet. The amount of water required to provide a universal flood, covering the Himalayas and all the rest of the world, would be very great, 'about eight times more water than we now have' (p. 166). God would have had to perform a special creation of water to furnish this much, but the scriptures give no hint of such a special creation. Equally difficult would be the problem of getting rid of all this water. The Bible makes it clear that the waters of the flood were removed by draining them away, but 'If the entire world were under six miles of water, there would be no place for the water to drain off'. A local flood would readily dispose of the problem. Again, devastating effects would have been exercised on marine life both by the mixing of fresh and salt water and by the enormous pressure of such a depth of water. Plant life would have suffered too: 'practically the entire world of plants would have perished under the enormous pressure, the presence of salt water, and a year's soaking'. Again, there would have been a multitude of difficulties connected with the animals, if the flood was a universal flood. How did the animals get from distant lands to the ark? Kangaroos, llamas and polar bears would presumably have had to make the long journey to Mesopotamia. There is no doubt that God could arrange this, but it seems doubtful whether this is really intended by the scriptural record. Again, after the flood was over all these animals, two by two, would have had to get back to Australia, South America and so on. An accident to only one of any species would have meant the complete extinction of that species. 'Once in the ark, the problem of feeding and caring for them would be enormous. The task of carrying away manure and bringing food would completely overtax the few people in the ark.' For these and similar reasons one should favour the view of a purely Mesopotamian flood.

Clearly, much good fun can be had from reading Ramm, but at the moment we are concerned to make only one point. The view of the world upon which Ramm relies at every step is the modern scientific view of the world. Through scientific methods he knows how much water would be needed for a flood of six miles' depth, he knows the effect this would have on water pressure, he knows that salt-water fish would die in fresh water and fresh-water marine life would perish in salt water. Again, 'the astronomical disturbances caused by the increase of the mass of the earth, if there was at one time a sheath of water six miles thick (from sea level), would have been significant, and could be detected by astronomers'. His entire approach to the problem depends on the full use of modern scientific knowledge. The total acceptance of this body of knowledge is presupposed throughout. The only question is: given the (unquestioned) fact that the flood was an external event that took place as described, how can it be understood to fit within the framework of our scientific knowledge of the world? Different theories can be discussed, but each of them depends upon some aspect of the world as scientifically known.

Thus, contrary to what many people would expect, the scientific view of the world is the one into which the Bible is fitted. The idea that one cannot do this to the Bible, because its world-view is different, is unknown to Ramm,[12] and rightly so, for if it were true it would mean that the Bible, contradicting the scientific facts, would be wrong. The biblical material is thus twisted to fit the various theories that can bring it into accord with science. For example, the merest beginner in the study of the Bible might have supposed that all men and animals perished in the flood except for the eight people who were in the ark, plus their animal guests. 'All flesh died that moved on the earth . . . they were destroyed from the earth; and only Noah remained alive, and they that were with him in the ark' (Gen. 7.21–23 AV). Not at all, Ramm tells us: the word *all* in scripture does not always mean every single one.[13] When the Samaritan woman said of Jesus 'he told me all that I ever did' it cannot mean that he recited her complete biography in every detail (John 4.39), and when Matt. 3.5 says that 'all' Judaea and the region about the Jordan went out to John the Baptist, it cannot mean that every single individual went out. Thus by Ramm's adaptation of the flood story to modern scientific knowledge its traditional meaning has been totally abandoned, in order to replace it with one that could be true as a real event in the world as known to modern science. In particular, the idea that the entire human race was wiped out apart from the eight who were in the ark has been completely abandoned. 'Man was destroyed within the boundaries of the flood; the record is mute about man in America or Africa or China' (Ramm, p. 169).

Ramm's treatment of the incident is so much a *reductio ad absurdum* that many conservative evangelicals may well want to laugh it off on the grounds that 'of course we don't believe all that sort of thing'. It is indeed very likely that thousands of people have never attempted to think out in any kind of detail what sort of event the flood may have been. But Ramm's interpretation cannot be pushed aside in this way. Similar lines are followed in standard works like *The New Bible Commentary* in both its editions and *The New Bible Dictionary*.[14] All of these survey the arguments for a local as against a universal flood. This is one of the things that conservative evangelicals are allowed to differ about: 'dogmatism is not reasonable, either way', as the dictionary article (p. 428a) delightfully reminds us. Moreover, Ramm's extensive bibliographical references and discussions show that a whole series of conservative writers are thinking along similar lines: whether they come down on the side of a universal flood or a local one, whether they relate it to glacial action and the weight of ice upon land masses (as in the dictionary article, p. 429a) or to some other phenomenon. The difference in Ramm is the naive openness of his statements in detail, but statements of the same logical status are implied in the others also. The common approach to all is the acceptance of the constitution of the world, as known through modern science, as the framework within which an explanation has to be found.

The other point is this: though much of Ramm's reasoning may be personally strange to many conservative evangelicals, he is doing no more than follow out the lines of interpretation and the doctrines of scripture which they themselves insist upon. They have no right to shrug off Ramm unless they are prepared to alter the doctrines of scripture and principles of interpretation upon which Ramm's reasoning is based and which he is logically following out. Conservative evangelicals have to face the fact: by the doctrines of inerrancy and methods of interpretation upon which they insist, they are bound if they are honest to come up against exactly these questions. It is, then, not only the idiosyncrasy of unusual individuals, but a general tendency among conservative evangelical interpreters, to accept entirely from science its picture of natural conditions in the world and to manoeuvre the interpretation of the Bible in order to find a place for its narratives within this picture. In saying this I do not suggest that Ramm, or other conservative interpreters, accept science, in the more theoretical sense, as the controlling arbiter of reality, for they do not: for ultimate principles, which might conflict with biblical faith or revelation, they go over to the latter; but for the simple account of how things are in the world, what forces exist and how they act, they totally accept the scientific picture and work within it.

More important is the following: fundamentalism's main conflict, in respect of its use of the Bible, is not with science but with historical method and literary discrimination. Historical method is at least in part a matter of probability, and literary discrimination is often a matter of taste: neither is able to offer decisive and irrefragable proofs, coercive even to the sceptic, in the way that science can do. And it is decisive proof that the fundamentalist demands: as in English law a man is innocent until he is proved guilty, they often say, so is the Bible right until it is finally and indubitably proved wrong, with the sort of certitude that was sufficient (in days of capital punishment) to hang a man, or indeed with a considerably greater degree of certitude than that. The argument is of course an absurd one, since it supposes that biblical criticism and modern theology are interested in proving the Bible wrong or guilty, a supposition that exists only in the fundamentalist mind; but, absurd or not, it shows the way people think. The fact that historical demonstration is probabilistic and not absolute is constantly exploited by fundamentalists in order to show that critical reconstructions are not certain; on the other hand, as we have seen, the same probabilistic element is exploited by their maximal-conservative argument in order to achieve at all points the most conservative picture possible. But *conservative* historical statements are not subject to the same limitations on the ground of their probabilistic nature. The judgment that the Bible contains inerrant information about Noah's flood, about the chronological situation of the Exodus, about Jonah's voyage in the belly of the whale and about the time when the Book of Daniel was written is a historical judgment, but is not subject to any limitations on the ground of its probabilism and hypothetical nature. Critical judgments are at the best hypotheses, which cannot be demonstrated unless the most final and coercive proofs are brought: conservative judgments on the same historical issues are fully reliable knowledge, and cannot be disproved except by the most final and coercive proofs. 'Possession is nine points of the law', as Wenham puts it, well revealing the kind of ideological basis that lies behind this principle.[15]

Historical reconstructions in a field like biblical studies depend to a large extent on literary reconstructions, and these in turn depend on matters of literary taste. Discernment of the differences between, let us say, the different sources of the pentateuch, and of the unevennesses and discrepancies that mark the transition from one source to another, are not matters where proof of an objective kind is obtainable. The differences between (say) the J sections and the P sections in Genesis consist sometimes in small details, sometimes in linguistic and stylistic differences, sometimes in differences of theological outlook. Anyone who looks at the text purely or even primarily from the point of view of its veracity in the sense of correspondence to external and historical reality will often easily push aside the whole set of distinctions. Much fundamentalist polemic shows clearly the literary philistinism of certain scientists and lawyers, just as their hostility to modern theology and its philosophical aspects, with its hesitations, questionings and uncertainties, represents their general antipathy towards the humanities.

This leads us on to a more fundamental point: the fundamentalist is often very much a secular man, very much at home in a secularized world. Prayer can and should be added to scientific medicine, but scientific medicine remains essentially untouched. Unworldliness is a virtue that some fundamentalists prize, but to many others it is strange. There may indeed be severe restrictions: some things may be disapproved of or forbidden, like dancing or drinking; and there may also be forbearance from certain enjoyments, but this with a distinct end in view, commonly to further the task of conservative-minded evangelism, perhaps with the use of money. But there is little asceticism and no monasticism, and there is little or no limitation on the enjoyment of food, the accumulation of money, for the sake of a world other than this one. The rituals of the Christian year, familiar in more Catholic Christianity, are largely lacking; Sabbatarianism still exists to some extent but is not a marked feature. Celibacy is rare.

Many observers have noted the way in which fundamentalists are at home in the world of money and profit. Again, one should not generalize, and not the slightest suggestion of wrong-doing of any kind is implied. Nevertheless the unashamed adoption of the techniques of salesmanship and advertising in the work of Billy Graham is not an exceptional case: rather, it symbolizes the relation of fundamentalism to the world in which we live.[16] The acute religiosity of the fundamentalist does not alter the fact that in another sense he almost fully accepts the secular and economic structure of that world. Some exception may be made for student organizations and youth groups: they, just because they are youth groups, have not yet fully developed the responsibilities and involvements that will later lock their members into the system of the environing world, and so they can show an idealism which is not always echoed in the daily life of conservative church members twenty years later.

It is true, indeed, that conservative evangelical teaching strongly insists that the influence of the faith must be felt in every department of the life of Christians. This is important, and people try extremely hard to make it so. But this does not alter what I say. The 'life' of Christians is defined by the religion in such a way as to provide for acceptance of the secularization of the surrounding culture. The Christian seeks to ensure that his faith in Christ, his dedication to his cause, and his obedience to the law of God are worked out in *his* disposition of the elements of power and wealth, opportunity and influence, which he holds in control. The secularized environment is not felt to constitute an obstacle to his doing this. And the religion does not require or even encourage any fundamental criticism of the forces in society which provide these elements of power and wealth, opportunity and influence. The Christian businessman must do his duty as a Christian business-man; but in doing this he is free to accept, and is indeed encouraged to accept, the dynamics and the ideology of the businessman. The position is well symbolized by two doctrinal axioms. The first is the principle that the world cannot be redeemed: the gospel operates upon the individual. 'The gospel is addressed to the individual. Society collectively cannot be redeemed. It can, however, be reformed according to the law of God . . .'[17] The second lies in the eschatology: as we have seen, the 'second coming' is fervently awaited, but this symbol negates any cumulative realization of God's will in the world in the meantime. This does not mean that the world is totally evil and should be left to Satan; but it cannot be redeemed either. The most to be hoped for is that it should be maintained as an effective functioning order of society, with a reasonable measure of justice but with no idea of any manifestation of Christian redemption within it. Such a neutral society is more or less a secular society. The religion, for all its fervency, does not interfere with, but if anything rather supports, the secularity of attitudes held within it. I am not concerned here to evaluate this secularity, to say whether it is right or wrong. I am only trying to explain the fact that seems to be quite evident, that this highly religious point of view, fundamentalism, appears to be reasonably well established in our secularized society and prospering well within it.

The secularity that can well accompany fundamentalist faith is well seen also in the strongly 'low-church' character of the movement. Little importance is attached to the official, canonical or institutional presence and influence of the church within society. Such presence and influence do exist, being expressed by (for instance) the position of established churches *vis-à-vis* the state, by the acceptance of 'civic religion', even apart from established churches, as a salutary thing, and by the general recognition accorded to clergy and other church leaders. All this may exist as a matter of fact, but the fundamentalist will not allow that much can depend upon it. The question for him is not whether there is an official representation of the church within society, nor what sort of effect is created by that representation, but whether church leaders and clergy are submitting themselves exclusively to the authority of the Bible as understood in fundamentalist terms. By fundamentalist mythology most of these church leaders are unreliable people, being influenced by 'liberal' theology, and therefore they cannot be relied upon to represent in society the true Word of God. The typical secularistic reaction of irreligious man, anti-clericalism, is echoed in fundamentalism with a kind of Christian anti-clericalism. The ministry as institutional embodiment of the church within society does not matter very much: what matters is the maintenance of a standard which stands outside of the ministry, the standard of biblical authority and inerrancy, which puts the fundamentalist laity above the official ministry in the sense that they are free to use this standard to judge it.

But the anti-clericalism of fundamentalists takes its most virulent form not in respect of the parish clergy but in respect of the theologians. Parish clergy, bishops and the like, though often not conservative, are not a positive menace in the way that the free intellectual activity of theologians is. The clergyman or bishop may be at least to some extent a valid official functionary and representative of the church within society, but the theologian as such, i.e. just because he is a theologian, is not at all a doctor of the church within society. In this respect fundamentalists somewhat share the secularist view of theology as an official-looking discipline the content of which is pure speculation, mere figments of the imagination. Fundamentalists want the church of course to have capable teachers of doctrine, but their task is not to work out freely their own thoughts, but to develop conservative doctrine under the control of the authority of scripture as fundamentalists understand it, and this means in principle that they should be under lay control.

As in so many things, however, there are paradoxes in this matter. Many fundamentalists will continue to look with veneration on (say) the Archbishop of Canterbury even when the holder of that office is not an evangelical. We shall shortly be noting ways in which on social and national issues the fundamentalist movement seems to hanker back to a society organized as a holy and theocratic Christendom, rather than as a secular society. I do not think that these aspects contradict the point I am making, namely that in many ways the fundamentalist is at home within a secularized society. This does not mean that he is quite unaffected by other visions of the world. As for the relation of clerical and lay, it can perhaps be argued that fundamentalism, while demoting the clerical, does so not by reaching a profounder understanding of the lay life of the Christian but by making the layman into a sort of cleric. The fundamentalist layman if properly instructed will and should do all the things that a clergyman should do, all at least that for the fundamentalist are essential.

He can interpret the Bible, he can 'preach', he can and must evangelize but, most of all, he can judge what is right doctrine and what is not, he can declare people to be unorthodox and heretical, he can declare that they do not belong to true Christianity. John Robinson suggests to me, in a striking phrase, that fundamentalists are thus 'crypto-clericalists'.

Another very important reason for the prosperous continuance of fundamentalism in an irreligious world lies precisely in the irreligiosity of that world. Some of the older 'liberal' theologies were motivated among other things by the idea that in the modern world outmoded conservative and biblical views were obnoxious to all educated people, so that only a more refined and reasonable Christianity, less bound to the exact words of the Bible, could win intellectual respect. Today, however, the secular rejection of Christianity, or indifference to it, has gone much farther. The more rational and philosophical forms of Christian belief are widely considered just as absurd, intellectually if not emotionally, as the most wildly irrational or the most unthinkingly biblicistic. Or, to put it in another way, since all Christianity is absurd, from the secular viewpoint it is all more or less fundamentalistic in character. Somewhat on the principle that one might as well be hanged for a sheep as for a lamb, this circumstance seems to reduce the difficulty of living in the modern world for the fundamentalist. Again, to those modern sociologists to whom religion is a subject of interest, extreme, narrow-minded, sectarian and fundamentalistic forms of religion are just as much a matter of research interest as are the mainstream churches and have to be looked on with understanding and sympathy as possibly viable forms of social and intellectual organization.

Changes in the pattern of education, as it affects biblical and theological studies, have also favoured the position of conservative evangelicals. Until fairly recent times there was comparatively little study of the Bible or of theology at university level except in theological faculties connected with the major denominations. But none of the major denominations have in recent decades been dominantly conservative evangelical in character, and on the whole they have not approved of fundamentalism. While that situation lasted, therefore, there were comparatively few people of markedly conservative evangelical views teaching either biblical studies or theology, except in those rather more limited institutions that were sectional or partisan conservative evangelical colleges. That situation has been altered by the secularization of many theological faculties and biblical departments, so that churches as such no longer have a voice, or much voice, in the choice of professors and lecturers. In biblical studies in particular many departments have grown up which from the beginning were not connected with any church or indeed with the teaching of theology as such. Correspondingly, there has been a marked increase in the number of individual persons teaching biblical studies at university level who have themselves never undergone a theological education. In view of the fact that conservative evangelicals are often deeply alienated from theology, this can well be significant.

I do not cite this change in the educational situation with any suggestion of complaint about it: on the contrary, the change was both right and necessary As a mere matter of fact, however, it means that there are probably more persons who hold markedly conservative views teaching biblical or theological studies today than there were a few decades ago. To this must be added a point which will be expanded later on, namely that many academics who are religiously conservative choose as their field not theology or biblical studies but rather environing fields, such as the languages and history of the ancient near east. But in general, in respect of higher education and opportunities within it, the secularized world has proved to be a not unfavourable environment for the conservative evangelical.

2. *'Culture fundamentalism'*

We have taken as our pattern for description a situation where conservative evangelicalism is in a minority position within the churches, or within the culture as a whole. But, as was indicated, this is not always the case, and certain parts of the world can be found where evangelical Protestantism of a conservative type is in fact the dominant religious form and one to which a large majority of the population are affiliated. From what has been said about conservative evangelical religion, one would have expected that its patterns would be greatly different where the main part of society was affiliated to that type of religion. Since there would be much less liberalism and modernism about, and little or no biblical criticism to worry over, and since the true gospel would thus have much more a monopoly of the religious scene, one would expect that the kingdom of God would be appreciably nearer in these territories and that the spiritual backsliding encouraged by liberal views would be notably absent. The facts of evangelical religion, however, make it quite doubtful whether this is the case. Even in those happy parts of the world where liberalism, modernism and biblical criticism have hardly been heard of sin seems still to be present, and on a scale not noticeably different from elsewhere; revival campaigns have to be held repeatedly in order to enliven the churches with an interest in the true gospel; and complaints of the hardness of heart and the unbelief of churchgoers are almost as loud as if Wellhausen and Bultmann had been stalking the land.

The point is a serious one for the general strategic picture of fundamentalism and what it could hope, if successful, to achieve. It suggests that for fundamentalists 'liberalism' and 'modernism' are no more than necessary myths, bogeys that have to be held up for execration and ritual contempt on every possible occasion, and that if they had their way and these evils were extirpated from the land things would not be one whit better. Even in a culture where the conservative evangelical reigned secure and supreme sin and un-belief would flourish as before. Or, to put a similar point, one suspects that, even where conservative evangelicals have a great numerical dominance, it is still a rhetorical necessity for them to depict their views as if they formed a minority position. Even where it is the main or the almost sole religious position known in a society, conservative evangelicalism pictures itself as if surrounded by numerous implacable enemies. Part of its preaching dynamic arises from the continual suggestion that its view is something that has not been heard before, that is unfamiliar to the hearers, that is in a minority position as against easy and comfortable opposing theologies, that is indeed practically stifled by opposition from its numerous foes – and all this even when it is easily the dominant religious form within a society. This picture, if I have depicted it rightly, would in turn help to explain why conservatives fail to draw the inference, from the situation of cultures where fundamentalism is dominant, that conservatism, when accepted in large zones of society, in fact presents no kind of religious solution satisfying even to its own supporters.

In societies where conservative evangelicalism is the dominant religious form there arises another question: to what degree is this numerical dominance used to enforce certain legal and social norms upon the society as a whole? This should be borne in mind when we come shortly to consider the social and political attitudes of conser-vative evangelicals.

3. *Roman Catholicism*

Conservative evangelicalism is an acutely Protestant form of religion. It is well known that, when the environment is dominantly Roman Catholic, Protestantism tends to become more acutely Protestant and often assumes a fundamentalist form. The two religious forms by their opposition polarize each other.

In this there is a good deal of paradox, for the official Roman Catholic position has for a long time had remarkable similarities to the fundamentalist position. 'Liberalism' could not have been condemned by the most ardent fundamentalist with more indignant disapproval than that which it received from a series of Popes, and the Pontifical Biblical Commission and similar authorities issued over a number of years a series of documents that declared with the utmost emphasis that the whole book of Isaiah was written by that prophet, that the fourth gospel was entirely written by John the son of Zebedee, that the human race was descended from the single original pair Adam and Eve, and such other decrees, all of which could only have delighted the hearts of conservative evangelicals everywhere. Indeed, as regards biblical literature and biblical criticism, Roman Catholics were until recently bound to a quite strictly fundamentalist position, and only with some difficulty have their scholars in more recent years been able to extricate themselves from it.

This fact should have been a cause of some worry to conservative evangelicals. They are accustomed to denouncing Rome with considerable fervour, though with hardly as much as they use in attacking 'liberalism' and biblical criticism; and it must come as something of a shock to discover that the Romans accept, or then accepted, the whole apparatus of fundamentalist belief as far as concerned biblical inspiration, inerrancy, critical questions and so on. Of course the overt similarity ends at this point: the setting of these doctrines within Roman Catholic life and thought is quite different from their setting within evangelical, and the Roman church has a complicated apparatus of tradition which appears to have no counterpart on the evangelical side. But even when this is admitted it would seem something of a shock that on the Bible, even if at no other point, the Roman doctrine came so extremely close to the conservative evangelical. Evangelical faith is supposed to make everything different: but in the handling of scripture it seemed to make *nothing* different!

The explanation for this, however, is simple. Although the official Roman doctrine has been as stated above, Roman doctrine as experienced and felt by evangelicals has commonly been quite different. Roman teaching, as it has been unfolded within popular controversy with evangelicals, has not stressed the infallibility or inerrancy of the Bible, nor has it emphasized the falsity of biblical criticism and the necessity of accepting the traditional ascriptions of books as by Moses, by Isaiah, by John the son of Zebedee and so on. Rather it has tended to play down the authority of scripture altogether: it has stressed that scripture can mean nothing without the authority of the church, that a man simply reading the Bible and interpreting it on his own can make absolutely anything out of it, that a biblical emphasis such as evangelicals would welcome is therefore quite excluded, and that the only real authority in the church is the Roman *magisterium*, which (it seems to evangelicals) can authoritatively interpret the Bible as it wishes. The result is that the vast majority of fundamentalists have not at all known that the official position of the Roman church, in respect of liberalism and modernism in theology and of the critical approach to the Bible, was one that they would, in itself, have welcomed with delight.

In fact it is extremely significant that these two opposite wings have or have had very similar views about the Bible. First of all, as many writers have noticed, the two have in common certain attitudes to the nature of truth. In both the emphasis is on the existence of correct statements which exactly state true doctrine and which give historical information exactly corresponding to the events reported. The second common element is the all-controlling conservatism of both. The most complete conservatism possible is the surest way of protecting the truth. In the latter part of the nineteenth century, when biblical criticism was a rising force and there was much anxiety about its effect on the life of the churches, the Roman church could well have exploited the situation in a very creative manner. It could have argued that the Bible was only one part of the total tradition of the church and that the totality of that tradition was a witness to God and to Jesus Christ, that this witness was theological in character but that it did not extend to and was not affected by such matters as the authorship of books, and that the total theological impact of the whole was so powerful that it could easily absorb critical views on literary and historical questions, even indeed on theological questions. This view would have given substantial freedom to biblical criticism without substantially altering the total dogmatic structure of the church, and such alteration of that structure as did take place could have been understood as legitimate and necessary development. That this was not done must be attributed to sheer conservatism, to the feeling that everything possible must be kept as it is, so that the church has to force upon its members an authoritative ruling about questions such as the authorship of books. The psychological character of conservatism in this case is identical with its Protestant counterpart in fundamentalism.

Protestant conservatives, indeed, feel that the comparison is a rather remote one in any case, because there are so many other factors: in particular, Roman Catholicism, excellent as its doctrine of scripture and its conservatism about historical matters may be, then goes and spoils the whole excellently conservative scheme by adding to the Bible the whole mass of church tradition as another major source of authority. The conservative evangelical, quaintly, thinks that he occupies middle ground in this respect: the 'liberals' depart from the true position about the authority of scripture by subtracting from it, the Roman Catholics by adding to it. But, as we have already implied, there is much more structural similarity between the Roman Catholic and the conservative positions than is at first apparent. Just as in the Roman church there is a tradition, and the system appears to ensure that the Bible will not say anything other than what is already present in the tradition, so it is in fundamentalism: the evangelical tradition of religion is from the beginning the accepted framework within which the Bible is interpreted, and no interpretation is carried out in such a way as to question this tradition. The insistence on biblical inerrancy, infallibility and so on is a shield set up to protect this tradition from criticism. Of course, the evangelical tradition grew up, long ago, under the assumption that this form of religion was dictated and required by the Bible; but that is true of the Catholic tradition also. The question is whether within the life of the community room is made for the questioning of the tradition by the Bible. The fundamentalist and the traditional Roman Catholic position have in this respect a similar structure, but the Roman position is much the more open and honest in that the place of the tradition is made fully explicit in doctrine, while conservative evangelicalism tends to conceal it: everything is represented as if it came solely and directly from the Bible itself. In both cases biblical interpretation has the task of bringing support from the Bible to the tradition; in both this is done by the use of varying interpretative techniques, literal at one point but vague, parabolic or allegorical at another; in both the

variations in interpretative techniques at any point are made in the
interest of the given religious tradition, which is the final governing
force.

4. *Social and political ethics*

We now come to consider the position taken by fundamentalist
Christians on social and political matters. Many observers have
noted that fundamentalism, which takes a very conservative position in matters of religion, is commonly accompanied by very conservative social and political opinions. Indeed, this is one of the
commonest of all observations made on the subject.

This observation, however, should not be made entirely absolute.
'One should not assume that political and religious "liberalism" and
"conservatism" are necessarily parallel.'[18] On a world scale, allowing for the variety of cultural situations, one cannot say that the
social and political consequences of fundamentalist faith are
monolithic. I have personally met several people who were convinced fundamentalists in religion and equally convinced socialists
in politics. In a society like parts of Wales, where the general culture
could be said to be a socialist culture, there may probably be many
who will adhere to a fundamentalist chapel but who are also loyal
Labour voters. Yet in such cases, though the same persons hold
both views, conservatism in religion and socialism in politics, it may
well be doubted whether any connection between the two is made
explicit: in other words, the two things may lie together as a matter
of fact, but it is not to be supposed that the fundamentalist faith is so
presented as to imply that it leads necessarily to a socialist political
position. Again, in some countries like Italy, where there is a long
tradition of Catholic-conservative government, I would not be surprised if a number of Protestants who in faith are more or less
fundamentalists will vote communist in elections; indeed I would be
surprised if they did not. Thus it is certainly possible for quite
extreme forms of fundamentalism to co-exist with leftish, or even
with far left, positions on the political scene. The Bible, read in a
certain way, could certainly provide the material for this: the image
of God in man, the economic laws of the Old Testament, the social
criticism of the prophets, the solicitude of Jesus for the poor, and the
primitive communism of the early chapters of Acts could all, if read
and interpreted on the principle that the Bible was entirely true and
divinely inspired, have provided the basis for a socially very concerned Christianity. And it may be that in various parts of the world

many people who read the Bible in that way do find in it an active and radical social message.

This does not alter the fact that the overwhelming preponderance of opinion among fundamentalists falls on the political right and often on the extreme right. This is most obvious in the United States.[19] At least within the twentieth century, and especially since the Second World War, American fundamentalism has commonly been strongly aligned with extreme political conservatism. Christianity is, in these circles of the far right, understood to give complete sanction to the capitalist system and to a *laissez-faire* approach to society, and government intervention in social arrangements, the welfare state, mildly reformist attitudes, higher criticism of the Bible, modern theology, radicalism, liberalism and socialism are all alike seen as forms of communism masquerading under another name. In such a milieu, though accusations of communism may be common coin (and even Billy Graham is said to have been called a communist by such extremists, or at least to have been accused of being 'soft on communism'), an actual socialist Christian, even a mild one, is as inconceivable among conservative evangelicals as a man with two heads.

In such circumstances the evangelical message does not only accept the capitalist society and the business ideology as a possible and tolerable way of life: it moves over into the position of lending positive and fervent ideological support to it. Not only actual communism, an entity almost totally unknown by experience to fundamentalists but bulking largely in their mythology, but mild socialist tendencies and even the occasional radical opinions of quite conservative Americans, are all alike a black mass of evil that threatens to engulf the world. From the religious point of view, the effect of this is suddenly to reverse the apparently radical claims of the evangelical gospel. The gospel and the biblical message in general, including that of the prophets, we are told, question and challenge all the systems of human security; all that man has relied upon is subject to question, for nothing is worse than that man should live by his own strength: and then suddenly we find that all this is abandoned, and evangelical religion assures men that the capitalistic system, the source of their strength and security in themselves, is in fact an ideal arrangement and that there is no question of God saying anything to disturb it; on the contrary, he says that it must not be disturbed. America is a sinful nation, so sinful that no other equally sinful could be imagined – and then suddenly it transpires that God looks very benevolently upon America, that

'Americanism' is a very good thing, something that ought to be supported and adopted by Christians entirely uncritically. In this form the religion looks with favour on the use of military power and presses for the maintenance of that power and for readiness to use it; and in more general terms the religion allows itself to be used as a pressure group to press right-wing policies upon the government. Thus on the one hand it tries to manipulate political force and rhetoric against its religious opponents, attacking especially the ecumenical movement as internationalist and communist-inspired; on the other side it tries to make good its own claim to be the genuine American religion and thereby to provide to its adherents the sense of really belonging in the United States. 'Despite the calls to people to come out of the world to Christ, being converted and joining an Evangelical church securely places the new members in a safe American-world context.'[20] Moreover, this sort of relation between evangelical religion and politics is not unique to America, though it is very prominent there; the situation of South Africa is perhaps in some ways parallel, although there are also many differences, since the traditional and dogmatic Calvinist tradition of South Africa has important dissimilarities from Anglo-Saxon evangelicalism.

It is not my purpose, however, to work out in detail the relations between conservative evangelical religion and right-wing social policies and ideologies. Let it suffice that we sum up the situation in general terms: the claim of the evangelical gospel to be a radical questioning of the inner bases of human self-certainty is suddenly reversed, when the religion becomes the ideological guarantor of the rightness of the existing social order. Or one might think of it as follows. One might expect evangelical religion to see the state and society, since by evangelical definitions they are not conducted by 'true Christians', at best in a neutral light as secular quantities, tolerable at most for true religion, and this would have fitted with the secularizing atmosphere within which fundamentalism often lives; but at a certain point this is reversed and evangelicalism of this kind is seen to hanker for a traditional and more or less mediaeval Christendom, a Christian country dominated by Christian values, using its military power in knightly style against the enemies of God and enforcing God's will through its laws and policies. Such a reversal or contradiction is not accidental in conservative evangelicalism, and we shall notice several analogous phenomena, not only where there is an alliance with right-wing politics.

One further brief note: it is hard to prove this, but there is reason to suspect that conservative evangelicalism fits well with nationalistic feeling. In the in-group national consciousness that is now becoming influential in many societies, and where the culture has a strongly Protestant background, as in Scotland, Northern Ireland and Wales, conservative evangelicalism may become a focus of nationalistic feeling, so that the evangelical groups within the church support the nationalistic trend. I do no more than mention this here; it will be significant later when we consider why fundamentalists are so hostile to ecumenical movements and endeavours.

If in certain cultures conservative evangelicalism is explicitly tied to a right-wing political position, at least this means that the religion has some kind of political awareness, however distorted it may seem to others. In the strain of evangelicalism that has been taken as typical for the purposes of this book, however, comparatively little is said about political matters, and it would be more correct to say that the tone is neutral than that it showed an inclination either to the left or to the right. Though I have listened to a large number of fundamentalist talks and addresses in Great Britain, I can hardly ever recall anything that sounded like right-wing political propaganda. On the whole the overt discussion of political matters is damped down. A book like Catherwood's *The Christian in Industrial Society* (Tyndale Press 1964), whatever its limits, gives at least some impartial discussion of the advantages and disadvantages of socialist and capitalist economic systems, and discusses with even-tempered calm such questions as the amount of compensation that should properly be awarded when industries are nationalized or socialized by the government. And Catherwood on religious and biblical matters takes a fully conservative evangelical line. His approach to social questions would be unthinkable in the atmosphere of politically right-wing American fundamentalism.

If the overt discussion of political matters is damped down, it is because prudent evangelical leaders, anxious to preserve the unity of evangelicalism, and rightly aware that politics is a divisive matter, seek to avoid involvement in political and social judgments that might be controversial. In such matters the practice of conservative evangelicals is governed by the character of the gospel. The evangelical gospel is the sole and essential means of salvation for man, only evangelicals can or will make it known, and their calling is to concentrate their time and energy on the performance of this vocation. The gospel is the absolute essential: political questions are in comparison optional subjects, not in the sense that they are unimportant for the life of man on this planet, but in the sense that political matters or any kind of matters can be seen in their right light only when the evangelical gospel has been known and accepted. Thus to introduce political and social concerns at a point before the character of the gospel had been made clearly known would invite confusion.

Moreover, political involvement is seen as an individual matter: not in the sense that the importance of collectivities is not at all seen, but rather that as a practical step the individual can take his political decisions as a single unit, while the church for the fundamentalist group cannot decide as a unit. Fundamentalists, we should remember, work to a large extent as a unit, each one speaks what is common doctrine to the group; they are not accustomed to working as a society in which a multitude of different voices are heard. The well-meaning attempts of bishops and church leaders to speak for 'the church' in civil affairs earn a good deal of derision from fundamentalists, and confirm them in the feeling that they as a body do not want to produce decisions, recommendations or plans for the advice of society. Even as a matter of practice, therefore, rather than of principle, it is good for the fundamentalist group to hold itself as a body apart from political and social commitments.

But behind this practical consideration lie more deep-seated theological convictions. The gospel is effective only through personal faith, acceptance and repentance, and by its own nature can be addressed only to individuals, or at least can be effective only through individual decision. It can indeed be preached 'to the world', but it is not intended to influence the world massively and collectively. These theological convictions need to be explored in more detail:

Firstly, there is no 'social gospel'. Even if the 'social gospel' may have found some echo in conservative pulpits in the last century or so, in modern evangelicalism the 'social gospel' has become a major bogey, exceeded in its obnoxiousness only by liberalism, modernism and biblical criticism. Indeed, it is taken to be more or less the reverse side of these coins: it is thought that, as people have been seduced away from the true gospel by liberalism, so they have gravitated towards a social gospel. This is an ethical gospel of improvement, reform and progress, supposed to be applicable to society as a whole. The ethic of Jesus is, it is supposed, the element that remained to liberals after they had stripped away the great biblical doctrines of sin, atonement, redemption, repentance and faith, and in the social gospel, as fundamentalists imagine it to themselves, this ethic is applied direct to society, as if it could be simply put into effect by people who have not yet put their lives in the hands of Christ by personal faith and surrender to him. According to conservative evangelicals, the ethical teaching of Jesus is not intended to work in this way, and it is not only useless but actually damaging if it is put before men as a way of life independently of the doctrines of atonement and personal faith. Any attempt to do so is clear testimony of an inadequate estimate of the power and iniquity of sin: human sin will frustrate the best ethical principles, and its power is not broken except by personal faith in Christ. In other words, the social gospel would be a religion of works rather than an appeal for faith in Jesus Christ alone.[21] Whether or not anyone actually holds or practises the social gospel as depicted by conservative evangelicals, there can be no doubt that it, or the myth of it, is cordially detested by them.

This is not to say, as critics of evangelicalism often say, that evangelicals have no concern for the common life of mankind, for the rebuking of sin in social and political matters, or for the support of necessary reforms and improvements. But they tend to put the emphasis upon the production of dedicated individual Christians. The dedicated Christian through his personal involvement in industry, in business and so on will then bring his witness to bear upon all sorts of relations in which he lives and works: this is much better than that the church as church should involve itself in saying what should or should not be done in the complicated and ever-changing social scene.

Another approach found among conservative evangelicals is that through 'common grace' and the 'social law'.[22] Though there is no social gospel, there is a law of God which forms a standard for society, and by it various sectors of society can be made more just, can be reformed. It is a Christian duty to press for this, and if one does not do so one is abandoning the world to secularism and humanism, if not to Satan. There is a 'common grace' given by God to the church and the world alike: God has not abandoned the world to evil, and he works to preserve good in the world, through conscience, through the divine institutions of government and family, and 'perhaps most forcibly of all through the explicit proclamation of God's law by the church'. But though this point of view is indeed found in certain currents of conservative evangelicalism, and especially where there is an influence from traditional Dutch Calvinism, one is entitled to wonder how much difference it really makes. When a form of religion concentrates its positive effort so much on the gospel as evangelicalism does, and when this kind of social interest is expressly classed not under gospel but under law, and when gospel and law are very strictly distinguished from one another, it is natural that the active dynamic of the religion should remain on the side of the gospel. And this suggests that, while the gospel may communicate general insights which are relevant for the ills of society, such as the universality and the seriousness of sin, the gospel in itself cannot be profitably brought into contact with particular social problems. This view, concentrating on the 'social law', can generate a sincerity in striving with social questions which should not be doubted, but it can still leave them in a place very secondary to the understanding of the gospel itself and, more important, quite separate from it. Thus we often come back to matters of the individual Christian's conduct in his working life, plus the opinions he expresses on social questions. The 'social law' often works out largely as the source of complaints over the generally low standard of morals, and these complaints are then fed mainly not into remedial social action but into the negative side of the preaching of the gospel: that is, they come to serve as exemplifications of the sinfulness of all mankind from which men have to be redeemed.

The limits set to any emphasis on the social dimensions of the gospel by conservative evangelicals are probably strengthened by their view of the Old Testament prophets. The social gospel, in so far as there is such a thing, has often leaned rather heavily on the prophets, because they made more explicit and continual reference to political and social matters than anything that can be found in the New Testament. That the prophets denounced sin and evil in their contemporary society would no doubt be common property to all shades of opinion. But the idea that this is the essential thing about the prophets, that their main function was their political and social impact on the society of their time, is a relatively modern idea, and one that was mainly worked out under the liberal and critical schools of the nineteenth century, and immediately taken up by the social gospel. The older traditional emphasis was not on the prophets as critics of the contemporary social order, but on the prophets as predictors of the coming of the Messiah, and it is probable that this older picture still has much influence among conservative evangelicals, while the newer picture has less.

But this leads on to another aspect of conservative evangelicalism which also makes it less interested in social action and in social questions than it might otherwise be, namely its eschatology, its picture of the relation between God and the future of mankind.

Here the idea of progress is sharply discounted by conservatives. When one looks back, indeed, it can occasionally be seen that some sort of progress has been made, and if this is so it is commonly attributed in fair measure to the influence of the Bible, the work of the Reformation, and the witness of evangelicals. But as a general principle progress is markedly disfavoured by conservative evangelicals: this is true whether one means that there has been progress in the past, that there will be progress in the future, or that progress is inevitable. The fall of man is much more striking than any progress he has made. The fact that some liberal theology, and some biblical criticism, worked with the idea of progress is a clear reason why one should be suspicious of it. The realization of God's will on earth will come not through any steady progress towards righteousness but by a cataclysmic act of divine intervention. Until then, far from seeing progress, one should expect things to get worse: wars and rumours of wars, increasing unrighteousness, and the incipient breakdown of the cosmic order are signs of the approach of the end. Within fundamentalism indeed the degree of emphasis on this sort of eschatology is diverse, and we shall later be considering some of the varieties. In some forms of fundamentalism these apocalyptic pictures are very heavily emphasized and when this is so people's thinking is quite dominated by this picture of a cataclysmic end at hand. Not all are so dominated by this picture; but among almost all fundamentalists this picture is strong and vivid enough to have a powerful negative influence on any vision of a social message, of social action, and of any interaction between the preaching of the gospel and the social situation. Thus the general impression received is that, apart from the necessary rebuking of sin and of low moral standards in individual and community, it is best to leave things alone. Any explicit programme for change is thus more likely to be resisted than any policy of keeping things as they are. Any attempt to introduce change, to plan things in another way, falls under the suspicion that the reformers are motivated by sinful pride in their own ability to do good, or that they really think of justification by good works rather than by faith. From this point of view the somewhat neutral political-social position of conservative evangelicalism as taken for the basis of this present study may be interpreted with some reason as a neutrality that is biassed towards the conservative through its own passivity. Admitting exceptions, and dissociating moderate conservative evangelicalism from the extreme right-wing partisanship that also exists, it remains broadly true that this type of religion favours conservative politics and policies or at least disfavours them much less than it disfavours their radical and socialist counterparts.

The question may, however, be asked: what about the great Evangelical leaders of the late eighteenth century and the nineteenth, such as Wilberforce and Shaftesbury, whose work in the abolition of the slave trade, the regulation of factories, the protection of children and the humanization of prisons is rightly honoured by all? Do not these demonstrate the deep social concern of the evangelical tradition? They do indeed demonstrate that a deep social concern may lie within the general evangelical tradition; but they equally show that evangelicalism has changed, they show how far modern conservative evangelicalism has departed from its evangelical forebears in this respect. It is true that certain elements, which are still central to the conservative evangelical viewpoint, were already fully emphasized by leaders such as Wilberforce: such was, for instance, the distinction between true and nominal Christianity. Fervency in prayer, continual study of the Bible, and consistent Christian living were all much fostered; 'rationalism' and 'ritualism' were much opposed. But this sort of evangelicalism was not then conservative in the sense that has now developed, and its theological emphases were not inexorably linked, as they are in modern fundamentalism, to hard and unrelenting insistence on the inerrancy of the Bible, especially in historical narration and in ascriptions of authorship. In other words, this older evangelicalism was more intellectually progressive: it is not clear that a man like Wilberforce would have rejected the critical study of the Bible, so long as its religious content was observed, and his religious emphasis was much more on sincerity of engagement in Christian living than on external purity of doctrine. The same can be said of other great figures of the time, like Wesley. In many respects the religious emphasis of the great eighteenth-century evangelicals came closer to what in the late nineteenth century and the early twentieth was liberalism. It was socially progressive, while much or most conservative evangelicalism of the mid-twentieth century has been socially regressive. What Wilberforces and Shaftesburys have been produced by the conservative evangelicalism of our own time?

We may conclude this section with some brief remarks about Catherwood's *A Better Way* (Tyndale Press 1975) as an example of conservative evangelical ethical thought, probably (so far as I know) the best work in this genre that has been produced. The strongly Christian surface atmosphere, conveyed by the numerous quotations from the Bible, plus occasional remarks such as the opinion (p. 70) that 'Adam had one wife and this seems to have been the early rule' (!), does not conceal the fact that as a basic ethical approach this work is not very evangelical and not very Christian at all. Fundamentally it is a rational and prudential ethic of eighteenth-century type to which a certain amount of Christian and biblical top dressing has been added. Christian arguments 'must be based on principle' (p. 45) and the biblical material is used to distil 'principles' for judgment in social matters. The rationalist atmosphere is strong. 'It is also a Christian principle that differences should be settled by reason. God is a God of reason and man is made in his image. The Christian message is a message of reason' (p. 81). Catherwood is a thoroughly good man and his ethic is full of good will. It is the nemesis of his conservative evangelical bias that he has paid no attention to non-conservative works on Christian ethics which might have indicated to him profundities of the Christian ethical position which to him are quite unknown. One example will suffice: the execution of Bonhoeffer. According to Catherwood, p. 88, Bonhoeffer 'entered into the plot against Hitler's life as a member of an influential Prussian family and not as a Christian pastor. It was for that that he was executed and not for his Christian faith.' This is not an accidental remark made in passing; Catherwood devotes an extra appendix, pp. 102 f., to the matter, and clearly it is personally important for him. Clearly also it does not occur to him that in the twentieth century, as in most ages perhaps, the true martyrs of the Christian faith will not die purely 'as' Christian pastors or the like but 'as' something else. There is surely no ethical instinct more deeply Christian and evangelical than this, that the question is not 'as' what you act, but *for whose sake* you act: The good and rational Catherwood has not enough insight into this to allow Bonhoeffer to rest as a Christian martyr. Partisanship wins in the end. Had Bonhoeffer been a conservative evangelical, he might have fared better. Catherwood really thinks that the ineffectiveness of German church resistance against Hitler was promoted by 'doubts about the authority of the faith (which the German higher-critical movement had certainly encouraged)'. In other words, it is implied, if they had all been conservative evangelicals, untouched by the doubts caused by higher criticism, there would have been much more resistance against Nazism. Illusions of these dimensions are past the possibility of confuting. All in all, the rational, and sometimes sensible, ethic of Catherwood shows only limited biblical or evangelical insight, while moments of serious conservative partisanship stain the fairness of the overall impression.

5. *The Jews and Zionism*

Among political issues of the present day there is one that is of special interest to fundamentalists, namely the return of the Jews to Palestine and the fortunes of the state of Israel. That the Jews should return to Palestine and that this should in some way (precise connections are not easy to find) go along with their conversion to Christianity and also be an event ushering in the last stages of world history and the coming of the end – all of this has long been for fundamentalists an attractive interpretation of passages in the prophets and the apocalyptic books. While many other strains of Christianity hold that all prophecies find their fulfilment in Jesus Christ, this particular current understands them, or at least some of them, futuristically, as predictions of great events which will actually occur, and that in the places specified in the biblical text: here once again we have an element in fundamentalist interpretation that is 'literal'. From this point of view the actual return of Jews to Palestine and their eventual establishment of an independent state was seen as a matter of cosmic religious importance. Indeed it is probable that shades of these religious expectations, however vague and shadowy, had some historical effect in the background of the Balfour Declaration itself: they formed part of the intellectual background for the British decision to establish a 'national home' for the Jews in Palestine.

'The Jews' are regarded as a uniform collectivity for the purposes of this trend of thought. When fundamentalists turn to this sort of question, they often, amusingly, reverse principles that are otherwise dearly held. Within the present scheme of things the gospel is preached for the faith of individuals, and God cannot do anything for great masses of people because their sin has not been removed, since they do not personally believe in Jesus Christ. In these eschatological expectations all this is abandoned: whole collectivities like 'the Jews' (ignoring the large numbers of them who stay in America or elsewhere) are marvellously moved about by God and their destiny altered. Here the supernatural really takes charge, not at all hampered by the failure of the persons concerned to become Christian conservative evangelicals. From time to time there is disappointment at the failure of 'the Jews' to embrace Christianity, which seems to eliminate one of the essential stages in the traditional eschatological programme; but in fact it seems that among fundamentalists the old conversionist interest in the Jews has become muted (as it has not when directed towards non-conservative Christians) and the sense of wonder at the destiny of Israel as the working out of an important part in the plan of God becomes paramount.

In such a milieu uncritical admiration for the state of Israel becomes common, and fundamentalist religion lends its ideological support to many of its policies, sometimes also to its conquests.[23] The conservative tone of some Israeli biblical scholarship is sometimes a further factor.[24] As we shall see, some conservative evangelical groups try to keep enthusiasm for such prophetic previews of history at a low level, on the grounds that these are speculations which distract from the Christian's main duty of witnessing to the gospel among his contemporaries of today;[25] other groups, by contrast, make this 'prophetic' element into the most important single element in their whole understanding of the Bible. The fact remains that conservative evangelical Christianity is one main source of pro-Israel feeling in the modern world,[26] and this is one of the matters of world politics on which it often takes an active stand. I shall make no attempt to discuss the rights and wrongs of the matter in itself: I place it here, not in order to stimulate discussion about the state of Israel, but in order to complete the picture of fundamentalism and its social-political views.

5 · Conservative Biblical Scholarship

1. *General*

It is indisputable that in recent decades scholarship has become more and more important for conservative evangelicals. At one time many of them might have been content to dismiss scholarship as a quite unimportant factor in the understanding of the Bible: after all, had not the apostle Paul declared that not many wise men after the flesh are called? Thus at one time one might have been happy to be a quite unlearned believer with no knowledge of any book other than the English Bible, but today there is visible a deep anxiety to have learning on one's side. Valiant efforts are being made to improve the standard of conservative publications. Works like *The New Bible Dictionary* and *The New Bible Commentary*, dubious as they are in many respects, are certainly a substantial improvement on what there was thirty or forty years earlier, and the same is true of some of the other conservative evangelical literature emanating from the same publishing houses. Books like Catherwood's *The Christian in Industrial Society* or his *A Better Way*, though naive and traditional in their understanding in many ways, are decently written and tolerably sophisticated works, and are not to be mentioned in the same breath with some of the pamphlets earlier produced for reading by conservative students, which did not differ in intellectual level from mission-hall tracts. The production of this better literature in itself indicates that an increasing number of conservative evangelicals are developing scholarly interests and are prepared to write articles and books which aspire to a scholarly level.

More interesting for our purpose perhaps is not the literature itself but the attitudes that go with it. Conservative evangelical literature about the Bible is not just scholarly literature, it is scholarly literature prepared, published and diffused with a particular purpose in mind: to provide literature that the evangelical student or reader can *trust*. The aspect of trust is all-important. In saying this I do not imply that the material is censored or that it is forced to conform to a partisan line: on the contrary, we shall see that there are glaring disagreements between writers, and that some of them substantially contradict positions that have generally been considered essential to the conservative evangelical faith. It is, indeed, to the credit of the conservative evangelical institutions that have arranged publication that they have not resorted to censorship of the opinions published. On the other hand, not too much credit should be allowed for this, because it probably has not been realized how far some of the opinions contradict or undermine the conservative evangelical approach. Anyway, the material published is perceived by the conservative evangelical reading public as material approved by this or that conservative publishing house or organization, and this in itself is a reason for trusting what it says. I do not suggest that publishers who are generally conservative never publish non-conservative books, or that all books that are conservative are published by conservative publishing houses. Nevertheless there is a sort of pool of known scholars and writers who are roughly identified with the conservative evangelical cause, and who can be trusted to follow a generally acceptable evangelical line and not to put things in such a way as to disturb the holder of conservative opinions. Conservative literature is written by people of this general type.

The attitudes of the writers and publishers have an echo in the attitudes of their readership. For conservative evangelicals, or many of them, a book is not the same sort of thing as it is to other people. Generally speaking, they will not want to read books that expound with sympathy critical, radical or sceptical views about the Bible. Books are therefore not things to be looked on impartially. Just as there is one book, the Bible, which is in all respects infallible and inerrant, so there are, on a secondary level, books that are 'sound' and wholesome because they *say* that the Bible is infallible and inerrant, and attack the critics who cast doubt upon this. What one ought to read is 'sound' literature. A conservative evangelical student, asked to read Wellhausen and discuss the reasons for his ordering of sources in the pentateuch, will not want to read Wellhausen and will try, if possible, to escape from the imposition: what he will want to do is to read a work which will tell him why Wellhausen was wrong. His pastoral advisers, if he has any, will counsel him to read this kind of book: they will not advise him to read energetically the works of Wellhausen himself, or of de Wette, or of Kuenen.[1] The approach to printed books among conservative evangelicals thus approximates to their approach to the spoken word among the speakers invited to their meetings: just as non-conservative speakers should not be heard, so non-conservative writers should not be read.

Modern developments have put at the disposal of the conservative reader a wide range of literature on all sorts of subjects. For a large series of questions he will soon have at his disposal a fairly complete series of assured conservative textbooks which he can read with the assurance that no writer of seriously 'unsound' views will have been asked to contribute: commentaries on books of the Bible, dictionaries of the Bible, works on the background of the Bible. On philosophy and theology in the general sense less is to be had, and it is of very mediocre quality, but perhaps something better will be forthcoming. Attempts are being made to provide books which, from a trustworthy evangelical point of view, give guidance on recent developments in art, on psychology, on comparative religion, on social ethics, on the new discipline of 'religious studies', and to this can be added all the books or pamphlets on practical questions like sexual behaviour, methods of personal evangelism, career guidance and all the rest. Perhaps the time will come when conservative evangelical publishing will have spread so widely that it will be possible to master any subject without reading any non-evangelical book.

Conservative books published in this way will often cite and describe non-conservative scholarly opinions, but this will always be done within the framework and under the scheme of presentation set up by the more or less conservative author. The conservative student will no doubt read, or will have to read, books representing other schools of opinion, but he will return again and again to the kind of book he can trust because he knows that its soundness is assured. Very likely he will press his professors to include some of these books on the syllabus of required reading for lectures and examinations. He will complain that scholars of other schools do not give enough recognition to conservative literature and that they thus exercise bias against it.

It is doubtful whether the evangelical readership has advanced in ability, knowledge and discrimination as fast as the publications destined for it have advanced in erudition. One might wonder whether the conservative evangelical reader, with his fairly simple Bible-centred faith, can really want or need as much information about the history of Egypt or Babylonia, or about Ugaritic, or about the history of the biblical text, as he is now being given. Here again the motivation which the literature serves is different from that with which books are commonly used. The erudition of the material is in practice often used to serve the function of giving assurance. It displays the fact that there are people full of erudition about these matters, who are yet fully reliable in their evangelical belief. This is a major way in which conservative evangelical scholarship functions: to the reader it functions very often as a display of learning which builds up trust within the religious consciousness. The student or reader perhaps does not understand all the facts or the arguments, and he certainly could not reproduce them or give his own justification of them, but he learns from the literature that there are learned men who do understand them, and that these men are either conservative evangelicals or at least do not openly oppose the things that conservative evangelicals hold to be true. In this sense the functioning of the literature is often propagandistic, and this function is confirmed by the reluctance to encourage people to read non-conservative literature for themselves, a reluctance that can be explained only by a propagandistic understanding of literature. I do not for a moment say that conservative scholars lend themselves intentionally to this sort of function: I only say that this is how the literature in fact functions within the sort of constituency to which it is addressed.

For the average fundamentalist reader, then, the function of conservative scholarship is to give him comfort and security, assuring him that the certainties of his religion will not be put in question. He has this comfort and security, however, because he does not understand how the conservative scholar really works. Moreover, the conservative literature itself refrains from telling him much about the way in which its own scholars work. If this was understood by the readership they would be less assured and comforted than they appear to be.

The material published as conservative scholarship falls into several categories. Only a certain amount of it belongs to, supports, or explicitly depends upon the old dogmatic fundamentalist arguments. Within this section it is accepted and expressly stated that the Bible must, on dogmatic grounds, be inerrant, therefore things happened just as described in the Bible, except where resort has to be had to non-literal interpretation in order to safeguard the inerrancy of the narrative. In this type of scholarship the supernatural may be directly invoked: according to it there is absolutely no reason why prophets should not have foreseen and predicted events hundreds of years after their time, no reason why there should not be miracles, a resurrection, a virgin birth. There is no difficulty with any of these things: difficulty only appears to exist because scholars through sheer prejudice ruled out the supernatural as the cause of events from the beginning. On questions of authorship and date of sources dogmatic arguments are freely used: the date of Psalm 110 is absolutely settled by the words of the citation by Jesus, and so on. This element in modern conservative evangelical scholarship is in complete agreement with a fully fundamentalistic understanding of the Bible.

A great deal of conservative evangelical literature about the Bible, however, has now come to be conservative rather than fundamentalist in its actual methodology. It works by historical methods and within historical categories. Writers who write in this way may personally believe the dogmatic, supernaturalist arguments and the results that are obtained by the use of them; but, whether they believe them or not, they do not use them as part of the overt structure of their arguments. They thus tacitly grant, and rightly, that these arguments, whatever one's personal attitude to them may be, do not belong within the structure of biblical scholarship. Perhaps they would call upon these arguments at certain extreme points, where nothing else would avail to validate a conservative interpretation; but otherwise, wherever possible, these arguments had best be kept out of sight. This attitude, according to which the dogmatic arguments are used only in the last emergency, is itself a tacit admission that they are invalid for use within biblical scholarship: for, if they dealt with the problems, they should be used continually and consistently. The average 'conservative' scholar actually reasons within an entirely historical methodological field. On all critical and historical questions there is, within modern biblical scholarship, a range of possibilities; the conservative scholar will survey this range, but he will then end up with the most conservative view reasonably possible; he will argue for that view and leave the reader with the impression that it is the best evidenced. The conservative reader foolishly prizes such interpretations because the *results* are highly conservative, without observing that in method this kind of scholarship already belongs to the non-fundamentalist world. Some of the conservative scholars whom the fundamentalist reader adores and whose contributions fill him with trust are in fact unconsciously undermining the doctrinal basis which motivates him to admire them; and some of them are probably preparing him gradually for a slow exit from the fundamentalist world.

In saying this I do not imply, and do not in fact think, that historically conservative scholarship of this kind is on the whole scientifically a good approach, for often it is not. Often it is clear that, though the dogmatic and doctrinal arguments in favour of biblical inerrancy are eschewed, the scholar feels himself bound to seek a highly conservative solution and supposes that such a solution is religiously more favourable than a more radical solution. Often it is clear that the evidence in favour of a conservative interpretation is being exaggerated and that the interpretation thus has a bias which seriously affects its status within biblical scholarship. This will be looked at again later. But in any case, whether these criticisms are right or not, the framework within which such conservative scholarship sets out its position, and the overt principles of demonstration that it uses, lie within a world that is largely shared with critical scholarship. Scholarship which lies within this world, however conservative, in fact ignores, and implicitly denies even if it does not expressly mention, the doctrinal grounds upon which fundamentalism is built: unlike all real fundamentalists, and unlike all scholars who share and actually work with the dogmatic positions of fundamentalism, these conservative scholars share the same universe of discourse with critical scholars and know perfectly well that they do. What they fail to do is to point out the fact, and its lessons, to their fundamentalist readership.

There is no question, then, that the sort of scholarship conservative evangelicals respect has improved in erudition and in ability to present itself on the historical level on which world scholarship exists. What has not improved is the awareness by this scholarship of the methods and principles that it itself follows; and what has actually deteriorated is its frankness with its own readership about the implications of these methods and principles.

Conservative readers, as we have seen, crave the assurance that there is real learning on their side. But conservative scholars, and especially the younger ones among them, equally crave intellectual respectability, recognition on the level of general biblical scholarship as against partisan apologetic. They may be perfectly willing to write material that may be *read* by a conservative readership as if it confirmed traditional views. But they write also with an eye to what will be at least up to a point justifiable on the level of general scholarship, which as they well know does not share the perceptions characteristic of their conservative readership. When they review the opinions of (say) Wellhausen, Noth, Pedersen and Engnell,[2] and then go on to opt for the most conservative option available, this is likely to be read by the conservative readership as an assurance that only the most conservative view has any basis and that it only need be taken seriously; but it is also written, in many cases, in such a way as to safeguard for the conservative scholar his membership of that same world which Wellhausen, Noth, Pedersen and Engnell also inhabit.

Thus recent conservative scholarship, in spite of the fact that it seems to uphold conservative results which are acceptable to convinced fundamentalists, is in fact highly equivocal in its relation to the basic convictions of that religious current. Modern works like *The New Bible Dictionary* and *The New Bible Commentary* contain side by side at least three types of material. There are, first of all, articles written by total fundamentalists who completely reject the entire apparatus of critical scholarship and who fully accept and rely upon the dogmatic arguments and evidences for scriptural inerrancy. Secondly, there is a great deal that is generally conservative, and that uses the maximal-conservative argument on historical issues; this material will naturally be read by fundamentalists as if it completely favoured the most highly conservative historical possibilities, but if read in another way it manifestly leaves open the line of retreat towards a more critical position, which is 'less probable' but nevertheless remains possible. Thirdly, there is quite a lot written by authors who have at some time had some contact with the conservative evangelical movement and who are quite willing to write for its publications. People like this may be mildly conservative on historical issues and are probably somewhat doubtful about the more radical trends in biblical criticism, but on the other hand they do not have any absolute polemic stance against critical scholarship and they may well be equally doubtful of the doctrinal position taken by fundamentalism. Such writers hold these opinions but do not make all this clear when they write, or do not make it clear in such a way as to express their substantial disagreement with the established fundamentalist line.

Thus current developments in conservative evangelical publishing, though regarded with complacency by the conservative reading public, are in fact quite equivocal in relation to the principles they hold so dear, and these equivocations are likely to lead to tensions within conservative evangelical religion in the long run.

Evangelicals are constantly being assured that scholarship is becoming increasingly respectful towards the conservative case. This is wishful thinking induced by their own propaganda. In a typical popular presentation of the matter, Michael Green assures his readers, concerning the 'liberal' method of approaching scripture, as illustrated by the customary analysis of the pentateuch, the priority of Mark among the gospels, the existence of the document 'Q', and the lateness and historical unreliability of St John's gospel: 'Though the scholars have to a large extent abandoned it [i.e. this approach to scripture], the minds of many people both within and without the Church are still affected by it.'[3] In this he is totally misleading his own evangelical readership, and the only excuse that can be offered is that he knows little about what is happening in scholarship and has allowed himself to be informed purely by conservative evangelical controversial literature, with its constant use of propagandistic methods.

One essential element in conservative attitudes has been the hope that criticism was a passing phase, that given time the new methods would just go away. The idea that their departure is already manifest is a wish-fulfilment dream assiduously diffused by writers like Green. The dream has nothing to do with actual study of recent developments in scholarship. On the contrary it is as old as the critical method itself. Pusey, who was no evangelical but was certainly a conservative and on biblical criticism held a position similar to that of modern conservative evangelicals, in his lectures on Daniel in 1862 was already giving the same assurance to his hearers, before Wellhausen's work had been done: 'That hacking school of criticism, which hewed out the books of Holy Scripture into as many fragments as it willed, survives only in a few expiring representatives. It reigned with an Oriental despotism in Germany for a time, but is now deposed even there.'[4]

The statement quoted from Green displays a complete ignorance of the facts of present-day scholarship. Of the four elements cited, the date and historicity of St John's gospel is the only one where some substantial movement of opinion might reasonably be registered. As for the priority of Mark and the existence of Q, not only do these continue to hold the support of the majority of critical scholars, but they are coming to be substantially accepted by conservative evangelical scholars too, as will be shown below.[5]

In general, far from the conservative case making an impact on scholarship, the world of scholarship has no respect for the dogmatic and supernaturalistic kind of conservative apologetic and rightly ignores it. As for scholarship working with the maximal-conservative type of argument, scholarship accepts it and admires it in proportion as it *fails* to be partisanly conservative; that is, it may be accepted and admired, but only in such measure as it does *not* do what conservative apologists insist that it must do and has done. In so far as it is seen as committed to a purely conservative line, it is discounted and unrespected. Thus the deservedly high reputation of some conservative scholarship rests to a large extent on the degree to which it *fails* to be conservative in the sense that the conservative evangelical public desiderate.

2. *Study in the environing fields*

A very striking characteristic of conservative scholarship is that, of the conservatively-minded people who take an interest in the Bible, a very large proportion interest themselves academically in the margins rather than the centre of the biblical field. Typically, they do not become scholars in the theology of the Old Testament, or in the concept of messianism, or in the Pauline doctrine of faith, or in the biblical concept of the covenant. Much more do they become scholars in fields like: textual criticism, the grammar of New Testament Greek, archaeology and the Bible, Coptic,[6] Semitic linguistics. Many take up as their field of study not even the periphery of biblical study but a field which, though separate from it, has some contact with it: so for instance Egyptology, Assyriology, Ugaritic studies. The presence in these fields of scholars who are also religiously very conservative is a well-known fact of the present situation, and one that deserves to have some discussion. Is it not strange if scholars, whose personal faith is deeply anchored in the Bible and its religious authority, choose to become specialists in the environment of the Bible rather than in the Bible itself or, within the Bible, to become scholars in the furniture and technical mechanics of the Bible, if we may so term them, rather than in the religious heart of the Bible?

The first reason is no doubt unwillingness to become involved with the critical problems. Entry into the exegesis of the Bible, or into its theology, means immediate contact with the critical positions taken up by scholars in their research. One might have supposed that evangelicals would be anxious to enter into these areas, to do battle with prevailing critical positions within them, and to show the results in the form of different exegetical and theological results. In fact this is seldom so: perhaps out of reluctance to be involved in controversy on these matters, perhaps out of a sense of pain at so many apparent obstacles, perhaps out of unwillingness to read the standard books which so often assume a critical approach, conservative students often prefer to seek expertise in a more technical field, or in one that belongs to the environment rather than to the study of the Bible itself and to its religious content. We can carry this point farther. The conservative mind, at least in its more recent manifestations, when applied in biblical scholarship, seems to seek a subject where a neutral and purely intellectual attitude is possible, a subject requiring the minimum of actual and direct theological involvement, a subject possessing the maximum possible grade of objectivity, the maximum possible separation from the theological issues that divide conservative studies from modern theology. The fundamentalist evangelical obtrudes his faith; the fundamentalist intellectual more often conceals it. But areas like the textual history of the Bible or the grammar of the New Testament have a much lower degree of involvement in personal and non-objective decision than subjects like historical introduction (deciding the date and authorship of books) or biblical theology; and, even where these areas require non-objective interpretative decisions, these are normally not theological or exegetical decisions: they belong to the level of historical, textual and linguistic science rather than to the level of religious content.

It may seem paradoxical that a religious current which strongly emphasizes personal faith and decision, and which has often been criticized for being basically emotional in its orientation, should in matters of scholarship seek the maximum possible of intellectual detachment and objectivity. Profounder analysis, however, should show that this, though paradoxical, is in fact characteristic of conservative evangelist faith and practice. Conservatism has a longing for validation on a strictly intellectual level, and we shall see that this fits with the general doctrinal approach espoused by it. It fits in with the conception of truth as lying in the correspondence between written formulations and external actuality – though as an intellectualistic view of truth this is only a shallow and elementary one. It shows up also yet another device of the conservative apologetic as a false argument: conservatives have often argued that, with the rise of biblical criticism, biblical truth is being betrayed into the hands of the intellectuals, who arrogate to themselves the right to decide and who seek to impose their esoteric schemes upon the church. This resentment against the accepted scholarship in biblical criticism is well expressed by conservative popularizers like Michael Green: to suggest that we should 'accept the assured results of modern criticism' is 'merely to replace the Pope on his throne by the Professor of Biblical Studies in his chair'.[7] Had conservative evangelicals in their own practice insisted on a very modest role for intellect in the handling of the Bible and emphasized the limited and tentative character of the results achieved by even the most intelligent and well-equipped scholar, there might at least have been some point in this argument. Its value is totally nullified, however, by the actual practice of conservative evangelicals in their evaluation of conservative interpretation, for their craving for intellectual recognition and their flaunting of the rationality and erudition of conservative apologists is one of the most unattractive features of their literature.

In recent conservative evangelical argument the scholar who is an expert in some environing subject, such as Egyptology or Assyriology, has come to play an increasingly important role. The lines of argument commonly developed are well illustrated by K. A. Kitchen in his *Ancient Orient and Old Testament* (IVP 1966). It is argued that evidence from the ancient near east confirms the historicity of the biblical narrative at countless points and makes the critical approaches now customary in scholarship totally unnecessary. (For the New Testament, similarly, analogous studies argue that documents like Acts fit in extremely well with the history of the period described; and it is urged that historians of this period, working from the Greco-Roman side, would never treat the circumstantial details of Acts with the historical scepticism that New Testament scholars show towards them.) The critical schemes and reconstructions accepted by critical scholars were worked out in a time when much less was known about the ancient world. Critical scholars treated the Bible as if it existed in a vacuum, and they arrived at their schemes of source separation within the Old Testament and the New because they paid no attention to such data as were even then available concerning the cultures of the environment. Biblical scholars and theologians, educated or indoctrinated in this critical tradition and totally wrapped up in it, and failing to keep up with modern research outside of the Bible itself, have failed to see that the difficulties and discrepancies found in the Bible by critics, and used by them for the identification of different sources, were unreal and that the source reconstructions proposed by them were totally unnecessary. 'Nowhere in the Ancient Orient is there anything which is definitely known to parallel' the sort of history of sources and redaction postulated by the documentary hypotheses of critical scholarship; and any attempt to apply to ancient near eastern literature the sort of analysis customary within the Bible would 'result in manifest absurdities'.[8]

Here again we find the assumption of an objectivist intellectualist attitude: there is no need to quote dogma, no need to indulge in heated religious controversy. One simply and calmly states the evidence from outside the Bible which shows how unnecessary and how completely wrong the entire series of critical questionings has been. Kitchen explicitly claims that '*no appeal whatsoever* has been made to any theological starting-point in the body of this work'.[9] But the personal sense of intellectual contempt held by the writer towards critical scholars shines through everything that he writes. And one may doubt whether the dogmatic and the personal is so far away. Appeal or no appeal to a theological starting-point, there is perhaps not a single book among the conservative evangelical works read in the research for this study (apart from Harrison's *Introduction to the Old Testament*) that so fully breathes the spirit of total fundamentalism as does Kitchen's work. And, as anyone experienced in theological discussion knows, the absence of any overt appeal to a religious starting-point is not the slightest reason why one should believe that writers are not motivated and guided by such a starting-point. Indeed, it is a necessity of the conservative argument from ancient near eastern evidences that it makes at least a pretence of impartiality. And I do not for a moment dispute the importance and the value of impartiality: but it is not to be expected, on these questions, from those for whom it is a vital matter of personal religious faith that critical scholarship should be wrong and should be discredited. And, finally, one other point, which fits in with what has been said on these last pages: probably none of the writers of conservative evangelical literature on the Bible *who are actual professional biblical scholars* can be found to be so completely negative towards the main trend in biblical scholarship as are those like Kitchen who look on the subject from outside. In view of all that has been said, this should not be surprising.

In any case this sort of approach to the problems of the Bible from outside the Bible has become an increasingly influential conservative strategy. In it we have once again a nice paradox: a form of religion which in itself depends so exclusively upon the Bible as the source of truth is turning increasingly to non-biblical sources, rather than to the internal religious and theological witness of the Bible, as the source from which the accuracy and inerrancy, and through these the authority, of the Bible may be vindicated. The approach is in essence not a new one: Dryden put it thus in 1682:

> If on the Book itself we cast our view
> Concurrent heathens prove the story true.[10]

Before we consider the arguments of conservative scholarship in greater detail, one further remark about the kind of position exemplified by Kitchen. It will come to conservative students of the Bible as something of a surprise to learn from Kitchen (and others who take the same line) that their teachers in biblical studies pay too little attention to the environment of the ancient near east. On the contrary, one of the chief worries conservatives often have is that the Bible is being too completely read in the light of ancient near eastern evidence. It is far from certain, therefore, that all conservatives will want to argue along the lines adopted by Kitchen: an important conservative case might be built up in exactly the opposite direction. This is true also in another respect. Not all conservatives will want to associate themselves with the purely intellectualist, apparently uncommitted, non-theological approach which we have just been surveying: some of them, as we shall later see, will take exactly the opposite position and attack critical scholarship for supposing that non-theological objectivity is possible.

3. *Some issues in biblical scholarship*

As we have already illustrated, conservative literature is full of assurances to its own readership that the great critical solutions concerning biblical literature, worked out in the latter part of the nineteenth century and the earlier part of the twentieth, are now breaking down and are in process of abandonment by those who previously held them. Now, even if biblical criticism is totally wrong and conservatism is completely right, conservative apologists are simply deceiving their own readership by giving them this sort of assurance. As a matter of fact, and whether we may like it or not, critical attitudes to the Bible and critical analyses of it remain deeply entrenched and widely accepted, and there is not the slightest sign of their breaking down. The steady production of critical introductions to the Old and New Testaments over the last two or three decades shows every sign of a full continuing confidence in the historical-critical approach. The lack of polemic against conservative attitudes is not because these are considered to be more strong and threatening, but because they are no longer considered to be a substantial or significant position, unlike the situation as it was in the nineteenth century. The increasing variety of critical positions put forward is not a sign that no assured critical position is to be found, but is rather evidence that assurance of the stability of the critical method in general encourages scholars to build up greater

variety within it. For the sake of conservative evangelicals themselves it should be desirable to face the reality of the situation in
scholarship and not mislead oneself with illusory dreams of a collapse of the critical movement. The facts are the reverse: it is
probable that conservatives are increasingly coming to accept elements of the critical position, as we shall see in a moment.

Take the case of traditional pentateuchal criticism: as generally
expounded, this has distinguished four main documentary sources,
named or styled J, E, D and P in the order of their supposed origin.
It is true that some modifications in the original scheme have been
accepted by many scholars. Many have come to doubt whether J can
really be distinguished from E, at least over large areas. Many have
come to think of blocks of oral tradition rather than of 'documents'
which were slotted into one another by a method irreverently
known as 'scissors and paste'. Many have ceased to believe that the
separation of sources can be carried out for every word and phrase.
Most have ceased to support theories that involve very large numbers of different sources and redactions. It was always easy to make
fun of a criticism that produced, let us say, ten sources, and that
could then distinguish every word so clearly that each word could be
coloured precisely to distinguish the source from which it had come.
But in the pentateuch most scholars work for practical purposes
with a much more simple set of distinctions. It is now usually
thought that the D source exists only in Deuteronomy and only
marginally if at all in Genesis–Numbers; and this means that for
these four books one has to reckon most of the time with only two
sources, which might be called J and P or might equally be called
'the older material' and 'the later material'. Thus certain adjustments in pentateuchal criticism have taken place and certain striking variations within it have grown up. To portray the various
discussions and disagreements involved in these adjustments as
signs that the acceptance of the general source distinction is now
uncertain is quite mistaken. The fact is that almost all serious
scholarship continues to this day to work with some kind of source
analysis of the pentateuch as a natural and inevitable working
instrument.

Moreover, it should not be thought that I am apologizing for the
critical approach by saying that it is really simpler than was thought
and that one does not really think of more than a minimal sort of
source distinction. If we are led to a complicated and detailed source
division, then one should make no bones about it: that is what we
think to be right. If we can discern ten sources or a series of ten

redactions by different hands within a passage, then ten sources it should be, and if we can discern the exact words of this or that, then we should say so. In other words, the *complication* of source analyses should not be, and is not, any valid argument against them. Unquestionably the complication of a source-critical solution to a problem can be a psychological shock to a reader when he first meets it, and this is one of the difficulties that often generate conservative attitudes. The reader, accustomed to reading the Bible as if it was one book at a time, that began at the beginning and proceeded through sequential temporal stages from earlier towards later, has to accustom himself to finding that one source succeeds another, that what goes before may be temporally after, and that a variety of writers or persons may be responsible for different parts. The critical approach therefore makes the Bible simply more difficult to read, as a text taken in itself. But this, though a psychological fact, simply has to be overcome by accustoming one-self to reading in a different way; it is in no way a reason against the critical separation of sources. And, as a matter of fact, far from it being the case that source-critical solutions are generally becoming simpler, the present tendency at least in Old Testament scholarship seems to be in favour of an increase of confidence in extremely minute and exact critical analyses.

Nor should it be supposed that critical procedures should be defended against conservative arguments on the grounds that they are not really very radical or drastic. Radical and drastic solutions should be, and are, part of the normal operating procedure of scholarship, just as much as mild or limited critical operations are. I do not myself commonly indulge in radical or drastic solutions but it must be made clear as against conservative timidity that these are in every way justifiable and acceptable as possibilities. Take the idea that some of the biblical Psalms originated in the Maccabaean period, a view that is sometimes quoted as a prime example of hyper-criticism. I do not wish to argue for a Maccabaean date for any Psalm; I think it rather improbable for the Old Testament Psalms. And I certainly do not think, as some have at times thought, that nearly all the biblical Psalms came from the Maccabaean period. But there is not the slightest reason why a Maccabaean date for biblical Psalms should not be considered, and there is no valid reason at all why such a dating should be considered shocking or hyper-critical. Those who argued for Maccabaean dates for certain Psalms had perfectly reasonable grounds for doing so. This is especially so if one adopts the 'historical' approach to these poems, 'historical' in the sense that they are understood to be referring to recent or contemporary real events. The interpreter then has to ask himself: in a poem like Psalm 79 or Psalm 74, when was there a time when the temple was defiled, when the blood of the servants of God was poured out, when the 'meeting-places' of God in the land (plural) had all been burned (Ps. 74.8: this was often understood to mean synagogues, which has of course an effect on the dating: so rendered already by AV), when there was 'no more any prophet' (Ps. 74.9)? The time of the attack upon the Jewish religion by Antiochus Epiphanes was a perfectly possible answer. Far from being the product of a modern unbelieving critical approach, exactly this was put forward as a suggestion for the 79th and 74th by no less stalwart a theologian than John Calvin.[11] Even if we abandon the 'historical' approach to the analysis of the Psalms, we can see very well the reasons which led some interpreters to a Maccabaean date. Moreover, we can probably take it that there was a continuity in the composition of Psalms in Israel, that ran down through the biblical Psalms into the post-biblical Psalms such as we know from Qumran. There is in fact not the slightest reason why a Maccabaean dating for some biblical Psalms should be considered an instance of extremism. As for religious reasoning, there is no valid religious consideration against the possibility that some biblical Psalms might be of Maccabaean date.

But what of the argument from archaeology? Is it not the case that archaeological evidence in the last thirty or forty years has increasingly 'confirmed the accuracy of the Bible'? Conservative literature ceaselessly presses this assurance upon its readers. This again is a propagandistic misuse of archaeology, which slants the subject in a purely conservative direction and quite conceals the limits of what can be demonstrated by this means. Perhaps the most striking instance, and certainly the one that is most often cited, concerns the picture of life in the age of the patriarchs, Abraham, Isaac and Jacob. It has at times been held by biblical critics that the story that told of these figures came from a time much later, and that it informed therefore not of things as they were in the patriarchal age, but rather of things as they were in the time of the writers. Against this it is now argued that archaeology has revealed evidence of customs among peoples of the second millennium BC which closely parallel customs and incidents narrated or mentioned in the book of Genesis. Incidentally, this is not strictly 'archaeological' evidence: that is to say, it is not the evidence of buildings, structures and artefacts, rather it is the evidence of texts found in the course of archaeological excavations; but this makes little difference. How much difference has this evidence about customs in the second millennium made?

A good example is the story, thrice repeated, of how a patriarch (twice Abraham, once Isaac: Gen. 12.10–20; 20; and 26.6–16 respectively), residing temporarily in Egypt or the Philistine country, feared that he would be put to death, because of the beauty of his wife (Sarah or Rebekah). So he gets her to say that she is his sister, in order that his life may be spared. The lady is taken into the house or harem of the local potentate, but various vicissitudes make it clear to him that this has been an unwise decision. The lady is released. There are a number of variations between the three versions. Why is the story here at all, and most of all why is it found three times? Neither the second nor the third contains a reference back: Sarah does not say, 'Well, look here, all this has happened already, do we need to go through it again?' or the like. For most people one of such a story would seem enough.

The American scholar E. A. Speiser sought to show that the incident fitted well with social customs evidenced in the Nuzi documents, fifteenth to fourteenth centuries BC. 'Abraham's efforts to pass Sarah off as his sister reflect the Hurrian practice whereby wifehood and sistership could be equated under certain conditions, with the significantly added feature that a "sister" enjoyed in such circumstances a greater degree of socio-political protection.'[12] This looks at first sight like a substantial piece of evidence in favour of the biblical narrative, if taken straightforwardly as history, and conservative polemicists have ceaselessly reiterated this.

Even if one granted the fullest concessions to the conservative argument from evidence of this kind, it is quite mistaken to suppose that the general critical assessment of Genesis is affected by it. All it would indicate is that aspects of social customs incorporated into the narratives had descended from ancient times in well-remembered tradition. This would not in the slightest demonstrate that there were real people Abraham, Sarah, Isaac and so on, who did exactly the series of actions described in the Bible, the real Abraham twice telling his wife Sarah to assure people that he was her brother. In any case it is quite erroneous to suppose that the critical separation of sources in Genesis is predicated upon, or logically depends on, the idea that the picture given of the patriarchs is inaccurate. Though this supposition has at times been held in company with the critical analysis, the latter is not in any way dependent on it. Even if these narratives had been shown by recent discovery to be historically accurate, which is not the case, this would have shown only that the older pentateuchal sources conserved better than others some memories of an older social situation. This recognition would not in any way have affected the need for a separation of the sources like D and P: indeed, it would probably support it. The conception that these discoveries destroy the case for the critical analysis of Genesis seems effective only if one looks at the problem with an established fundamentalist outlook from the beginning. In fact, though this evidence has been much discussed and has certainly been taken seriously by scholars, I do not know of any scholar whose evaluation of the critical analysis of the pentateuch has been modified by it.

If we press the matter further, even more interesting results emerge.[13] The reader has to understand what Speiser is saying. He is not saying that the biblical narrative, taken as it is, fits in with the phenomenon known from Mesopotamia. Rather, he is using both the biblical material and the Mesopotamian material to reconstruct a picture which establishes contacts between the two but which also, in his mind, explicitly replaces the biblical account. Speiser's argument is itself a critical reconstruction. He wants to establish what happened to the patriarchs, but for him the reliable sources are not the biblical narratives but the contemporary social evidences. 'Of the two interpretations, one based on original and contemporary records of a society that is closely involved, and the other in much later literary narratives, the first is obviously to be preferred.'[14] Thus according to him the actual situation was totally garbled in the biblical account. The Bible represents the incident as a deception for the sake of the safety of the patriarch; but in reality according to Speiser these were diplomatic visits of Abraham and Isaac to neighbouring capitals. But, most important, the biblical conditions are reversed by this interpretation in one essential respect: what in the Bible is a lie or a deception is according to Speiser the truth.

All three stories make sense only on the understanding that the woman, if she is a sister, would therefore not be a wife, and therefore it is safe for Pharaoh or the King of Gerar to take the woman without becoming involved in adultery and consequent divine punishment. Each of the three stories builds independently, that is, with different detailed emphases, on this basis. If there was a society in which a woman on becoming married also became a sister, or where this was reasonably normal, then the entire stratagem of Abraham and Isaac would not have worked in that society. Thus, if we follow Speiser, we may indeed find that the passage reflects a real and ancient social custom, but we shall also be saying that the Bible gives a totally distorted and misleading picture of what was happening. Speiser, I repeat, is not to blame for this: he did not pretend to be upholding the narratives of Genesis as correct historical narratives. We here have a familiar phenomenon of modern conservative argumentation: in its anxiety to prove the Bible 'true' as against some critical point of view, it produces an explanation that in fact proves the Bible untrue in another respect. Anxiety to overcome the suggestion that the social customs of Genesis did not genuinely reflect the patriarchal age caused conservatives to rush to an explanation along Speiser's line; they ignored the fact that this explanation did not set out to be an interpretation of the Genesis passages as they are, and that if taken as an account of them it made them historically quite false in another respect.

There is a further question, namely, whether in fact the Mesopotamian evidence has been rightly assessed and used, and whether it is in fact of any value for the understanding of Genesis; but I shall leave this aside. It should be clear, in any case, that the enterprise of proving the accuracy of Genesis, or of other parts of the Bible, on the basis of parallels in other ancient near eastern cultures can be a precarious and complicated undertaking, and that the evidence cannot be used for this purpose without very careful consideration.

One general methodological point, however, should be mentioned here: it belongs to the way in which ancient near eastern materials and biblical texts are brought into contact. In a great deal of work done in the past the investigator of oriental texts (or ruins) has been interested from the beginning in possible relations of his material with the Bible; not only so, but he has used the Bible as a source of hints for the interpretation of his ancient near eastern material. This does not mean that he takes the Bible as inerrant: it means only that he hopes to find in it hints and suggestions, doubtless garbled, but such as will perform a useful heuristic function in relation to the interpretation of his new material. Such a procedure is not in itself absolutely faulty, but it is easy to see how it can be the cause of over-hasty identifications of relations between the Bible and ancient near eastern material. The very concept of (say) 'biblical archaeology' ought to be looked at critically in the light of this. Generally speaking, ancient oriental material is more reliable when its meaning and interpretation has been established strictly on its own merits and separately from any application to the understanding of the Bible.

One other point about the use of archaeological evidence should be mentioned here, because it is relevant to the total assessment of fundamentalism as a religious phenomenon. The belief that the Bible has been 'proved true' is not necessarily a particularly religious belief at all: it is widely entertained by people as a form of quite secular credulity, and the satisfaction of this credulous appetite is one of the obvious phenomena of our times. People like or want to believe that there is somewhere some one book that is absolutely true or correct, and if there is to be such a book, in our society it is likely to be the Bible. Now real fundamentalism has a religious core and it starts out from that core, even if in the wrong direction, when it makes its approach to the Bible. But the question remains, whether it sufficiently distinguishes itself from the quite non-religious appetite for belief in a true Book, and whether it does not, in spite of itself, pander to these same emotions and draw from them some of its own power to convince. Doubtless the best-known example of a work that plays to these appetites is Werner Keller's *The Bible as History* (Hodder 1956), which makes no attempt at any sort of religious message, apart from some hostile references to theologians and biblical critics, but is packed full of imaginative pictures and reconstructions designed to encourage credulity. Of Noah's ark (p. 58) someone has been supposed to have seen 'a great wooden ship' on Mount Ararat; in 1833 a report mentioned the 'wooden prow of a ship which in the summer season stuck out of the south glacier'. Of Lot's wife (p. 97), 'anyone who escaped alive from the scene of the disaster might well be suffocated by the poisonous fumes which spread over the countryside. And everything in the neighbourhood of the Salt Sea is even to this day quickly covered with a crust of salt.' On pp. 179–80 Keller tells us of a British officer in the First World War who, discovering that he was in the neighbourhood of the biblical Michmash, remembered from the biblical account what the topography of the land beyond the skyline must be, and utilized this knowledge, gained from his knowledge of the Bible, to mount a successful manoeuvre and defeat the Turks. Stuff of this kind belongs entirely to credulity and not to faith; its genre is gossip rather than serious comment on the Bible. But the fact remains that many of Keller's explanations are quite similar to those we find in conservative evangelical works, and indeed it is probable that he got many of his ideas from that tradition.

Conservative evangelicals, then, are totally misled by their own literature when it tells them that changes in the emphasis of critical scholarship are signs of its coming break-up or abandonment. In the

Old Testament there is no indication that the general Wellhause-nian position is going to be substantially abandoned. If critical scholars lay less emphasis on this position than was the case thirty or so years ago, the reason is probably not that they value it less, but that they have moved on to other forms of critical study which presuppose it and supplement it. These other forms of study – form criticism, redaction criticism and so on – are now much more the centre of current interest. In general, in so far as scholarship may modify the Wellhausen position, or any other position that is now fairly standard, it is likely to move to a position not more like the conservative point of view, but farther away from it. Any shift from the 'classical' solutions of critical scholarship is likely to be even more deplorable in the eyes of conservatives than are the existing views. Fundamentalists already give clear indication of this in the violent antipathy they show towards form criticism in the New Testament. These moves beyond source criticism are in many ways more important for biblical study than the basic source criticism itself. Most fundamentalist argument, however, is stuck at the source-critical stage. This fact is a main reason why in this book attention has been given primarily to the source-critical stage. The fact that the cutting edge of scholarship in this century has long lain elsewhere has meant that scholars have not been attending to the task of meeting and overcoming the arguments of fundamentalists as much as they should, and this, curiously, is one of the reasons why fundamentalism has been able to show so much vitality in the last decade or two.

It is interesting to note, however, that there seems to be a marked difference in this respect between Old Testament and New Testa-ment studies. In the literature I have been able to survey, the opposition between conservative evangelical and critical points of view is very much more severe in the Old Testament than in the New. As we have already seen, there are several reasons in the structure of fundamentalism which makes its problems more acute in the Old Testament. The difference can be easily traced in the ethos of two major conservative evangelical Introductions: R. K. Harrison's to the Old Testament and Donald Guthrie's to the New, (both IVP 1970). Guthrie's work, while conservative, is irenic and understanding throughout. Even his treatment of form criticism of the Bultmannian type, a sort of scholarship with which Guthrie is manifestly unsympathetic, is equable and calm. Guthrie points to scholarly difficulties in the Bultmannian and the form-critical approaches, but at no point does he sweep these approaches away by asserting that they are built upon non-Christian presuppositions, denials of the supernatural and so on. It is evident that Guthrie belongs in the same world with critical New Testament scholars and accepts his membership of that one world.

With Harrison it is quite otherwise. The book is full of special pleading and the burning personal antagonism of the writer against the critical approach is evident throughout. Critical scholarship is repeatedly attacked for its presuppositions and critical scholars are represented as filled with prejudice and incompetence. They never had the slightest good reason for their decisions, all of them are made on the basis of mere preconceptions, which they violently and forcibly imposed upon the evidence. The attacks on the presuppositions and the methods of Wellhausen are so personal and violent that one wonders in what sense that blundering and incompetent person deserves to be called a 'gifted scholar' (p. 507), for clearly, by Harrison's own account, he was nothing of the sort. Harrison does not share the same world with critical scholars; there is no room for them in the same world with him.

Now, this might have been considered a mere difference of personality, but it is probably more than that. There is strong evidence that leading conservative New Testament scholars have moved the conservative position much closer to the critical position within the New Testament. A few pages ago we saw how Michael Green dismisses several well-known critical positions, including the priority of Mark and the existence of the document Q.[15] He particularly resents the suggestion that these positions are 'assured results' or 'assured findings', a phrase which has always excited the particular wrath of conservatives. In the last few years, Green tells us, all these 'assured' results 'have been heavily assailed by capable scholars'. In this Green is simply repeating the traditional line of conservative evangelical polemic. But in repeating his well-worn lines he has omitted to look and see what 'capable scholars' in conservative evangelical books are saying. *The New Bible Commentary Revised* (C. E. Graham Swift on Mark) tells us (p. 851a) that 'it is now almost universally agreed that Mark's Gospel is the earliest of the four', and this universal agreement seems to go so far that the writer does not feel he has to argue for the position at all; he simply accepts it. On the next page (p. 852a) he talks again of 'the established priority of Mark'. Note the word 'established'! Similarly, F. F. Bruce in the same work, in the article 'The Fourfold Gospel' (pp. 64–70), and in the article 'Gospels' in *The New Bible Dictionary* (pp. 484–8) appears fully to accept both Marcan priority and the existence of the source Q. The priority of Mark is one of the 'findings' (the very word!) that 'command a much greater area of agreement than others' (*Dictionary*, p. 486a), and 'the supposition that the "Q" material was derived from a common source by Matthew and Luke involves fewer difficulties than any alternative supposition' (ibid., p. 486b). And, to return to Guthrie's Introduction, the common documentary analysis of the synoptic gospels, much as it would be maintained by non-conservative scholars, is set forth without any hesitation. Even so very hypothetical a critical reconstruction as Proto-Luke[16] receives a warm welcome and recognition. Though in the end Guthrie is doubtful about the value of the Proto-Luke theory he does not at all try to sweep it away as if its presence were an outrage or something to be rejected on principle.[17] On the synoptic problem as a whole Guthrie, though carefully and mildly conservative, sets forth an exposition that is fully in line with critical scholarship and leaves entire room for all the considerations that critical scholarship on the same subject might want to bring to bear.

This all leaves conservative polemicists like Michael Green without a leg to stand on, for the scholarship in which they trust has in fact adopted the critical positions which he repudiates. It is not to be doubted that a shift in scholarly position has taken place, and that Michael Green represents the older conservative and fundamentalist position. The earlier *New Bible Handbook* (IVP 1947) is much more negative towards the customary critical solution. The treatment is vague and imprecise, but the following points seem to be made: firstly, there is no real reason to suppose that Mark was the earliest of the gospels in the sense of the normal 'Marcan hypothesis'; the facts behind this hypothesis 'only show' that one of the chief sources of the synoptic tradition is the apostolic preaching as recorded by Mark. Secondly, the material common to Matthew and Luke can be designated as Q, but this does not mean that Q ever existed as a separate document. Thirdly, and positively, the view encouraged is that each of the three gospels goes straight back to the apostolic preaching and teaching.[18] Similarly, Douglas Johnson, in a typical expression of authoritative rigid conservatism from 1953, was arguing that there were no real literary relations between the gospels, no clear evidence for Marcan priority, no clear evidence for Q, and that Matthew was probably the first gospel to be written. This view of the critical approach to the synoptic problem, though vaguely expressed, would undoubtedly mean to a conservative readership that the whole thing should be ignored and that all four gospels alike went straight back to eye-witness reporting. The most that is admitted is that 'careful, reverent and conservative scholars' do exist who think there is sufficient evidence of literary dependence between this gospel and that.[19]

At least on the synoptic problem, then, the accepted conservative scholarship has shown a marked slide towards the critical position. I do not want to exaggerate this, or to say that it betokens any conscious increase of acceptance of critical methods. It may well be that on some other questions, such as the historicity of the depiction of Jesus in St John's gospel, or the historical accuracy of Acts, no such shift of opinion has taken place. But at least within the synoptic gospels the movement of opinion has been very striking.

But this at once leads us to the question: if all this can be granted within the synoptic gospels, why can it not be granted within the pentateuch? Why, if we can have Marcan priority, Q, and possibly even Proto-Luke, can we not have D and P? For one cannot see that there is any aspect at all in the logic which led to Marcan priority, to Q and to Proto-Luke, that is different from the logic that led to J, D and P in the pentateuch. In both cases the previous history of the documents is based on no direct evidence other than the evidence of the texts that have emerged at the end of the process, that is, our gospels and our pentateuch as we have them. In both cases the new documents postulated are reconstructed purely on the evidence of the final texts. In both cases the differences between one extant document and another are explained as a result of, and thus as an evidence of, a reconstructible previous stage in the tradition, the existence of which would not be known but for the peculiarities and discrepancies existing within the final texts as we have them. There is absolutely no procedure involved in the customary solution of the synoptic problem, as modern conservative scholars present it, that is not equally involved in the customary critical solution of the pentateuchal question. Yet in the New Testament case conservative scholars set out their survey of the situation without the slightest hesitation, and without the slightest suggestion that their approach might offend against inexorable dogmatic prohibitions. When critical scholars do the same with the pentateuch, on the other hand, they are assailed by the violent hostility of a Harrison or a Kitchen, who do not only reject the particular solutions proposed but attack the entire attempt at a critical solution as illegitimate.

Are Harrison and Kitchen going to turn their violence on to Guthrie? And if not, are they not admitting that their own anti-critical vehemence is no more than pure partisanship? One sees, in fact, that the admission of even a very little critical perception can cause many consequential difficulties for conservatives. They might have been better to stick to their own principle, that one must not let the camel get his nose into the tent, for then it will not be long before he occupies all of it. In the case of the synoptic gospels, however, he has already got his nose well into the tent, and it is not likely that that nose will be withdrawn.

One way I can see in which fundamentalists could accept the critical approach to the synoptic gospels, while denying the legitimacy of the same when applied to the pentateuch, would be by stressing traditional ascriptions of authorship. They would have to say something like this: the gospels of Matthew, Mark and Luke do not expressly *say* anything about their own composition: they do not say which was the first to be written, whether one of them used another as a source, and so on. It is therefore legitimate to construct hypotheses which on the basis of the literary relations as we see them in the extant gospel texts reconstruct the previous history of the tradition, written or oral. In the case of the pentateuch, however, it actually says that the Lord spoke the words to Moses, e.g. Num. 36.13, or that these were the words that Moses spoke, e.g. Deut. 1.1. It is on this ground illegitimate to consider any possible sources other than Moses himself.

This position might indeed be taken. If it were taken, however, it would be a return to a total dependence on the dogmatic argument. It would mean that all ascriptions of authorship or composition are finally true, assuming they are within the Bible. If this is so, however, then there is no more to be said. If ascriptions of authorship are final, then there are no critical questions to discuss, except in those (many) books in which there is no such ascription. It is doubtful whether even extreme conservatives want to become dependent solely on the argument from ascriptions of authorship.

Or perhaps it might be taken in another way. In the gospels we begin from multiple documents. There are three separate gospels, four if we include John. It is some kind of an open question how all these are related to one another, and literary dependence, Marcan priority, the previous existence of sources like Q, are all possible paths to an explanation of the multiplicity that we have in any case. After all, a critical solution of the synoptic problem might need no more than four original sources – Mark, Q, L, and M (M is the symbol for the material peculiar to Matthew) – and numerically four is not so much different from the three gospels from which we began. But in the pentateuch the fundamentalist may see it differently. Here is one single narrative; there are not (as he sees it) three or four parallel pentateuchs. To divide it up into J, D and P is to introduce divisions and separations where previously none existed. Pentateuchal criticism is therefore totally illegitimate, while a critical solution to the synoptic problem is quite a different matter.

This may well be the opinion that underlies fundamentalist attitudes. The difference it establishes is, of course, quite illusory: in a gospel like Matthew, following the critical procedure, one has to go through verse by verse, saying that this element came from Mark, this from Q, this from M and so on; in other words, the procedure in analysing any individual gospel is the same as that used in a critical analysis of Genesis or Exodus. The fact of beginning with three parallel gospels, though psychologically perhaps different, makes no logical or methodological difference. One can perhaps picture it in this way: if the Diatessaron had been a success, and had driven the separate gospels out of circulation, we would have a situation in the analysis of the gospel material analogous to that which in fact obtains with the pentateuch.[20]

To sum up this point, whether through merely personal differences or otherwise, conservative literature has been moving markedly towards the acceptance of standard critical procedures and results in the New Testament, but much less in the Old. This fact is likely to create new problems for conservative polemic.[21]

4. *The presupposition question*

Conservative writers of recent years continually attack critical scholarship on the grounds of the philosophical and theological presuppositions which the critics are supposed to have accepted and which are alleged to have controlled their work. Polemicists like Kitchen and Harrison represent the scholars who worked out the critical analysis of the pentateuch, or similarly of other parts of the Old Testament, as entirely controlled by a framework of philosophical presuppositions. They never looked at the Old Testament itself, it seems, they saw it only through the spectacles of the philosophy of their time, which they accepted uncritically and unthinkingly. This is a very bad thing. Merely to hear this about Wellhausen or other such critics is sufficient to persuade the conservative reader that such people are not worth reading, especially since that is what he believes when he starts in any case. Conservative scholars, it is implied, are quite different. They are not at all affected by the philosophies of their time. Indeed, though they often belong to a religious stream in which the Bible is considered to be inerrant, they want us to believe that theological factors do not affect their judgment either. Conservative scholars are affected only by the *facts*: the facts of the Bible and its environment, but, all in all, facts only, with no ideological attachment of any kind.

Now, according to this criticism, the customary critical analysis of the pentateuch was built upon an intellectual foundation that was (*a*) evolutionistic and (*b*) Hegelian. It was suggested that religion had evolved continually from lower forms to higher, so that higher forms would necessarily be found only at late stages in the process. Evolutionism, it is supposed, was so completely dominant in the nineteenth century that scholars just could not avoid being controlled by it. Some critical scholars have indeed traced within the Old Testament a development in religion from animism, through polydaemonism, to henotheism (where one god was worshipped but it was not denied that others existed) and finally to monotheism or (still higher) to ethical monotheism. This scheme according to conservative apologists is totally false; it is a theory bearing no relation to the realities whatsoever. The argument about Hegelianism, if we are to dignify it by calling it an argument, was somewhat the same. Wellhausen was a pupil and follower of Wilhelm Vatke, who had used an explicitly Hegelian scheme in his approach to the religion of Israel. This was essentially a developmental scheme, using the pattern thesis-antithesis-synthesis supposed to be characteristic of Hegel. Another line of biblical study in the nineteenth century that used a Hegelian pattern was the Tübingen school in New Testament studies.[22] The discussion of this argument must be undertaken from several sides.

First of all, it was not an unreasonable criticism when the evolutionary theories of the development of Israelite religion were attacked. This particular criticism was one made not only by true conservatives but also by many within the 'biblical theology' movement, which we shall be considering later. A highly evolutionist approach to Israelite religion, such as that found in the widely-used textbook of W. O. E. Oesterley and T. H. Robinson, *Hebrew Religion: its Origin and Development* (SPCK 1930), was in many ways unsatisfactory: in particular, it tended to see many aspects of the religion as 'survivals' from an earlier stage, and did not get far beyond identifying them as such.

It was wholly mistaken, however, to suppose that evolutionary views of this kind were logically and intrinsically connected with the source analysis of the pentateuch or of other Old Testament documents. It is true that scholars who held the evolutionistic view of religion often also held the documentary source hypothesis, but one is not founded upon the other. In fact scholars who have quite abandoned the evolutionary view of the religion have generally continued to maintain the critical analysis of the pentateuch.

As for Wellhausen himself, the criticism for an uncritical evolutionism is almost grotesquely misdirected. Far from it being the case that he believed in a unilinear evolution from the lower to the higher, with the highest stage necessarily coming at the end, the most valid criticism of Wellhausen would be almost the opposite: he was particularly moved by the contrast between the free and natural life of the early Israelites and the fixed, hardened and defined lines of life in the priestly hierarchy with which the Old Testament ended up. The movement was thus in the end a degeneration, much more than an evolution necessarily moving from the lower to the higher. One cannot doubt that those who have attacked Wellhausen for acceptance of a deterministic evolutionary philosophy have taken little trouble to study his actual works. When Kitchen writes:

> The evolutionary theories of development of religion (drawn from philosophical premises, not facts) required a unilinear development of concepts from 'primitive' to 'advanced': therefore, the Old Testament writings (especially the Pentateuch) *had* to be split up and the resulting fragments rearranged in a sequence to fit this theoretical scheme[23]

he is simply making clear his complete lack of acquaintance with the intellectual history of the critical movement – something not surprising in a writer who so vehemently opposes everything about it.

The violence of conservative opposition to evolutionary theories of the religion of Israel, however, goes beyond what can reasonably be explained as an element in their attack on Wellhausenian criticism. We have already seen that fundamentalists, after their stalwart resistance to evolution as a biological theory, have surrendered on this front and accepted evolution, to all intents and purposes, as an account of the biological descent of man. As an account of anything else, however, evolution is absolutely wrong and must be rejected. 'Evolution, if it be true, is a law of biology. It is not a law of the elements, nor of social institutions, nor of man's higher powers . . . Evolution as a biological theory cannot be artlessly transmuted into metaphysics, epistemology, and *religion*.'[24] It is probable that the conservative abhorrence of evolutionary explanations in the history of religion is a visceral survival of the violence of their hostility to biological evolution. This, in turn, may be a partial explanation of their hostility to pentateuchal criticism, at a time when analogous critical operations on the gospels are quite tolerated. The gospels by any account cover only a short expanse of time; the pentateuch covers a long period, within which evolution might get a hold if it were allowed to do so. Here again we have to stand against the conservative position: even if we do not favour an evolutionary account of the religion of Israel, we must say categorically that there is no reason in principle why such an evolutionary account should not be attempted. The conservative position in this respect is a clear attempt at denying freedom of research, only the latest in a long series of such attempts from the same quarter. In other words, to say that an account of Israelite religion is evolutionary is not in the slightest to make a valid criticism of it.

In fact all students of the Old Testament must be aware that some kind of change and development along a scale of time takes place within the religion of Israel: even the most conservative can hardly fail to grant this. Even if it were possible, let us say, to think that the entire pentateuch came from one man and one time, we would still have clear evidence of religious change within the pentateuch – for instance, between Abraham and Moses – or after the pentateuch – for instance, between Moses and Ezra. It is not clear that even on conservative principles no element of an evolution within this history could be admitted. In fact, when this point is put, conservative apologists usually change their ground from an attack on evolution to an attack on 'unilinear evolution', i.e. an evolution that goes in only one direction, from lower to higher. But since the vast majority of critical scholars have never supposed that there was an evolution of that kind, even in the most 'evolutionary' days of the discipline, we can ignore that argument.

As for Wellhausen's supposed Hegelianism, much as this criticism has been repeated, parrot-fashion, by all sorts of persons over several decades, it is sufficient to say that no good evidence for Wellhausen's Hegelianism has ever been produced and there is no reason to suppose that recent conservative apologists have any to produce.[25] Within normal fundamentalism, one must remember, this Hegelianism functions simply as a bad word. Conservative students say that Wellhausen was a Hegelian without looking at his writings at all: they simply find it as an accusation in Kitchen or Harrison or another conservative source. They probably know nothing about Hegel either and would not have known if he was a good thing or a bad thing but for the fact that he is used in an attack on critical scholarship. There is, however, one extenuating circumstance. The attack on Wellhausen for Hegelianism has been made not only by conservatives, but also within non-conservative scholarship. Conservatives are therefore not too deeply to blame. In any case, it can now be agreed that the whole diagnosis of Hegelianism in Wellhausen was perverse. The world's chief expert on Wellhausen, Rudolf Smend, wrote in 1965: 'People have been pleased to ascribe to Wellhausen influence from Hegel. Nothing could have been more perverse: if one has to offer names that have influenced him, then it would have to be, more than any others, Carlyle and Burckhardt.'[26]

And in the same year Lothar Perlitt produced his lengthy and detailed study *Vatke und Wellhausen*, in which he shows in detail how, in spite of Wellhausen's veneration for his teacher Vatke, he remained unimpressed and unaffected by the philosophical aspects of Vatke's thinking.[27] In fact anyone who reads Wellhausen with a will to discover how the man's mind worked will see that he was above all a historian, with an interest in the detail of texts and evidence, and that he was the last man to be carried away by philosophical theories, as conservative writers depict him. Harrison goes farther than involving Wellhausen with Hegel, and resorts to ethnocentric railing at 'the German mind'.[28] But this can all be left aside: the entire argument was never other than a lot of nonsense, and all that can be done is to forget it.

One final note, however, should be added. This matter has brought forward the question, whether philosophical trends should have an influence upon biblical scholarship. Even if it had been true that Wellhausen's analysis was dependent on the philosophy of Hegel, this would not constitute any sort of criticism unless either (*a*) it was held that all biblical interpretation must be done in an atmosphere free from any philosophical influences whatever or (*b*) it was held that philosophical influences were permitted but those of Hegel were for some reason exceptionally pernicious. Do conservatives claim to work with no philosophical (or theological?) assumptions at all? Or do they claim that there is a right philosophy for the carrying on of biblical study, and that they hold this right philosophy? In fact they generally say nothing about the matter, and this strengthens the view that their criticism of the supposed philosophical preconceptions behind biblical criticism is simply irresponsible carping. We shall return in a later chapter to the question of the philosophical position held by conservative evangelicals.

5. The influence of W. F. Albright and others

No scholar has been more frequently quoted by conservative writers in the last decades than the late Professor W. F. Albright (1891–1971). Albright, long professor at the Johns Hopkins University in Baltimore, made a deep mark on scholarship in the United States and throughout the world; he created a recognizable 'school', notable for its deep respect for the insights and views of the master; and in many ways he hewed out a distinctive approach and a recognizable personal attitude to the problems of biblical scholarship. Moreover, many of his opinions were, in contrast with those generally held at the same time in biblical scholarship, quite conservative. Many texts were dated by him extremely early: on almost any document he argued that it was very old, much earlier than had generally been believed, and so on. His widespread archaeological researches were often stated in such terms as to suggest that new information from the ancient east was flooding in, almost all of which tended to confirm the Bible's own picture as against those widely held by scholars. He was highly critical of the Wellhausen type of critical scholarship and joined in the chorus of disapproval of it on the grounds of 'evolutionism'. On the early history of Israel he tended very strongly to take as historical the depiction of the patriarchs in Genesis, as against the influential group of German scholars who thought that real historical knowledge of Israel begins only with the entry of Israel into Canaan. The conflict of the two principles can be easily traced in the two works, Martin Noth's and John Bright's competing histories of Israel.[29] All in all, then, Albright sought to push biblical scholarship into a more conservative orientation, in respect of dates, reliability of narratives, authorship of books and so on. There are, however, several reasons why readers should not allow conservative writers to push them into a more conservative position through the citation of Albright.

Firstly, Albright's judgments, often dogmatic and categorical, often ran far beyond the area in which he had any real expertise: so for instance his judgments about the early date of St John's gospel and the idea that 'there is no fundamental difference in teaching between John and the Synoptics'.[30] On a matter of this kind Albright was not in the slightest degree an authority; judgments of this kind were oracular pronouncements very often, not backed up with the detailed study one would obtain from any average New Testament professor, conservative or critical, and there is no reason to take them as more than quick judgments based on Albright's inveterate conservatism about documentary questions. Secondly, even where Albright had done substantial study of the question at issue, it is by no means clear that he was right. Even on the basis of his own judgments it can easily be seen that he changed his views very frequently, though always asserting that all existing evidence favoured the most recent view. In fact many of his judgments on particular issues are very liable to criticism as being no more than individual hunches justified by evidence that is in fact quite ambiguous.[31] Thirdly, it is fair to say that Albright was not a scholar who worked on the massive phenomena of the biblical text at all. In this he differed from the fathers of biblical criticism, who were above all scholars of the text, scholars of the biblical literature. His constant work in archaeology and in multiple aspects of the cultures of the oriental environment, and his voracious reading, furnished him with evidence as a base from which he conducted raids of research into biblical scholarship. But comparatively little written by Albright on the Bible receives the kind of meticulous foundation in the evidence of the total biblical text, such as was normally given by the fathers of the critical approach. Fourthly, in any case, and this in itself shows how the conservative exploitation of Albright's arguments over-reaches itself, for all that Albright said against the foundations of the critical documentary hypothesis on the pentateuch, *he himself continued to adhere to it.* This aspect of Albright's total scholarly viewpoint is little heard of in conservative literature.[32]

The paragraph just written is not intended in any sense to depreciate the very real greatness of Albright as a person and as a scholar. Criticisms would not be necessary were it not for the use of his name and reputation in conservative apologetic, which has often idolized Albright and deified his every opinion, little noticing that he cannot in fact be forced into a true conservative mould.

This leads us, however, to a yet more important point, which is very well illustrated by the instance of Albright. Though Albright frequently spoke in favour of conservative datings and assessments of evidence, he had none of the other marks of the conservative evangelical. His total philosophical, religious and theological position is one rather difficult to define, but it would be perhaps most naturally defined as a broad universal liberal humanism, in which the Bible took its place among many other grand intellectual forces as a prime and central channel in the development of ideas. A liberal humanism! There is no reason to suppose that doctrines dear to conservative evangelicals, such as the inspiration of scripture or the deity of Christ, had any significant place in his scheme of things.

Albright is thus the most important, though far from the only, example that illustrates how conservatives are ready and delighted to draw support, on questions like the dating and historicity of sources, from scholars who do not share their religious principles – but only so long as their historical opinions are conservative.

This makes a great deal of difference to the argument about presuppositions which we surveyed in the last section. Perhaps conservative evangelicals will want to say that this is an instance of the open-mindedness of conservatives, their readiness to see the truth in any man's academic views, quite independently of religious convictions. But such a disconnection between conservative evangelical faith and rightness about historical questions must raise tensions within the total structure of that faith: if one can be historically right without being evangelical in faith, indeed without being Christian at all, might one not also be evangelical in faith without being conservative in historical matters? The fact is, there is no reason to see any open-mindedness in the matter at all. What it suggests is something totally different. When scholars hold critical historical opinions, their work is attacked on the grounds that they hold presuppositions that are philosophical, theoretical, non-supernaturalist and anti-evangelical; but if scholars hold historically conservative opinions, even if these opinions are integrated into a total ideological scheme entirely different from conservative evangelical religion, their work is evaluated as the purest of pure scholarship and their non-evangelical ideological failings are ignored. The question thus uncovers one of the central facts about the scholarly side of the fundamentalist movement: *in matters of historical judgment and biblical criticism, historical conservatism is more important than evangelical Christianity*. Though at first sight paradoxical, this fits in with a whole series of aspects of fundamentalism in its intellectual aspects. And the argument about presuppositions, as used by conservatives, is mere hypocrisy: they will accept any presuppositions, so long as they seem to lead to a conservative result.

6. Conclusion

Leaving aside sophisticated argument, the question that ordinary people most often ask about critical scholarship is a practical one: does it leave us with any certainty? Can the historical circumstances, which so profoundly control the understanding of the Bible, be allowed to vary as uncontrollably and as unpredictably as seems to be the case with the critical approach? Can we really accept a world in which St John's gospel is according to one scholar more or less the autograph of the Beloved Disciple himself, according to another a work from a late stage, well on in the second century and thus from a time quite remote from the realities of Jesus' ministry in Galilee? Do we not need a greater certainty?

Now the answer to this lies in several parts, and not all of them can be discussed at this point. But one part of the answer is this: in so far as we have come to hold that the interpretation of the Bible is a matter of history, then the manifold vicissitudes and possibilities of history must be our destiny: there is no getting out of that. Moreover, this is no exotic critical point of view: the modern generation of conservatives think this too and have already committed themselves to it by their own working methods. The wide differences between scholars are a necessary mode in which the manifold variety of possibly relevant historical evidence, and of possible structures made out of that evidence, is put before us; and we have no means of avoiding this except by opting out of history as the category within which the Bible is studied and our faith is expressed – or even, if we were to say that history is not the only such category, even if it were one such category this would be enough to decide the issue. There is therefore no certainty to be had, if it depends on some device that would simply cut off historical debate. Even if some historical interpretation becomes so discredited that people cease even to discuss the evidence for and against it, there is absolutely nothing to prevent some scholar from coming forward and taking up the case again.

Thus even if we were miraculously transported back to the beginning of the process, to a time when biblical criticism had not begun, the question of certainty would not be answered; we would only be starting off again with the simple yet often profound questions that the deists raised.[33] Modern conservatives sometimes make fun of these questionings; but an opinion is not discredited because it was held by a deist, and the question remains, what answer does one have to the question that he asks, what explanation do we have for the evidence on which he rested his questionings? And from another point of view we can see that conservatism cannot give any better assurance of certainty than criticism offers. On the one hand, examples cited in this book will show the reader how often the conservative interpretation of a passage, far from being the sort of natural interpretation that the ordinary man would think of, and that would thus make him feel as if he could really understand what was going on in interpretation, is a highly artificial interpretation that the ordinary man or the ordinary churchgoer would never have thought of. And the second reason is this: conservatism as an option for the ordinary man is not just a way of reading the Bible: it is a part of fundamentalism, it means sinking oneself in that religious form and belonging to it. Though there are perfectly good possibilities of taking a conservative position as a matter of mere scholarship, this is not the reason why anyone advocates conservatism to you as a way of life; the missionary impetus of conservative study comes from fundamentalism, and unless it takes you into that religious form it has not made any real difference.

Brief mention may be given here to form criticism. The conflict between conservative and critical opinion first took shape very largely over the issues of 'literary' criticism: questions of authorship, unity of books, diversity of sources and dates; and in fact, as this book will have shown, the conflict remains more or less stuck at that level to the present day. Though modern scholarship accepts a considerable series of critical positions on the level of literary criticism, this sort of literary criticism has long ceased to be the cutting edge of scholarship and research has passed on to more advanced methods. This, incidentally, is probably one of the reasons why conservative opinion has been able to rally its opposition to the literary-critical positions. These positions have somewhat lost their freshness. They no longer hold the interest they held when they were first developed, and the most original research is no longer that devoted to them. In any case, the most important of the strata of scholarship that have been developed in this century is form criticism. Form criticism does not attempt to deal with questions of sources, authors and dates, or that is not its primary object. It studies the form patterns of narratives, poems, bodies of teaching and so on, and it seeks to understand the 'situation in life' within which a particular pattern was used. It has thus often been used in the attempt to penetrate into stages of tradition earlier than the earliest written sources. It is particularly well known for its application to the gospels, where it has been used to penetrate behind the earliest written sources, like Mark and Q, into the life of the oral tradition, where individual stories (rather than a complete written gospel or source) were handed down. It has also been used with great effect in the Psalms, where it was always very difficult in any case to date poems on the basis of content, historical allusions and the like.

One of the chief differences in form criticism is that it is concerned with community authorship and transmission rather than with the 'writing' of a 'book' by an 'author'. At first sight it might seem that this approach would reduce the danger of a sheer collision that had existed between conservatism and critical scholarship over literary questions. The conception of oral tradition, and the view that the oral period, rather than the actual writing down of documents, was the main formative moment in the biblical tradition, has probably done something to reduce tension. Moreover, in some fields the use of form criticism has resulted in generally more conservative results: the Psalms are the most striking instance. The use of form criticism has been accompanied by a wide agreement that many or most of the Psalms belong to the period of the Solomonic Temple and were used in the liturgy there. Conservatives will probably welcome this. On the other hand, under form criticism the idea that David personally 'wrote' Psalms becomes not so much impossible as just rather silly. If form criticism were widely accepted among conservatives, it might mean that they would come to attach less importance to ascriptions of 'authorship' to particular persons such as David or Peter.

The area in which form criticism has been most influential, however, is the gospels, and here the situation is difficult to explain concisely, because there is a certain difference between what is necessarily entailed by the form-critical method and the way it has been handled by particular practitioners. Some positions taken up on form-critical grounds have been fairly welcome to conservatives: for example, it is supposed to have made impossible the quest for a 'historical' Jesus, which means more or less a Jesus separated from the Christological conceptions of the later church.[34] But the main problem for conservatives has been over its relation to historical narrative. The instance of the Psalms had been easier in this respect, because the Psalms are generally not historical narratives at all, or not in a sense comparable with the gospels. In the gospels form criticism has often gone along with a rather sceptical view about the historicity of the material. And even form critics who are not particularly sceptical will still look at the stories from the point of view of their function: how was this story *used* within the early church? Some stories, it is thought, are of types that were used, and therefore developed, in missionary preaching, others in controversy, others in liturgy, and so on. This raises for conservatives the spectre of a suggestion that the narratives were not only *preserved* in the church's consciousness through their use, let us say in missionary preaching, but that they were even *generated* by the church's consciousness for that purpose. Here conservatives refuse to follow, except perhaps in abnormal examples. If a passage is narrative, its form for them is generated by the fact that things happened in that way; the form of the story is thus a form brought about by the form of an external event. This aspect of form criticism comes under bitter opposition from conservatives, and indeed to some of them form criticism is the most serious enemy, much worse than the multiple sources of the pentateuch or the Deutero-Isaiah theory. On the whole, I suspect, it is the more advanced and liberal conservatives who get to the point of worrying about form criticism; the main body of conservative evangelical literature still has its lines drawn essentially on questions of literary criticism, sources, dates and authorship. Some slight recognition is given to form criticism for the aspects in which it is supposed to have made certain liberal quests impossible; but this can be taken as a mere debating-point, not indicating any willingness to go with form criticism along its own way. At present all indications, at least in Britain, are that conservative evangelical scholarship will continue to dig and deepen its trenches along the lines of literary and historical questions. In this they can with some justification rely on some support from scholars who, though not at all conservative in the theological sense, take a conservative position about the historical character of narratives, mainly in the New Testament; and this emphasis is said to be strong in British New Testament scholarship.

Form criticism raises for fundamentalism a problem more serious than the accuracy of historical reporting in the gospels. It raises a completely different perspective on the origin of scripture. Scripture, it becomes possible to imagine, arose out of the church. So long as there were a few identifiable 'writers', it was possible to think that they were specially 'inspired' in distinction from all other persons in the church: though they received their experience within the church, as writers they spoke authoritatively, from outside as it were, to the church. But once the scripture comes to be thought of as the product of whole generations of nameless people the idea of the inspired writers becomes not so much false as irrelevant. Fundamentalist doctrine was formed, of course, at a time when nothing of this had been taken into consideration, and all its conceptual apparatus remains geared to the idea of 'writers' who received their material by inspiration from God. It may be that fundamentalism will have to form a new front against this aspect of form criticism, and that this will make much of its traditional apologetics irrelevant;

but at present there is little sign that this has been realized.

We have said all along that conservative opinion on matters of history, authorship of books, authenticity of sayings ascribed to Jesus, and so on is not necessarily fundamentalistic: there can be a legitimate conservative case on all these grounds that is quite distinct from a fundamentalist case depending on a full belief in the inerrancy of the Bible. On many points I would consider myself to take a conservative position of just this kind. And yet it is important to be discriminating and self-critical about these conservative judgments. Merely to say that it is not fundamentalistic is not a sufficient reason to show that conservatism in biblical interpretation is a perfectly good thing, lying beyond all criticism. Conservative tendencies in interpretation may have to be looked at from several sides. Some conservatism, though clearly distinct from fundamentalism, can still be fairly diagnosed as residual fundamentalism. A scholar, realizing the hopelessness of the strict fundamentalist position, with its attendant fuss over Balaam's ass and the number of generations from Adam to Noah and so on, becomes ready to abandon all that, but he thinks that the broad lines of what fundamentalism had upheld can still be upheld. Criticism is, then, legitimate, and we can have sources in the gospels, perhaps sources in the pentateuch also: but, allowing for all that, Jesus can still be taken as having said all the sayings attributed to him, the whole pentateuch is still somehow, though more vaguely, tied up with Moses, who must after all have been a historical figure, and the whole book of Isaiah is still somehow linked to the prophet of that name. In conservatism of this kind a good measure is the question: how far does it make itself expressly distinct from actual fundamentalism? How far does it make clear to fundamentalists that a quite different understanding of the Bible has to be sought and found?

This leads us on to what is perhaps the other main way of looking at conservatism: how far does it lead into fresh theological exploration? In general it must be said that, at least in the English-speaking world, conservatism about the Bible has gone along with the idea that historical questions come first, theological ones only later. And this often means that the theological questions do not come along at all. If the Bible is being studied primarily historically, and if this process leads to no fresh theological explorations, it probably means a falling back on traditional positions. Conservatism of this kind, while far removed from actual fundamentalism, can nevertheless stifle the sparks kindled by the existence of a critical approach to scripture.

Questions of this kind are very apposite at a time when John A. T. Robinson has just produced a book, *Redating the New Testament*, SCM Press 1976, in which he seeks to prove that all the New Testament books were written before AD 70. Now Robinson thinks that his work will not give comfort to fundamentalists: 'I trust it will give no comfort to those who would view with suspicion the application of critical tools to biblical study – for it is reached by the application of these tools.'[35] Grateful as I am for the insights that Robinson has kindly granted me for my use in this book of mine, I must say that I find this assurance naive and unfounded. For the position of fundamentalists, as should be plain to all readers of this book, is not that critical tools must not be used, but that when they are used they will produce conservative and traditional results; so long as conservative results are produced, they do not care what sort of tools are used, indeed the more critical the better so far as that goes. The main question posed by Robinson's book, however, is not that posed to the fundamentalist but that posed to the average churchgoer and Bible-reader. By all means let it be admitted that the conservative results of this book might be right and that such an intepretation, dating the entire New Testament extremely early, is an entirely legitimate enterprise. But let those beware who think that thereby their faith will be strengthened, their certainty made greater. On the one hand there is no reason to suppose that this swing of the pendulum towards a conservative side will be permanent, and every reason to expect that it will only call forth a new series of late datings with contrary evidences. On the other hand, it is important to understand that a faith that is strengthened by the publication of books advocating an early dating is just not Christian faith. Faith is indeed related to historical data but it is not related in that way. One of the main lessons which the existence of historical criticism of the Bible has given to the church is the awareness that faith cannot be built upon such things as datings and authorship of books; yet this lesson has been so poorly learned that we are constantly in danger of forgetting it.

And this brings us to the conclusion of this chapter, with a point of central importance that arises from all this. It is a great mistake to suppose that the essential difference between the fundamentalist and the critical-theological approaches to the Bible lies in the historical and literary questions usually subsumed under 'introduction' – questions like whether Deuteronomy goes back to the time of Moses, whether Isaiah 40–66 goes back to the original Isaiah, whether the Book of Daniel was written by an actual Daniel who lived in the time of Nebuchadnezzar and Cyrus and was physically thrown into the lions' den, whether Timothy and Titus were written by St Paul, and how many of the sayings ascribed to Jesus in the gospels were actually spoken by him. All of these are in fact side-issues, and in the following sense: even if, as a matter of historical opinion, critical scholars were to come around to the most conservative opinion on all these points, the situation would not be altered one whit. For the essence is, not that this date or that should be earlier or later, but that the understanding of truth and meaning as applied to the Bible has become thoroughly different; and even if on almost every question of history and literature the conservative answer came to be accepted, the understanding of the Bible that has grown up in the tradition of modern critical scholarship and modern theology would remain totally different from that which conservative evangelicals want us to adopt. Thus the whole elaborate apparatus of conservative apologetic for early date, traditional authorship, avoidance of source divisions, and the like, though we have here done it the courtesy of discussing it, is a waste of time. The issue lies elsewhere.

6 · Fundamentalism and Theology

It has been suggested that the real conflict of fundamentalist faith is not with critical biblical scholarship but with theology. Even if every critical position on historical questions were to be abandoned, every biblical book deemed to have been written by the author to whom tradition ascribes it, and every sentence attributed to Jesus agreed to have been actually spoken by him, the conflict between fundamentalism and the main stream of theological interpretation of the Bible would not in the slightest degree have been mitigated. The dates, authorships and sources assigned by critical scholarship are not the essential: the essential is rather the quite different way of looking at the Bible, and at truth, to which theology as a whole has been assisted by the presence of critical scholarship. Again, biblical study, though a field of deep conflict between fundamentalist and critical approaches, is at least a field where some common study is done and where there are some common questions to differ about. In theology, on the other hand, the alienation of fundamentalists is so complete that almost no worthwhile contact remains in existence. Within conservative evangelical literature the works on the Bible achieve a reasonable standard of learning and sophistication: practically all they say about theology or philosophy can only be described as abysmally poor in comparison. The profound personal alienation and absence of sympathy, and the failure of intellectual understanding, are two sides of the same coin. A recent book like J. N. D. Anderson's *A Lawyer among the Theologians* (Hodder 1973) could suitably be condensed into one sentence: the author has no understanding of what modern theology is about, and hates everything to do with it. But phenomena like this are not a result of mere personal intransigence: they are the signs of deep-lying structures of thought which are basic to fundamentalist Christianity.

In a certain sense fundamentalism could be described as a theology-less movement. I have already suggested that its anticlerical secularist tendencies direct themselves with a special negativity against the theologian. What is intended by the theologian as an attempt to restate the gospel in categories that can be understood by the modern world is perceived by the fundamentalist as a quite gratuitous attempt to foist upon the church and the world the personal and professional fashions of a theological caste. The principle of scriptural authority, formulated expressly as a matter of inerrancy, means in effect that any Christian with his Bible, so long as he believes the latter to be inerrant, can completely discount the arguments and opinions of any theologian who does not fully accept that principle. Most theologians do not, and this means that for fundamentalism they have no positive function or usefulness. But to fundamentalists this is no great loss, for the fundamentalist faith does not greatly need theologians, even if they were on its side. There is, as a matter of fact, not much for them to do.

Fundamentalists have theological views, of course, and in that sense they could be said to have a theology; we have already spent considerable space on depicting its outlines. Yet, if we call it a theology, there are three qualifications that have to be made. Firstly, if it is a theology, it is a fossilized theology. The fundamentalist movement took the theology of the evangelical revivals or, more correctly, built up a theological position which was believed to have been that of the evangelical revivals, and in part also of nineteenth-century Calvinism, and sought simply to conserve these theological views. Secondly, it is a fragmented theology. The older orthodoxies taught and required a 'system' of doctrine, in which all interrelations were carefully stated in full and with great detail. Fundamentalism picked out from this older theology a few essential points, which had to be believed. The perception of the interrelations is markedly lacking in fundamentalist faith; and it is these interrelations that are peculiarly the sphere of operation of the theologian. Thirdly, the theology of fundamentalism is an inactive theology. If there is a theology, there is nothing for it to do. This is an immediate and complete explanation for the third-rate theological productivity of conservative evangelical writing: there is no new work for the theologian to do. In so far as there is a need for theologically competent thinkers at all, their task is essentially apologetic: they must defend the evangelical faith against doubts within and attacks or criticisms without. Sometimes it might be doubtfully admitted that they should also restate it in more modern forms, but even that must be held strictly in check: it is very doubtful if even the outward forms and phraseology of conservative evangelical belief can be openly and publicly subjected to criticism in order to ensure their restatement in more modern form. A certain amount of change and shifting of positions does indeed occur; but it commonly occurs not as a result of open criticism and a call for change, but rather as the result of a slow and secret process, the change being completed before anyone admits that it is needed, and the fact of change being concealed after it has taken place. Because the active task of theological work in fundamentalism is so restricted, it is understandable that able and active young conservative theologians are found to be grasping at the coat-tails of the more conservative elements in other theological positions such as neo-orthodoxy and the biblical theology movement.[1] These are positions which, while not intrinsically or wholly conservative, at least have elements that are capable of being used in a generally conservative direction. This gives conservative biblical theologians some freedom of movement and something at least to think about. Within true fundamentalism there is no real task for theology other than the conservation and reiteration of a tradition believed to have existed in the past and in any case now taken as immovably fixed.

In these senses it would be possible to say that fundamentalism has a sort of theology; but I suggest that a better picture is given if we say that fundamentalism has *doctrines*. This is the way in which they themselves put it, and I think rightly. There are certain things that are taught, doctrinal structures that are extremely important; but it is not necessary to talk of these as a theology, and indeed this is not generally done. Fundamentalism with its limited but strongly-held series of doctrines thus stands as a solid and clearly marked entity against the wild, vague and speculative theologies of the main stream of Christianity. The main character of fundamentalist doctrine will be discussed in a later chapter.

Now the most obvious characteristic of the fundamentalist position *vis-à-vis* theology is its quite total complacency and lack of self-criticism.[2] On every point at every time the conservative evangelical position has been totally right. In no respect at any time has any non-conservative argument, viewpoint or position been in the slightest justified as a statement of Christian faith. Nowhere in the British conservative evangelical material that I have used for the research for this book have I found any evidence of self-criticism in the face of others. Conservative evangelicals are not, indeed, believed to be perfect, and sometimes indeed they show signs of severe faults: but all of these come to the same thing, that is, to the fact that they have not been sufficiently conservative evangelical in their point of view. There is never any acceptance that really different theological positions, and especially any liberal position, have had anything at all to say that stated any aspect of the Christian faith better than the conservative evangelical position. The rejection of the theologies labelled as liberal or modernist is total. There never was the slightest good reason why these theologies were propounded; there never was, and is not, the slightest biblical evidence that could legitimately tell in their favour; they were all alike thought out by men who were indeed clever but who merely spun out of their own heads total fancies and speculations, none of which had the slightest justification from within the Christian faith. On every point of difference there was from the beginning, as there is now, a conservative and 'orthodox' answer which made the liberal and modern approaches unnecessary and wrong; sheer perversity caused theologians to ignore these perfectly satisfactory answers and go off in another direction.

In other words, in fundamentalism all relations with non-conservative theology are purely polemical. The conception of a catholic community of theological thinkers seeking by joint discussion with one another to state the truth within the totality of the Christian faith in all its varieties, is entirely repudiated. The main reason for this lies in the fundamentalist position, that the question of scriptural authority is *the* one question of theology, that takes precedence over all others. Though fundamentalists take great pride in their trinitarian orthodoxy and emphasize their belief in the triune God, this does not mean that they stand in theological fellowship with theologians just because the latter believe in the Holy Trinity. Not at all: belief in the Holy Trinity, though better than unitarianism or than believing in no god at all, does not in the slightest entitle one to expect that one's theological opinions will be respected within fundamentalist circles. The same applies to the virgin birth, the resurrection, the necessity of the work of the Holy Spirit and all the rest. The doctrine of the authority of scripture is the overriding consideration, it is the sole final consideration. Yet, peculiarly, the authority of scripture would never in itself have justified a split between fundamentalist faith and mainstream theology. What fundamentalism has always insisted is not just that scripture should be received as authoritative, which most or all theologians would in some sense, and most of them gladly, have agreed, but that its authority should be grounded upon its infallibility and inerrancy and defined in these terms. In practice therefore fundamentalists so define their doctrinal position that the true theological community for discussion is constituted by one party only: fundamentalists. All relations with other points of view are in principle solely polemical. Once again we see that this arises not from personal intransigence but from the doctrinal structure itself; but it means, of course, that for fundamentalists this doctrinal structure is dearer than the possibility of fellowship with Christians who think differently.

The picture of non-conservative theology, as cherished by fundamentalists, is interesting and important. Here again we are dealing with mythology: the fundamentalist picture of what non-conservative theology is like is not based on any deep study of the latter, indeed, it is usually based on a complete absence of study of the latter. Nowhere in the conservative evangelical literature have I found evidence of any serious attempt to understand what non-conservative theologians think.[3] This is not surprising, since we have already seen that the ethos of fundamentalist religion discourages the sympathetic study of the works of such theologians. The picture of what non-conservative theologians are up to is within fundamentalism a matter of faith: a picture of what this theology must be like is current within the religion, indeed is a necessary part of the religion, for opposition to 'liberalism' and 'modernism' is an essential constituent of it. Non-conservative theologians and theologies are simply classed by the fundamentalist as mildly varying forms of this picture. The global negative picture of non-conservative theology is like the fundamentalist doctrine of sin: it is a necessary general and negative assumption, used to justify the claim that only a purely fundamentalist gospel can save.

The most striking characteristic of the fundamentalist picture of other theologies is its failure to discriminate, perhaps its inability to do so. All of them come to the same thing. There is, no doubt, Schleiermacher, and there is Ritschl; in more modern times there is Tillich, and then there is Bultmann, and there are many others. Indeed, conservatives suppose that the very variety between different non-conservative theologies is a reason why one should stick to a conservative position: at least it is (they think) only one, while the others are many. But this variety makes no real difference to them: from the viewpoint of fundamentalism, they all come to the same thing. They do not expressly begin from the authority of scripture, understood and defined as inerrancy, and thus they can all be classed together.

Thus the inability of fundamentalists to understand other

theologies, indeed their reluctance even to attempt to do so, is not the consequence of ignorance or lack of native intelligence: on the contrary, it follows naturally from the intellectual and doctrinal structure of fundamentalism itself. It is a natural result of the fundamentalist view that the question of authority, expressed as the inerrancy of scripture, is the sole overriding criterion for distinguishing between one theology and another.

In any case, whether this explanation is accepted or not, the practical facts are easily seen: there is, within fundamentalism, very little or no understanding of what non-conservative theologians actually think, and no incentive to find out. It is a psychological necessity of membership in the fundamentalist organizations that one should be convinced that everyone outside is completely 'liberal' in theology, or at least that he has no stable defences against the adoption of a totally liberal position.

Professor Lefferts Loetscher, talking about the once famous conservative polemicist J. Gresham Machen, once wrote:

> The argument of Dr Machen's book was partly vitiated by the fallacy of the 'undistributed middle'. This book, as well as many of his public utterances and other writings, described 'liberalism' in terms of the most radical naturalistic implications, and then, by implication at least, included in this classification all those who differed from traditional orthodoxy even on subordinate points.[4]

Quite so; but Dr Loetscher need not have been surprised by this, for it is nothing peculiar to Machen; on the contrary, the same procedure is entirely normal in conservative evangelical and fundamentalist circles.

What is the pattern upon which the fundamentalist picture of the non-conservative theologian is constructed? Commonly it is supposed that a liberalism, such as Harnack's, is taken as the model.[5] I would suggest that the pattern goes much farther back in history. It is drawn, as it seems to me, from the deists of the late seventeenth and the eighteenth centuries. It is in deism, and not in later liberalism, that one finds an element that is deeply engraved on the fundamentalist soul: the attack on the verbal form of the Bible as part of an argument that Christianity, as a revealed religion, was not true. This is the element, I would suggest, that has remained central to the fundamentalist perception throughout all this time. A model of this kind could not have arisen with Harnackian liberalism or with any other sort of classical liberalism. On the contrary, the model was already there much earlier, and when liberal theology appeared in its late nineteenth- or early twentieth-century forms it was simply assimilated to the model, as was neo-orthodoxy even later, and Bultmannian radicalism after that, and so on. None of these people had the slightest idea of attacking Christianity, or of attacking it as a revealed religion. All this exists only in the fundamentalist mind. That mind has remained stopped with the deist model with which it took its start: criticism of the Bible is an attempt to undermine Christianity as a revealed religion. All forms of critical discussion thus come to the same thing: whether it is the pointing out of discrepancies between different parts of the Bible, or doubts about the morality of passages in the Old Testament, or questions whether miraculous events could have taken place as narrated, or suggestions that books were not written by the authors named or at the times traditionally accepted, all of these are alike attacks on the Bible and on the basis of Christianity as a revealed religion; all of them are intended to show that the Bible is totally untrustworthy and that Christianity should and must therefore proceed on a non-biblical, non-revelatory basis, which will be dictated by the theologians on the basis of their own ideas. Fundamentalists see all non-conservative theologies as varying realizations of this model.

Thus, even as seen from its own point of view, conservative evangelical polemic loses much of its possible effectiveness because of its failure to understand what non-conservative theologians think. This weakness is compounded and increased by another striking weakness, to which we shall return again, namely the failure of fundamentalism to see theologies as wholes, to concern itself with the interrelations between the doctrinal elements affirmed. This weakness is encouraged by the position within fundamentalism itself, where, as we have seen, it is customary for a few nodal points, a few vital truths, to be enunciated as essentials of belief and tests of orthodoxy. These points function like items on a check-list: you must believe in the Trinity (tick), you must believe in the virgin birth (tick), you must affirm the infallibility and inspiration of holy scripture (tick) as originally given, and so on. The doctrinal standard requires and insists upon the affirmation of the whole list of elements. It does much less to indicate what interrelations between the elements have to be affirmed, or on what grounds the elements have to be connected in this way rather than in that. Though the whole list is set up in order to avoid and exclude liberalism, it is naively supposed that liberalism is sufficiently negated by these affirmations, while liberalism can perfectly well survive as a mode of correlation between the conservative affirmations, and we shall later see how this is so. In general, the failure to see doctrinal affirmation as a whole, the centre of which is in the interrelations rather than in a list of particular affirmations, is built into the doctrinal structure of fundamentalism itself and makes it unsurprising that the same attitude is transferred to its outlook on non-conservative theological viewpoints.

The same position is seen when conservative evangelical apologists seek to enlist the church as a whole in support of their tenets. A writer like Green will tell us that ecclesiastical authorities, let us say the assembled bishops of the Anglican communion, have reaffirmed the traditional position of scripture as conservative evangelicals understand it.[6] 'The Church is not *over* the Holy Scriptures, but *under* them . . . The books were recognized as giving the witness of the Apostles to the life, teaching, death and resurrection of the Lord . . . To that apostolic authority the Church must ever bow' (cited from the Lambeth Report of 1958). So, Green continues, 'in so stressing the supreme authority of Scripture over both Church and Reason, our Bishops have merely been following the lead of the Church from the beginning'. But Canon Green knows perfectly well, that though the bishops are very happy to make a declaration stating the authority of scripture over the church, their reasons for doing this, that is, the interrelations between this affirmation and their understandings of doctrine in other areas, are entirely different from the conservative evangelical point of view, and that the bishops in conclave are not in the slightest reaffirming the latter view; indeed, considering the bitter complaints about the apostasy and unbelief of the church and its leaders which conservative evangelicals diffuse and devour, it would be very remarkable if such an assembly were to reaffirm the view that conservative evangelicals hold. The fact is that they did nothing of the kind. Green has extracted the affirmation of scriptural authority from the interrelations in which it stood, and this, as we have seen, is typical of the conservative evangelical approach to doctrinal matters. Many other instances will be seen below.

But, thirdly, the same weakness is seen when non-conservative theological positions are described. These are inspected with the same check-list approach: does he affirm the virgin birth, does he hold scripture to be inerrant, does he look forward to the personal return of the Lord? On the one hand this approach is swiftly effective in condemning most theologies as non-conservative evangelical and therefore wrong; on the other hand it is an effective bar against understanding how the minds of actual theologians work and what considerations motivate them.

All this is very important when we come to consider the question whether fundamentalist doctrine should be counted as 'orthodox'. Conservative evangelicals consider themselves, indeed, to be orthodox and take great pride in this. The type of fundamentalism that has been taken as the model of research for this book is of course more or less orthodox by definition: but that means that it is an 'orthodox' type of fundamentalism as against more deviant types, and it does not mean that it is orthodox in the sense that it is a valid continuation of the main orthodox tradition in the churches. It means, rather, that it aspires to be orthodox, that orthodoxy is its ideal. Its claim to be orthodox is not, however, to be taken very seriously, and the main reason is the one we have just been discussing. Conservative evangelicalism takes a few elements out of traditional orthodoxy and affirms them, but the elements are interrelated in a way that does not at all correspond to any past orthodoxy. Even if we follow the usual conservative evangelical viewpoint and take as our standard that stream of the early fathers which is usually esteemed as orthodox, plus the main Reformers and the classic confessions of faith of the Reformation period, one could not suppose that fundamentalism is orthodox by this standard except in a very selective way. Though the Trinity is a basic affirmation of modern fundamentalists, even they can scarcely affirm that the essentials of modern conservative evangelicalism were upheld by (say) Athanasius or Augustine. 'Orthodoxy' for these fathers was something of total shape and content entirely different from the religion of modern fundamentalists; the relation between scriptural evidences and Trinitarian or Christological formulations was quite dissimilar from what obtains among them. But the same applies if one moves to the Reformation period, to the Westminster Confession or to the Thirty-Nine articles. It is just not true to say that fundamentalists hold to the 'essential' affirmations of these documents. For the fundamentalist 'essential' means that which he (and his modern tradition) has extracted as suitable and essential for today. But these extractions would not have been legitimate in terms of the orthodoxy of that time. It would have been unthinkable to extract isolated elements, such as the affirmations about the Trinity or holy scripture, without at the same time affirming the clauses about predestination, election, and the relations between church and state. The most one can say, then, is something like this: at those points at which modern conservative evangelicals affirm an 'orthodoxy' which agrees with some element in ancient orthodoxy, there they are at least aspiring to be in accord with that more ancient orthodoxy. But all sorts of other things that were equally emphasized by ancient orthodoxy are simply ignored by conservative evangelicalism. And even where doctrines are affirmed which did in fact exist as elements in ancient or Reformation orthodoxy, the reasons for any one element, and its interrelations with other elements, may well be, and commonly in fact are, quite different in modern conservative evangelicalism from what they were in that older orthodoxy. Fundamentalism is thus, even in intention and in practice still more, orthodox only selectively and occasionally.

In terms of traditional orthodoxy, there is at least one major point at which the fundamentalist faith can probably be considered heretical or unorthodox, and that is the view of the person of Jesus Christ. Many observers have argued this and I do not propose to press the point very far. While traditional orthodoxy holds that Christ is both God and man, and while that position is taken by correctly-informed conservative apologists, the emphasis of fundamentalist religion falls heavily on the deity of Christ. He is indeed man, but the essential thing to affirm is that he is God. This becomes stronger when one turns away from informed conservative apologetics and looks at the ordinary fundamentalist believer. He has probably never heard of Athanasius and knows nothing of the idea that Jesus Christ is equally God and man. What he believes about him is that he is *God*. He is God walking about and teaching in a man's body. Everyone knows that Jesus is a man, no virtue and no value is to be got from recognizing that he is a man; it is the recognition that he is God that counts, that makes some difference. The personal affirmation of faith in fundamentalist organizations is often in 'Jesus Christ as my Saviour, my Lord and my God'. If the last term 'my God' were missed out, as in some ecumenical formulations, the affirmation would be of lesser value. The essential thing for popular fundamentalism is that Jesus is God. To put it negatively, and fundamentalist affirmations have to be seen negatively in order to see what they mean, any approach to Jesus that starts out from Jesus as *man* falls under suspicion and has to be rejected, unless it is immediately qualified with an even stronger assertion that he is God.

It is hardly necessary to point out that this affects the whole character of the religion. The approach to the atonement, for instance, naturally takes the form of God (the Son of God) suffering on our behalf, and not of other conceptions of atonement such as that of the man Jesus making reconciliation as leader of a new manhood. It affects also the balance between the cross and the resurrection and fits with the emphasis, already mentioned, on the crucifixion as God taking our judgment or punishment, more than on the resurrection as man breaking forth from the bonds of death and entering into new life.

Still more does it affect the reading of the New Testament. The New Testament does not approach the presentation of Jesus with the bald statement that he is God, or even that he is Son of God. The question arises, why it preferred to present him in other terms, often as 'Lord' or as 'Son of Man', or in a way that suggests that he was not 'Son of God' in a timeless unchanging fashion, but was designated 'Son of God' through the resurrection (Rom. 1.4)? Why did it not say, from beginning to end, that Jesus was God, in these exact terms? Because fundamentalism insists that the central affirmation is that Jesus was God, it is forced once again to a major harmonizing operation. On the one hand all passages which fail to say that Jesus was God, and had been so from the beginning through incarnation and through a virgin birth, are read as if they did say so. On the other hand a heavy emphasis is laid on these passages which most expressly represent Jesus as 'God'. The effect of this is to obliterate the meanings of terms like 'Son of Man', which are actually widely used in sources like the synoptic gospels. These are assimilated to trinitarian doctrine; it is supposed, perhaps, that Jesus was both God and man, and that to say 'Son of Man' is a reference to this double nature and is thus in effect a designation referentially equivalent to 'Son of God'. Moreover, it is felt as important to avoid the impression that the plain designation of Jesus as 'God', and the use of divine imagery about him, occur only in marginal books like Titus (e.g. Titus 2.13, 'our great God and Saviour Jesus Christ') or in St John's gospel; this is another reason for the anxiety to prove that these books are authentic works of Paul and John the original disciple. In other words the understanding of Christ as God is one main reason that contributes to the basic fundamentalist position about authenticity of books. All this is very well known and need hardly be pursued.

The most powerful reason, however, for the fundamentalist distortion of the orthodox picture of the nature of Jesus Christ is that which works in the opposite direction. We have just seen that, in order to make it clear that Jesus is really affirmed to be God, a fundamentalist view of certain books is desirable. But much more, conversely, as we have seen, the fundamentalist view of the Bible as a whole is very much grounded upon the teaching of Jesus: Jesus taught that David wrote Psalm 110, that Jonah was in the belly of the fish, that Daniel spoke the prophecies named after him: and in order for this teaching to be infallible and inerrant it has to be teaching that comes from God. It is wrong to say that Jesus didn't know, or was wrong about these things, or didn't care, or did not mean to say anything about dates, authorships and origins of books. His teaching on such matters was infallible because he was God and shared in God's infallibility; to say he was wrong would be to say that he was not God.

This is a very familiar matter and not much time need be spent on it. Jesus becomes, according to this picture, more like God dispensing eternally correct information through a human mouth than a man speaking under the conditions of his time and situation. He is separated from the limitations of the human situation and made into a superhuman and inhuman person, who cannot be supposed to have thought about the book of Jonah or Psalm 110 just what every other person of the time thought. In fact, I do not think that there is any disagreement about the facts here: the only question is what is orthodox and what is not. Packer, for instance, writes a sentence, following Warfield, which makes it clear that the weight and emphasis in the doctrine of Jesus Christ should fall upon his being God: 'The right and scriptural way in Christology is to start by recognizing the unity of our Lord's Person as divine and to view His humanity only as an aspect of His Person, existing within it and never, therefore, dissociated from it.'[7] Similarly, he thinks, by analogy the Bible is really a divine book, and its character as a human book should be studied 'only as one aspect of its character as a divine book'. Whether this is orthodox concerning the person of Christ, I leave to readers to consider. I think it is unorthodox but do not think much will be gained by pursuing this line, as will be indicated below.

On the matter of Jesus as a teacher about books, persons like Jonah and so on, we would do better to consider the matter in a different way. The traditional discussion has operated with the two categories of divine and human, and has argued whether the balance between the two is preserved or upset by the position characteristic of conservative evangelicals. Might we not do better to put it in this way: Jesus' teaching is time-bound and situation-bound, not because of his humanity, because of his being man, but because of the functional character of his teaching. What he taught was not eternal truth valid for all times and situations, but personal address concerned with the situation of Jesus and his hearers at that time. It is therefore entirely to be expected that what he says about himself in his early preaching will be different from what he says about himself from what the church says about him after his resurrection. That the teaching is functionally related to the ministry, death and resurrection is a good evangelical insight, which is however quite abandoned when fundamentalists come to talk about the teaching and use it to validate assertions about literary and historical questions. Thus I put this question not in terms of divine and human, or in terms of ancient times as against our own time, but in terms of the function of Jesus' teaching in the various changing situations of his own life and the early church. It is possible that this approach will do something to loosen the log-jam of this question.

In any case it is clear that here, as everywhere in fundamentalism, everything has to yield to the overriding necessity of the principle of inerrancy. Christological orthodoxy has to go too. I would put it this way: I do not really know, nor do I much care, whether Packer's formulation is orthodox or not; and the question would involve the further problem, by what standard of orthodoxy? But I do not believe that either Packer or Warfield would have taken this stand about the person of Christ but for the pressure of the issue of biblical inerrancy. That is the obvious and only motivating power for the argument they present. If biblical inerrancy is in difficulties, Christological doctrine has to be so defined as to give the maximum possible shelter to inerrancy.

In any case, whatever our judgment on the question about the relation of divine and human in the person of Christ, we have seen ample reason to discount the claims of orthodoxy made by fundamentalists in a whole series of other matters, and the whole assertion of orthodoxy can be dismissed. I do not argue this, however, in order to suggest that conservative evangelicalism can be or should be criticized by others on the grounds that it is unorthodox or heretical. Obviously one could not so argue unless one was prepared oneself to take orthodoxy as the ideal and the measuring-staff, and I am not. On the person of Jesus Christ, it may well be that any formulation that would satisfy our present understanding, whether in conservatism or in modern theological currents, would be unorthodox or heretical in terms of the ancient discussions, which after all lie some fifteen hundred years in the past. But when a movement like fundamentalism prides itself on its orthodoxy it is quite proper to point out that this form of self-congratulation is quite misplaced.

We can now perhaps leave the question of orthodoxy and discuss the wider question of the general continuity of fundamentalist faith with the older faith of the church. Fundamentalists believe that they are only conserving and preserving the faith that has been there always; some critics have tended to suggest that, in spite of that conservative aim, fundamentalists have in fact worked out a quite new form of faith, one that did not exist until modern times. There is something to be said on both sides.

Some of the reasons why fundamentalism should be regarded as a modern phenomenon have already been mentioned. One is its relation to secularity and, if the argument put forward is correct, to a scientific and materialistic idea of truth. Another is the point made just above that, although fundamentalism affirms certain elements taken from the older tradition of doctrine, it does not interrelate these elements in the same way. A third point is the deliberate regressive direction of fundamentalism. Where a revolution in the understanding of a subject takes place, it is one thing to live before that revolution, and another thing, after the revolution has taken place, to turn one's back upon it and say that it was entirely wrong. As Alan Richardson puts it:

> The position of a man who insists after the Copernican revolution that the sun goes round the earth is not really the same position as that of the pre-Copernican astronomers. He has in fact taken up an attitude to evidence which the pre-Copernicans had not been able to consider, and which would in all reasonable probability have caused them to modify their Ptolemaic views, if they had had access to it. His attitude to the authority of Ptolemy is quite different from theirs; for them Ptolemy was the only known standard of truth, and accepting Ptolemy did not involve rejecting Copernicus.[8]

Theologians of before the critical era had not seen biblical scholarship as it later developed; but they had not turned their backs upon it. One can see the difference already with Calvin. We have already noted that he contemplated with equanimity the dating of some Psalms in the Maccabaean era, an opinion now regarded with horror by conservatives, and that his own inclination was to believe that II Peter was not written by the apostle Peter. I do not wish to exaggerate the importance of this evidence. It is clear that Calvin was ready to make, in the spirit of the Renaissance, some critical literary judgments on biblical texts. The fact that these limited steps could be made at all suggests that he might have gone farther along this line; in any case it fully demonstrates that he had no idea that such steps were forbidden or contrary to the faith. We cannot, however, go far in this direction, and for the following reason: the problem of critical scholarship, as it in fact developed, was the matter of scale. Calvin had no means of knowing the scale of the changes that would have to come about when not an occasional one or two, but many hundreds and thousands of such questions were to be asked and answered on a critical basis. Though these occasional critical decisions were given, they seem to have made no substantial difference to Calvin's total theological method, and they thus remain as isolated particles.[9] But even taken so, and understood minimally and negatively, the fact that Calvin could make them at all sets a huge qualitative difference between him and the modern conservative, for whom it is of the dogmatic essence of the faith that such critical proposals must be rejected, because for him they deny the veracity of God himself. Thus the anti-critical aim of modern conservative evangelical doctrine, an aim which is not only part of that doctrine but is the supreme and overriding architectonic principle of it, is quite absent from a person like Calvin. In saying this I readily admit that in other aspects Calvin used much of the language which modern fundamentalists use or imply – the exact words of God, dictation, and so on. But his doctrine of scripture, intense as it was, was not organized as an anti-critical defence.

In this I am not in the least seeking to use Calvin as an evidence of the legitimacy of modern critical biblical studies; on the contrary, I do not think that he can give us any kind of decision upon such a question. I merely seek to illustrate the fact that theology in the pre-critical period was not animated by the anti-critical animus and passion of modern conservative theology. Matters of discrepancies between texts, minor contradictions and so on were taken very easily. This is true of Luther also. He scorned the harmonizing devices which were necessary in order to bring various passages of scripture into exact agreement with one another.[10] Indeed, the tradition whereby minor errors, discrepancies between parallel texts, and so on were taken easily, being regarded as of no serious moment, as constituting no problem for Christian doctrine and therefore requiring no special harmonization, was still dominant until well on in the nineteenth century and was expressed by the impeccably conservative Charles Hodge in a famous passage.

> The errors in matters of fact which skeptics search out bear no proportion to the whole. No sane man would deny that the Parthenon was built of marble, even if here and there a speck of sandstone should be detected in its structure. Not less unreasonable is to deny the inspiration of such a book as the Bible, because one sacred writer says that on a given occasion twenty-four thousand, and another says that

twenty-three thousand, men were slain. Surely a Christian may be allowed to tread such objections under his feet.[11]

It is probable, in fact, that many conservative evangelicals would very much like to get back to this position; but meanwhile they have saddled themselves with a doctrine which will not permit even the occasional 'fleck of sandstone'. But that doctrine, with its rigid insistence on absolute inerrancy, was a development of the later nineteenth century. Far from being the traditional doctrine of the church before critical scholarship came along, it was a doctrinal position that was worked out because critical scholarship was already there.[12] In respect of its picture of the Bible as practically perfect and divine, fundamentalist doctrine has its closest precedent in one limited period of tradition, namely the scholastic Calvinism of theologians like Turretin (*Institutio*, 1701); but this is different in two respects that have already been named. Firstly it is pre-critical rather than anti-critical and is therefore not at all organized on the basis or with the motives found in modern fundamentalism; and secondly it is a total system of Calvinistic dogmatics, which could not be taken over for the purposes of modern fundamentalism, for the simple reason that most fundamentalists did not believe what that system contained. All this development will be considered further in a later chapter. From all this point of view it is quite justified if we hold that fundamentalism is a modern phenomenon. It contains elements which are found also, and indeed strongly asserted, in the older theological tradition of the church: but the characteristic organization and shape of fundamentalism is modern.

There is another important way in which modern conservative evangelical doctrine appears to be related to the older theological tradition: it relates itself to older doctrines through a process we may call formalization. Doctrinal elements from an older theology are conserved, but they are conserved formally: an element is conserved in such a way that it must be affirmed, but the affirmation does not mean that the doctrine in question plays a very great role or conveys a great deal of meaning. The function of the doctrine is to act as a sign of the correct conservatism of the believer, his rejection of 'modern' and 'critical' ways of thinking. The clearest example is the doctrine of the virgin birth of Jesus. Conservative evangelicals do not think about the virgin birth so very much; it does not play a major part in their preaching. It is there as a test case. Since the virgin birth is known from only very few biblical passages, and since there is no compelling reason for believing in it apart from these passages, a person who says he believes in it is demonstrating his willingness to believe in a quite extraordinary event on the basis of scripture alone. Conversely, if someone is going to dispute the apparent evidence of some part of the Bible on the grounds that certain extraordinary narratives cannot be taken as actual fact, or on the grounds that other parts of the New Testament managed to exist without knowing of this doctrine or at least without saying anything about it, or on the grounds that the doctrine, even if found in two of the gospels, still seems to make no sense in relation to the total structure of the faith – for any such person the virgin birth is likely to be the first obvious large-scale obstacle in traditional Christianity. It functions therefore as a test case, and historically has often been used exactly as such. Conservatives therefore emphasize the virgin birth very heavily in their doctrinal statements: it is the net that will catch the most slippery fish. But this means that the virgin birth within conservative religion is strongly formalized. There is no Mariology and little theological meditation in which the virgin birth provides an important source of imagery for the religious imagination, unless in Christmas services; but there the imagery is in any case non-distinctive, being used equally by the rankest liberals. The virgin birth is thus an emptied and formalized doctrine, emphasized not for its own content but because it furnishes the best test case for the authority of scripture on fundamentalist terms.

It might be suggested, perhaps, that the virgin birth does carry an important functional load within fundamentalist religion because it provides the basic evidence for the deity of Christ. A moment's thought should show that this is not so. Fundamentalists do not derive their belief in the deity of Christ particularly from the virgin birth passages; on the contrary, they suppose that there is a wide variety of biblical evidence showing that Jesus is God. The virgin birth passages function negatively in this respect: if a person says he is unwilling to affirm the virgin birth (and this is also a classic test case, since exactly this step has been taken by persons unwilling to accept conservative control in various churches), then he is understood by conservatives to be denying the deity of Christ. Here again the doctrine functions as a test rather than as a source of intrinsic content.

This matter of formalization of doctrines can be widely extended. The doctrine of the Trinity is another example. Fundamentalism shows no depth in understanding of the Trinity or meditation upon it. It shows no awareness of how the trinitarian doctrines were worked out or what they meant in their own original situation. The Trinity is a bare fact, which must be affirmed. The final reason why it must be affirmed is not that the traditional faith of the church has been trinitarian, or that the Fathers worked out a noble trinitarian doctrine – as far as these considerations count, fundamentalism would no doubt have been happy to take up a unitarian position, and indeed it is a basic and a justified argument for unitarianism that trinitarian doctrine is much more thinly evidenced in the Bible than traditional Christians think – but because it is there, as fundamentalists see it, in the Bible. Since trinitarian doctrine within the Bible is admittedly rather scanty and imprecise, and since exact formulations on the matter are patristic and much later, this helps us to understand why fundamentalists may easily be unorthodox on such issues: precision is attainable only through making excursions outside the field where biblical citations can settle the matter.

Sin is another doctrine that is heavily formalized in fundamentalism. Nothing is more constantly emphasized than 'the fact of sin'. Sin is different from a doctrine like the virgin birth: while the virgin birth is comparatively little used and carries a low functional load, sin carries a heavy functional load. It comes into everything or almost everything (one or two exceptions will be cited below). Sin is the reason why Christ had to die; it is the reason why the gospel has to be preached and heard; it is the source of all troubles and temptations in the Christian life. It therefore occurs in a large number of connections. Nevertheless it is formalized in another way. In fundamentalism sin has a sort of presuppositional status: it provides the reason why certain things are said and believed. If you ask what is the reason why one should be a conservative evangelical, rather than some other sort of Christian, the answer will very likely be: because of sin. Sin is so powerful and so bad that conservative evangelicalism is the only faith that faces up to its awfulness. Sin is the reason why we have a Jesus Christ, why we have a substitutionary atonement, why we have a Holy Spirit, why we need a second advent. It is, in short, the reason why we have got to be conservative evangelicals. Sin is a valuable intellectual resource to this form of religion: without it, it could not get anywhere.

But, precisely because sin thus works as an argumentative principle, we have to ask more closely what sort of understanding of it is actually to be found. Personal experience and study of the literature make it clear, in fact, that there is no evidence for a more profound or radical understanding of sin in conservative evangelicalism than in other branches of Christian faith. The contrary is the case: study of conservative writing on personal and ethical problems shows a strong tendency towards the trivialization of sin and evil. Simply to repeat the word 'sin' is not to demonstrate any deep analysis of what it is or what it does. The perpetual conservative evangelical boasting about their emphasis on sin should be severely discounted; there is no reason to accept the assertion that this is profoundly understood. This being so, all arguments that seek to validate the conservative evangelical religion on the grounds that it takes sin more seriously should be ignored.

Two examples can be given. If the idea of sin is to be profound and not merely moralistic and superficial, it must be applicable to the self of the religious man. It must have sufficient depth to show that the man of faith, in the very form of faith which he chooses and follows, is still subject to the force of sin, so that sin is an influence working upon and through his own religiosity, through his affirmation of his own form of faith. Does conservative evangelicalism teach that a man in and through his adherence to conservative evangelicalism may be following out his own sinful impulses, or that conservative faith may itself be a structure vitiated by the deep and all-pervading sinfulness of mankind? Of course it does not. Sin may be found in religion, but not in conservative evangelical religion. Sin is to be found in liberalism, in Roman Catholicism, and of course in non-Christian religions. This polemical approach to the matter blinds the fundamentalist to the presence and activity of sin in his own religious attitude. The understanding of sin in these regards is unashamedly partisan. Conservative evangelicals may suffer from the pressure of sin and temptation, but this is only because they are not as fully and consistently conservative evangelical as they might be. All in all, the doctrine of all-pervading sin is used as a premise to support the exclusive and partisan assertiveness of conservative evangelicalism, but there is no suggestion that this all-pervading sin may be a basic and deep-lying factor within that faith.

The second example is in the biblical writers themselves. The Bible is the holy of holies of fundamentalist religion. But, if sin is as profound and all-pervading as we are told, presumably it affects the Bible also? Not at all. The biblical writers were, indeed, sinners, justified sinners, but this did not at all affect what they wrote. Personally they could be very troublesome people, doing all sorts of things wrongly; even St Peter, according to St Paul, 'stood condemned' on a certain unhappy occasion (Gal. 2.11). But as writers of scripture, as distinct from their personal position, they were quite free from the distortion of sin. The moment they took pen in hand, sin fled out of the window, and what they wrote was a perfect expression of the will of God, in no way distorted by human sin. The idea that biblical writers may have been affected by personal animosities against one another, by misunderstandings and polemics, by partisan loyalties and pride, is entirely ignored by fundamentalist theory. But this means, necessarily, that sin is not so very serious after all. It does not affect the things that for fundamentalists are the ultimate principles. It is doubtful whether for them it affects even the reason, as we shall see: they tend to take rather the optimistic position that, though reason can be brought into servitude to sin and then misused, of itself it works perfectly well and is not necessarily in servitude to the passions.[13]

We sum up, then: though fundamentalists continually congratulate themselves on the belief that their form of religion takes sin more seriously than others, this assurance should not be believed. On the contrary, though the doctrine of a universal, all-pervading, totally horrific sin is a common argumentative premise in fundamentalism, there is no reason to suppose that it in fact contains any specially deep or serious insights into sin. In fact, it tends very easily to let sin be understood as specific lapses from conformity, or else in its personal advice to trivialize everything into minor matters. There is no reason to suppose that a fundamentalist Christian has deeper understanding of the way in which sin works in the heart and life of the average person than any Roman priest or any mainstream Protestant clergyman. The pretence of fundamentalism to a more profound and radical doctrine of sin is a bluff which should now be called.

But the fullest evidence for the formalizing character of fundamentalist faith comes, as we have already seen, from its treatment of the Bible. The essential thing in so many interpretations is that the event actually took place. Even if the event is emptied of significance, or if the significance attached to it in the interpretation is quite different from that which the Bible itself attaches to it, or is quite trivial and theologically unimportant, the all-important thing is that the Bible has been shown to be true. So many instances of this occur in the interpretations surveyed in this book that it is not necessary to cite specific instances here.

There are therefore many respects in which modern conservative evangelical doctrine represents a novelty in the history of Christianity, as many observers have maintained. It is only by looking at its affirmations in a formal way, without considering their interrelations and the total structure and motivation of belief, that they can be made to appear as if they corresponded with the position taken in older traditions of theology.

It is an exaggeration, on the other hand, if this point is pressed too far. From the point of view of the critic of fundamentalism this makes it too easy; and it tends to represent fundamentalism as a sort of strange and unforeseeable excrescence, suddenly appearing without warning in the body of Christendom, and (some might hope) likely to disappear equally suddenly. I fear that this is not so, and that there are deep roots for fundamentalism which stretch far back in the history of the church and probably back into the Bible itself. It was not until the time was ripe, in modern times, that these roots brought forth the fruit that we now perceive. But we cannot understand fundamentalism unless we take account of the intrinsic problems and structures, deeply built into the whole Jewish-Christian tradition, which have occasioned its birth.

The problems and structures I have in mind include the following. Firstly, the formation of 'holy scripture' in the first place was a fateful process: it led, not directly, but under certain conditions, to the appearance of the fundamentalist problem. The traditions that went into the corpus of material eventually known as the Bible contained a great deal of historical or history-like matter, including dates, names of persons and places, and synchronisms, and some of these were of great importance because they provided a locus in space and time for great events in the salvation of mankind. They also contained a great deal of doctrine which was understood to be the purest form of doctrine for true religion, along with specific ethical guidance, advice about one's way of life and so on. Not only that, but they contain also many discourses which are represented as having been the actual discourses of God himself, whether they are mediated through persons like prophets or not. In addition to this the Bible contains all sorts of other material describing social customs, traditional legends, customary moral reflections and so on. It includes speeches against God, as well as speeches by God, and it includes speeches by the wicked, as well as speeches by prophets and servants of God. To us it is obviously important and necessary that we should separate out the various kinds within this mixture. But we cannot be surprised that the men of the Bible themselves had no interest in doing anything of the sort. As the material slowly grew closer and closer to the status we now know as that of scripture, the tendency was for the entirety of materials within the sacred text to receive the same sacred status, and this tended to be the highest of the theological roles we have mentioned, the status of pure doctrine for the true religion, nay more, the status of a message actually formed and communicated by God himself. Though words of God were only one element in the mixture, the entirety came to be thought of as the 'Word of God'. The fact that there were passages, like the Ten Commandments, which were fairly close to the status of pure doctrine and which were supposed to have come direct from God himself, was extended into the supposition that the whole corpus came from God in the same way.

Thus the character and formation of 'holy scripture' gave an impression, already in ancient times, that everything contained in a book had the status of truth actually enunciated by God.

This fact was further reinforced, secondly, by the process of exegesis and interpretation, later stages of scripture interpreting earlier, and post-biblical ages interpreting the whole. Interpretation certainly rightly caught the broad outlines of the biblical message, and it is fortunate for us that it did so. But it also made use of the minutest details, and it not seldom acted as if any word or word group, whether an intelligible unit or not, and whether taken in context or not, and whether taken in its original sense or not, was a valid theological unit for the establishment of a doctrinal or exegetical point. It also allowed, over long periods, wide variety in general interpretative principles: one might take the 'plain' meaning (for which, unfortunately, no quite clear criterion existed), but one might also use allegory, and then there was typology, and so on. And, since the entire scripture, once that entity became established, was alike authoritative, interpretation built up highly complex relations between one part of the Bible and another. As far back as Origen a list of names or places in the book of Numbers was already surely some kind of divine message, full of theological content, for God would certainly not have enunciated such a message unless he had something important to say through it. Thus anything within the scriptural text could in principle be of vital importance; and that meant that reverence and authority must extend to it all.

Thirdly, however, in this interpretative process one element was lacking until a very late stage. That element was the process of historical and critical investigation. In Greek historiography, and in the tradition of classical literary studies, this element was present and active from an early time. It was said: this story is told, but I do not believe it; or, this story is told, but it is contradicted by this other; or, this story is told, but I do not believe it goes back to the person about whom it is related. Jewish and Christian interpretation of the Bible contained many and violent disagreements, but this particular type of critical investigation scarcely figured among them. Apart from very occasional flickers of critical questioning during the Middle Ages, it was not until post-Renaissance and post-Reformation times that critical investigation of this sort got a grip. It then came in, partly through contagion from the critical methods being used on other, and especially classical, literatures, and partly through theological conflicts, in which the rise of new theological positions both encouraged, and was encouraged by, the critical approach to the Bible. But by this time an understanding of the Bible, in which this critical approach had no place, had a millennium and a half of established authority to go on.

The fourth element that comes from sources deep within our tradition and which is built into fundamentalism is the tradition of doctrinal exclusiveness. In Israel one is moving in this direction as far back as Deuteronomy, and in the New Testament it is appearing in the later marginal writings. In neither Testament is it at the centre of the religion in its time of maximum growth and creativity; but in the canonical Testaments, as they lie before us as finished books, it is evident enough. And in the church thereafter, for many centuries, the degree to which doctrinal conformity was exacted, and the concepts of heresy and excommunication employed, was very extensive.

In other words, the basic patterns that permitted the much later rise of Protestant fundamentalism were there at an early stage. They go back into the Bible itself, the nature of its formation and the conceptions which people had of it, as far back as the time of Deuteronomy and Ezra. This fact is one reason for the phenomenon already mentioned, that attitudes to holy scripture which have some similarity to Protestant fundamentalism are to be traced also in Judaism, in Islam, in Roman Catholicism and in Greek Orthodoxy. In none of these, however, did these built-in features of the biblical tradition and its interpretation go on to produce a full fundamentalism of the Protestant type, because in all they were modified by other factors that were present: for instance, by the presence of a developed and explicit philosophical theology, by the use of allegorizing exegesis, by the acceptance of the authority of tradition in the synagogue and the church. Only in Protestant evangelicalism, from the eighteenth century on, did it transpire that the ground was ready for the birth of full fundamentalism. In it these other, modifying and restraining, factors had been eliminated. From the Reformation it had inherited a doctrine of 'by scripture only', which eliminated the authority of church tradition as a serious rival. It no longer had any basic philosophical theology or philosophical dialogue with the world. The wide-ranging allegorical exegesis of scripture had been greatly curtailed, and the emphasis was left on two great elements: the things that had taken place, in correspondence with the narratives about them in the Bible, and the doctrines that were enunciated as infallible teaching. On top of this came the loss of confidence in the existing church institution as the sphere in which salvation is to be found, something hardly to be traced back before the eighteenth century. Add to this the idea, also coming from eighteenth-century evangelicalism, that instead of theologies and complicated intellectual doctrinal systems you can work with a simplified list of essentials, and the nineteenth-century materialistic emphasis on the mere happening of events, rather than on their significance, as the central form of truth. Set alongside this the fact of rising critical scholarship, cutting right across this inherited set of attitudes to the Bible and dividing up the whole cake in a quite different set of slices, and pressing upon church and theology in the Anglo-Saxon countries especially in the latter part of the nineteenth century – and you have the intellectual pedigree of fundamentalism. And fundamentalism from the beginning considered itself entitled to apply to itself the principle of doctrinal exclusiveness, and to treat non-conservative doctrinal positions just as so many heresies and deviations had been treated throughout much of the history of the church.

Thus fundamentalism has roots that lie deep within our traditional heritage and go back into the Bible itself. Even fundamentalists will, I think, see that in saying this I am not saying anything to justify their position. On the contrary, my argument goes in the other direction: precisely because there is an element within the Bible and within our tradition which can lead and has led to fundamentalism, it is important that we see the Bible in a different way. Or, again, I am not saying that the Bible in any way lends its authority to fundamentalism. We are not talking in terms of authority here, but of the history of religions. I am not citing evidences which justify fundamentalism, but considering materials within the Bible and later tradition which help to explain it. Our purpose is understanding, not the establishment of authority. Or, if we must put it negatively, those elements in the Bible which can lead and have led to fundamentalism are elements upon which we today have to look critically. Not simply because they have led to fundamentalism: this would hardly be sufficient reason for such a critical look; but rather because these are elements which, not necessarily but at least potentially, block out our understanding of other, deeper-laid, more basic, and more creative strata within the Bible itself.

So, to return to our basic question, it is not fundamentalism, but the main stream of modern theology, including its involvement in critical biblical scholarship, that really stands in continuity with classical theology, whether of the Bible, the Fathers, the Reformers or the period after the Reformers and coming up to the beginning of modern times. There are things in fundamentalism that grew out of the older history of Christianity, but its inner structural continuity with that history is very limited. There are things in modern theology that differ from what was there in the older history of the faith, but modern theology stands in real continuity with that past.[14]

To argue and expound this in full would go beyond the space available and also beyond my own competence. I shall express it in a simple way only. The critical historical method, as used upon the Bible, did not grow up as a mere technical device, purely scientific in purpose. It grew up in the context of theological questionings and conflicts, and people developed some of the methods as tools for use in these religious difficulties. The critical method and the positions characteristic of modern theology grew up together, and it is often very hard to tell which of the two came first in application to any particular problem. The changing theological understanding and the use of the critical approach to the Bible stimulated one another. Conservative apologists are often very bitter because critical scholars regard the critical method as 'scientific', as if it had grown up without any theological presuppositions at all.[15] Their complaint is to be rejected, firstly because critical scholarship does not depend on such a justification, and secondly because the complaint is mere hypocrisy, since exactly the same claim is made by conservative scholarship.[16] As far as being scientific goes, the position is not that critical methods were worked out without theological and philosophical presuppositions but that they continue to stand, once they have been worked out, with other theological and philosophical presuppositions than those with which they were worked out. Thus, even if it had been true, as it is not, that the analysis of the pentateuchal sources had been worked out on the basis of Hegelian and evolutionary assumptions, this would not matter. It would matter only if the analysis depended logically upon these assumptions, in such a way that all persons holding to the analysis must hold these assumptions. Since this is not so, and even conservative apologists have not even tried to show this, the matter can be forgotten. The main reason why some major critical analyses can and should be regarded as stable is that they are upheld by a large variety of scholars who hold quite different philosophical and theological assumptions.

The critical position is thus an *open* position, in a respect in which the conservative evangelical one is a *closed* position. In so far as the latter works at all, or seems to work, it works solely and exclusively for people who as a matter of fact are fundamentalists in their religious life and in their doctrine of scripture. Pieces here and there will be found to be shared or agreed with persons whose ideological background is different; but where will a person be found who is not a fundamentalist and who yet affirms the ensemble of interpretations that I have quoted from conservative evangelical literature?

But this is not the present point. My point is this: the questions and difficulties which led to the critical approach did indeed arise within the bosom of theological change and the asking of them was often motivated by the drive for theological change. But this is entirely right! This is a sign of the fact that the older theology had difficulties and inner contradictions. These had their outward expression in theological conflicts: but their inner reason was the fact that the biblical basis (and the post-biblical historical basis) was seen no longer to fit the conclusions that were based upon it. The following up of these questions was a right, necessary and proper way of standing in continuity with that older theological tradition. Many of the early questions of critical study of the Bible were raised by deists, rationalists, liberals and so on, and conservatives tend to point to this as if this was some sort of reason why answers arising from these questions are vitiated. This is not at all so. An opinion may have been voiced by a deist, but it simply leaves the question: what do we say to the evidence that the deist put forward? If there was a shift from (say) eighteenth-century orthodoxy to nineteenth-century liberalism, there were very good reasons in the structure of the former which caused people to move to the latter. And none of this was done, as conservative apologists pretend, by the working out of a totally theoretical and preconceived theology, which was then simply imposed upon the facts and details. Never have the facts and the details of the Bible been so carefully sifted as in the period of shift from eighteenth-century theology to modern theology with its close alliance with critical method.

Thus the very change as we pass from older orthodoxy to modern theology is itself a sign of the living continuity of the latter with the former. But the fundamentalists have perhaps been right in one major point, more right, indeed, than the main body of Christian opinion. They have perceived, however dimly, that modern theology and the critical study of the Bible have initiated, and are initiating, massive changes in the way in which Christians understand

God and Jesus Christ. Well-meaning persons, dazed and perplexed by the fury of fundamentalist attacks on modern developments, have often answered that no essential of the faith is changed. The new critical approach, they have argued, has immensely illuminated the Bible, making it possible for us to see it as a human book in its true historical and geographical setting; it has incidentally caused us to change the sort of formulations in which the authority of the Bible was expressed; but, these things being so, everything else could stay as it has been. Belief in God, the understanding of Christ, the character of faith, the ethical demands of Christianity – all of these in their essentials could remain as they had been in the past. Conservatives are perhaps right in their instinct that this is not so, and that major changes are taking place, with perhaps even greater ones to come. But I would say: firstly, these changes, real as they are, are changes for the better, not for the worse; secondly, these changes are a continuation of a line which was already traceable in Christian theology before they took place, and indeed are in part a consequence of that earlier line of development. The conservative appeal back to a fixed past orthodoxy, which should never have been allowed to change, is an appeal back to a fictitious past that was never there. It is, interestingly enough, the absence of a doctrine of tradition within fundamentalism, and therefore a lack of loving care for the truth of the past (apart from the Bible), which allows it to live by such a fictitious past.

7 · Variations and Conflicts

It should not be imagined that conservative evangelical faith possesses a monolithic unity. On the contrary, some marked conflicts and tensions may lie within it at any one time. The idea that evangelicals are in principle at unity with one another, though pleasant as an ideal, has often been difficult to translate into actuality. On the contrary, conservatives have been on the whole a remarkably quarrelsome segment of Christendom, and it has required considerable talent on the part of the leadership from time to time to prevent violent conflicts from breaking out. These efforts indeed have not been always successful. Vehemently held doctrinal views, fed by the principle of doctrinal exclusiveness, can easily produce deep personal enmities and schisms. This has been particularly noticeable in the United States. Bob Jones, a leading conservative and the founder of Bob Jones University, is said to have stated that Billy Graham had done more harm to the cause of Jesus Christ than any man alive.[1] According to Erickson, after Machen and his group, withdrawing from Princeton, had founded the Orthodox Presbyterian Church and Westminster Theological Seminary, a group led by Carl McIntyre withdrew and founded the Faith Seminary and the Bible Presbyterian Church. 'Soon Faith Seminary was also rent asunder and Covenant College and Seminary was founded in St Louis. The continual splintering of conservative Christianity has brought disrepute upon the church.'[2] It will not be the purpose of this chapter, however, to dwell upon such drastic instances of conflict, but rather to point to variations of importance which do affect the total understanding of fundamentalism. Moreover, not only are there disagreements or difference of emphasis which may at any time lurk under the surface of conservative evangelicalism as a whole, but the movement itself is probably changing through time, adopting some new forms and discarding some old. A few examples of these variations and changes will be discussed in this chapter.

1. *Calvinism and Arminianism*

A prominent illustration, to begin with, is furnished by the contrast between the Calvinist and the Arminian[3] theological traditions within evangelicalism, a contrast which in the English-speaking world can best be traced back to the differences between Whitefield and Wesley respectively among the great eighteenth-century evangelists.[4] As is notorious, ideas of election and predestination belong to the Calvinist side: man cannot help himself except in so far as God has already chosen and called him, and nothing that man can do can of itself alter his standing with God. To the Arminian tradition this seems to derogate from human freedom and responsibility: salvation is certainly made available by God, but man has at least the task of accepting or appropriating it. The grace of God is not irresistible, as some Calvinists held, and man can reject it; thus a man can be a Christian and yet later fall from grace.

At least in the Anglo-Saxon world, in spite of some significant exceptions,[5] conservative evangelicals tend towards the Arminian side. In this they are probably influenced for the most part by the strategic needs of evangelism: Christ died for all men, but he calls them to come to him, they have to take the decision to accept him, and if they do not accept then they are rejecting. God will not save automatically, but only if the gospel is preached and then is accepted. This emphasis is very strong in most types of evangelization. The stress on human decision and on the creating of the necessary conditions for it are sometimes so strong as to earn, both from the more Calvinist side and also from non-conservative opinion generally, the judgment that evangelistic movements, like that of Billy Graham, are in the end humanistic and man-centred, rather than God-centred, in their implications. In the common Arminian-style evangelization, the biblical passages about election and predestination, far from being taken literally or with their natural force, are sharply down-graded, as one would expect – yet another case where theological difficulties mean that the Bible is not 'taken literally'.

To this we may add another contrast that in part overlaps with the one just discussed, though it is harder to define. There is one side of conservative evangelicalism that is more doctrinal and controversial in its approach, another that is more interested in inward piety and the cultivation of the spiritual life. A parallel can be drawn with older stages of religious development: we can compare the older Protestant orthodoxies of the seventeenth and eighteenth centuries, with their extremely detailed dogmatic definitions and their highly controversial form of discourse, and the reaction of pietism, with its emphasis on the religion of the heart as against doctrinal formulae and dead orthodoxies.[6] Both of these traditions have flowed into conservative evangelicalism as we know it, but the distinction of type and emphasis can still be made between them. The more 'pietistic' wing of conservative evangelicalism can be seen in the movement often styled 'conventions for the deepening of spiritual life', of which the best-known example is the Keswick Convention. Such movements do not differ substantially in belief from the more doctrinally and apologetically-conscious aspects of conservative evangelicalism. They believe the same things, but the emphasis is different. The stress in the 'pietistic' wing is on inward piety, on prayer, on quiet Bible-reading, on the attainment of personal sanctification, rather than on exact formulation. 'Liberalism' and biblical criticism are met more with tearful sorrow than with angry controversy.

I shall do no more than mention one issue that has sometimes appeared in this context and troubled the waters of conservative evangelicalism, namely the question whether perfection is attainable by Christians in this life. A faith stressing personal sanctification might well strive towards such an end, while a more Calvinistic emphasis would deprecate the whole quest. For our present purpose this may be important because of the various 'holiness' movements of the present century. If I understand it rightly, holiness movements will hold fundamentalist views of the Bible, but the stress will move from questions of conflict with liberalism and modernism to a much more inward and personal question, how the ordinary Christian can pass into the state of sanctification and possess holiness. I have not, however, been able to do any research along this line. More 'orthodox' evangelical currents will sometimes regard these endeavours as dangerously optimistic or illusory; critics will say that the illusion of perfection can lead people to underestimate the power of sin and temptation and actually lead them into grossly immoral behaviour.

These are just some of the differences in emphasis to be found within conservative evangelicalism. No more need be said about them at the moment, except that we should note how a common fundamentalist view of the Bible does not succeed in providing a clear or unitary basis for faith. Even within a strictly fundamentalist outlook, indeed a good deal more within it than within a critically-informed reading of the Bible, there can be a wide divergence of religious emphases, according as one stresses one element of the Bible or another.

2. *Millennialism*

A more important area of tension is that concerning eschatology, the expectation of the end of the world. All conservative evangelicals lay considerable stress on the second advent of Jesus Christ. But a great deal depends on the emphasis with which this is done. The emphasis may be on the personal relation of the believer with Christ, his readiness for the end, the relativization of all earthly goods and status because of the imminent coming of the Lord. But for many fundamentalists the interest in the future goes much farther: it becomes an all-embracing passion for schemes that will work out the time of the end, the order of the various events of the final sequence, the detailed interpretations of books like Daniel, Ezekiel and Revelation, and the exact identification of figures like the Antichrist and periods like the millennium. A distinction commonly used is that between 'premillennial' and 'postmillennial': the former means that Christ will come before the beginning of the thousand years during which the saints are expected to reign with him, and the latter means that the millennium takes place first.[7]

Such schemes have their point of origin in the common fundamentalist religion, as we have outlined it; but when they come to be sufficiently emphasized, they alter the balance of that religion. The forecasting of the end comes to be the central preoccupation, and other things fall into the background. The dominant element is so-called 'prophecy', that is, the working out from the apocalyptic texts of a scheme for the second advent and the end of the world. The stress shifts from the death of Christ, conversion, forgiveness and justification to the apocalyptic elements: the secret 'rapture' of the saints, the identification of Gog and Magog (figures from Ezek. 38–39, cf. Rev. 20.8) and the location of Armageddon, the final battle between the forces of light and of darkness.

Millennial speculation cuts across the field of fundamentalist religious life in many ways. The more orthodox conservative groups often seek to damp down at least the overt expression of millennial enthusiasm, mainly because they realize, and rightly, that it is a serious obstacle to the main task of presenting the evangelical gospel to the average man of the present day. For instance, the conservative literature researched for this book seems on the whole to avoid giving positive encouragement to millennial enthusiasm in the interpretation of books like Daniel and Revelation.[8] Millennial interest is also a dangerous threat to the unity of evangelicals: millennial schemes are many, and quarrels among their adherents are often bitter. The conflicts between them illustrate once again that the fundamentalist approach to the Bible is not by any means a way of reaching an agreed understanding of it. And, though millennialism is often not actively encouraged, it remains a constant threat to moderate conservative evangelicalism, and a temptation to which evangelical faith by its own logic may very easily succumb.

Of the various millennial schemes, none has been so influential as the so-called dispensationalism, to which we shall devote some greater and more detailed attention. The scheme is associated particularly with J. N. Darby (1800–82), at first a Church of Ireland clergyman and later a main founder of the Plymouth Brethren, which movement was long convulsed by his violent quarrels over millennial doctrine with his fellow-millenarian B. W. Newton. It is best known, however, and most influential, through its presentation in the *Scofield Reference Bible* (OUP), prepared by the American C. I. Scofield and first published in 1909. The influence of the Scofield Bible has been historically enormous. It is said that two million copies were sold in the first generation. From my own experience I would say that in many conservative evangelical student groups, as they were in the early 1950s, perhaps a half, and among those who had been brought up in conservative evangelical homes a larger proportion, were well accustomed to the Scofield Bible and regarded its interpretations as normal, often being surprised to discover that any other interpretation is possible. The text is the ordinary King James text, but its divisions and its notes impart a very decided interpretation. The casual reader will hardly notice this; but a careful study will soon reveal the drastic effects which this presentation has upon the meaning of the Bible. 'The *Scofield Reference Bible* combined an attractive format of typography, paragraphing, notes, and cross references with the theology of Darbyite dispensationalism. The book has thus been subtly but powerfully influential in spreading those views among hundreds of thousands who have regularly read that Bible and who often have been unaware of the distinction between the ancient text and the Scofield interpretation.'[9]

Dispensationalism is a premillennial scheme, that is, the second advent of Christ takes place before the millennium (but see a further complication in a moment). There are seven dispensations, different succeeding systems of relations between God and man:

they are Innocency, Conscience, Human Government (beginning with Noah), Promise, Law (from Moses to Christ), Grace (the age of the church) and Kingdom (the Millennium). The church is a purely spiritual fellowship of true believers and is quite distinct from the empirical ecclesiastical bodies commonly known as churches. At a time known only to God the true church will be secretly 'raptured' (a key word in the whole scheme) out of the world and taken to 'meet the Lord in the air' (the central text for this all-important concept is I Thess. 4.17).

Even more characteristic is the following. The church is a mystery. It is so much a mystery that it had been hidden even from the prophets of the Old Testament. 'Israel had been a worldly kingdom with material promises and blessings. The Messiah had come to fulfil that worldly kingdom but had been rejected by his people. When that happened, God had broken the continuity of history, stopped the prophetic clock, and instituted the church. When the church is raptured out of this world, this clock will start again and God will return to the task of dealing with the earthly problems of Israel.'[10] This is an essential feature of dispensationalism: the age of the church is a sort of afterthought, an interim stage between two stages in which God works through Israel, through the Jews.

Now this approach means that the events predicted by prophets like Daniel will take place, and in the future. But one of the major difficulties that had brought many millenarians to disaster is avoided. Many of them had sought, by reference to the figures and images in Daniel and Revelation, to work out the date of the second advent, only to be embarrassed when the stated date came and nothing took place. This was because they had worked by the so-called 'historical' mode of interpretation, that is, they had reckoned periods straight forward through history, ending up with a date such as 1843 or 1844. This type of interpretation had two great disadvantages: firstly, it was a disappointment when the date came and still no end of the world but, secondly, if the date was still far in the future, eschatological expectation could only be dimmed, since by the timetable one might have many years to wait. By the Darby-Scofield scheme, since the age of the church was not included in the figures of any prophecy, the time of the rapture is not predictable; it may be at any moment. Actually, the position is still more complicated, for it is common to distinguish between the rapture, when the living believers are suddenly and secretly taken out of the world and go to meet the Lord, and the second advent, which is a public event, visible to all the world, and occurring later.

Still more important for the structure of dispensationalism is the contrast between the church and the kingdom. The kingdom, to which the Bible looks forward, is a completely different matter from the church: it is a restored Jewish kingdom. The events of the end, the great tribulation, Armageddon and so on, come after the church has been removed from the world in order to reign with Christ. The final events, being concerned with a restored Jewish kingdom, are set in the Holy Land and connected with wars and persecutions there, and with the conversion of the Jews to Christianity. The church is thus an interim stage between two stages of the kingdom, promised to the Jews but then postponed because of their rejection of Christ. In this scheme Old Testament prophecies naturally play an important part. These are taken 'literally', in the sense that a reference to 'Israel' remains always a reference to Israel, the Jewish people, and can never be transferred to the church; similarly, reference to events of the last times in places in Palestine must mean real future events in these places. The fact that such events had not yet occurred, precisely as described, before New Testament times is one unchallengeable proof that these prophecies have still to be fulfilled, which leads naturally to the entire scheme of a new age, after the church, in which God will once again work through Israel.

But the most drastic effects of the entire scheme fall upon the picture of Jesus and his teaching. The dispensation of grace, the age of the church, begins with the death and resurrection of Christ, and the doctrine of grace and of the church is therefore not to be found in the teaching of Jesus in the gospels, but in the epistles. 'The *doctrines* of grace are to be sought in the Epistles, not in the Gospels . . . The Gospels do not unfold the doctrine of the Church.'[11] It is true, there is some limited degree of overlap, which depends upon complicated exegetical principles which need not be gone into here. But basically Jesus, in much or most of the teaching recorded in the gospels, is talking to Jews on the basis of the law, and not to the church on the basis of grace.

The implications of this for the understanding of his teaching are devastating. 'The Sermon on the Mount in its primary application gives neither the privilege nor the duty of the Church. These are found in the Epistles. Under the law of the kingdom, for example, no one may hope for forgiveness who has not first forgiven. Under grace the Christian is exhorted to forgive because he is already forgiven.' Again, in St Matthew's gospel 'it is the Gospel of the kingdom which he preaches. The Gospel of Grace is something different'.[12] Or, most strikingly, 'as a rule of life, it [viz. the Sermon on the Mount] is addressed to the Jew before the cross and to the Jew in the coming kingdom, and is therefore not now in effect'.[13] People not accustomed to dispensational doctrine will be equally taken aback to find the Lord's prayer also under something of a shadow. Though it is 'an incomparable model for all prayer', in its primary sense it does not belong to the church age: 'used as a *form*, the Lord's prayer is, dispensationally, upon legal, not church ground; it is not a prayer in the name of Christ; and it makes human forgiveness, as under the law it must, the condition of divine forgiveness; an order which grace exactly reverses.'[14] As a consequence there are people who consider it improper to use the Lord's prayer in the church.

I have stated the dispensational position very simply here, since this is sufficient for the purposes of our present discussion; but readers should not suppose that it is in fact simple. On the contrary, the task of fitting this general scheme into the detail of the biblical text requires an extremely complex apparatus of distinctions, discriminations and explanations, which form the main content of Scofield's notes. In addition to the seven dispensations already mentioned, the reader has to know about the eight covenants with the distinct relation of Christ to each one of them (Scofield, note to Heb. 8.8), about the eleven greater 'mysteries' (Scofield, note to Matt. 13.11), about the seven sorts of resurrection to be found in scripture (Scofield, note to I Cor. 15.52) and so on. Exact verbal phraseology can often be very important: the church is not often so named, as everyone knows, in the gospels, and the reason has already been indicated, namely that the church did not commence as a stage during the gospel period. In the supremely famous passage (Matt. 16.18) Jesus says 'upon this rock will I build my church', and the future tense, 'I *will* build it' indicates clearly that he is not going to build it now: in the next dispensation he will be building it, and the verse figures in Scofield's index accordingly as 'the church, predicted by Christ' – it is a prediction of what he is going to do later on. Sometimes verbal distinctions are taken to indicate real theological distinctions, and the most characteristic and important of these concerns the key term 'kingdom'. All readers know that some sources speak of the 'kingdom of God' and others of the 'kingdom of heaven'. One might be disposed to think that this was a stylistic difference, both phrases designating the same theological reality; but not so in dispensationalism. In it the kingdom of God is a different reality from the kingdom of heaven. The kingdom of God is universal and includes celestial beings like angels, but the kingdom of heaven, paradoxically, is earthly and Davidic; but since 'the kingdom of heaven is the earthly sphere of the universal kingdom of God, the two have almost all things in common' (Scofield, note on Matt. 6.33; cf. notes on Matt. 3.2 and 13.11). In fact, in order to apply the doctrine of the kingdom to the detailed texts a mind-boggling series of distinctions and complications is required.

And this is the first point about which something must be said when we consider the significance of millennialism for the difference between general fundamentalism and critical scholarship. One of the most popular fundamentalist arguments against biblical criticism is based upon the plain man's dislike of the complex and apparently artificial nature of the distinctions it sets up within the Bible: distinctions between early texts and later texts, between J and D and P, between different theologies, between the opinions of later redactors and those of the original writers. No one who tolerates dispensational millennialism – and fundamentalists generally tolerate it, even if they do not espouse it – has the right to complain about the artificiality and complexity of J, P and D. The distinctions and separations of critical scholarship are models of clarity, simplicity and naturalness when compared with those involved in dispensational or other millenarian schemes.

To say this is not to sneer at a system like dispensationalism. On the contrary, Darby-Scofield dispensationalism is a remarkable achievement of the mythopoeic fantasy. As a feat of the imagination it might well compare with the apocalyptic poems of Blake, and indeed these latter may have done something to influence its origin. Not that dispensational writing counts as literature; this was hardly to be expected when its genre of literary expression is something like Scofield's annotations. Whatever one thinks of it in relation to truth, and even if one looks on it as a mass of myth and fiction, dispensationalism is a remarkable and in many ways original approach to the understanding of the Bible. Though fully fundamentalist in almost every aspect, dispensationalism has originality and creativity of a sort that is lacking in 'orthodox' fundamentalism. It offers something new. Its most fervent devotee can hardly boast that dispensationalism is the faith which all the saints through all the ages have professed. On the contrary, it is something quite different: at a time when fundamentalism of orthodox type can be only merely conservative, recalling us to truths that were acknowledged before liberalism came along, dispensationalism reveals a total and peculiar system of interpretation about which no one knew before the mid-nineteenth century.

But, whatever may be said about its creativity, when it is considered as a statement of Christian theological truth dispensationalism creates for fundamentalist faith a difficulty in the opposite direction: for it can scarcely be doubted that dispensational doctrine is heretical and should count as such, if the term 'heresy' is to have any meaning. If dispensationalism is not heresy, then nothing is heresy. In comparison with it, many of the traditional deviations commonly branded as heretical, such as Pelagianism, Monophysitism, Nestorianism and the like, are no more than minor disturbances in the flow of the entire doctrinal current of Christianity. Dispensationalism is more like Gnosticism among the traditional heresies, in that it creates almost an entire new mythology of its own, though this mythology takes the outward form of biblical interpretation. I am not saying this as a form of attack on dispensationalism itself. The question concerns fundamentalism itself and in general. Although fundamentalism prides itself on its orthodoxy and freely uses the charge of heresy against supposedly deviant opinions, it is extremely lenient towards dispensationalism. There are many conservative scholars who are quite opposed to dispensationalism, and who go to some lengths to show how it is wrong; but they seldom or never turn upon it the violent and hostile attacks they direct towards deviations in a liberal sense. Liberal and modernist deviations are worse than heresy, they are not Christian positions, even deviant ones, at all; they are completely beyond the pale of true Christianity. This is the normal fundamentalist attitude in doctrinal discussion. Nothing of this violence can be found in the criticisms of dispensational, or other millenarian, doctrine by these same writers. E. J. Young, for instance, a scholar of an unbending conservatism, writing on Daniel 9, reviews the dispensationalist interpretation and tells us that 'the difficulties which this view entails are very great'.[15] Similarly Ladd who, again from an extremely conservative viewpoint, but having a deeper acquaintance with critical scholarship, devotes a whole book to an examination of the question, also generally uses the word 'difficulties' about the dispensational approach.[16] Difficulties! It is clear that many conservative scholars, even when they do not support the dispensational scheme, consider it a permitted option or variation. The idea that it is thoroughly destructive of Christian understanding of the Bible seems scarcely to occur to them. No far-reaching criticism of its effects on faith and doctrine is attempted; rather, its interpretations are rather respectfully examined on their own merits, and dropped only because of their 'difficulties'. The case cannot be understood otherwise: conservative writers, though their nose is very sharp for any heresy or unorthodoxy that tends in a liberal direction, are quite insensitive to the possibility of it when it comes from a conservative direction. Their claims for 'orthodoxy' are a sham: they add up in the end to no more than that all conservative positions are possible, but all liberal deviations are utterly wrong. By allowing dispensationalist millenarianism as a permitted variation, conservative evangelicals are on their own terms making themselves answerable for it even when they themselves do not accept it.

To avoid misunderstanding, let it be clear what I mean. I do not criticize dispensational millenarianism on the ground that it is heretical. This is not my own position on the matter. Personally, I believe that the concept of heresy has ceased to be functionally useful for the evaluation of present-day theological opinions. When we say that this or that is heretical, all we are saying is that, in those days in which there was such a thing as heresy, when heresy was a useful functioning concept, this opinion would then have been heretical. Conservatives and fundamentalists themselves, however, use orthodoxy and heresy as positively functioning concepts for the present day; and just because they do so, their toleration of dispensationalism shows that they do not in fact apply these concepts strictly towards deviations that are also conservative in their attitude to scripture.

Dispensationalism is a totally fundamentalist scheme. Liberal and critical analyses lie almost entirely below its horizon. While 'orthodox' fundamentalism is very busy in polemics against modern criticism, once we get into the dispensational world we are in a very different atmosphere: here liberal and critical perceptions scarcely need to be combated, because they scarcely exist. If your main concern in life is in the secret rapture of the saints and its relation to the great tribulation, you do not need to bother your mind much with J, D and P. Orthodox fundamentalism has to trouble about J, D and P because it comes a good deal closer to critical scholarship in its methods: because it understands the Bible in some degree as a human product, conditioned by the stylistic and cultural conventions of its time, it has to combat those who carry that same understanding farther and produce splits and cleavages in the Bible that fundamentalism will not tolerate. Dispensationalism, on the other hand, though it may say with general fundamentalism that the Bible is in principle a human book as well as divinely-inspired holy scripture, in fact goes a good deal farther in treating it as a direct transcript of the divine will. The surface markings of the biblical text, though they have to be interpreted under the guidance of the dispensational hermeneutical guidelines, once this has been done are a direct transcript of God's work and his future plans. The order in which elements appear, the number of times they appear, and the verbal distinctions which accompany them on one occasion as against another – all of these may be completely direct indications of different realities of the theological world.[17]

But, in spite of its total and unquestioning fundamentalism, the dispensational scheme paradoxically has a certain analogy or kinship with critical scholarship that is lacking in 'orthodox' fundamentalism. The whole dispensational framework is in a certain mad way an attempt to cope with problems and facts that were being dealt with by critical study at the same time in a completely different mental world. Dispensationalism gives some sort of recognition, however distorted, to the fact that what Jesus says is not the same as what Paul says, that the gospels have a different theological role from the epistles, and that the idea of the kingdom of God does not easily fit into the customary structures of Christian doctrine. It recognizes that there are basic differences here. But, because it does not in the slightest think of explaining them as human differences, as differing ideas and images held by different persons at various times, it has to reify the differences and understand them as separate real stages in the actual plan and work of God. It is thus a little less bound to harmonization than is 'orthodox' fundamentalism. On all minor and historical points, indeed, it follows the same kind of harmonization as is found in general fundamentalism:[18] but on certain major theological issues, where the dispensational scheme will allow, it can permit important differences of emphasis which 'orthodoxy' would often want to harmonize away. Thus the idea that the doctrine of Paul is significantly different from the teaching of Jesus, which for most fundamentalists is a shocking liberal idea, is within certain limits recognized in dispensationalism: not, of course, as a matter of different understandings, but as exact transcripts of the divine truth for two different dispensational stages.

Critical separations depend on the identification of human authors and their ideas, and the ordering of sources along a scale of time; the dispensational scheme assumes full divine origin and full correspondence with divine actuality for all scripture alike and in all its details, but it has to construct a speculative future timetable, destructive of the central theological truth of the Bible, in order to marshal the 'prophetic' texts into some kind of unity. Thus millenarianism illustrates to a very high degree the way in which interpretation does not simply emerge from the Bible but is imposed upon it through the application of a highly rigid conceptual framework. One of the main services of critical and historical scholarship has been to soften the rigidity of these frameworks. As critical study sees it, much of the variety within the Bible is accounted for through human diversity of ideas and situations and through historical development. Even then a theological framework is needed, in order that we may deal with the Bible as a theological guide for today. But a theological framework working under the circumstances of critical study does not have to provide a theological account for everything. The less the influence allowed to critical study – and in dispensationalism this reaches the point of nil – the more rigid and elaborate the dogmatic system that is required.

Now, it would be a mistake to exaggerate the degree of influence that dispensationalism and other millenarian views exercise upon the conservative evangelical movement as a whole. No doubt there are many quite extreme fundamentalists who not only do not hold millenarian views but do not even know that they are held at all. Such people, while believing steadfastly in the second advent and holding the expectation that God in Christ has an important future purpose for the world, as evidenced in the eschatological passages of the Bible, have no interest in working out the details of that future or making it into a hard and fast scheme. For them the passage of Acts 1.7, 'It is not for you to know the times or the seasons, which the Father hath put in his own power', is sufficient. Whether this is a sufficient force to put a stop to millenarian speculation, once one has met with it, is another matter.

The influence of millenarianism on the conservative evangelical movement as a whole goes far beyond what can be measured by numbers alone. First of all, millenarianism has historically been a very important force in the development of modern fundamentalism. Sandeen has argued, and very convincingly in my opinion, that the fundamentalist position from the beginning was not 'only a conservative restatement of doctrines traditionally accepted by the church'.[19] On the contrary, the position was worked out through an alliance between millenarians and non-millenarian conservatives, an alliance called into being by their common hostility to biblical criticism. All five articles on biblical inspiration in *The Fundamentals* were written by 'veteran millenarians' and much of the leading and directing force in the whole enterprise came from millenarians.[20] This seems to me to be very probable; but even if Sandeen's judgment, as a matter of American church history, should require modification, the following remarks are not derived from it and can stand independently of it.

One can easily see a reason why millenarian views may lie at the foundation of much fundamentalism. Millenarian doctrine entails a much more violent rejection of all modern theology and all biblical criticism than is necessarily entailed by the general doctrine and experience of evangelicals. For example, deep scepticism towards the existing church institutions could arise from well-understandable experience: but it is in millenarianism that an almost total negativism towards the existing church becomes almost an ideological principle, a matter of necessary doctrine. Similarly, there can be good reasons for scepticism about the idea of progress: but it is in millenarianism that the idea of progress becomes totally hateful and abominable, for it contradicts the view that everything will and must either stay the same, or else get a good deal worse, until God intervenes to alter the dispensation. Again, one might have good practical reasons for scepticism about the hope for an ethical interaction of church and world or the hope that such interaction would somehow fulfil the eschatological promises and perspectives of the Bible: but, when these hopes are considered not only idealistic or optimistic but foul and horrible, this violent rejection of the interaction probably comes from millenarian belief, for it is essential to at least some forms of it that the destiny of the church is to be taken totally out of the world. Yet again, where millenarian influence is present, fundamentalism is likely to be much more socially conservative: though millenarianism may have been socially progressive and even revolutionary in the seventeenth century, in the twentieth it is emphatically socially reactionary. In general, then, where it is difficult to explain why the hostility of fundamentalism to non-evangelical views is as violent as it is, the influence of millenarianism may well be the explanation.

This is particularly so in the matter of biblical criticism. We have already remarked that it is hard to see why conservatives should reject so completely and so violently even the simpler suggestions made by biblical critics: what would be lost to evangelicalism, we have asked, if it were admitted that Titus were not by St Paul or Deuteronomy not by Moses himself? Such suggestions require, it is true, some small adjustment, but they cannot be said in themselves to involve any great theological upset. Even fairly extreme conservatives might be induced to contemplate these possibilities with some equanimity. For millenarians, however, it is otherwise. The millenarian is not seeking to understand the human thoughts or theology of the writers of Daniel or Revelation. Rather, he is seeking to project a series of future events, the sequence of which will correspond precisely with the sequence of elements in the texts, and the characteristics of which will be closely connectable with details, names and figures as stated in the texts. For him this is not just one element within the Bible, it is the most important element. This being so, it is really out of the question that one should even begin to account for the thoughts of the writers in terms of normal human relations within their knowable historical environment. If, for instance, the writer of Daniel was talking about events which were not only future to him but are future still to us and which may take place today or tomorrow but may equally well not take place for yet another thousand years, then there is nothing in the historical and mental background of the writer that can elucidate the text for us: the text must be explained, not on the basis of what the writer thought, but on the basis of the actual events in the plan of God which, though divinely communicated through the writer, are not explicable on the basis of thoughts within his mind in his own situation in life.

We can put the point in this way also: traditionally, the issue between conservative and critical analyses of the Bible has been expressed in terms of the reporting of *past* events. Was the Bible accurate, or not, in its reporting of the story between Adam and Noah, or of the story of the Exodus, or of the story of Jesus and his teaching? The differences between conservative and critical opinions on such matters, though very great, can at least sometimes be represented as a matter of degree. But when we suppose, as millenarians do, that the most important events referred to in the Bible are *future* events, the gap between the conservative and the critical approaches widens almost to infinity. If, for instance, the passage in Ezekiel concerning Gog and Magog (Ezek. 38–9) refers and refers solely to an event in the distant future, taking place only after the end of the church age and the return of Jesus in glory to the earth, when a Jewish 'remnant' in Palestine, apparently believing in Jesus as Messiah, will be besieged by a force of 'the northern (European) powers, headed up by Russia',[21] then an explanation of this kind will not need or require any explication on the basis of the human and historical situation of Ezekiel himself. It is no longer a matter of degree. There is no common ground at all between such an interpretation and a historical-critical study of Ezekiel. This being so, it is understandable that millenarians should take up a totally negative stand towards the very idea of critical scholarship.

A similar point is as follows. Millenarianism depends upon the idea of a complicated network of 'prophetic' texts, especially in the Old Testament, which, it is understood, have not yet been fulfilled, and which will therefore be fulfilled in the series of final events – in the dispensational variety, after the secret rapture of the church. But the validation of these future prophecies rests in considerable measure upon intra-scriptural prophecies, that is, passages in the Old Testament which are understood to have predicted events in the New, and passages in early parts of the Old Testament which are understood to have predicted events in the later parts of it. The existence of these 'past' prophecies is taken as a clear evidence that the Bible is a closely-woven network of prophecies and fulfilments, and the fact that such prophecies have been fulfilled exactly as they predicted is taken to be a clear reason why all other prophetic texts will in due course be fulfilled exactly as they predicted. This being so, one of the basic foundations of all millenarian faith would be badly damaged if the thought were even for a moment entertained that some of the biblical predictions were prophecies after the fact, or that the prophet did not mean the same thing as the 'fulfilment' brought about, or that the passage was not spoken by the prophet to whom it is attributed. This may help us to understand why the Deutero-Isaiah theory is so strongly rejected:[22] if Isaiah 40–66 was in fact composed by the original prophet Isaiah, it would be one of the prime cases within the Old Testament itself for an exact prediction, made about two hundred years before the fulfilment, and with the names like Cyrus and Babylon actually included in the wording. If Isaiah 40–66 is made contemporary with the return from exile in Babylon, this important instance of exact long-range predictive prophecy, with names and details given, is lost.[23]

All in all, then, the completeness of the rejection of critical methods and results by fundamentalism is most easily understood if we suppose that millenarianism has had an important role in the intellectual history of that rejection.

It is probable that millenarianism continues to have much more influence within conservative evangelicalism than would appear on the surface. Many conservative evangelical leaders have a background deeply touched by thoroughly millennial literature and indoctrination, such as is found in the Scofield Bible. From a source like the Scofield Bible many elements of the distinctively extreme millenarian attitudes can easily be absorbed, without the reader becoming a fully-fledged dispensationalist himself. And this background is not easily lost, even when it becomes wise to show reserve about millenarianism, as evangelical leaders often do. Moreover, it is likely that many conservative evangelicals personally entertain strongly millennial ideas, even when they know that it is not expedient to put them in the shop window. Finally, even those who are moderate, reserved or even negative in their attitudes to millennialism probably experience some considerable pressure from circles which are powerful within conservative evangelicalism and which are also explicitly and devotedly millenarian. In these circumstances the absence of explicit millenarian statements is not enough to show that conservative evangelical spokesmen are definitely disengaged from millenarian influence: considering the explicitness with which they reject 'liberal' theology and biblical criticism, a real disengagement from millenarianism is not to be judged probable unless actual words of dissuasion and rejection against it are to be found, and this is not very often. As has been suggested, even moderate conservative evangelical discussions commonly treat dispensationalism and similar positions with respect and go no farther than to say that it is 'not certain', 'less probable' and the like. A central spokesman like G. T. Manley, surveying the possible relations between the advent and the millennium, is firm that a premillennial view 'is the only view which does full justice to the text', but seems uncertain about the precise dispensational position, pointing out 'problems' in it and 'difference of opinion'.[24] Clearly he is not certain; but he leaves plenty of room for anyone who holds a full dispensational view. The shattering damage done by it to central Christian doctrines goes here, as generally in conservative literature, unremarked.

The fact is that fundamentalism does not include any conceptual instrument that is capable of controlling millennialism. There are perhaps two arguments which might achieve this. One is the argument from the central structure of the Christian faith, let us say, from the nature and work of Christ: such an argument would maintain that peripheral materials like Daniel and Revelation, and peripheral questions like speculations about a future millennium, must be kept firmly in subjection to our knowledge of Christ as a person and the problems of faith in him in this present world. The other is the argument from what the biblical authors, understood in the context of their own lives, situations and backgrounds, on a basis of normal and knowable human relations, could have thought: this approach might involve the use of extra-biblical information, might suggest a distinction between what the biblical author thought and what we can actually believe, and might lead to a critical separation between one biblical author and another, between one source and another in the same book. The first is an argument from the central structure of Christian theology; the second is an argument from the critical approach to biblical literature. Fundamentalists cannot freely use either of them. The first creates great difficulties for them. It would suggest that there is an antecedent structure of Christian theology, which has to be inherited from earlier ages and applied to the Bible, in order that one may know which parts of it are the essential ones. This would be an impossible position for fundamentalists, who would be faced by dispensationalists arguing that doctrine must not be applied *to* the Bible but derived *from* it.[25] It would, moreover, be an admission that some biblical texts are peripheral: and if this were admitted, then there would be no safeguard against 'liberals' who might put the virgin birth narratives or the texts about the inspiration of scripture into this category.

These arguments, then, cannot be used, or cannot be freely and openly used, by fundamentalists, and this means that they have no effective means of contradicting a resolute dispensationalist. In fact conservative critics of millenarianism have at times used parts of these arguments, but they have not done so freely or openly, for the reasons stated. Such conservatives as have attempted radical critiques of millenarianism have probably been dependent, in the last resort, on the argument that millenarianism distorted the true balance of elements within the Christian faith: but if they had had to say how one knew the true balance, their answer would have had to be that one knew it from the Calvinist or Lutheran doctrinal tradition; or else they have had to resort to arguments belonging to neo-orthodoxy or to biblical theology, arguments therefore which did not really belong to the fundamentalist world.[26] There seems to be no satisfactory methodological or hermeneutical ground on which millenarianism can be properly combated by fundamentalists who deny its validity. Allis and others have pointed to the literalism of dispensational interpretation, and then gone on to point out how it is not consistently literal, but sometimes literal and at other times non-literal.[27] This is a valid observation in itself but has no controversial value, since we have seen that the same is true of all fundamentalism, whether millenarian or not.

Thus in general conservative evangelicalism, through its own doctrinal principles and still more through its repudiation of the critical approach to the Bible, has no real answer to millenarianism: the best it can do is to hope that it will go away or, once away, that it will not come back. And very many conservative evangelicals accept substantial elements of the millenarian outlook, even if they do not pursue it very far.

I have already pointed out that, while evangelical faith tends to place a strong emphasis on the human assent to and acceptance of the gospel, all depending on human decision for its effectiveness, in eschatology the situation seems to be the reverse. Fundamentalism generally emphasizes that the gospel is preached for individual decision; but in fundamentalist eschatology generally, and most of all in dispensationalism, all this is reversed and great masses of people are moved about by simple divine decree. Determinism takes over. The humanistic side of fundamentalist religion, with its stress on human acceptance and decision, disappears, and expectations become sheerly supernatural: a whole series of earth-shaking events will be brought about by direct divine agency, with little or nothing that man can do about it. Thus the communal in the end takes revenge on the individualism of the religion. As a popularized and sensationalized version of dispensational doctrine puts it:

> After the Christians are gone God is going to reveal Himself in a special way to 144,000 physical, literal Jews who are going to believe with a vengeance that Jesus is the Messiah. They are going to be 144,000 Jewish Billy Grahams turned loose on this earth – the earth will never know a period of evangelism like this period.[28]

In this striking picture one aspect is left quite vague, indeed nothing is said about it at all: the possibility that this number of Jews will decide not to believe in Jesus as the Messiah at all. In the present world no one can be a Christian without making a free – and therefore unpredictable – decision for Christ; in the events of the end everything will work in another way, and God will simply arrange that the requisite number of Jewish believers in Jesus will become available.

With this shift of emphasis the valid theological core of evangelicalism is increasingly lost: the centrality of Christ as saviour, the call for personal faith in him, the need for personal discipleship and obedience – all of this becomes less prominent. The centre lies increasingly in the working out of a sequence of future events, in which Christ appears no longer in the role of a saviour calling all men to him but rather as a kind of automaton or switch, whose actions introduce each new stage of the apocalyptic sequence. In general, though millenarianism grows quickly upon the religious soil of conservative evangelicalism, it also quickly bears fruits which cannot but be offensive to the religious core of mainstream evangelical religion.

Fundamentalism, then, is unable to discipline its own millenarian offspring.[29] Millennial enthusiasm can rise and fall in waves. The fact that the main literature of conservative evangelicalism at present damps down the millenarian note or at least does not give it much positive stress may be a sign that millenarianism is waning. On the other hand it is doubtful whether the wary don't-rock-the-boat prudence of moderate leaders is sufficient to prevent conservative evangelicals from spilling over into a wild millenarianism, when there is no effective barrier against it and when it follows as a natural, though not a necessary, development from the methods and ethos of fundamentalist biblical study in general. One event that may well have stimulated millenarian interest is that already mentioned, the foundation of the state of Israel. The restoration of the Jews to the Holy Land was already a central element in the millennial programme as seen over a century ago. The realization of such a hope seems to some people to vindicate the millenarian approach. According to Lindsey's widely-read book, past attempts to make a contemporary history fit with prophetic texts erred because the correct datum line for the beginning of the events of the end was not known: in fact, only after Israel was once again a nation in the land of its fathers did the prophetic clock begin to tick again.[30] Thus, though all past millennial schemes have gone wrong, we can be sure that this one will go right. How far this argument will be accepted I do not know. G. T. Manley discusses the question, and obviously does not know the answer.[31]

That there is an interested market for all sorts of futuristic speculations in our present cultural situation will be readily granted. An appetite for witchcraft, for the irrational, for the exotic in religion, can easily find room for millennial speculations about the end of the world. The question is not whether such speculation is popular, but whether it will continue to have any connection at all with a respectable form of religion like conservative evangelicalism. It is more likely to become part of a great secular appetite for magic and the irrational, cut loose from the whole basis in traditional religion and in careful biblical study within which traditional fundamentalism lived and in which the older millenarianism grew up. The work just cited, *The Late Great Planet Earth*, which claims to have had twenty-six printings in the first year and a half and to have more than 1,700,000 copies in print at that time (December 1972), is an excellent illustration. On the one hand the racy journalese in which it is written should not conceal the fact that this farrago of nonsense is in essence little different from traditional premillennial dispensationalism.[32] On the other hand it is obvious from title, style and presentation how close a work like this has moved towards the genre and interest of science fiction, how consciously it relates itself to astrology and the occult. The addition of some three pages of traditional Christian sermonizing at the end cannot disguise the fact that the work as a whole attracts (if it does attract) as a secular science fiction fantasy, which contributes nothing to the Christian faith and has no intention of doing so. In general, even if millenarian speculation should come to be favoured by our era, it is possible that this tendency will carry it beyond the grasp and control of religion, even of fundamentalist religion, and that any benefit it brings to religion will be even less than it was in the past.

3. *Pentecostalism and the like*

Millenarianism, however, is far from being the only deviant form into which fundamentalist religion may easily be diverted. Another direction into which much fundamentalist religion spills over is that of faith-healing, glossolalia or speaking with tongues, the charismatic movement as it is now generally called; and with this we can consider also the so-called Jesus movement. These types of religion are not absolutely tied to fundamentalism, and sometimes they spring up within quite other streams of Christianity. Nevertheless they often have a close kinship with fundamentalism and a considerable attraction for fundamentalist people. Healing and speaking with tongues both commend themselves fairly naturally on the grounds that they represent a recovery of the original state of the New Testament church. If one is to be a true Christian of New Testament type, one ought to have personal experiences such as those described in the earliest church: one should see the sick healed through prayer and faith, one should have a fresh and overwhelming experience of the Holy Spirit after one has been a Christian for some time, one should speak with tongues, in a sort of ecstatic prayer expressed in the utterance of language not normally intelligible (for St Paul's views of this, see I Corinthians 12–14). Thus, though the charismatic movement does attract people from all streams of Christianity, it is likely that fundamentalist background is there in a very high proportion of cases. In any case, charismatic Christianity, in so far as it is not fundamentalist or near to fundamentalism, falls beyond the scope of the present enquiry.

The doctrine of most Pentecostal groups seems to be uncompromisingly fundamentalist, and in this sense probably more extreme than the mainstream type of conservative evangelicalism taken as typical in this book.[33] Modern theology and biblical criticism are often violently repudiated. There are however some groups and individuals who repudiate fundamentalism and take a relatively free position towards the Bible.[34] This, if right, is to me not surprising. As I see it (and my experience in this regard is very limited), Pentecostalism and related movements differ from mainstream orthodox fundamentalism in that they have something extra and positive to offer, and this extra thing, whether it is speaking with tongues, healing, or something else, is for them the real centre of the religion. Mainstream fundamentalism is in comparison quite negative: all it can offer is an old-fashioned traditional orthodoxy as it would have been (it is supposed) if biblical criticism and modern theology had not come along. Thus to fundamentalism, especially on its more intellectual side, opposition to criticism and modern theology is almost the total goal and purpose of the movement. It would seem understandable if a Pentecostalist, though repudiating modern theology, nevertheless concerned himself much less with it. For in a charismatic community there must surely be a displacement of emphasis: the stress must fall less on orthodoxy of doctrine and more on personal experience. The intellectual polemic and apologetic aspect, so obvious about mainstream fundamentalism, may well be much reduced. In Germany, according to Hollenweger, fundamentalist circles (called Evangelical in the English translation of his book) have bitterly attacked the Pentecostal movement, branding it as diabolical or satanic in inspiration.[35] I do not have any information about official judgments of Pentecostalism by conservative evangelicals of the sort whose work has been taken as typical in this book.

The Jesus movement similarly has many of the features of evangelicalism: the basic evangelical picture of Jesus is celebrated and enjoyed in speech and song. But the solemn and intellectualist weighing of doctrine, the endless apologetic arguing over biblical detail, is considered rather irrevelant.

It seems at present impossible to tell whether the presence of these new and active movements will alter the character of conservative evangelicalism as described in this volume. It is possible that, just at a time when the intellectual leadership of conservatism, especially in literature and biblical scholarship, becomes more prominent, it may at the same time become more irrelevant, because the actual popular interest may be attracted away into another direction, more concerned with experience and emotion than with doctrine and apologetics. It is, on the other hand, also possible that movements that are at present fairly fluid and doctrinally relaxed may move towards an intellectual rationalism of the normal fundamentalist type, and some observers have remarked on this as a tendency in Pentecostalism.[36] From the point of view of conservative evangelicalism, the outlook for the future may well be uncertain. Its principle of biblical inerrancy and infallibility does not in fact succeed in controlling the extremes of doctrine and interpretation, and the outbursts of seeking after personal experience, which may occur. It remains now, more than ever before, a question whether the central, mainstream, relatively orthodox fundamentalism which we have taken as the pattern for our discussion will survive, or whether it will in the future be displaced by its own more extreme offspring. Fundamentalism is, in the end, a religion of the old world: in doctrine, in philosophy, in personal outlook it looks back to the eighteenth century. It may well succeed in disciplining and overcoming the newer religious impulses that have their origin in the modern world; but then, on the contrary, it may not.

4. *Modern translations of the Bible*

One aspect in which conservative evangelicalism is changing along a scale of time is its relation to the English translations of the Bible.

Until quite recently conservative evangelicals were extremely closely tied to the Authorized (King James) Version. The symbolic and practical importance of this tie with a particular and traditional English version is difficult to exaggerate. This was not, indeed, a matter of doctrine: no one laid down that only the Authorized Version should be used or cited. But in practice the Bible was very seldom quoted in any other form. The exact wording of this version was prized as if it were the holy of holies, and any phrase quoted from it was carefully demarcated in print by quotation marks to make clear what were the exact biblical words as distinct from mere human comment and discussion. Titles of books, pamphlets and talks might often highlight a sacred phrase, as in *Heirs Together* and *'A Time to Embrace'*, two pamphlets on sexual ethics. Theoretically it was known that this version was only a translation and that a Hebrew and Greek text lay behind it; but in experience it was rare for anyone to appeal to these originals against the AV. Mere jokes, like that about the man who said that he would stick to the Authorized Version because it was the version read by St Paul, can be set aside; but, quite apart from such exaggerations, and admitting that some fundamentalist leaders were learned men with a good knowledge of biblical languages, for fundamentalist society as a whole the Authorized Version functioned as the direct and immediate expression or transcript of divine revelation. Even where leaders had a good knowledge of Greek or even Hebrew (and I am less sure about Hebrew), it is not clear that this made a great deal of difference. In the nineteenth century, and even more before that time, it was still possible to command the grammar and vocabulary of these languages and yet read them as if they produced a semantic pattern identical to that laid down by traditional Christian understanding as exemplified in the Authorized Version. The learning of biblical languages was in at least some centres, and possibly continues so to the present day, not a critical process designed to help the reader to understand the Bible in a different way, but a sort of biblical zeal, an anxiety to know everything possible about the detail of holy writ, and in the end something that produced a total impression not much different from a study of the English. To put it in another way, it is not clear that a wide difference of ethos existed between those conservatives who knew the biblical languages well and those others, of whom there were many, who did everything on the basis of the English. It is certain that large areas of doctrinal and interpretative work were done entirely on the basis of the English: this would be true of a great deal of the development of millenarian doctrine.

The importance of this fixation upon the Authorized Version, as it actually functioned within fundamentalism, was very great indeed. Because a form of words was there which corresponded directly to the will of God, the degree to which one had to search the mind of the author, in his historical setting, in order to interpret his words was minimized. Naturally, it could not be entirely eliminated, and in the case of writers whose personality seemed to emerge clearly, like St Paul, one could talk about what he intended in his historical situation, as a clue to the understanding of his words. But this did not alter the fact that the words and sentences of the English Bible, that is to say, the semantic effect of these words as directly formed in the mind of an English reader, formed a direct and not a mediated transcript of God's intention. Moreover, since the accepted recourse in all difficulties was to 'compare scripture with scripture' (both, of course, in English), and since practically no room was given for the illumination of the text from extra-biblical sources, the universal use of one single translation had the effect of damping down and discouraging any thought of stressing the mind of the author in his historical situation, as against any other author, in interpretation. The virtual use of only one English version, and it one originating within very traditional early seventeenth-century Christianity, thus indirectly but very powerfully supported the alienation of the fundamentalist public from, and its opposition to, the positions, interests and methods from which all biblical criticism grew and on which it depended.

In more recent years the sole domination of the Authorized Version in the fundamentalist movement has suddenly disappeared. *The New Bible Commentary* had in its first edition (1953) taken the King James text as basis for the commentary, though sometimes citing also the wordings of the Revised Version of 1881–5. *The New Bible Commentary Revised* (1970) took as its basis the Revised Standard Version (New Testament 1946; complete Bible 1952). This is very interesting because it shows how mainstream conservative scholarship has decided to ignore the storm of hatred and opposition with which ultra-conservatives, at least in the United States, had greeted this version. The group of scholars who worked on the revision had the reputation of being liberal, and perhaps some of them, unlike most of those whom fundamentalists regard as liberal, were really liberal. On top of that they were ecumenical, and the whole venture was sponsored by the National Council of the Churches of Christ in the USA. The translation was therefore not surprisingly attacked as a liberal-communist plot. F. F. Bruce cites pamphlets with such engaging titles as *The New Blasphemous Bible* and *The Bible of Antichrist*, and tells us that 'One American preacher is reported to have burned a copy of the RSV with a blowlamp in his pulpit, remarking that it was like the devil because it was hard to burn.'[37]

It is still difficult to say how far the general acceptance of newer translations like the RSV has gone; but the action of the revisers of *The New Bible Commentary* would seem to indicate a very substantial measure of acceptance. However slow one may be in realizing this, this must imply: there is no reason why conservatives should not use and cite as their normal practice a translation of the Bible which came from scholars who were presumably all ecumenical in spirit and in at least some cases were liberal, that is, liberal by even non-fundamentalist terms of reference. F. F. Bruce writes:

> The committee of revisers . . . was sufficiently broadly based to make it unlikely that the version would promote any particular or sectional interest. And in fact it has found widespread acceptance in the years since its appearance in a great variety of Christian communities,

theologically conservative as well as theologically liberal. No change in Christian doctrine is involved or implied in the readings and renderings of the RSV; every article of the historic faith of the Church can be established as readily and as plainly from it as from the older versions in whose tradition it stands.[38]

That this should happen at all must indicate a lessening of the bitter suspicion with which conservatives in the past so often regarded any and all doings of the liberal and ecumenically-minded.

But the example is important not so much for itself, but rather as an indicator of a wider trend. In principle, this cannot be a switch from one version to another which will be as central as the Authorized Version was. Once the unique primacy of the Authorized Version has gone, the implication is that there can be many translations. Less and less can any English form of words be taken as a direct transcript of the mind of God. More and more must the question be put, what can we know of the mind of the author that can decide the questions of interpretation? For, once the idea has been lost that the Authorized Version is the direct transcript of the mind of God, it will be found that even the Greek or Hebrew text cannot be taken as the direct transcript of the mind of God either. Thus the change of attitude to the English translations in the last decade or so may typify and be proleptic of a yet greater shift of emphasis in conservative faith.

There remains another question which is posed for conservative interpretation by the work of biblical translation. Any respectable translation contradicts a substantial number of the conservative interpretations that come under discussion in this book. We shall later be considering the suggestion that the number 603,550 at Num. 1.46 should be understood to mean 603 'captains' with their troops or 603 'families' with their few members.[39] But the RSV gives us the figure of 603,550. One can scarcely dismiss this as a mere liberal misunderstanding, for the AV gives us the same: 603,550. Turn to the NEB, the Jerusalem Bible, or the New American Bible, and what do we find? 603,550 in them all. Thus the commentator on the passage in *The New Bible Commentary Revised* is offering an interpretation that contradicts not only the translation which his commentary takes as basis but also all other known translations of the Old Testament. Take again the matter of the 'long day' of Joshua. Conservative interpreters have often assured us, as we shall see, that there was no lengthening of the day, but a miraculous hailstorm that prolonged the night.[40] But when readers turn to the passage in their RSV, what do they find?/

'Sun, stand thou still at Gibeon . . . and the sun stood still, and the moon stayed, until the nation took vengeance . . . The sun stayed in the midst of heaven, and did not hasten to go down for about a whole day' (Josh. 10.12f.). And again the same is found when they turn to the passage in the AV.[41]

In other words, even to the most conservative reader of *The New Bible Commentary Revised* it is going to occur sooner or later that, interesting as the interpretation offered in the commentary may be, the Bible as he reads it does not say what the commentary would like it to mean, and that this is so whether one turns to the ancient and revered text of the AV or to the modern version of the RSV, or indeed, probably, to any other. Sooner or later it is going to strike him that this may be because all linguistic evidence favours the understanding represented in the translations, and none of it favours the interpretation proposed in the conservative commentary he is reading. And in this, of course, he would be quite right.

In the end, therefore, conservative evangelicals might have to face the choice of either producing a translation of their own, which would follow the interpretative tendencies of their own commentators, or tacitly allowing the suggestions of their commentators to be forgotten. Everything suggests that they will take the latter course. The movement towards a purely conservative evangelical translation of the Bible would be a step in exactly the opposite direction from that which has just been made in accepting the RSV. A modern translation of this kind would be a sectarian and partisan production to a degree unparalleled in the past history of Bible translation. It would on the one hand be wonderfully conservative in doctrine, and on the other hand it would tactfully eliminate a good number of the biblical miracles which flourish conspicuously in the Authorized Version. The mere attempt to produce such a version would soon convince of its impractibility. As we have seen, you can use the RSV and still remain thoroughly conservative in general doctrine; but if you use the RSV intelligently, it must reduce your confidence in some of the interpretations which conservative commentators offer. Curiously and paradoxically, the matter of the translation of the Bible is the first field in which a sort of ecumenicity is being forced upon fundamentalists.

5. Neo-orthodoxy, biblical theology and the new conservatives

We now have to consider a change that may be coming over conservative theology. The loss of the uniqueness of the Authorized

Version is something that affects the general functioning of fundamentalist society; the theological shift is something that affects the leaders, or some of them. In order to understand this shift we have to look outside conservative theology and consider the pressure that was brought to bear upon the conservative world by certain elements in modern theology. The elements I have in mind are neo-orthodoxy, as exemplified by Karl Barth,[42] especially on the right wing of those who were influenced by him, and 'biblical theology', a movement that was found mainly among biblical scholars or was expressed on the level of biblical scholarship but which nevertheless reflected on that level many of the same interests and aspirations as did neo-orthodoxy on the more dogmatic level.

Neo-orthodoxy was bound to be of interest to conservatives because it was, like their own position, sharply opposed to liberalism. The entire direction of liberal theology, it appeared from Barth, had been totally wrong. As against the liberal emphasis on religion, he laid the emphasis on revelation. Christianity was not man's increasingly refined ideas of God, but God making himself known in his own way to man. The old doctrines of the classical faith could come into their own again: the Trinity, the two natures of Christ, scripture as the Word of God, election and predestination, all of these had vital and central theological tasks to perform. All working out of doctrine had to be done in the closest possible relation to the exposition of the Bible. Conservatives, who had dismissed much other modern theology, could hardly escape from at least listening to some of this or coming under some pressure from it. The polemic of neo-orthodoxy against liberal theology was infinitely more effective than that of traditional conservatism, because Barth and his associates, unlike conservative apologists, had thoroughly studied liberal theology and knew what it was.

The revelation of God, according to the Barthian line of thought, was uniquely witnessed to in the Bible. The Bible, however, was not itself the revelation of God, but only a witness to that revelation. The Word of God was in the first place Christ himself, as witnessed to in the scriptures and preached in the church; in the second place the scriptures, in that they witness to Christ and are preached in the church; and in the third place the preaching of the church, in so far as it witnesses to Christ on the basis of the scriptures. The Bible can be thought of, like the person of Jesus Christ, as having a divine and human aspect, neither of which cancels out or overweighs the other. This does not mean that parts of the Bible are divine and parts are human: rather, the entire Bible is human, subject to the strains and weaknesses of any human product, but at the same time all of it is from God, in that it says something that does not arise from human culture and is not immanent within it. The revelatory content is not the Bible, its words and sentences, but the persons and acts to which it testifies; ultimately, what God reveals is himself, not books and verses.

Moreover, the centrality of the Bible in Barthian neo-orthodoxy was greatly increased by Barth's attack on natural theology. Natural theology is a scheme whereby it is supposed that, since God created man and the world in a certain ordered mode, something can be known of God by analogies and reasonings that take their departure from this world, from man and from his reason. Many classical schemes of theology had had an element that might be known of God on the basis of natural theology, ascending from below as it were, while beyond this all was dependent on revelation, descending from above. According to Barth, natural theology was totally wrong and, since all previous systems of theology had had at least some infection from it, a radical programme of purgation was required. As Barthians saw it, if any natural theology was admitted at all, even only in an ancillary role, it then dominated the entire structure of belief. This meant that a very serious view was taken of the effects of sin upon man's ability to know God. Natural theology would have been all right if there had been no Fall. Though God had created man in his image, the distortion of the image of God in man as a result of human sin was so great that nothing could be achieved by a theology that sought to reach up to the knowledge of God through structures based upon the world as it is. The effect of this is to increase the centrality of scripture, as a means of attaining to the knowledge of God, to a point probably higher than it has ever had in the history of Christian thought. One might have expected conservatives to take some interest in this.

But the polemic of neo-orthodoxy was as hot against traditional conservatism as it was against liberalism. For one thing, the apologetic character of conservative argument came under fire. Apologetics, the attempt to prove on the basis of human knowledge, reason and experience that such and such things were true of God, was contemptuously dismissed by the neo-orthodox. The endless attempts of conservatives to prove the Bible right by demonstrating from historical evidence the accuracy of its story of Abraham or the fact that the resurrection had really taken place were contemptible and absurd. They were not only in themselves useless and wrongly-conceived, but they destroyed the very thing they sought to establish. By making the authority of the Bible depend on pettifogging arguments about the genealogies in Genesis or the 'long day' of Joshua or the 'historical evidence' for the resurrection, they were admitting that the Bible just in itself did not have the authority that they themselves wanted it to have. They were not willing to rely on the Bible, they had to prop it up with their scaffolding of proofs, harmonizations and evidences. This conservative approach was in itself a clear proof that traditional conservatism, far from being a biblical form of faith as it boasted, depended throughout on a natural theology. Far, therefore, from being a radical opposition to liberalism, it actually shared the basic liberal fault, differing from liberalism only by standing at the other end of one common spectrum, of which the basic insights and methods were shared by both.

Thus the whole conservative attempt to maintain the authority of the Bible by combating the movement of biblical criticism had been totally wrong; the critical reading of the Bible was in itself a quite justified procedure.

Neo-orthodoxy also strongly attacked the conceptions of faith and truth in conservatism. Faith in Christ was a personal relation, and Christ was the true and only revelation of God. Conservatives were so anxious about the Bible that they allowed it to usurp the controlling position in theology and faith that belonged to Christ alone. In this sense they made the Bible into an idolatrous object. Their conception of faith, at least as it worked out in their views of the Bible, was no longer one of a personal relation with a person, it was one of true statements or propositions. For fundamentalists the only ultimate question was: is this statement true or not?, while for neo-orthodox thinking the ultimate question was rather: is he, to whom this statement points, the truth? The fundamentalist position about the Bible, much as it boasted of being truly Christian, was in fact destructive of Christian faith: it made it into an assent to infallible biblical propositions, rather than a personal relation. The result was that conservative orthodoxy corrupted equally all the other traditional doctrines that it sought to keep alive: the Trinity, the Holy Spirit, the church.

In general, then, neo-orthodoxy accepted the human and historical character of the Bible, but did not find this to conflict with its function as mediator of revelation. It subordinated the Bible to the higher reality of the self-revelation of God, but continued to maintain the essential role of scripture in all decisions about what is or is not revelation.

The movement known as 'biblical theology', working on the biblical rather than the systematic level, took a parallel course. Firstly, it emphasized the historical events which formed the centre of the biblical narrative. These were the 'mighty acts of God' through which salvation was achieved. The reporting of these might be quite inaccurate, but it was these events, and the theological interpretation of them, rather than the correct reporting of them, that constituted revelation and the way of salvation. It was characteristic of the Bible that its theology was expressed in the recital of events and not in static terms of true doctrines, true statements, eternal truths or correct propositions.

Secondly, the emphasis lay on the distinctiveness of the theology of the Bible and the concepts from which it is built up. For many workers in this field, the Bible had a way of thinking distinctively Hebraic, built upon personal relations and events in time, and quite different from the thought of traditional Western theology (including conservative thought and its argumentative apparatus). Conservatism, based upon late and rationalistic patterns of Western thought, had completely failed to think in the dynamic terms in which the Bible itself thought. Its stress on the factual historical accuracy of reports, often theologically peripheral, was only evidence of its failure to understand anything about the biblical way of thinking. Though the revelatory core of the Bible lay in the events in history which lay behind its witness, its theological authority was centred not in the accuracy of its reporting but in the distinctiveness of its way of thinking. Since this way of thinking was essential to the Bible, the understanding of it had to be present before the Bible could be understood correctly.

The emphasis on the distinctiveness of the Bible enabled biblical theology to separate the Bible very markedly from its environment. It was felt that much scholarship in the Old Testament had seen the latter too much as a variant of ancient oriental culture, and that the New Testament had similarly been too much assimilated to its background in the Greco-Roman world. On the contrary, it was now maintained, the Old Testament stood out markedly as a quite different cultural type from the mythological cultures that surrounded it; and, as for the New Testament, though it existed in the Greco-Roman World it was not *of* that world, for its controlling concepts were those that had been worked out in the life of ancient Israel. Thus, though the language of the New Testament was Greek, its content of ideas was Hebraic.

This in turn enabled biblical theology to emphasize the unity of the Bible. Most biblical theologians continued to accept the critical approach, and did not deny the methods which had led to the identification of many sources, or to the late dating of certain books; these things did not concern the movement very greatly. But on the whole it remains true that biblical theology was an expression of weariness with a merely analytic approach: it sought to establish a synthesis. It was weary with the work that had separated one source from another, the prophets from the law, the Old Testament from the New, Jesus from Paul. In this sense it was indeed a reaction against the dominance that the critical approach had had in the previous generation of scholarship. But the sort of unity it found was one that had no precedent in conservative scholarship. It was not a unity formed because all biblical texts were alike inspired by the one God; it was a unity discovered through detailed research into the human and historical forms of thinking that had animated the biblical writers and their milieu.

The above is a very simplified account of a period of study that was in fact much more variegated and complicated. In what follows I can indicate only some broad lines of influence which this whole movement had upon the problem of fundamentalism.

Neo-orthodoxy, though at first sight poised between liberalism and conservatism, was in fact more conservative than it wanted to be; and this was especially so in the English-speaking countries. Barth himself had been both a liberal and a Christian socialist; but his inheritance in the English-speaking world fell, very often though not always, into the hands of people who would never by any stretch of the imagination have been either liberals or socialists at any point in their lives. In their hands the neo-orthodox arguments, though admitting in principle the legitimacy of the critical study of the Bible, could still doubt whether it had any positive value. Granted that it might be legitimate to say that Titus was not written by St Paul, what could possibly be gained by such an argument and what sound motives could a person have for pursuing it? Though a theologian like Barth fully accepted the need for a 'critical' reading of the Bible, he tended to redefine the meaning of 'critical' in such a way that it no longer coincided with what was generally understood by critical scholarship. And, though Barth contemptuously rejected the entire fundamentalist attempt to prop up the authority of the Bible upon its accuracy in historical details, this in itself scarcely provided a strong positive rationale for the necessity of a critical approach. I once heard Professor John Baillie tell how he had Barth in his study for several hours, and had pressed him to admit that

Methuselah had not really lived for 969 years. Barth was, as always, contemptuous of the conservative approach which would have sought to 'prove' the biblical figure 'right' by arguing from evidences, internal or external. But this did not mean that he would admit that Methuselah had not lived for 969 years. What possible valid theological reason could there be for anyone to want to know that this figure was not correct? What use could it be to theology to declare that the figure was a legendary one? At the end of several hours of conversation, Baillie told me, Barth had still not been persuaded to admit that Methuselah had not in fact lived for 969 years. In general, the right-wing Barthian approach, in spite of its rejection of the fundamentalist doctrinal structure, discouraged any inclination to make critical questions very significant for theology and created an intellectual atmosphere in which they could easily be evaded.

The more conservative side of Barthianism could thus come quite close to the conservative evangelical kind of position and, as more and more attention began to fall on the conflict between the more 'orthodox' side of neo-orthodoxy, as represented by Barth, and the much more radical approach represented by Bultmann, which had started from somewhat similar origins, the possible sympathy between Barthian theology and conservative evangelicalism seemed to become greater. The rejection of liberalism and the insistence on biblical authority among right-wing Barthians could be so strong that they felt quite at home in the conservative evangelical sort of movement. Conversely, a roughly or vaguely neo-orthodox position agreed with the general religious aims and character of the conservative evangelical movement much better than the normal conservative doctrine did. A neo-orthodox position, while insisting very strongly on the authority of the Bible and giving little or no positive encouragement to biblical criticism, discouraged the emphasis on inerrancy in historical details, dates and authorship of books; its dislike of apologetics meant that evangelicals stopped trying to argue people into Christian faith in a living person, which agreed with the deepest religious roots of evangelicalism; and its view of faith and truth, being personal rather than doctrinal and rationalistic, gave much greater freedom and flexibility in the proclamation and understanding of an evangelical message. On the one hand, then, a neo-orthodox position could be quite conservative, indeed very conservative, and could feel a closer kinship with the conservative evangelical people than with any other grouping; on the other hand, the basic religious impulses of evangelicalism could be better expressed and better served by a neo-orthodox approach than by the traditional conservative doctrine, apologetic and biblical interpretation.

This is not just theory: something of this kind actually happened. The student evangelical group in Edinburgh University took roughly this course during the later years of the 1940s and into the beginning of the 1950s, and a stirring of similar ideas probably occurred elsewhere. People were mostly not 'Barthians' in any very well-informed sense, but the general atmosphere and impulse of some evangelical groups was as I have just described. This allowed much greater freedom and flexibility in the use of the Bible than was permitted by the fearful and restrictive policy of the national conservative evangelical organization, and eventually the latter was successful in isolating and finally silencing the deviant line of action. It was probably to the interest of conservative evangelicalism to have followed a roughly neo-orthodox sort of line, but it did not; its rejection of Barth was almost total. The absurd title of Cornelius van Til's book against Barth, *The New Modernism* (James Clarke 1946), shows how neo-orthodoxy was classified, like all other non-fundamentalist theologies, as a liberal development. The reasons why Barth was repudiated by conservatives come down to two: the first is that he was not absolutely conservative about the Bible. No position about the Bible, however much it emphasized the authority of scripture, was acceptable to traditional conservative evangelicals unless it was absolutely conservative in their terms, that is, unless it made specific conservative affirmations about historical inerrancy, dates of books, authorships and so on. Secondly, Barth, and neo-orthodoxy generally, thought in a quite different way from traditional conservatism. Their processes of reasoning were quite different. They thought in a basically theological mode, while conservatism was predicated, as we shall see, upon a rationalistic pattern of thought, and gained its security in fact from reason.[43] Barth's attack on natural theology and on the use of reason to argue from worldly evidences to the reality of God was thus a deep threat to conservative ways of thinking. As always, conservatism was more important to conservatives than the authority of the Bible, and their rational-apologetic approach more important than freedom and flexibility in the understanding of the gospel and of faith.

The situation within theology has in recent years somewhat altered. Neo-orthodoxy has lost its leadership and initiative, and the biblical theology movement has fallen into severe difficulties. I myself have been one of the severest critics of misuses of evidence, principally linguistic evidence, within biblical theology.[44] It is amusing to find a conservative polemicist like Kitchen taking up these criticisms and using them as one stick among others wherewith to beat biblical criticism and the use of the Bible in modern theology.[45] It is of course pleasant to receive warm commendation of one's arguments from a scholar of Kitchen's distinction in Egyptology. Unfortunately, however, he has failed to see the direction of my argument; perhaps the vehemence of his antipathy to critical scholarship has obscured his understanding. Nowhere in the works I wrote on this subject did I suggest or suppose that the linguistic faults of biblical theology arose from or were connected with its acceptance of the tradition of critical scholarship, and nowhere did I suggest that these faults underlay the critical analysis (say) of the pentateuch by Wellhausen. My opinion was exactly the contrary. Though I did not express it in this way, my feeling about biblical theology was that it had gone wrong because it had moved too close to a modified fundamentalism in its use of biblical evidence. Though it did not hold a fundamentalism of the historical details in the traditional conservative manner, it produced something like a fundamentalism of the biblical concepts. The analysis which broke down this concept-fundamentalism was a critical analysis analogous to the earlier source-analysis of the pentateuch or the gospels but on a different level. Or, to put it in other words, I thought at the time, and still think, that biblical theology would not have run into so much trouble if it had retained sufficient respect for the analytic methods of Wellhausen and other pioneer critics. In any case, whatever its defects and faults, the position taken in biblical theology, like that taken in neo-orthodoxy generally, was a hundred times better in every possible way than the position of traditional conservatism.

Moreover, in spite of the difficulties into which neo-orthodoxy and biblical theology have run, it is likely that they will long continue to exercise pressure upon conservative thinking. On the one side, neo-orthodoxy performed the very important service of a bridge by which people of very conservative tendencies were enabled to cross over into the main stream of Protestant Christianity. Without neo-orthodoxy it is hardly conceivable that this would have been possible: how many fundamentalists would ever have been attracted, shall we say, by the appeal of Harnackian liberalism? Since neo-orthodoxy was, intellectually speaking, infinitely more developed and advanced than the traditional conservatism of the mid-twentieth century, it provided a route for those who wished to avoid liberalism and at the same time find a theological position that was intellectually respectable. There is no reason to doubt that this is still going on. Barth, after all, is still there to be read.

More important still is the emergence of a group which may be loosely classified as the 'new conservatives', or 'new evangelicals', especially in the United States. It is interesting that, if neo-orthodoxy and biblical theology began to decline about 1960 or so, it is from about the same time that the new conservatives begin to be noticed. It is indeed possible that the more conservative sides of neo-orthodoxy and of biblical theology have been in part taken over by this new alignment. Hordern puts the question: 'Will this movement produce the real inheritors of Barth's theology?'[46] Whether this is so or not, it is clear that some of the questions asked and the positions taken up in neo-orthodoxy and biblical theology are being re-echoed by these Americans.

The most striking feature of this group is its self-critical approach. The title of one book is itself striking: *The Uneasy Conscience of Modern Fundamentalism* by Carl Henry (1947).[47] In the mainly British conservative evangelical literature read for the present study, as already remarked, I have not found one word that might suggest an uneasy conscience; the complacency of conservatism, as this literature has presented it, is total.[48] It is conscious of no weaknesses and no failures; in all respects the conservative evangelical case has been entirely right and its opponents have never had a shred of justification on their side. Practically never is it suggested that traditional arguments are faulty or that cracks and contradictions run through the conservative arguments and interpretations. In this respect the self-critical attitude of the American new conservatives, even if limited, is a breath of fresh air. The scholars who have impressed me in this regard are Beegle, Ladd, Mickelsen and most of all Carnell.[49]

These scholars are clearly to some extent influenced by the general neo-orthodox argument (whether they learned it from neo-orthodoxy or not) that revelation is revelation of God himself, rather than the writing down of infallible doctrinal statements. They see that the emphasis on personal encounter and events in history is the one that fits best with the best part of the evangelical tradition. They are aware that man is saved, not by the acceptance of doctrines infallibly revealed, but by his personal relation with Jesus Christ. They are aware that the idea of the inspiration, infallibility and inerrancy of the Bible is full of difficulties and uncertainties, and they are critical of many ways in which these time-honoured conceptions have been handled by the traditional conservative leadership.

The 'new conservatives' have been particularly conscious of the need for conservative theology to say something positive. Conservative writing has been in an extreme degree defensive and negative. On the one hand it has tried to defend the inerrancy of the Bible; on the other hand it has made endless bitter and negative criticisms of all other theological directions. To many younger evangelical scholars, unlike the traditional apologists, this sort of argument has seemed in the end wearisome and useless. Even if non-conservative theology is wrong, something positive has to be done to construct a viable alternative. Carl Henry, not exactly a liberal, wrote in 1966:

> If evangelical Protestants do not overcome their preoccupation with negative criticism of contemporary theological deviations at the expense of the construction of preferable alternatives to these, they will not be much of a doctrinal force in the decade ahead.[50]

Such an opinion comes as a revelation to anyone who has worked through the morass of British conservative evangelical literature. Practically nowhere does the latter suggest or admit that any positive or constructive task has to be carried out. On the contrary, conservative faith stands already complete and perfect, and the only task is to embrace it wholeheartedly, while pointing out the gross defects of all those who have advanced any other kind of doctrinal position. In this respect the American new conservatives certainly merit the title 'new'.

Theologically the strongest in the new conservative group seems to be E. J. Carnell (1919–67). Carnell is hardly to be regarded as a non-conservative scholar; on the contrary, he is deeply conservative (or orthodox, which is the word he prefers to use). He sets forth one of the most poignant formulations ever written of the argument that, since Jesus recognized the authority of the scriptures (i.e. of the Old Testament), to deny their accuracy is to destroy the credibility of Jesus in all regards: 'The orthodox apologist rests his case on this single datum [that Jesus accepted the Old Testament as the inspired Word of God]. Not to recognize this . . . would imply *the loss of his Savior*.'[51] No conservative could carry the argument farther than that. Nowhere in Carnell does one find evidence of concessions to liberalism, to biblical criticism, or to neo-orthodoxy. But criticisms of the traditional conservative arguments simply pour forth from him. Inspiration for him is not an answer, rather it is a problem. 'Although orthodoxy stoutly defends the doctrine of inspiration, it has never devised an official view of inspiration.'[52] 'The problem of inspiration is *still* a problem.'[53] 'Orthodoxy does not have all the answers; nor does it always ask the right questions.'[54] 'Unless the claims of orthodoxy are spelled out with care, they may connote an odious Biblicism.'[55] All in all, there are three directions in which Carnell's questions seem to go:

Firstly, he opposes the normal conservative argument, whereby literary questions, like the date and authorship of books, are dogmatically settled on the grounds that Jesus referred to such and such a book under the traditional authorship: 'Purely literary questions *cannot* be settled by an appeal to Christ's testimony. Whether The Book of Judges was composed by one inspired author, or whether it is the work of several redactors, is a question of criticism, not Christology.'[56]

If this is true, then a vast amount of conservative argumentation is a waste of time; for we have seen that the appeal to the testimony of Christ is not only one argument, but the main argument, used by standard apologists for traditional authorship. If Carnell is right, all this means nothing.

Secondly, Carnell looks critically at the major line of conservative doctrinal development, associated with Warfield, and he seems to prefer, in opposition to it, the position of the Scottish theologian James Orr, whom he describes as 'an outspoken critic of the Princeton theology'. The positions of Warfield and Orr will be discussed in a later chapter. At this point it will be sufficient to remark that Orr's ideas bore some resemblance to what was later to count as neo-orthodoxy.[57]

Thirdly, Carnell was acutely aware of the many detailed passages which created difficulties for the dominant conservative doctrine of inspiration. He had gone back over the debates between Warfield and the critical scholar Henry Preserved Smith (1847–1927) and noted the many detailed instances, adduced by Smith, which tended to bring the normal conservative doctrine of inspiration not into disproof but into ridicule. It was all very well to say that God had given inspired formulations of the truth, but what of the places where the words of the Bible were speeches of Satan or of false prophets or other enemies of God? All one could say in such cases was that inspiration gave us an infallible account of error. The same was the case with the discrepancies between Samuel/Kings and Chronicles. Carnell set out in two columns the parallel figures for numbers of chariots, cubits, persons slain and so on in a series of parallel passages. The conservative apologetic, according to Carnell, had explained these as follows: the figures had somehow become confused in the ancient public archives from which either one or other of the biblical sources had drawn their material. The biblical writers were inspired, and there was no error in what they wrote. But, on this hypothesis, Carnell suggested, inspiration meant no more than that the Bible gave us an infallibly accurate reprint of erroneous figures.[58]

Again, it has been repeatedly urged that the formula 'as it is written' in the New Testament is evidence of the complete submission of Jesus and the apostles to the truth of God as already written in the Old Testament. But, if so, what about a case like I Cor. 3.19: 'For it is written, "He catches the wise in their craftiness" ' (RSV). Clearly the apostle is here submitting himself to the Word of God as expressed verbally in the Old Testament text. But in fact the passage quoted comes from the speech of Eliphaz *against* Job (Job 5.13); and of Eliphaz we read in Job 42.7, 'The Lord said to Eliphaz the Temanite: "My wrath is kindled against you and against your two friends; for you have not spoken of me what is right, as my servant Job has." ' Thus not only can inspiration mean the infallible reporting of error, but that error, once infallibly reported, can be taken as the truth of God for the establishment of doctrine in the New Testament. Now it is not to be supposed that Carnell is siding with Henry Preserved Smith, a critical scholar who, though apparently originally conservative, was eventually forced out of his chair by conservatives in the American Presbyterian church.[59] He is simply pointing out that there are facts, as alleged by Preserved Smith and others, that the traditional conservative doctrine fails to cope with. The effect of these facts is not to disprove the traditional doctrine, it is rather to make it ludicrous.

Perhaps the other main issue raised by neo-orthodoxy and still felt among the more self-critical new conservatives is the matter of propositional revelation. This is a somewhat confused matter. Certain writers in the biblical theology movement had made repeated and vociferous attacks on the idea that God had made himself known through doctrinal statements expressed in propositional form.[60] This was not always a purely anti-conservative argument, for it tended to be directed rather indiscriminately against systematic or doctrinal theology in general. But, as against the doctrinal stratum of conservative evangelical theology, it certainly hit the mark, for there is no doubt that the propositional view was the one openly taken in the dominant current of opinion. Thus, for instance,

Charles Hodge writes: 'Truths, to be received as objects of faith, must be intellectually apprehended . . . In believing we affirm the truth of the proposition believed.'[61] It is not so clear, however, that this in itself expresses the actual religious sentiments of evangelicals. Though their doctrinal leaders might speak of assent to propositions, the rank and file might well concentrate on personal adherence and loyalty to Jesus Christ. Event, encounter, personal decision, rather than propositions, might be the basic stuff of daily worship in a fundamentalist community.[62] Thus the move from propositions to events and encounter was not in itself a clear move against the fundamentalist position: it might, indeed, be considered otherwise, as a move away from the scholastic level of fundamentalist leadership and back towards the religious grass roots of the same movement. There is good reason to diagnose certain elements in the biblical theology movement in just this way.

A further complication was the fact, mentioned above,[63] that biblical theology in moving away from biblical propositions tended to do one of two things: either it moved from authoritative propositions to authoritative biblical concepts, or else it moved from one type of authoritative propositions (those stating unchanging essences and substances) to another type of authoritative propositions (those containing a reference to historical events). Thus the attack on conservatism for its propositional view of truth, though in many ways justified, was also very confused and ambiguous.

In reply to this criticism, some conservative apologists, surely rather foolishly, let themselves be trapped into saying that revelation was indeed propositional and nothing else. 'The Word of God consists of *revealed truths*', says Packer, rushing cheerfully into the net.[64] 'the biblical position is that the mighty acts of God are not revelation to man at all, except in so far as they are accompanied by words of God to explain them.' Propositional revelation, the disclosure by God of truths about himself, is a necessary part of his redemptive activity. God's word in the mouths of the prophets and apostles was propositional in character. 'Christ and the apostles regularly appealed to Old Testament statements as providing a valid basis for inferences about God, and drew from them by the ordinary laws of grammar and logic [*sic*] conclusions which they put forward as truths revealed there.' Thus, Packer thinks, 'the Bible confronts us with the conception that the Word of God which it embodies consists of a system of truths, conveying to men real information from God about Himself.' The death of Christ would have been a complete enigma unless it had been interpreted to us by 'a spoken word from God'.

Here once again we see the automatic regressivism of the conservative apologist. It is not at all certain that conservatives, now that the issue has been raised, will want to accompany Packer back to a 'system of truths' and faith as an assent to 'real information' sent from God about himself in propositional form. Many conservatives have felt the incongruity of this with any Christian conception of faith, and they know that much evangelicalism as a form of personal religion does not work in this way. It was well enough for Hodge, a century ago, to talk of assent to propositions, but perhaps he said this without seeing that there was any question about the matter; and perhaps he might have modified this had he known the contrary positions as we know them today. It is quite doubtful therefore whether Packer is really speaking for most conservative evangelicals who have faced the issue at all.

But there is a much greater difficulty for those who want to go along the road of propositional revelation with Packer. Let us for the moment grant that God has set out certain propositions which are revelations of himself in that they tell the truth about God and interpret his 'mighty acts', which acts would otherwise remain unintelligible. This may or may not be so; but it is irrelevant to the issue as between critical and conservative views of the Bible. It does not justify the inspiration of *the Bible*. At the most it justifies only those texts within the Bible which convey information about God and interpret his mighty acts. But this is not the issue between critical scholarship and conservatism; in that controversy passages that may be regarded as 'interpretations' of God's mighty acts are not at all the centre of the problem. For instance, it is common ground, and not disputed territory, that the letters to the Romans and the Galatians are interpretations, and authoritative interpretations, of God's acts in Christ. This is indeed one of the few points where there is some degree of agreement.

When one turns to the passages that are centres of dispute as between conservative and critical opinion, one sees that many of them are passages that cannot on any intelligible basis be understood as 'interpretations' of God's acts at all. God did not interpret any mighty act by saying that Moses wrote the pentateuch, or that Jonah spent three days in the belly of the whale, or that Balaam's ass spoke to Balaam, or that Ishmael was a teenager when Isaac was born, or that Methuselah lived for 969 years. The view (not expressed in the Bible in any case) that the fourth gospel and Revelation were both written by John the son of Zebedee is not and could not be the explanation of any mighty act, nor could the view that all chapters in the book of Isaiah had been written by that prophet.

Packer's argument, as he unfolds it, might lead us to the position that the *theological* assertions and interpretations of the Bible are divinely inspired, and this is of course quite a popular position, but also quite a liberal position. This is, of course, not what Packer intends. What he really wants and needs to say is that *all* propositions in the Bible are divine propositional revelation. But he has already excluded this by his own argument. Once we take revelatory acts as the basis, even if revelatory propositions are needed in addition, we have introduced a differentiation which makes impossible the conclusion Packer wants to reach. Packer has got himself into the position where he must argue that, because some propositions in the Bible are revelatory propositions, therefore all propositions in the Bible are revelatory propositions, and inerrant even in matters that do not count as revelation by any criterion.

In fact Packer has ruined his argument as soon as he admitted revelatory acts as the primary basis, and thereby admitted also a diversity of functions for propositions. In an older conservatism like that of Hodge this kind of difficulty did not arise. The view was a general overall one: faith is, or includes, the affirmation of the truth of a proposition. This would apply, presumably, to any truth believed: particular facts, particular Christian doctrines, the Bible as a whole.[65] Revelation might be propositional or might not, and this would not make a difference to the truth of the Bible, for the truth of the Bible was not derived from or dependent on antecedent revelatory events, whether interpreted or not. Such revelatory events were of course believed in, but the truth of the Bible was not derived from its relation to them: it was derived from the inspiration of the writers, inspiration which made them infallible as teachers. That older conservative doctrine might be wrong, but at least it saw the target at which it aimed: what it said, if valid, was valid for the Bible as the book it is.

Packer well illustrates the total negativism as against neo-orthodoxy common or normal in British conservative evangelical writing. Yet it is not clear that, by separating out revelatory events in the first place, he has not already conceded too much to the neo-orthodox position. In any case, it is not probable that the newer current of evangelical opinion will follow Packer. On the contrary, his espousal of the propositional revelation position is likely to discredit it even more. Too many evangelicals know that their own faith is not a matter of assent to true propositions and they do not want it to be so. I would expect the majority of younger conservatives to lay the emphasis on the opposite side from Packer. Packer lays all the positive stress on the propositional revelation and does everything he can to depreciate any possible independence of revelation through events or through personal encounter. Many conservatives will go the other way. They will agree, along with neo-orthodoxy, that the primary and basic reality is revelation through events and personal encounter, and that personal faith relates itself to this. To this they will add as a secondary but also important aspect the propositional character of theological interpretations given in the Bible. But they will not thereby take the view that revelation is in essence propositional and still less that faith is assent to a system of truths operated upon by the ordinary laws of grammar and logic.

Certainly the 'new conservatives' are likely to go in a different direction from unbending hardliners like Packer. Ladd writes:

> God has acted in the events of redemptive history to make himself known to men. I cannot assent to the older orthodox view, which still has its adherents, that 'Revelation, in the biblical sense of the term, is the communication of information'. While I do not deny that revelation includes the disclosure of truth, this is too limited a definition. It is more accurate to say that 'revelation moves in the dimension of personal encounter . . . This is indeed the end of all revelation, to see the face of God.' What God reveals is not only information about himself; he reveals *himself*. This self-disclosure is not self-evident in historical events but requires the word of God to understand it as revelation.[66]

Of Beegle Hordern writes: 'Beegle believes that neo-orthodoxy has rescued the biblical meaning of faith, but it is in danger of overlooking the importance of propositional truths.'[67] And similarly, of another recent American writer:

> Kantzer affirms that revelation is through divine acts and culminates in Christ. All of this can be taken as a debt that conservatism is ready to acknowledge to neo-orthodoxy. But Kantzer goes on to insist that revelation is not complete without interpretation. If God acts, it is still necessary for God to interpret the meaning of his act. Thus, argues Kantzer, 'The God of most contemporary theologians can act but does not speak.' The conservative maintains that the Bible contains not only the history of the events in which God acted, but also the inspired interpretation of the events and this is why the Bible is the sole means of revelation.[68]

It is very likely then that many conservative evangelicals will in the next decade take up a position like those just cited from Ladd and Kantzer. This will probably bring some alleviation to the conflict between conservative and non-conservative types of Christianity. However, not too much should be hoped for in this direction. The line between personal or event revelation and propositional revelation was never well, carefully or clearly drawn and does not in fact coincide with the line between fundamentalism and other types of Christianity. To me it seems probable that a more careful analysis would divide not between propositional and non-propositional views, but between different classes of linguistic expressions, some propositional and others not, and that all of these expressions, whether propositional or not, would be related to the personal dimension and/or to events. If this is so, then we would end up with a totally different alignment. The question as it was traditionally discussed over three or four decades was probably badly confused. Conservatives would have been justified in saying that many of those who attacked propositional revelation took a much more propositional view than they admitted, or that the emphasis on biblical concepts in the biblical theology movement had something of the same kind of total effect. On the other hand it seems clear that one can hold revelation to be personal or through events and still maintain the entire series of fundamentalist tenets. Finally, it is likely that the key position, accorded by both sides in the recent discussion to the concept of revelation, is now due to be reconsidered;[69] but it would take us too far afield to follow this up in this book.

Apart from the matter of propositional revelation, perhaps the most striking thing about some of the 'new conservatives' is the way in which they are taking up the heritage of the biblical theology movement. This is particularly evident in the work of Ladd, who follows out with great devotion the type of biblical theology which took the history of salvation (*Heilsgeschichte*) as its centre. Among the various strains of *Heilsgeschichte* theology it is to a highly conservative line that Ladd attaches himself, one akin, if I am not mistaken, to the position taken by Otto Piper. The approach involves an attack on the sufficiency of the historical-critical method. This attack is made by means of a plentiful use of the presupposition argument, already surveyed above.

> The historical-critical method itself did not emerge as the result of open-minded, neutral, objective study of the Bible, but was motivated by rationalistic presuppositions which had no room for the biblical claim to revelation and inspiration.[70]

But this does not totally invalidate the critical method:

The method as such is not hostile to an evangelical faith, but the method as employed within certain non-evangelical philosophical presuppositions about the nature of God, history, and revelation.[71]

This may or may not be so, but the way it seems to work out in Ladd's approach remains highly conservative in regard to historical and literary matters. Authorships seem to remain traditional. Second Peter is written by Peter.[72] John, on the other hand, after a rather vacillating discussion, seems to have been written 'late in the first century to refute a gnostic tendency in the church'; it is not made clear who the author actually was.[73] Divergent theological emphases between John and the synoptic gospels are not glossed over.[74] But the general impression given by Ladd's work is highly conservative on the historical and literary questions. His free use of the presupposition argument probably blocked off for him many critical possibilities: that is to say, though he himself says that the critical method is not necessarily wrong, he is so suspicious of its presuppositions that he can hardly ever bring himself to make an actual critical decision.

But, for all its conservatism, the tone of Ladd's work is markedly different from that of most conservative evangelical writing.[75] Unlike most conservative writers on biblical passages, he does not take an apologetic approach. He does not seek to prove by historical evidence that events took place as narrated; on the contrary, as we have seen, he approaches the Bible from the other direction, arguing its uniqueness precisely because its events can *not* be proved through normal historical methods. He is sufficiently in line with common theological opinion to argue that the gospels, even the synoptics, do not attempt to set out the actual words spoken by Jesus. John's gospel is thus strongly theological interpretation, and not mere history. But this does not mark it off clearly from the synoptics, for they are not straight history either. Thus Ladd seems to direct attention to the documents as theological documents rather than as historical records. But he does not go far with this before he remembers that this should not be allowed to imply that the events narrated in them did not happen. 'If John is a theological interpretation, it is an interpretation of events that John is convinced happened in history.'[76] In general, though hesitant, Ladd looks at the documents from a much more theological angle than the average conservative evangelical commentator.

One has the impression that the main question for Ladd is not: are these narratives historically true? but: on what basis can one write a biblical theology? This means that many of the interests and values represented in the biblical theology movement are taken over, with a certain limited conservative adaptation, by Ladd. Though the position is not clear, it seems that his main message is: one cannot write a biblical theology on the basis of the historical-critical method, because that method implies presuppositions which cannot cope with the realities of the Bible, and this is because the realities of the Bible go beyond what is subject to normal historical explanation. Biblical theology is thus the end; the means is a method other than the historical-critical. What actually emerges from these methodological reflections seems to be in fact very largely a piece of ordinary biblical theology, with the historical-critical elements subtracted from it. This, if it is a right diagnosis, produces some rich paradoxes. One of the main reasons for attempting a biblical theology was, while accepting the results of the historical-critical method, to go beyond it to a synthetic operation; this particular conservative version accepts the goal of a biblical theology, but cuts out the historical-critical elements the presence of which was the reason for attempting the whole thing in the first place.

In any case, it is clear that certain strains in conservatism are happy to take over substantial elements in the biblical theology movement and its ethos. That this is attempted at all shows a considerable degree of sympathy and overlap with what is done in non-conservative biblical studies; and a corresponding degree of difference from the normal polemic and apologetic conservatism, with its inability to recognize anything of value in any non-conservative scholarship. But another thing is clearly displayed: in all this sort of operation conservatives are simply hanging on to the coat-tails of the non-conservative work in biblical theology. I cannot see any sign that conservatives who undertake this sort of work have any distinctive method or approach to put forward. They simply accept the plans, aims and categories of non-conservative study, and then modify (or spoil) these in the detailed execution by pulling everything into a somewhat more conservative direction.

It is sometimes pointed out that conservative writers quote non-conservative scholarship a great deal. In the field of biblical theology this is true. Some have suggested that this means that the conservatives are really much more open-minded than has been thought.[77] This is highly doubtful. In the biblical theology field conservatives are in fact accepting their categories and their basic ideas from scholars like Cullmann, von Rad, Piper, George Ernest Wright and others, because the whole leadership in biblical theology lies and has always lain in non-conservative hands. Non-conservative names and books are therefore constantly quoted in this field. But it is still only a small minority among conservatives who are willing to work in the terms provided by biblical theology, and the hard core of fundamentalism probably stands ready to repudiate this whole approach if need be. Similarly, works of commentary and introduction, dictionaries of the Bible and the like, quote non-conservative scholars a great deal; but much of this is either because the writers are not real conservatives at all, as explained above,[78] or because the conservative writer, though he knows the names and the work of critical scholars, quotes them in a purely polemic way, or else in the limited areas where there just is no disagreement. The reading and citation of non-conservative books by conservative writers, especially in the field of biblical theology, has been no sign of a genuine reduction in hostility towards critical scholarship. On the whole, the attitudes have remained as they have always been, dominantly polemical, except for those scholars who, though writing for conservative publications, do not really belong to the total conservative position. Biblical theology is indeed an area where some real overlap takes place; but it may be a case of conservatives taking over a field that was once non-conservative, rather than a case of fresh willingness to accept the methods of critical scholarship.

To sum up, neo-orthodoxy and biblical theology have been means by which some significant interaction between fundamentalism and non-conservative theology has taken place. These movements presented a deep and serious challenge to the fundamentalist position. On the other hand, the far right wing of these movements also had certain important overlaps with fundamentalism. Some conservative scholars, either influenced by these movements or thinking in parallel with them, have succeeded in introducing some welcome variety and movement into conservative thinking. It is possible that this will have wider repercussions in the future. But the hard core of conservative evangelical writing, the work of the apologists and polemicists, has as yet shown little or no sign of being affected by these developments. Its rejection of neo-orthodoxy remains, as it was, almost total; there is no sign that even the most conservative version of biblical theology has caused it to change its mind in any way; and, all in all, it seems still determined to reiterate the rigid polemical positions which have been repeated for a century or more and which were already traditional before neo-orthodoxy or biblical theology came upon the scene. Though

the 'new conservatives' are far more lively and creative than traditional conservatism has been, they are quite likely for exactly that
reason to be repudiated by conservatism and to lose influence
within the conservative world. One should therefore not hope for
too much.

8 · Miracles and the Supernatural

One of the most common charges made against critical scholarship by conservative apologists is that by some *a priori* prejudice it rules out the possibility of miracles. It simply assumes that miracles do not happen and cannot happen and that the supernatural must be left out of account in the making of judgments in biblical criticism. This totally unwarranted assumption shows how completely prejudiced critical scholars are and how unwilling they are to look at the facts for themselves. Because they rule out the possibility of miracles and similarly discount such possibilities as the divine inspiration of prophets and of writers, and the prediction of the future, they necessarily fall into the position of seeing all sorts of difficulties and discrepancies in scripture, none of which are genuinely there at all. These difficulties and discrepancies are created by the dogmatic and wholly unscientific assumption that miracles do not happen and that the intervention of the supernatural must be discounted.

A passage often quoted is this from Bultmann:

> The historical method includes the presupposition that history is a unity in the sense of a closed continuum of effects in which individual events are connected by the succession of cause and effect . . . This closedness means that the continuum of historical happenings cannot be rent by the interference of supernatural, transcendent powers and that therefore there is no "miracle" in this sense of the word. Such a miracle would be an event whose cause did not lie within history . . . It is in accordance with such a method as this that the science of history goes to work on all historical documents. And there cannot be any exceptions in the case of biblical texts if the latter are at all to be understood historically.[1]

Now this is an interesting position and perhaps it is a very logical and consistent basis for the historical approach to biblical criticism. It is very unlikely, however, that more than a small percentage of those who have practised the critical analysis of the Bible have actually believed this. Thunderings against criticism, on the grounds that it has assumed what Bultmann holds it to assume, are therefore vain, for most critics have assumed nothing of the sort. Certainly very many of them would have disagreed with Bultmann when he goes on to say that 'An historical fact which involves a resurrection from the dead is utterly inconceivable.'[2] I am sure that very few of them have in fact denied the possibility of miracles and of divine intervention in the course of history. Indeed the theological utterances of many of them show that they take these possibilities very seriously indeed for some purposes; and the vast majority have in fact believed in some sense that Jesus rose from the dead.

What critical scholars have probably believed is something quite different. They have not in the slightest 'assumed' that miracles, the resurrection and the supernatural are to be ruled out on principle, on the grounds that these things just cannot happen. What they have thought is that these cannot usefully be invoked as explanations for literary and historical questions in the dating and authorship of biblical books. Because this is the centre of the conservative case against critical scholarship, conservatives are not simply arguing in general that one should believe in miracles and the supernatural; they are arguing specifically that the belief in these things makes a difference to the historical and literary questions dealt with by biblical critics. If we accept that miracles really happen, then that will allow us to give greater historical value to a stratum in the gospels that contains miracles; if we accept supernatural intervention in history, and previous forecasting thereof by divine inspiration, then that will enable us to date Isaiah 40–55 in the time of the original Isaiah and the book of Daniel in the sixth century BC. This is the sort of application that conservative scholars have in mind.

The position that most critical scholars have probably taken, then, is something like this: we believe that 'supernatural' events, like the more important miracles and the resurrection of Jesus from the dead, can occur and have occurred; this is part of our Christian faith, which we do not deny or diminish, though we have no universally agreed understanding of how such events can take place or what we should make of them. It is not clear, however, that this belief of ours can be incorporated within, or regarded as part of, the historical and literary task of explaining the origins of the various biblical books. This, on the contrary, is a different matter and stands on a different level. We believe in the resurrection and in some degree in other miracles also; but we would spurn the idea of using this belief as a *deus ex machina*, as a device to establish an early date for Isaiah 40–55 or the book of Daniel.

Bultmann was thus a godsend to conservative polemicists, for he exactly confirmed their standard model of critical scholarship; and Bultmann is at one with the conservatives in failing to recognize what critical scholars have generally believed. In this Bultmann is not to be blamed. Firstly, I am not saying that Bultmann is wrong in his view of how historical criticism operates. All I say is that his description of the critical operation does not describe what a large number of scholars operating with critical methods have thought. Secondly, Bultmann was not seeking in any case to present a survey of what his colleagues have thought; he is speaking for himself and describing the critical procedure as he understands it. There is therefore no question of misrepresentation on Bultmann's part. Conservatives, on the other hand, are certainly guilty of misrepresentation in this entire matter. Their assertions about the 'assumptions' of critical scholars are simply the restatement of their own traditional model, which they apply to all modern theology and critical scholarship. When these assertions are made, they are not backed up by any attempt to discover what critical scholars have thought about miracles and the resurrection, or about the supernatural.

The historical-critical approach to the dating and source-criticism of books has been one that establishes a detailed network of normal human relations connecting the various books, their authors and the circumstances in which they are thought to have lived. The approach should not be expressed negatively as Bultmann does, when he says that it entails a denial of miracles and the supernatural, but positively: it is a network validated by the fullness and completeness of the account it gives of things in terms of normal human relations. What scholars have in fact found, as critical study of the Bible has progressed, is that, even where miracles and supernatural events are related, the historical and literary questions can be and should be treated as a matter of normal human relations and not resolved by means of an appeal to the supernatural or to miracles. The validity of this approach is supported by two considerations. Firstly, conservative scholars themselves, apart from actual conservative polemicists, probably share this approach to a very great extent, though they do not say so. Secondly, even on the most extreme conservative position, the number of places where miracles and the supernatural have to be invoked in order to settle literary and historical questions is very small. That is to say, the strength of the critical approach is not that it works because miracles and the supernatural are excluded as impossible, but that it works in the same way, for the vast majority of cases, whether miracles and the supernatural are accepted or not. I shall give ample evidence of this shortly. But one instance, already quoted in another connection, will illustrate what I mean. The gospels are full of miracle stories and apparently supernatural interventions. Critical scholars, who according to conservative belief exclude all miracles and the supernatural as a matter of principle, have worked out the analysis of these gospels into several sources, like Mark, Q and L. Obviously the elimination of miracles and the supernatural will have caused deep distortions in the analysis of evidence. Yet, when we turn to conservative New Testament scholars, who though not extremists certainly believe in the reality of miracles and the resurrection, what do we find? Exactly the same analysis is accepted, with small variations at the most. It is clear that, for the purposes of literary analysis, critical and more conservative scholars are at one in agreeing that, difficult as is the question of miracle in itself, that question can be bracketed out for the purpose in hand.

Thus writers like E. J. Young and R. K. Harrison who use the supernaturalist argument and rule out of court any work on the dating and historicity of biblical books that 'denies' the supernatural leave us with no case that needs or deserves to be answered. Conservative introductions like theirs seek, like a critical introduction, to construct an account of the relations between authors, dates and books on the basis of normal human relations. They invoke the supernatural not as part of a general theological argument about miracles, but as an *ad hoc* device to justify without further discussion the conservative position on finite points of literary history, such as the authorship of Isaiah 40–55 and Daniel. The effect of this is to establish a gross discontinuity between the main mass of the introduction and the quite discordant picture produced at the points where the supernaturalist argument is invoked.

Before going farther we may say something about the general theological character of the supernaturalist argument.[3] The view that Christian faith implies belief in a supernatural, a world controlled by divine power and inaccessible to normal human methods of understanding and investigation, is an honoured one of noble pedigree, even if it is now old-fashioned. It is a position that can be perfectly well used by, let us say, a Roman Catholic scholar who unites conservative views of the Bible with (say) a traditional Thomism in philosophy and theology. The reason why it cannot be consistently followed by Protestant conservative evangelicals is that they apply it only to the Bible. Outside the Bible their perception of the world is not in the least supernaturalistic; on the contrary it is often bitterly sceptical and secularistic. Miracles have to be believed – but only if the miracles are narrated in the Bible. Even a miracle that has only the most dubious and tenuous connections with any moral or doctrinal values for Christianity must be taken very seriously, if it is found within the Bible: for example, the story in II Kings 6.1–7 of the axe-head which fell into the water. Elisha threw in a stick and made the iron float. Because this is a biblical story, anyone who ruled out the actuality of the miracle would probably suffer violent attacks from conservatives.[4] But a story of a miraculous healing, if narrated in an apocryphal book or a mediaeval source, is treated with scornful contempt, even if the story is set in a context of fully Christian doctrine. It is this confinement to a zone identical with the Bible (excluding the Apocrypha) that makes the supernaturalist argument, as it is used by Protestant fundamentalists, a superstition. Their use of the supernatural is occasionalistic and opportunist. They do not have and do not advocate a general supernaturalist outlook; the supernaturalist argument is one upon which they fall back at those points where it is the only way of establishing a necessary conservative position in the literary history of the Bible.

There is, however, an even more convincing ground why we should not take seriously the conservative argument from miracle and the supernatural. Though conservative apologists continually appeal to miracle as a means of attacking and discrediting critical scholarly methods, there is no evidence that conservative biblical scholars themselves can use miracle as an explanatory device any more than critical scholars do. On the contrary, the explaining away of miracle stories and the rationalization of them into something less than miraculous is a common and normal, though not a universal, feature of the conservative scholarly literature of recent times. Take the incident of the crossing of the Jordan by the incoming Israelites as related in Josh. 3.13–17. The incident takes place at a time when the Jordan is in full flood. But Joshua told them (v. 13) that when the priests carrying the ark of the covenant set foot in the waters the waters of the Jordan would be cut off: 'the water coming down from upstream will stand piled up like a bank or heap (Hebrew *ned*)'. So it happened: the moment the priests put their feet into the water, the water coming down from upstream was brought to a standstill; 'it piled up like a bank for a long way back, as far as Adam, a town near Zarethan' (NEB). Now let us see how *The New Bible Commentary Revised* (Hugh J. Blair, p. 237) deals with the matter:

An interesting parallel to the event recorded in this chapter has been found in the pages of an Arabic historian, describing how in AD 1266 near Tell ed-Dâmiyeh, which many experts have identified with Adam, the bed of the river was left dry for ten hours in consequence of a landslide. Other parallels have been quoted: in 1927 an earthquake caused the west bank to collapse near the location of Adam, and the Jordan was dammed up for more than twenty-one hours.

In other words, we have here, in a standard conservative evangelical commentary – and plenty of further examples will be cited shortly – an excellent instance of the explaining away of a miracle by a naturalizing and rationalizing explanation. Were the blockage of the Jordan, related by an Arab historian, and the one caused by an earthquake in 1927, miracles? Of course they were not. They were absolutely normal events brought about by natural causation. The aligning of the biblical incident in the same series with them decreases or totally abolishes its miraculous character. It is a completely natural event that takes place at a very fortunate time for the Israelites. This is a quite common type of conservative evangelical procedure: an explanation is adopted which will support the belief that an event took place as narrated, but without worrying about the consequence, namely that the event as thus explained ceases to be a miracle. The veracity of the report, and not the miraculous character of the event, is what counts for the conservative interpreter.

The same treatment is given to a large number of miracle stories in *The New Bible Commentary Revised*. The manna given by God to feed the children of Israel was also a natural substance, easily to be found by travellers in the region of Sinai. Anyone who goes there at the right time of year will find it. As the commentary says, 'The season in the western Sinai peninsula begins at the end of May and continues into June and July, the time when the Israelites were in the desert' (J. A. Thompson, p. 181). 'It (the manna) was, no doubt, a divine provision, but none the less it may have been a natural substance.'[5]

What about the crossing of the Red Sea by the Israelites in the Exodus story? The same is the case here. 'The crossing is miraculous in the sense that God uses a natural agent (a strong east wind) with positively supernatural results (dividing the waters)' – so Hywel Jones, p. 128. On p. 129 the same writer gives a similar interpretation to the quails which arrived and gave the Israelites plenty of food: 'The common quail migrated across the Red Sea in large numbers at this time and, faint after a long journey, could be caught with ease. The miraculous element consists in the time of their arrival.' In Num. 11.32 it is the same, though this time the commentator is J. A. Thompson: 'The Lord sent a wind which brought quails from the sea, probably the Gulf of Aqabah. This is a natural phenomenon and still today the quails migrate in the spring ... '

Now the writers who deal with miracle stories in this way at times show some awareness that they are really de-miraculizing the miraculous. Thus Blair (*The New Bible Commentary Revised*, p. 237) tells us that 'These events may indicate a "natural" explanation of what happened centuries earlier, but to accept that explanation does not detract in any way from the supernatural intervention which opened the way to Israel just at the moment when they needed to cross.' This is in essence the same as the argument about the quails, already quoted, to the effect that the miraculous element consisted in the timing. What must be emphasized is that this sort of argumentation, whatever its intrinsic value, is essentially liberal argument. Liberal! One could go farther and say that it is rationalistic and deistic argument. It reduces what seem on the face of it to be gross divine interventions into very limited providential concatenations of natural forces. 'Miracles' of this sort are not in any way essentially abnormal: they are only rare combinations of factors all of which are provided by normal environmental forces. The only thing God has done is to arrange that this rare combination takes place at the right time. God is not really upsetting the natural order very much. This position is in fact identical with the commonplace rhetoric of the liberal pulpit. It is a combination of fundamentalism and liberalism: the biblical report is understood in fundamentalist fashion, for it is essential that the event took place as described in scripture, but the treatment and explanation of the miracle is liberal. The irritation of the interpreter with the complaint that a miracle thus naturalized is not a real miracle at all is a truly liberal sentiment.

An even more impressive naturalization falls upon the plagues of Egypt. 'The nine plagues manifest natural phenomena which occur in the Nile Valley, and the miraculous element in them is to be found in their timing, intensity and distribution.' Only the last of the ten plagues, the death of the first-born, is a real miracle and 'belongs wholly to the realm of the supernatural'; the other nine 'demonstrate God's use of the created order for his own ends'. The whole thing began with an unusually high inundation of the Nile. Kitchen writes:

> Thus, the excessive inundation may have brought with it microcosms known as flagellates which would redden the river and also cause

conditions that would kill the fish. Decomposing fish floating inshore would drive the frogs ashore, having also infected them with *Bacillus anthracis*. The third plague would be mosquitoes, and the fourth a fly, *Stomoxys calcitrans*, both encouraged to breed freely in the conditions produced by a high inundation. The cattle-disease of the fifth plague would be anthrax contracted from the dead frogs, and the 'blains' on man and beast (sixth plague), a skin anthrax from the *Stomoxys* fly of the fourth plague. Hail and thunderstorms in February would destroy flax and barley, but leave the wheat and spelt for the locusts whose swarming would be favoured by the same Abyssinian rains which had ultimately caused the high inundation. The 'thick darkness' would be the masses of fine dust, *Roterde* (from mud deposited by the inundation), caught up by the *khamsin* wind in March.[6]

The interpretation is, in other words, a total naturalization and rationalization of the story. The miraculous is reduced to the absolute minimum in order to obtain a sequence that has plausibility as a series of events that could intelligibly have taken place in nature. The sequence is so perfect that it seems a pity that God did not use the natural order to kill the first-born as well.

The instance is an amusing reversal of the situation evoked by conservative polemicists. If they are to be believed, critical scholars refuse to believe in miracles, and because they discount miracle they have to consider the Bible full of errors and they have also to invent source-critical theories in order to explain how all these errors came to be put together in the form actually found in the Bible. In fact conservative scholarship, as we see it here, reduces the miraculous to vanishing point in order to obtain a 'true' narrative, which hangs together by a series of scientifically plausible connections totally absent in the biblical story. Far from defending the biblical story as against a modern or scientific picture, the conservative interpretation just reviewed depends totally on non-miraculous but scientifically plausible connections, all of them quite absent from the biblical text. If one uses on it the terms that fundamentalists use upon interpretations offered by critical scholars, it has clearly stated that the biblical version of the incident is false. The entire atmosphere and the detail of the biblical narrative are abandoned. In the biblical text God intervenes separately for each plague, and each one is introduced by threats communicated through Moses, or by the stretching out of Moses' rod: in the new 'conservative' interpretation each plague follows directly from the previous one by natural causation. In the Bible God turned the water of all Egypt into blood; according to Kitchen he did nothing of the sort, all that happened was the production of flagellates which 'would' redden the water.

The dependence of the interpretation on modern scientific connections is made clearer still by another aspect of Kitchen's argumentation. Some critical scholars have thought that some of the ten plagues came from one source of the pentateuch, some from another. Kitchen emphasizes that it is the whole unitary argument that corresponds with observable physical phenomena.[7] That is to say, if one separated out a group of three or four plagues, supposed to belong to the source J, and another few that belonged to P, neither of these sets would make any sense, because they would not possess the chains of natural causation that make the complete set of ten so plausible. How wonderful and how final an argument against the separation of sources! The 'conservative' argument depends on natural causation, and therefore on the absence of special divine intervention to bring about this plague or that; the 'critical' argument can take them in any order, since it sees them as direct divine interventions. It is the supposedly 'conservative' argument that depends for its effectiveness on scientific causality and the absence of explicit miracle within the series of nine.

Readers might think a case like this so obviously absurd that I must be picking out occasional examples, and that the real tendency of conservative evangelical interpretation may be towards affirmation of full-blown miracles. I assure them that this is not so, at least in the literature studied by me. Another major example from the Old Testament may be cited; it is the passage about the sun 'standing still' during the battle of Aijalon, Josh. 10.12–15. The average reader of this passage will suppose that Joshua commanded the sun and moon to stand still, and that this gave him adequate time to complete his victory. 'The sun stayed in the midst of heaven, and did not hasten to go down for about a whole day. There has been no day like it before or since, when the Lord hearkened to the voice of a man' (Josh. 10.13–14 RSV). Blair in *The New Bible Commentary Revised*, p.244, tells us that it has usually been assumed (!) that Joshua prayed for the day to be prolonged, to enable him to overcome his enemies fully. In fact, according to Blair, it was a night attack, and what Joshua really needed was that 'the darkness should continue and the night be prolonged for his surprise attack'. There was therefore no change in the astronomical behaviour of the sun and moon. 'The answer to his prayer came in a hailstorm which had the effect of prolonging the darkness.' So in the darkness of the storm the defeat of the enemy was complete.

Thus one of the major miracles of the Old Testament is rudely eliminated by the conservative protagonists of an 'inerrant' Bible. Blair, the commentator, realizes that his readers might feel that he has explained the passage only by explaining away the miracle, and so he goes on:

> One is not disparaging the miraculous nature of the occurrence by suggesting that there was a less spectacular divine intervention than is postulated by the more customary interpretation, which takes it that the day was lengthened. It was still God who lengthened the night by a miraculous intervention on behalf of his people.[8]

In other words, his evangelical readers ought to feel that a God who arranges for a heavy but quite natural hailstorm is just as good a God of intervention and miracle as one who stops the movement of the sun in the sky. Well, they may or may not accept this argument, but they are simply foolish if they are unaware that in accepting it they are passing over entirely into the liberal-rationalist position and type of argumentation. If this was the way in which conservatives understood biblical miracle stories there would be no reason for them to quarrel in this respect with liberal and rationalist interpreters.

Two notes should be added in respect of this interpretation. Firstly, those who understand the story in this way adduce what is supposed to be linguistic evidence, to suggest (for example) that the text said the sun should stop *shining* rather than stop *moving*.[9] Thus they really think, or suggest one might think, that the passage actually does not say anything about the stopping of movement or the lengthening of the day. Those who wish to may believe this.

Secondly, the 'long day' of Joshua is one of the most difficult miracles of the Bible for fundamentalists of today, and with it goes into the same category the story of the 'return' of the shadow on the dial of Ahaz (Isa. 38.8; II Kings 20.11). Older fundamentalism would have felt no difficulty: God simply moved the sun or moon backwards, as he could perfectly well do, having created them in the first place. But awareness of modern astronomical knowledge, along with total acceptance of it by fundamentalists, has changed this. If God had really stopped the movement of the sun (in fact, of course, the movement of the earth), as Ramm with his engaging frankness puts it, 'the disturbances on the earth and the solar system would have been enormous'.[10] No doubt all houses would have fallen down, seas would have shifted, who can tell what would have been the consequences? Beyond all doubt there would be clear evidence of this enormous disturbance of the solar system available through astronomical investigations to the present day. There is, however, no such evidence. The scientific evidence therefore compels fundamentalists to the belief that God did not in fact perform this miracle. He could of course have done, as Ramm makes clear, and kept the solar system and the universe from disintegrating, but would it have been worth doing? Most students 'feel' that the record 'does not call for a miracle of such gigantic proportions'. In other words, the entire discussion of the matter within fundamentalism assumes scientific knowledge as a basic datum, and simply gets rid of the miracle in its biblical form when it is found that this will not stand against the scientific evidence. The thought that there might have been a legend that God had stopped the sun or moon, and that this picture, though legendary in our terms, is essential to the biblical narrative, receives little or no notice at all.

The examples taken up to now have been from the Old Testament. In the New Testament the commentators in *The New Bible Commentary* may take a similar line, but it is often hard to tell, because in many miracle stories they simply relate the incident and comment on the passage, without making any attempt to specify whether in their opinion the event took place or not, or whether it was miraculous or not. Another astronomical example is the star perceived and followed by the Magi (Matt. 2): they followed this star until finally it stopped above the place where the child Jesus lay (2.9). R. E. Nixon in *The New Bible Commentary Revised*, p. 819a, tells us: 'There is no certainty about the astronomical phenomenon but it may have been the close conjunction of Jupiter and Saturn in 7 BC.' This means, of course, that the 'star' was a perfectly normal and regular astronomical phenomenon, traceable from modern observations and mathematically predictable. Far from the star being specially sent or arranged for by God, God would have had to fit in his timing for the birth of Jesus to agree with the movements of the star – unless perhaps he had set the solar system in motion at its beginning in order to synchronize with the future birth of Jesus. So here again there is not much of a miracle, if this explanation is true. Ramm, however, though he knows and respects this interpretation, goes in another direction.[11] The conjunction specified is only a very loose and imprecise one, and the biblical text requires something much more precise. No conjunction of planets, nor any other known astronomical phenomenon, could provide us with a star so precise in its movements that it could indicate the very house where Jesus was. As Ramm, ever realistic in his scientific observations, says, 'a star so close would have scorched the populace to death for hundreds of square miles around'. He thinks therefore that this was a 'special luminous manifestation', specially created for the birth of Jesus and seen only by the Magi – presumably, therefore, not traceable by modern astronomy. How did the Magi know about it and understand its meaning? They were told this supernaturally.

The instance is an interesting one. The interpretation given by Nixon implies no miracle at all in the provision of the star. Ramm considers this with respect but observes that the biblical text requires something more specific than this rationalizing interpretation can offer. In this case he therefore in the end goes over to a sheerly supernaturalist explanation: God made, specially for the occasion, a 'manifestation'. Does this 'luminous manifestation' satisfy the requirements of the biblical text? Hardly, because the gospel clearly states that it was a 'star'.

The case is interesting because it demonstrates the problems that appear when a completely uncontrolled appeal to the supernatural is adopted. If historians do not use the supernatural as a category of explanation in the writing of history, it is not necessarily and not in fact because they deny the existence of the supernatural; rather, it is because with the supernatural anything at all can happen. There is thus no means whatever of controlling statements that purport to state events that are explained as supernaturally caused. Ramm illustrates this well with his interpretation of Jonah and the fish or whale.[12] Ramm pays no attention to the possibility that the story of Jonah might be a legend or myth; he does consider the possibility that the book of Jonah might have been allegorical but follows Aalders in concluding from the literary form that it was not allegorical. Nothing is now left but to consider the nature of the fish or whale. There are whales which could hold a man alive in their air tract, and so it is impossible to deny that Jonah might have been carried in a normal whale as described in the story. But Ramm himself goes another way:

> The record clearly calls the creature a *prepared fish* and if this means a special creature for a special purpose we need not search our books on sea creatures to find out the most likely possibility. It would be a creature created of God especially for this purpose, and that is where our investigation ends. The evangelical accepts a supernatural theism, and the centrality of redemption and moral values. The necessity of getting the message of redemption to Nineveh is the sufficient rationale for God to have made such a creature.

This shows us well what can happen when the sheerly supernatural is taken as a means of historical explanation. From the wording of the King James text, 'Now the Lord had prepared a great fish', Ramm extracts this imaginative account of a specially created creature, different from all other fishes or whales.[13] No doubt it had a primitive form of air-conditioning for the well-being of the prophet. Perhaps it contained a writing desk with inkpot and pen, similar to those actually found at Qumran, so that the prophet could indite on the spot the prayer which he recited (Jonah 2). These are not exaggerations for comic effect: in sober truth there is absolutely nothing to control speculation once the extreme supernaturalism of Ramm is accepted. There is no means of saying what is more or less probable, what is justifiable and what is not. The only limitation is that such a supernaturalist speculation should have some sort of scrap of biblical evidence to hang on to. Ramm is not quoted here in order to be dismissed: he is far more intelligent about these matters than conservative evangelical apologists usually are. Though he thinks that Jonah's sojourn in a normal and natural whale is possible, he knows that it remains a very precarious supposition: it is really easier to think of God creating a special creature than to rely on Jonah's spending three days within a normal whale or fish.

These last two instances are cases of very extreme supernaturalist interpretation. The general tendency, however, in conservative evangelical literature is in the opposite direction, and numerous cases have been cited. Far from it being the case that miracle and supernatural causation is a fully accepted principle of interpretation in conservative scholarship, that scholarship makes very considerable efforts to rationalize and to eliminate miracle, reducing it from its biblical dimensions to something more like the picture of a deity who from time to time arranges favourable conjunctions of natural phenomena. Though the sheerly supernatural explanations just illustrated from Ramm would probably be respected, and would certainly not be scorned, by most conservative interpreters, they do not in fact generally go in this direction. The rationalization and naturalization of miracle narratives in deist and liberal style is a quite normal and frequent feature of conservative interpretation.

Surely, readers will say, this is rather surprising. Is not fundamentalist interpretation strongly opposed to rationalism? In order to understand this an important difference should be noted. There are two kinds of rationalization applicable to stories of this sort. One is a sceptical and mocking explanation which explains the miracle away altogether, making it into a lie, a pretence or an illusion. Interpretations of this sort are always or almost always rejected by conservative interpreters, but sometimes they are at least mentioned. At the capture of Jericho, for instance. *The New Bible Commentary Revised* (p. 239) warns us that there is no basis for such an anti-supernaturalist and minimizing view as that the marchers served to distract the attention of the watchers on the walls while Israelite sappers were undermining the ramparts. Quite so. Again, it is wrong to suppose with the 'rationalists' (p. 865b) that at the feeding of the multitudes by Jesus the people actually had provisions in their pockets, so that the 'miracle' consisted in no more than the fact that at Jesus' indication they produced these from their pockets and ate them. The story of the resurrection is full of such attempted rationalizations, e.g. that the 'angels' were people in white robes and so on, but the *Commentary* usually does not even mention these. Amusingly, it does mention (p. 835b) at Matt. 14.25, where Jesus came towards the disciples 'walking on the sea', the possibility that the expression should mean 'on the sea shore'. This would of course be a marvellous rationalization. It would mean that the gospel did not say that Jesus walked on the water but only that he was walking on the shore. This interpretation, however, says the commentator (R. E. Nixon) is 'unlikely in the context', perhaps the most monumental understatement ever to be made in a conservative evangelical commentary. Unlikely! If this is not more than 'unlikely', miracles and the supernatural are certainly receiving a thin and inhospitable treatment from modern conservatives.

In any case, it is generally true that conservatives reject rationalizations that make the event narrated into a non-event, a pretence or an illusion of some kind. But it is equally clear that they welcome those rationalizations that make the event historically true but explain it as a natural event, God doing no more than to arrange a favourable concatenation of natural forces. This is fully intelligible, because we have seen throughout this study that their main interest is in securing an interpretation which, whatever its modes and presuppositions, will agree with the idea that the Bible is inerrant. A reduced and rationalized miracle, such as these interpretations give us, may be some sort of a weak and watery miracle, but it is no longer a biblical miracle and the God who arranges it is no longer the God of the Bible. Moreover, the interpretation has in many cases still not succeeded in its prime aim, that of showing that the Bible is without error. Many of these interpretations make the Bible inerrant in one aspect, perhaps in that an event really occurred to which the narrative refers, but they do this at the cost of producing new errors in the Bible. These explanations abstract from the biblical narratives many or all of the features that caused the story to be regarded as a miracle in the first place.

For example, in the damming up of the Jordan for the Israelites to cross, it would not be counted as much of a miracle if the story had simply said what Blair makes out of it, that when the Israelites arrived at the Jordan they found it blocked by a landslide upriver. This would be good fortune for them, perhaps it would be divine providence, but it would not be a miracle. In fact, however, the biblical story contains much more. Firstly, Joshua had already told the Israelites exactly what would happen: this makes it a good deal more than a 'natural event'. Secondly, the story is quite precise about the occurrence: it was at the moment that the priests put their feet into the water that the current was cut off. This again is a bit more than one can attach to the category of common landslides. Thirdly, the story says nothing at all about the Jordan being blocked by a landslide or any kind of physical obstacle. What is said is that the water piled up like a heap or *ned*; that is, it was not blocked by a natural force, it simply piled up, in a way that water, a quite familiar physical substance, does not do. The idea that God works through natural forces, whether theologically acceptable or not, is attained in these interpretations simply by disregarding the particular form of the biblical texts. The same is true of the idea that at the Exodus God used a natural agent, a strong east wind. A strong east wind can have physical effects but it does not do what the Exodus narrative says: the water was a 'wall' to them on each side, the sea bed was turned into dry land. Here as often, the conservative interpretation, far from being literal, is quite abandoning the literal form of the text. Similarly, in the plagues of Egypt, the text does not tell us that flagellates would redden the river as a result of an unusually high inundation, but that the water was turned into blood. In order to attain a non-miraculous and therefore apologetically tenable interpretation this biblical statement is simply ignored.

At the risk of boring readers, another illustration from the Old Testament will be offered. The very large numbers of the children of Israel on their march from Egypt to Canaan may not constitute a miracle, but at least they seem to be a very remarkable situation. According to Num. 1.46 the total number of males, twenty years old and upward, fit for war, was 603,550. This and similar figures have often evoked apologetic problems. If this was the number for adult males, another million or two must be added for women and children. Sceptics have pointed out that if this were so, the column on the march would have been so long that when the head of it was entering the promised land the rear part would still not have got out of Egypt. What does the modern conservative have to say about this? Is he boldly upholding the accuracy of the Bible, relying on the power of God to sustain this great multitude by miraculous feedings? Not in the slightest. On the contrary, he is doing all he can to find a way to cut the numbers down. According to J. A. Thompson in *The New Bible Commentary Revised*, p. 169, 'the exact numerical value of the terms is unknown'. Perhaps, he suggests, the consonants of the Hebrew numeral meaning 'thousand' should be revocalized to give us another word with a sense like 'leader' or 'captain'; it might then, one supposes, mean only a few hundred captains (plus their, presumably few, followers); or else it might be taken to be another word meaning 'families'. Perhaps, if the words were not originally numbers, 'a later compiler of ancient source material misunderstood the true meaning of the terms and, assuming them to be numbers, simply added them up and arrived at the total 603,550.' R. A. H. Gunner takes a similar line in *The New Bible Dictionary*, p. 896.[14]

Here again it seems that the trend towards the rationalizing explanation has been increasing in recent years. The older *New Bible Handbook*, p. 145, correctly notes that any attempt to get rid of the high numbers by such devices as finding another word instead of the word 'thousand', while getting rid of some difficulties, only introduces others. The text emphasizes the exceptionally high numbers of the people and the need for miraculous provision for them; the large number and the miracles have therefore just got to be accepted. Similarly, E. J. Young in his *Introduction to the Old Testament* (Tyndale Press 1964), p. 85, also sticks to the figures as they stand. It cannot be doubted that the position taken by these older sources is the more honest and integral one. The more recent conservative writers, however, seem not to be going in that direction.

Once again we have to note the contrast in atmosphere as between the Old Testament and the New. Conservative evangelical commentators on the Old clearly feel very often that they have to give an account of a miracle narrative in terms of the actuality of the event: sometimes they do this by a rationalizing explanation, sometimes they go in the other direction and say that a total miracle has to be accepted. In works like *The New Bible Commentary Revised* the New Testament commentators often leave such questions undiscussed. This may correspond to the fact that conservative New

Testament interpretation, when done by professional scholars in the field, comes rather closer to critical methods than corresponding work in the Old Testament. Critical scholars in a commentary often leave undiscussed the question of what exactly happened in a healing miracle or other miraculous story. Conservative commentaries often leave the same information undisclosed. This means that their fundamentalist readers will commonly read the commentary with the understanding that the events took place exactly as narrated, while more critical readers can use them on the assumption that this question is simply bracketed out for the purposes of the commentary. Where something explicit is said about miracle stories, it can oscillate, as in Old Testament commentaries, between the use of rationalizing explanations and the denial of them, with a consequent resort to total supernaturalism. For example, C. E. Graham Swift, writing on Mark, and dealing with the stilling of the storm by Jesus, gives us the hoary information, beloved of the liberal pulpit, that there are frequent sudden storms on the Sea of Galilee. This information tends to reduce the supernaturalism of the story by making it more likely that there is a sort of naturalistic basis for it. Storms come and go very suddenly, so no very great miracle is needed for Jesus to have stopped one (p. 861f.). In the well-known instance of Jairus' daughter, where Jesus says (Mark 5.39) that 'The child is not dead but sleeping', some have taken advantage of this to produce the interpretation that she really was asleep, not dead, which obviates the need for a miracle of the magnitude of the raising of one dead, and which also enables the words of the Lord to be taken as exactly correct and inerrant. It is not quite clear from Swift's wording (p. 863b), but it looks as if he gives respectful consideration to this view but himself goes in the other direction, taking it that the girl was really dead. On the feeding of the multitude (p. 865b) he uses the dogmatic argument, that is, that if we believe that Jesus was 'incarnate Deity' there is no real difficulty in believing that he carried out the miracle. These are a fairly representative sample from among cases where comments on miracles and the supernatural are made.

We have now done enough to survey the character of fundamentalist opinion about miracles and the supernatural, as it is to be seen in actual comment on particular passages. It has been shown that the actual attitude to miracle stories and the use of the supernatural is totally in contradiction with the general assertions made about the subject by conservative polemicists. It remains to gather up the subject with some general remarks.

First of all, it can easily be seen that the position of miracles and the 'supernatural' is better safeguarded in critical scholarship than in the sort of conservative apologetic we have been discussing. Conservatives seem not to have seen a point that to most Christians must be sufficiently obvious: the problem of miracle cannot be solved by simply saying that anything can happen, or even that anything can happen so long as it is in the Bible, because if anything can happen no happening will be a miracle. Far from it being a necessity of Christian faith that one accepts as true the story of any miracle narrated, the miraculous character of occurrences is preserved only if miracles are regarded as in high degree improbable if not impossible. Only when miracles cannot happen do we have some reason to wonder at them when they come to pass. If conservatives had their way and we solved the problem by simply believing that the supernatural exists as a world beyond our own in which God can do anything, then of course anything could happen and there would be no intrinsic improbability in the raising of someone from the dead; on the contrary, it would be one's duty to suppose that, though such things do not happen often, there is absolutely nothing to prevent them from happening. This is the necessary implication of what is repeatedly said in conservative polemic against critical scholarship. But of course, as we have seen, conservatives themselves do not believe this argument, or not most of the time. They are likely to be quite sceptical about miracles and such things except for such incidents as are narrated in Bible. And, as we have seen, even within the Bible they tend to reduce the miraculousness of the miracles, sometimes however going off entirely in the other direction and increasing it. They do not want to prove that, because there is a supernatural, any miracle, of even the greatest magnitude, can happen at any time. They pull in the argument about the supernatural, as a rule, where they have no other means of validating apologetically some particular miracle story within the Bible. But their whole procedure shows that they do not want to press the supernaturalist argument beyond the necessary minimum. In fact the only way to put biblical miracles into a good light and see them as real and precious signs from God is to exercise towards them the cool and critical reserve that has long been characteristic of modern theology and of critical biblical study.

The idea of the supernatural entertained by conservative apologists seems to me to be as follows. Experience is like a jointed rod; some pieces are of iron and some of brass. One piece is natural, the next is supernatural. Unlike the great consistent supernaturalist systems of the past, fundamentalism does not hold the supernatural away from this world and its experience. The supernatural is thus reduced to the same level as the natural. One segment of experience follows the patterns of the natural world, the next follows those of the supernatural. One thus simply goes back and forward from one to the other. To put it in another way, the concept of the supernatural is borrowed by fundamentalism from a philosophy in which it itself does not believe, and it is borrowed in order to be used for one sole purpose: to provide a polemical weapon against critical attitudes to the Bible and the sort of theology that is informed by these attitudes. It is the Bible that ties the whole thing together, and not the ideas or the theology of the Bible, but the inerrancy of the Bible. In order to validate so far as is possible the inerrancy of the Bible, the interpreter constructs a continuum of experience where at one moment everything has a naturalistic explanation, at the next everything is sheerly supernatural. This is the only way in which I can understand how the same interpreter can give a thoroughly naturalizing and rationalizing interpretation of a passage and on the very next page invoke a principle of complete supernaturalism. The effect of this is to assimilate the supernatural to the natural: it is much bigger and better as a set of potentialities, but it is really the same sort of thing. Or, to put it in another way, it trivializes the God of the Bible, who becomes a sort of larger-than-life manager of the world, arranging at one moment for flagellates to appear in the Nile, at the next raising someone from the dead, at another supervising the movement of quails, at another creating out of nothing bread for a multitude to eat. If one wants a God who is 'supernatural', who is something other than our own kind of experience, then the most sceptical and critical kinds of modern theology have far more to offer than conservative evangelicalism has.

Apart from the general question of miracle, some brief attention should be given to the question of prediction. Conservative arguments frequently hold it against critical scholarship that it denies the possibility of prediction. Norman Anderson recently castigated scholarship for, as he thought, assuming that 'there can be no such thing as a prediction of the future by anyone'.[15] R. K. Harrison blames the critics for their 'insistence that there was no predictive element in prophecy'.[16] How important is this?

Firstly, the attention given to the question seems to support the suggestion, made in these pages, that conservative evangelicals use a deist model for their understanding of non-conservative biblical study. The 'argument from prophecy', i.e. the argument that certain things in the future had been predicted by prophets and had come to pass as predicted, was one of the traditional arguments for the existence of God and for revelation. The criticism of this argument by the deists was one of their ways of (as it was then seen) discrediting the claims of Christianity to be a revealed religion. The sensitivity of conservatives over prediction to this day is probably a survival of this way of looking at the matter.

Secondly, we have already noted the extreme importance of predictive prophecy in millenarian versions of fundamentalism. In this approach it is not only mere prediction of particular future events, but a large-scale forecasting of wide-ranging sets of events, that is essential, and is indeed the most important element within the Bible. It is not surprising if anyone who allows millenarianism to be even a possible form of fundamentalist belief will be very anxious to uphold the reality of predictive prophecy.

Thirdly, older traditional Christianity thought of the prophets primarily as those who foretold the coming of Christ. It was with the move to a critical approach in the late eighteenth century that they came to be seen primarily as men who spoke for their own generation, and the result was certainly a reduction in the predictive understanding. This shift of emphasis was in any case entirely right, since even if the most complete acceptance of prediction is granted prediction cannot be regarded as the content of more than a very small fraction of the prophetic sayings.

Fourthly, the idea that critical scholarship denied or minimized prediction on principle, that is, because it was supposed that prediction depended on the supernatural and was therefore impossible, is quite unjustified. Even if individuals said this, there is no reason to suppose that this is the position logically required by critical scholarship. What is more likely is that passages which had traditionally been regarded as predictions of the future came under critical scholarship to be explained in a different way. It is only conservative prejudice that interprets this as motivated solely by the desire to avoid prediction. Equally, it is only conservative prejudice that wants to forbid us to see a passage, which on the surface appears to be a prediction of the future, as a prophecy after the fact. There is not the slightest reason why explanations as a prophecy after the fact should not be entertained.

Fifthly, the question of predictions and the question of the supernatural cannot be identified. If one denies that a passage is a prediction, this is not at all necessarily because one 'denies the supernatural'. Many of the predictions, or future statements, within the Bible, as without it, have the opposite difficulty, that one can make them or could have made them perfectly well without any supernatural aid at all. Journalists, politicians and others make predictions every day, and many of them, especially their predictions of ruin, chaos and general deterioration are quite likely to come true. The Holy Spirit is not at all needed in order to make a true prediction.

Sixthly, of the many statements about the future made by prophets or by Jesus himself, it is doubtful whether many, or indeed any, are treated with dignity if they are considered as 'predictions'. One has to consider how many of them are better classed as warnings, as judgments, as promises, and as indications of the will of God. It would be easy to argue that the category of prediction is a non-biblical category, or one which was suitable for only extremely few cases within the biblical material. This might mean that prediction, though not altogether absent, was marginal and theologically rather insignificant.

Seventhly, where detailed study can be made of biblical statements concerning the future, and where this can be checked against what happened in due course, a highly varied pattern emerges, which would further discourage any simple theological commitment to 'prediction'.[17] There are prophetic statements about the future which are, however, dependent both on the future will of God and also on the possible repentance of the people. According to Jer. 22.18–19; 36.29–31, Jehoiakim king of Judah was not to be buried, but his dead body thrown out in the heat and the frost, 'buried with the burial of an ass'; but the natural meaning of II Kings 24.6 is that he in fact had a normal burial: he 'slept with his fathers'.[18] A still more striking instance is Ezekiel's prophecy about Tyre. In Ezek. 26.7–14 we hear that God will bring Nebuchadnezzar against Tyre, and the place will be destroyed and never rebuilt; but in 29.17–20 we have the remarkable phenomenon of a substitute prophecy: Nebuchadnezzar made his army labour hard for Tyre, but they gained no profit, and therefore the Lord says: I will give him the land of Egypt 'as his recompense for which he laboured, because they worked for me'. It is clear that there is no simple 'predictive' relationship between future-related prophetic statements and their 'fulfilment'.

Eighthly, it must be considered doubtful if even fundamentalists want to commit themselves too fully to prediction as a necessary category. Prediction and fulfilment carry with them serious philosophical consequences, for prediction, if it implies the exact knowledge of distant future events, implies also determinism. It must be considered doubtful whether evangelical religion can go far along that path, or wants to do so, unless it wants to be swallowed up in millenarianism, for that is the natural and historical fundamentalist form of predictive determinism. Exact predictions, involving (for instance) the names of persons and places far in the future, involve fundamentalism in another problem: they can be understood only on the basis of a mechanical or dictation view of inspiration, which fundamentalists are very anxious to repudiate. Finally, it is doubtful if even fundamentalists themselves, apart from convinced millenarians, consider more than a very small number of passages to require explanation as prediction requiring supernatural inspiration.

The matter of prediction, then, to sum up, though it is a traditional ground of conservative accusation against critical scholarship, is probably of little consequence. There is little evidence that conservative scholars are themselves able to make creative exegetical use of the principle of prediction. It is probable that they understand the texts more or less naturalistically, that is, on the basis of what the prophet or speaker could have understood or surmised as a normal human person in his own historical situation, and bring in supernaturally-guided prediction only as a *deus ex machina* for those limited cases where nothing else will avail to sustain a fully conservative explanation.

As in the case of miracles, so in the matter of knowledge of the future, we find the conservative exegete using naturalistic explanations a great deal of the time and discounting the supernaturalist modes of interpretation which polemicists would demand from scholars. Take the case of the death of Moses in Deuteronomy. One of the most elementary of all critical remarks is the assertion that Deut. 34 could not have been written by Moses, because the passage describes his own death. When we turn to conservative commentaries, what do we find? Moses wrote Deuteronomy, or almost all of it, but of course not chapter 34, because he could not have written the account of his own death. Why not? On fundamentalist exegetical principles there is not the slightest reason why he could not have written the account of his own death. Indeed, he hardly needed supernatural aid in order to do it. He could have felt inwardly that this was the day of his death and written the chapter before he expired, forecasting that he would be buried and mourned and that no one would know the place of his burial. Add to this the supernatural, and it becomes easier still. Yet conservative scholars, in spite of the fact that the name of Moses is attached to this book, and that no other writer is mentioned, tell us that someone else wrote the chapter.

Enough, then, of prediction; we return to the general question of miracles.

There remains one further point of importance: the relation, in fundamentalist thought, between miracles and historical evidence. Why should one believe, after all, in any miracle? One approach would be to take the Bible as dogmatic authority: it says there was such and such a miracle, therefore there was that miracle. But many conservative polemicists take another path: they use the Bible, but not as dogmatic authority, rather as evidence. The biblical text, taken as historical evidence, shows beyond all doubt that such and such a miracle took place. Norman Anderson, for instance, in his *A Lawyer among the Theologians*, works almost continually in this way. The New Testament texts present, according to him, such strong historical evidence of the resurrection of Jesus from the dead that no one could question the actuality of this event except for biblical scholars, who (apart from conservatives) have been indoctrinated with false presuppositions.

The point about this is the insistence that miracles not only happen but fall within the normal processes of historical reasoning and substantiation. The demonstration that a miracle like the resurrection actually took place is a process quite analogous to that of showing how a motor accident happened and who was responsible, or of showing that such and such a man committed a burglary. Little more need be said about it, other than the remark that this is a further way in which the favoured and cherished supernatural is assimilated in character to the natural. In any case, though this argument is endlessly used by conservative polemicists like Anderson, it is doubtful whether it has much effect in the actual operations of conservative biblical scholars. Polemically, the strategy is often as follows: the evidence of the New Testament texts, treated as a matter of historical validation and substantiation, is supposed to prove that Jesus really rose from the dead. Once this is believed, it is argued that this one great miracle is so tremendous as to validate belief in more or less all other biblical miracles – or such as still require validation, after the rationalizing treatments that conservative apologists give them. As for really far-out ones like Elisha's axe-head, probably no one will trouble the enquirer about them unless he presses the point.

We might take this opportunity to return to a remark of Bultmann's which was quoted earlier.[19] When he says that 'an historical fact which involves a resurrection from the dead is utterly inconceivable', this is understood by fundamentalists as 'denying the resurrection'. But surely the statement may deserve to be understood in a sense relevant to the matter of evidence which we have just been discussing. Bultmann is saying, or we can say whether he says it or not, that, if there is such a thing as a resurrection, it belongs to a category of events which do not take a normal place in the sequences of historical explanation and cannot be accounted for in its terms. There may be difficulties in this, but it is a far more Christian, and also a far more 'supernaturalist', approach than the one through historical evidence just discussed.

The matter is interesting from another angle also. There are probably two competing and contradicting conservative approaches. G. E. Ladd, who though very conservative has a far greater theological depth and scope than a writer like Anderson, comes at the problem in a very different way.[20] He quotes from II Macc. 3.25–28 the story of how, when Heliodorus came to Jerusalem to confiscate the Temple treasure, he was prevented by a divine intervention. A horse with an armoured rider and two other splendidly dressed young men attacked him with such violence that he fell to the ground in a swoon. Now, is this miraculous story true? Ladd seems to think it is not. 'Practically all ancient records contain such elements of imagination and legend, mythology and superstition.' Ancient records have to be investigated critically. The historical method which does this excludes the reality of divine interventions. Here Ladd cites the passage from Bultmann which we have cited above.[21] According to this there is no room for miracles in scientific history. So Ladd seems to be moving rather fast towards the Bultmannian camp.

For ancient history, it seems, Ladd is perfectly happy with Bultmann's scheme. There seems to be no 'supernatural' which might have been working in the story of the Maccabees or in the history of Athens and Sparta; he gives no thought to that possibility. History really seems, therefore, to exclude the supernatural. The problem is when you try to apply this historical model to the Bible. Here it will not work. Why not? Because 'there is, according to the New Testament witness, no "historical" explanation for the resurrection of Jesus from the dead; it is a direct, unmediated act of God, without "historical", that is, human explanation, and without historical analogy.' A few pages later Ladd is writing again (pp. 186–7) that, if such an event occurred, it is without historical explanation or historical causality and analogy. This is precisely what Christian faith affirms.

It seems that Ladd is approaching the problem from exactly the opposite direction to Anderson. His reason for giving a special status to the resurrection is precisely that you cannot do with it what for Anderson is the main path to belief in it: you cannot demonstrate it from historical evidence, because it does not lie within the analogies and sequences that constitute historical evidence. It is very probable that the two approaches represent a split of outlook within conservatism, with Anderson pressing continually the traditional historical-apologetic arguments and Ladd seeing the matter in a way more theological and more related to the thought of mainstream theology. The difference is not an accidental one but probably represents a real mental split within conservatism, some seeking to go by one path, some by the other, and the movement as a whole hoping to gain something from both, and failing to see that the two cancel each other out.

Some of these more philosophical points will receive further attention in the next chapter. To summarize again our main point, the argument concerning miracles and the supernatural, which is often put forward by conservative polemicists as if it was one of their strongest weapons, is completely valueless. Conservatives take a very confused and contradictory position on this matter, not so much in that their theoretical statements are contradictory, but in that their practice totally contradicts their principles. Considering the large-scale rationalizing and naturalizing of miracle stories in conservative literature, their many bitter accusations, to the effect that critical scholarship assumes that miracles are impossible and that the supernatural can be neglected, are a mountain of hypocrisy. Conservative apologists have re-echoed their old slogans, without giving thought either to what their own scholarly commentators were doing or to what was actually thought by critical scholars and modern theologians. Of all the conservative arguments, none is a more disastrous one for its proponents than this; none is so completely void of justification; and in so far as there is any point in the question, it tells against the conservative case, for it demonstrates their willingness to use any argument, however contrary to their religious convictions, to support a conservative position about biblical inerrancy, however religiously trivial.

9 · Doctrine; Philosophy; Textual Variation

1. *Doctrine*

One of the most characteristic features of the conservative evangelical doctrine of the Bible, as we have already seen, is the extremely narrow ground upon which it is based. To a very large extent, the doctrinal statements of modern conservatives base their position about the Bible on one single point: the Bible is authoritative, inspired and inerrant because the Bible itself says so. Because the Bible itself says so, we have to believe it, and if we do not, then nothing in the Bible would have any value. This argument is repeated again and again in the literature. Thus Bromiley writes: 'If the Bible did not make that claim (to inspiration and authenticity) we should have no call to believe it. Nor could we have general confidence in the teaching of scripture.'[1]

The position is not altered if one says that Christ himself, or St Peter or St Paul, 'claimed' that the Bible is authoritative and inspired: for this means only, Christ, Peter or Paul as depicted in the biblical texts. This is only a restatement of the same argument. Notice the exclusivism of Bromiley's argument: there would be no call to believe in the authority or inspiration of the Bible unless the Bible itself asserted it. No reason whatever? Can this really be meant?

It is extremely improbable that this narrow and exclusive doctrine of the ground for belief in biblical inspiration represents the actual religious sentiments of conservative evangelicals. They do not believe in the inspiration of scripture purely and solely on the grounds that such inspiration is asserted within the Bible. Indeed, they would probably believe in that inspiration even if it was not asserted within the Bible, and this is just why they are not much perturbed by the paucity and marginality of biblical sources that do assert it. They believe in it because of a multitude of reasons: because it fits in with their experience as evangelicals, because through it they have come to know faith in Christ and peace with God, because it seems to them to hang together as a total picture of God's works and will, because preaching based upon it is effective, because life can be patterned upon meditation on it: all in all, for them the position is the reverse – far from there being only one sole reason for belief in biblical inspiration, there are to them so many reasons that no one single reason would particularly enter their mind. What would be difficult for them would be to think of any reason at all why one should not believe in it. There seems, then, on the face of it, to be a sizeable gap between official conservative evangelical doctrine and the actual religious perception of things by conservative people themselves. Can this peculiar split be explained?

If there is such a split, it cannot be doubted that the true evangelical, Reformed and in the fullest sense catholic position is that taken by conservative evangelical people rather than that taken by their official doctrinal polemicists. The Westminster Confession, a revered source of authority on these matters, says:

> We may be moved and induced by the testimony of the church to an high and reverent esteem of the holy scripture; and the heavenliness of the matter, the efficacy of the doctrine, the majesty of the style, the consent of all the parts, the scope of the whole (which is to give all glory to God), the full discovery it makes of the only way of man's salvation, the many other incomparable excellences, and the entire perfection thereof, are arguments whereby it doth abundantly evidence itself to be the Word of God; yet, notwithstanding, our full persuasion and assurance of the infallible truth, and divine authority thereof, is from the inward work of the Holy Spirit, bearing witness by and with the Word in our hearts.[2]

Thus there are many reasons why the Bible is supremely and uniquely authoritative, and all of these are intrinsically and necessarily linked with other essential doctrines. But, though numerous factors come together to confirm the authority of scripture, the fullest and finally the most effective one is 'the inward work of the Holy Spirit.'

In order to understand what has happened here we must go back to the Princeton theology of the nineteenth century, to Charles Hodge (1797–1878), to his son A. A. Hodge (1823–86), and most of all to B. B. Warfield (1851–1921). The vast majority of fundamentalists, no doubt, have never heard of the Hodges and Warfield, and even those who have heard of them have probably never read a word of what they wrote. Nor do fundamentalists agree with the Princeton theology in its entirety – far from it, for in its entirety it was a high Calvinist theology, a full system of doctrine in which predestination was a controlling, or the controlling, notion.

But at least in respect of the doctrine of scripture it was this tradition, and especially the contribution of Warfield himself, that moulded the set of ideas we now know as fundamentalism. A conservative evangelical bibliography will almost certainly have Warfield's name on its list of authorities for the doctrine of scripture: and any other names there are will in all probability have got their thoughts from Warfield. Warfield himself wrote for *The Fundamentals*. The conservative orthodoxy of the Princeton theology was impeccable.

Now the Westminster Confession, as has been seen, accepted multiple reasons for the conviction of the divine authority of holy scripture, the most important however being the inner witness of the Holy Spirit. In the Princeton theology this has been replaced by a single reason. In Hodge this is inspiration: 'The infallibility and divine authority of the scriptures are due to the fact that they are the word of God; and they are the word of God because they were given by the inspiration of the Holy Ghost.'[3] But this meant, already for Charles Hodge, that guidance on the subject of inspiration should be found exclusively in what the Bible taught about inspiration. Instead of providing an explication and a doctrine of his own about inspiration, in other words an account of it which would relate it to the other doctrinal elements which he believed in, he relied directly on what the Bible itself says about inspiration. Rather than offer his own doctrine of inspiration, he takes what the Bible says about inspiration as being already doctrine, already complete. But then the question arises: how do we know that what the Bible teaches about inspiration is true? In other words, can any sort of reason be given why this biblical doctrine of inspiration should be accepted? Hodge's answer is that it lies beyond the sphere of Christian theology to discuss that question. 'After showing what the Scriptures teach on the subject, it would be necessary to show that what they teach is true. This, however, is not the position of the Christian theologian' (p. 166). That is to say, it is a presupposition of any activity calling itself Christian theology that it accepts, without even asking for a reason, the teaching of the Bible on a question like this. Already in Hodge, and increasingly in Warfield, this position is made to stand upon the authority of the apostles, and of Christ, as teachers of doctrine. They teach that the Bible is inspired: if we deny that teaching, indeed if we even question it, then by association we question all their teaching. If we accept their assurances about the resurrection of Jesus and its consequences for men, then why should we not accept what they say about inspiration? And if we doubt what they say about inspiration, then surely we deny the reliability of all they say about the resurrection, about justification, or about anything. With this we are already in the midst of a field of argument absolutely familiar to us from modern fundamentalism.

But Hodge, as we have already seen, though firm on the infallibility of the Bible, did not insist that this was absolutely congruent with its inerrancy. I have already quoted the passage in which he maintains that a few flecks of sandstone do not mar the exquisite marble of the edifice. A matter of a hundred years here, a thousand men there, was of no importance and could be ignored. But Warfield did not allow this relaxed approach to stand. Errors in scripture could not be tolerated, however minor they might seem, because they threatened the total fabric of its inerrancy. Any one 'proved error' therefore threatened the inspiration of scripture and thereby the reliability of the teaching of the apostles on any subject and thereby the total credibility of the Christian faith. 'A proved error in Scripture contradicts not only our doctrine, but the Scripture claims and, therefore, its inspiration in making those claims.'[4]

There is every reason to believe that the stiffening of the doctrinal position between Hodge and Warfield was caused by the increasing pressure of biblical criticism.[5] The number of flecks of sandstone in the marble of the biblical Parthenon was becoming too great to permit the easier-going attitude of Charles Hodge to continue. Either one had to admit to fairly substantial discrepancies, and so to soften the doctrine of inspiration, or one had to harden it up in such a way that no real errors at all were admitted. This latter course was the one taken by Warfield.

And this brings us to the most obvious characteristic of the Princeton doctrine of scripture in its complete form. The Bible was inerrant because it was inspired or, conversely, to admit errors of any kind whatever would be equivalent to saying that it was not inspired. But why was it inspired? Because it made inspired (and therefore inerrant) statements that it was inspired. That the argument was circular is clear. I do not point out its circularity in order to suggest that it is therefore wrong. The point I want to make is the social character of this sort of doctrine. It was a doctrine made by fundamentalists for fundamentalists. It was a doctrine that worked perfectly well, so long as one was a fundamentalist in the first place. Outside of this circle it did not look. It showed no interest in, and paid no attention to, the idea of a consensus of differing opinions and schools within the church. It made no attempt to accommodate the growing practice of biblical criticism within the doctrinal framework. It made no attempt to adjust doctrine to allow for the many within the (Presbyterian) church who were influenced by the new approaches to the Bible. It was not a doctrine designed to meet half-way those who thought otherwise. Rather, it was a doctrine designed to prevent those who were already fundamentalists from abandoning that position, and in that aim it was, perhaps, relatively successful.

This helps us to understand why the multiple grounds for the authority of scripture were reduced to a single ground, and in particular why the inward witness of the Holy Spirit was so little emphasized. In part this depended on the philosophical background of the Princeton theology, which will be considered shortly. On the one hand, it did not want to rely on inward and apparently 'subjective' evidence; on the other hand, biblical evidences counted to it as hard 'facts', so that a doctrine of inspiration advanced in the Bible was a 'fact' that had to be recognized and faced. But the most important consideration was this other: all the multiple grounds for biblical authority were compatible with the critical approach to the Bible. Critical study does not make it difficult to hold that 'the heavenliness of the matter' or 'the efficacy of the doctrine' or 'the consent of all the parts' are grounds for the authority of the Bible. Worst of all, the inward witness of the Holy Spirit might perfectly well testify, and indeed does testify, to the authority of the Bible in the lives of persons and of churches that fully accept the critical approach. It is thus highly probable that opposition to biblical criticism was not the result of the doctrine, but was the reason why the doctrine was formulated as it was. The narrowing down of the grounds of biblical authority to one single ground is thus a characteristic fundamentalist line of thinking: it means that the conservative resistance against critical study is more important than any other consideration. Seen from the fundamentalist viewpoint, this narrowing down actually hardens and strengthens the doctrine. If the only ground for the authority of the Bible lies in its inspiration, and if the only ground for believing in inspiration is that certain biblical texts say so, then the fundamentalist has proved to his own satisfaction that only fundamentalists can affirm the authority of the Bible. This is exactly what he wants. While to others the acceptance of manifold grounds might seem to confirm and strengthen the doctrine of biblical authority, to him the narrowing to one single ground improves it because it makes it above all exclusive.

It might seem, therefore, as if fundamentalist doctrine was strengthening itself by abandoning all possible sources of strength but one. The paradox involved in this is greatly increased when we observe a further element. In fundamentalist doctrine, the inspiration of the Bible, far from being deeply grounded in the essentials of the Christian faith, is almost accidental in its relation to them. This is not only an outsider's comment but is the position that Warfield himself affirmed and repeated several times. Biblical inspiration was not an essential of Christianity, and if inspiration had not been there Christianity would have been in every respect true and valid: 'The verities of our faith would remain historically proven to us . . . even had we no Bible.'[6] But, Warfield held, all this lies in the realm of hypothesis: we do in fact have a Bible, and it teaches a doctrine of inspiration, and therefore that doctrine must be believed. The doctrine is not a necessary part of Christianity, and therefore is not a necessary implication to be drawn from the other doctrines; but, since it is in fact taught by scripture, if it were not believed, we would be denying the authority of the teaching by which all the other doctrines are known. The fact that inspiration is not necessarily grounded in the nature of divine revelation makes no difference to its essentialness as a doctrine to be believed. Since the Bible teaches inspiration, to deny inspiration is to deny the doctrinal validity of the Bible as a whole.

Now this element in Warfield's thought is not well known to the conservative evangelical world and is given little publicity in its literature. The idea that biblical inspiration might be accidental in relation to God's total plan of salvation is not calculated to encourage the average fundamentalist believer. The impression it must make, if it were known, would be of the great distance that lies between fundamentalists and the man whose doctrine of scripture, apart from this sole element, they have so largely taken as their guide. The balance of elements within Christianity was quite different for the Hodges and Warfield from what it is for the average fundamentalist. To them the 'divine decrees', the eternal inner decision of God whereby a finite number of persons were destined for salvation and a finite number for damnation, were an essential part of Christianity; it was unthinkable that there should have been a Christianity without this, for this was the way God necessarily was, from all eternity. The inspiration of scripture did not have anything like the same status. Nevertheless scriptural inspiration must be believed, and it was defined in such a way as rigidly to exclude the critical approach to the Bible. All in all, the Warfield argument has an air of almost deliberate fantasy about it. It is somewhat as if one declared it was known how many angels could stand on the point of a pin. This number could not be deduced from other truths of Christianity nor could it be related to them. Nevertheless it had to be accepted, since otherwise the authority of all teaching on any question was put in doubt.

Though Warfield's actual opinion in this respect is little known among conservative evangelicals and not at all publicized by them, it actually has a deep affinity with the social constitution of fundamentalist society. The doctrine of inspiration is one worked out by and for the conservative position. It does not give reasons, for the non-conservative, why biblical inspiration should be essential, apart from the fact that the Bible says so, which is a proof only for those who already hold a fundamentalist position in the first place. The argument is one designed for, and produced by, those within the conservative position, and for their own benefit only. The argument is not only logically circular; it is circular because it is meant to be. It forms a tight circle into which the outsider can break only by totally abandoning his objections and accepting in entirety the world-view of those within. Equally, it forms a tight circle which encloses the existing conservative believers; they can escape from it only at the cost of a deep and traumatic shattering of their entire religious outlook. This is exactly what is intended.

Socially, this is exactly what happens. Evangelical faith is not fundamentally faith in the Bible or in its inspiration; it is faith in Christ as Saviour. Even fundamentalists do not suppose that one is saved and forgiven through believing that Moses wrote the entire pentateuch, that Isaiah wrote the book named after him, or that Titus was written by St Paul. The gospel they seek to present is that of Christ as personal saviour, with (it appears) no other conditions than repentance and faith in him. This, however, soon turns out not to be so. The person who experiences the beginnings of such faith, within a conservative evangelical community, soon finds that he has to live within a group which also holds as essential a whole lot of other things and, in particular, the inspiration of scripture in a form that necessitates the rejection of critical opinions about date, authorship and so on. The personal dynamics of the group are used to enforce conformity with these opinions. Opinions about authorship, dates of books and so on are accidental and not necessary in relation to the total scheme of salvation by faith in Christ: nevertheless fundamentalist practice ensures that these accidental elements are made essential for fellowship in the community of Christians. Thus the doctrinal pattern of Warfield's doctrine of inspiration, in its relation to Christianity as a total plan of salvation, is quite in agreement with the normal social pattern of personal experience within fundamentalism.

And this leads in turn to one of the other major questions. Warfield's doctrine of inspiration depends, as we have seen, on inspiration as the biblical writers 'taught' it. This involves us in questions of exegesis. What evidence is there that a biblical writer (like II Peter) who used the word translated as 'inspired' expressly and definitely intended this to mean 'without error in all matters of history, geography, scientific fact and so on, including authorship of books, dates and the like'? How did Warfield, and after him the main conservative evangelical tradition, show that this was the intention of scripture? The answer, of course, is that they did not. The essential connection between inspiration and inerrancy is formed by one link only: their own opinion. They thought that if a passage said scripture was inspired then it must mean also that it was inerrant in historical matters, and since they could not conceive that the biblical writer might have thought in a way different from their own they considered this final. The grand demand for proof, so important in their apologetic method, worked in one direction only. In order to prove error one had to prove with the utmost rigour of proof and beyond all possible doubt that the biblical writer had deliberately and expressly intended the sense that was erroneous. But there was no need on the reverse side to prove with the utmost rigour of proof and beyond all possible doubt that the writer of II Peter, in saying that all scripture was inspired, had deliberately and expressly intended to affirm that it was historically inerrant in such matters as the genealogies of Genesis, the figures in Chronicles, the authorship of Isaiah, of the pentateuch or of Titus, all of which were subjects totally unknown as themes of debate in his time, and that he included exactly and only the canonical books of the Bible, leaving none of these out, and excluded exactly all of the Apocrypha. There is in fact not the slightest reason to suppose that the writer of II Peter intended any of this, much less that he intended all of it. But, since the conservative evangelical of modern times is vitally concerned with these latter questions, he cannot imagine that the writer of II Peter cared nothing about them and that his remarks do not refer to them. Thus, at the heart of the doctrine of inspiration, the insistence on reference to historical and literary matters was simply imposed upon the biblical writers by modern conservative argument. The idea, later so strongly urged by biblical theology, that biblical thought-forms were different, had little or no effect.

The demand for 'proof' of discrepancies and errors in the Bible in

Warfield's doctrine, as in conservative evangelicalism of today, was completely biased in a conservative direction. A conservative position scarcely required proof at all: it simply had to be asserted. Any allegation of a defect in scripture required an incredibly exhaustive process of 'proof'. Indeed, this was one of the aspects in which Warfield's position reached a final state of absurd unreality. In order to show that any real discrepancy or error existed in scripture, even in the tiniest regard, it had to be 'proved' that each such statement 'certainly' occurred in the original autograph text, i.e. the text as written by the hand of Moses, or St Paul, or whoever it might be; it had to be 'proved' that 'the interpretation which occasions the apparent discrepancy is the one which the passage was evidently intended to bear'. A mere difficulty is not enough for Warfield, for it might be caused by our defective knowledge of the circumstances. 'The true meaning must be definitely and certainly ascertained, and then shown to be irreconcilable with other known truth.' On top of this it had to be 'proved' that the true sense of the original text is 'directly and necessarily inconsistent with some certainly known fact of history, or truth of science, or some other statement of Scripture certainly ascertained and interpreted.'[7]

In other words, Warfield has stiffened the conditions for possible demonstration of errors or discrepancies in scripture to the point where it becomes impossible to attempt it. Since the original texts are long lost, and since 'proof' of the absoluteness required by Warfield, when attempted or undertaken as against the highly unwelcoming audience of Warfield and others who thought like him, would be impossible, the demonstration of discrepancies in the Bible has become a methodologically impossible undertaking. But by proving so much Warfield only shows that he has proved nothing. He has only defined the question in such a way that no position other than an absolutely conservative one is possible.

I pointed out earlier that fundamentalism displays to a high degree the character of formalization of the doctrines which it tries to take over from an earlier orthodoxy. It is now evident that the doctrine of scripture itself can well be added to the list of examples. The stress on scripture is found also in earlier theologies, for instance in Calvin or in Calvinistic orthodoxy, but in such earlier systems it had a set of connections quite different from that which it has in fundamentalism. The doctrine is thus emptied of the relations that give it meaning: it is affirmed purely on the grounds that an affirmation of it appears in the Bible itself. On the one hand this enables the doctrine to be used as a test, and we have seen that fundamentalist 'doctrines' are often in fact only tests. On the other hand it means that the stress falls on the formal assent to the doctrine, which leaves the possibility that the content of biblical authority will not be filled in in any consistent way. This fits in with the fact that fundamentalists stress elements of historical introduction, like dates and authorship of books, exactitude of historical information, and so on; they can do this in a way that quite ignores the theological content, or they can fill up the content in a quite liberal and rationalistic way or, if they have serious theological interests, they are found to be following the leading-strings of neo-orthodoxy, biblical theology or some other movement which they formally reject. The doctrine of scriptural inspiration in fundamentalism is in the end an empty doctrine.

The Princeton theology, as personified in Warfield, is indeed not the only doctrinal alignment that fundamentalists might take up. An alternative position is that taken up by James Orr, a Scottish professor (1844–1913). Orr was severely critical of contemporary movements in biblical scholarship and attacked it passionately. He wrote for *The Fundamentals* and is hardly to be classed as a non-conservative. But his thought about biblical authority was markedly different from that of Warfield. He emphasized that, as he put it, inspiration grew out of revelation and was a ground for the positing of the latter. It was suicidal to suppose that all revelation would be destroyed by some minute error to be found somewhere in the Bible. On the contrary, inerrancy was 'not a point in the essence of the doctrine of inspiration'.[8] Rather, it was a doctrine of faith, a deduction from an inspiration established independently of it.

It is clear, in fact, that Orr represented ahead of the time some of the positions that were later to become known as neo-orthodox. Among 'advances in later thought' which had made it easier to understand the inspiration of the Bible he lists first of all the 'clearer distinction between revelation and the Holy Scripture'.[9] Secondly, he says, we now understand revelation as something primarily historical. It was not simply or exclusively a communication of ideas and truths, its essence was in the divine acts: the work of the apostles stood in an interpretative relation to this. He was thus opposed to the approach to revelation in terms of revealed doctrine or inspired doctrine. Orr adduced, as a sign of recent progress, a 'more dynamical view of inspiration': rather than concentrating on the writing of the books, he talked of 'the entire process by which the inspired record has been produced'. In the last resort the proof of the inspiration of the Bible is to be found in the life-giving effects which the message has produced.[10] And so, following the Westminster Confession, Orr considered an important ground of belief in inspiration to lie in the internal witness of the Holy Spirit.[11]

It is scarcely to be doubted that Orr's doctrine comes closer than Warfield's to what most evangelicals in fact believe. As we have seen, biblical authority is far more central to their faith than can be represented by any doctrine that derives it solely and exclusively from that Bible's own 'claim' to inspiration. For them, its roots lie in personal faith, in the experience of salvation, in what seems to be confirmation by the Holy Spirit. They do not for a moment believe that the Bible is in any way in error; but they do not express this in so exclusive a way as to suggest that errors in the figures in Chronicles, or even substantial differences between one gospel and another, would mean the total destruction of all biblical authority and thereby of their faith.

For this and other reasons, there are some signs that fundamentalists would like to enjoy some of the advantages that might come from Orr's type of doctrine rather than Warfield's type. It would enable them to take more relaxedly the possibility of errors and discrepancies in the Bible. Yet it is not probable that a substantial move toward the Orr type of doctrine will take place. First of all, it would mean that fundamentalists would have to give up their mode of arguing that the Bible is inerrant and infallible because Christ and the apostles said so, and they are clearly so fond of that argument that they do not think of abandoning it. Secondly, it would leave them at a loss to explain why, if they accepted Orr, they repudiated neo-orthodoxy with such hostility as they did. Thirdly, there might be a yet more unpleasant consequence. Orr, though a passionate foe of biblical criticism as he saw it in his time, was willing to consider that a time might come when one would have to accept that it was 'of God' (following the equally reluctant remarks of Gamaliel about Christianity in Acts 5.39);[12] and modern fundamentalists still do not want to think that criticism might be 'of God'. Fourthly, and perhaps most of all, though many fundamentalists might like to have the more comfortable results that would follow from Orr's approach, they will stay with Warfield because they think like Warfield. This brings us to the question of the philosophical position assumed in conservative evangelicalism.

2. Philosophy

It would seem, on the face of it, a difficult task to try to state what sort of philosophical position is implied in fundamentalism. The average fundamentalist seldom or never makes a philosophical statement, nor does he read a book of philosophy. He follows, no doubt, the advice of Col. 2.8: 'beware lest any man spoil you through philosophy and vain deceit, after the tradition of men, after the rudiments of the world, and not after Christ' (AV). Philosophy, he perhaps thinks, is wild and uncontrolled human speculation. It is likely to put forward views of reality – of God, of the nature of man, · of sin, of morality, subjects on which the conservative evangelical already has full information from the Bible; and these views are likely to compete and conflict with the gospel. So, generally speaking, the less heard of the whole matter the better.

On a rather more sophisticated level, this tradition of negativity towards philosophy is carried farther in those attacks upon biblical criticism and modern theology on the grounds that they have been influenced by this or that contemporary philosophical trend. We have already discussed the zest with which the charge of Hegelianism was used as a means of undermining the intellectual authority of Wellhausen. Obviously those who used this argument implied either that any acceptance of influence from philosophy in such matters was wrong, or that, while some kinds of philosophy were right, Hegelianism was wrong. Which of these is meant, however, is never made clear. Similarly, the idea, widespread in popular presentations of conservative belief, that liberal theology seeks to make 'reason' the controlling authority in Christianity, seems to mean that liberal theology took its orders from philosophy or at least from that faculty in which the impulse towards philosophy is located.[13]

This, however, is only one side of the matter. When one leaves the realm of popular evangelicalism and turns to the levels that are doctrinally conscious, one finds that conservative evangelicals are far from being so negative towards philosophy as this might suggest. In the neo-orthodox period, when evangelicals influenced by Barth insisted that philosophy had absolutely nothing to do with faith or with theology, and that natural theology was a totally destructive poison, conservatives drew back in dismay. This kind of sole reliance upon the Bible was something they were not prepared to venture upon. Their embarrassment was amusing. They did not want to admit that they themselves assumed any particular philosophy; but they were quite unwilling to say that one should resolutely do without one. The idea that doctrines supposedly based upon the Bible should be drastically purged of their philosophical elements and rethought in biblical, rather than in philosophical, categories, was far from welcome.

Clearly, one cannot prove what all fundamentalists have thought, but it is not difficult to show what certain leading figures in the movement have thought, and in the case of people like the Hodges and Warfield a good deal of this is plainly set out in their writings. It cannot, I think, be doubted what philosophical position they held: it was a pre-Kantian eighteenth-century empirical rationalism. The following sketch is based on Charles Hodge.

Hodge thought that there were two contrary streams of error, mysticism and rationalism as he called them. All views depending on intuition and inner light belonged to the former. The latter, the deist position, so elevated reason as to dethrone revealed religion and seek a Christianity on the level of natural religion alone. Hodge and the Princeton theology in general rejected both, but they rejected the 'mystical' tendency completely, while against the 'rationalists' they contested only the *misuse* of reason. In this respect therefore they stood on the same ground as the deists: the only difference was that, within the same set of questions, they maintained that reason correctly used would show the deists to be wrong.

This being so, the confidence of Hodge in reason is unbounded. In a series of clearly stated paragraphs he tells us that reason is 'necessary for the reception of a revelation', that reason 'must judge of the credibility of a revelation', and that reason 'must judge of the evidences of a revelation'.[14] This last is perhaps the most striking, and I shall quote a larger part of the relevant paragraph:

> As faith involves assent, and assent is conviction produced by evidence, it follows that faith without evidence is either irrational or impossible ... This evidence must be appropriate to the nature of the truth believed ... In many cases different kinds of evidence concur in the support of the same truth. That Jesus is the Christ, the Son of the living God, for example is sustained by evidence historical, moral, and spiritual so abundant that ... the wrath of God abideth on them [that reject it] ...
>
> As we cannot believe without evidence, and as that evidence must be appropriate and adequate, *it is clearly a prerogative of reason to judge of these several points. This is plain* (my italics).[15]

Equally interesting is Hodge's notion of science and of 'facts':

> If natural science be concerned with the facts and laws of nature, theology is concerned with the facts and the principles of the Bible. If the object of the one be to arrange and systematize the facts of the external

world, and to ascertain the laws by which they are determined; the object of the other is to systematize the facts of the Bible, and ascertain the principles or general truths which those facts involve.[16]

Hodge did not think there was any ultimate conflict between religion and science. Theologians should learn the lesson of the Copernican revolution, and know that it is unwise to array themselves needlessly against the teachings of science. One should let science take its course, assured 'that the Scriptures will accommodate themselves to all well-authenticated scientific facts in time to come, as they have in time past'.[17] The wording, that the scriptures would 'accommodate themselves', is worth noting. 'Facts' were powerful for Hodge, and in a section entitled 'The Authority of Facts' he wrote:

> The relation between revelation and facts is one thing; the relation between revelation and theories is another thing. Facts do not admit of denial . . . To deny facts, is to deny what God affirms to be true. This the Bible cannot do. It cannot contradict God. The theologian, therefore, acknowledges that the Scriptures must be interpreted in accordance with established facts. He has a right, however, to demand that these facts should be verified beyond the possibility of doubt.[18]

On the relation between philosophy and theology, Hodge held that the two occupied common ground. 'Both assume to teach what is true concerning God, man, the world and the relation in which God stands to his creatures.'[19] But the methods are different. Theology works by authority, philosophy 'by speculation and induction, or by the exercise of our own intellectual faculties'. Both are legitimate. And this leads us to the following remarkable piece of natural theology:

> God is author of our nature and the maker of heaven and earth, therefore nothing which the laws of our nature or the facts of the external world prove to be true, can contradict the teaching of God's Word. Neither can the Scriptures contradict the truths of philosophy or science.

Philosophy and theology, Hodge thought, should strive after unity. This meant that theologians should not insist on an interpretation of the Bible which brought it into collision with the facts of science. On the other hand, it meant that philosophers should not ignore the teachings of the Bible. 'It is unreasonable and irreligious for philosophers to adopt and promulgate theories inconsistent with the facts of the Bible.' Where the two contradict, philosophy must yield to revelation. Though revelation cannot contradict facts, and the Bible must 'be interpreted in accordance with what God has clearly made known in the constitution of our nature and in the outward world', real contradiction is not to be expected. The distinction between fact and theory provides for this. Revelation and the Bible cannot contradict facts; but much of what passes for philosophy or science is not fact but theory, 'merely human speculation'.

Only a few comments on Hodge's position need be given. The position of reason, as we have seen, was extremely strong. For the Princeton theologians it was, if I understand them rightly, essential that reason should not be the architectonic authority for theology, that reason should not set itself up against revelation. But, this being allowed, they left it open for reason to be the operative control in all matters of interpretation. Reason had a free rein in deciding what was meaningful, what was credible(!), what was evidence, and in what direction that evidence led. Reason as a methodological principle is given a free hand. As Sandeen rightly remarks, no influence of Kantian thought is visible.[20] The data of the Bible were 'facts' from which the theologian had to extract the principles or general truths, on the analogy of the natural scientist extracting from the facts of the external world the laws by which they are determined. The Kantian 'critical' idea that facts are recognized and understood only through the imposition upon them of categories furnished by our minds was unrecognized. Applied to the biblical 'facts', the reason works unhampered in drawing conclusions, formulating general principles and deciding about meanings and implications. From the smallest biblical 'fact' the reason was free to draw the implications that it saw.

This whole position is surely aligned with Hodge's understanding of what philosophy does. He sees it as something that works in parallel with theology. It deals with the same things as theology does: it tells about God, about man, about the relation between God and his creatures. Philosophy is a sort of shadow theology; and in this role it has to be carefully watched, though it is entirely justified as an enterprise. But he does not seem to think critically about philosophy as a method of working, or an analysis of methods of working and thinking, within any other discipline. The activities of reason, in the service of biblical interpretation, thus escape the net of his criticism altogether. No doubt reason could be misused in biblical interpretation, but then a better use of reason would set things right.

Now, we need not pursue the study of Hodge in this respect. What has been said is surely sufficient to indicate at the least that the fundamentalist position has not been a non-philosophical or anti-philosophical one, but one built upon a strong and clear philosophical position, in which a very powerful, indeed a practically unlimited, role was accorded to reason in the vital matter of biblical interpretation. It is also an indication, if yet another were needed, that the basic fundamentalist orientation is not an emotional one, as is so often thought, but a strongly rationalistic and intellectualistic one.

It is by no means my purpose to show that all fundamentalists think like Hodge in this respect, and it is certain that very few of them have ever given conscious thought to these matters as Hodge did. But one cannot pass on without noting how remarkable is the agreement between aspects of Hodge's philosophy and things we have already noticed in modern conservative interpretation. For example: the apologetic approach to matters like the resurrection, through argument from the historical 'evidences', very marked in the work of an apologist like Norman Anderson; the readiness to 'accommodate' biblical narratives to scientific realities as soon as these latter come to be recognized as 'facts' and no longer 'theories'; the correspondingly unhappy status of biblical criticism, since it deals not with the 'facts' but spins out speculative 'theories'; the lack of influence from the rise of historical method, facts and reason being seen on a basis not yet illuminated by that method; the status of the biblical passage asserting inspiration as a 'fact', which on that ground alone must justify a full doctrine of inspiration; the doctrine of a God-given concord between the laws and facts of our world and the teaching of the Bible, which exactly justifies the reluctance of conservatives to jettison natural theology along with Barth. In all of these ways Hodge provided or expressed assumptions upon which the course of modern fundamentalism is readily intelligible.

Another point, mentioned just above, is the tendency to look at philosophy not as a guide in logic and method but as a kind of shadow theology, producing ideas about God and the nature of man which stand in parallel with those of theology. Such meagre studies of philosophical questions as I have been able to find in the conservative evangelical literature confirm this judgment. They do not really ask: what is philosophy and how does it work? The question that interests them is: what did this or that philosopher say about God and religion? An engaging instance is given by Colin Brown, who on introducing Kant says: 'The general reader who has no special interest in Kant's view of knowledge may be advised to skip the next few paragraphs.'[21] Quite so. The rest, after the 'view of knowledge' has been skipped, is about what Kant thought of God and religion. Certainly, if Kant's view of knowledge is to be 'skipped', little real understanding of philosophy among conservative evangelicals is to be looked for. Probably for a long time they will look on the subject as a parallel, an accessory and a possible rival to religion. Their failure to look critically into their own position and to consider whether it has involved, or still involves, philosophical elements, is total. Brown in the book referred to, in spite of its dominant interest in religion, and in spite of the completely conservative evangelical perspective from which it is written (the author puts Cornelius van Til and Francis Schaeffer into the same category with Karl Barth as three examples for 'Philosophy and Reformed Theology' in this century), makes no attempt to identify and discuss the philosophical positions that have been held by conservative evangelical leaders. As a result of this the attacks on 'the disastrous results of the liberal espousal of Hegelianism or Kantianism' are un-self-critical and valueless.²² But, though the quality of the work is mediocre, it is as good an indication of conservative evangelical opinions on the subject as we can find, unless we go back to Hodge and Warfield.

It is probable, moreover, that those conservative evangelicals who think seriously about the matter are contemplating not a theology or a faith quite separate from philosophy but a Christian philosophy or a biblically-informed philosophy which would be a suitable handmaid for theology. Ramm, for instance, is quite clear that a 'Christian philosophy of nature' is a necessity, and something on the analogy of neo-Thomism on the Catholic side is envisaged.²³ Similarly, a good deal of interest is shown in the 'Christian philosophy' of Herman Dooyeweerd.²⁴ Where this will lead one cannot say. It suggests that this highly Protestant form of religion is, through its aversion to modern theology and modern biblical studies, hankering after some sort of restored mediaeval situation. But most likely nothing will ever come of this. There is not sufficient interest in live philosophical questioning within fundamentalism to generate any movement. A particular philosophical pattern, born in the eighteenth century, has through a set of unusual circumstances been able to survive and to give remarkable stability to the fundamentalist religious pattern, without more than the slightest recognition being given to the fact by the adherents of this religious form.

Two other philosophical points have been mentioned in earlier chapters and need only to be briefly resumed here. The first is the concept of divine perfection. When conservatives say that the Bible is inspired by God, this means for them that it is completely without faults, failings, errors or discrepancies of any kind, or that such as exist are so absolutely minimal as not to count. What is the basis for this conclusion? There is no biblical or exegetical ground upon which it can be made, and conservative apologists do not even pretend to attempt an exegetical demonstration of it. The implication is a philosophical one. The nature of God is to be perfect; and if he involves himself in something, as he would do in inspiring a collection of books, these books would partake in the divine qualities of perfection.[25] That is not to say that the Bible is fully perfect; but it cannot have more than the tiniest faults, failings, errors or discrepancies.

This way of thinking about God does not come from the Bible. In the Bible God is presented above all as active and personal: he can change his mind, he can regret what he has done, he can be argued out of positions he has already taken up, he operates in a narrative sequence and not out of a static perfection.[26] The picture of God which presents perfection as the essence of the doctrine of God is clearly of Greek origin and is well represented in the Platonic and Aristotelian traditions. It was incorporated into Christian thought at a very early date and has remained extremely influential. It is probably particularly powerful in the Anglo-Saxon tradition of Christianity. It is not at all surprising, therefore, that fundamentalism assumed this way of thinking to be automatically valid. In doing this they were not doing anything specifically fundamentalistic, for the same idea is endemic throughout much of liberal and moderate Christianity. In so far as modern Christianity has been able to escape from this idea, it has been through the influence of the historical approach to reality, represented by biblical criticism and historically-oriented theology. Just at the point when there emerged a possibility of escape from it, however, fundamentalism turned its back upon these new and liberating developments and made the situation worse by extending the perfection-centred perception from the idea of God, where it at least has some apparent justification, to apply also, even if in lesser degree, to the Bible.

The second point is the conception of the supernatural.[27] Here again fundamentalism ties itself to a piece of traditional philosophy. But there is no attempt to present any coherent or thoughtful account of what it is to be 'supernatural'. Indeed, when one discusses these questions about miracles and the like with fundamentalists, though they often begin by vehemently asserting the supernatural (as against critical scholarship, which they suppose to neglect the supernatural), they soon allow the natural/supernatural distinction to break down. What is the difference after all? How can you tell one from the other? If God brought about the plagues of Egypt through a chain of natural causation involving flagellates, bacilli and so on, what point is there in trying to pin this down as if it was natural or supernatural? Either way, God did it. Perhaps one can put it like this: the real basis for the fundamentalist affirmation of the 'supernatural' is theological: they believe that there is, not only a God, but also angels, devils, heaven, hell and so on: these form part of a supernatural world. But little thought is given to this supernatural world as something that continues to run along on its own, independently of our world. What interests the fundamentalist is when these entities become involved *in* our world. When they do this he no longer cares much about the difference between natural and supernatural; the distinction is no longer important. The necessary continuum of experience is constructed not out of the distinction between natural and supernatural, but out of the inerrancy of the Bible. The role of the philosophy of the supernatural is thus ancillary and accidental. It comes in here and there for polemical purposes and is used eclectically; but it is not really very important. Fundamentalists would be much embarrassed if they were forced to work out their own category in this respect, and explain how far the supernatural can work naturally, where the natural ends and the supernatural begins, and so on. Once again we see that a major argumentative category of fundamentalism is actually accidental in relation to fundamentalism's own internal structure. This poor relation is a partial explanation of the totally incoherent character of fundamentalist traditional arguments about miracles, as outlined above.

To sum up, the element of philosophy is extremely important for the understanding of the Princeton theology and for the intellectual heritage of fundamentalism. The Hodges and Warfield aspired to teach only traditional Calvinist doctrine. In fact what they produced is considerably different from either Calvin's own teaching or the theology of the post-Calvinian orthodoxy. In this difference there is no more important factor than the philosophical position taken. The Princeton theology started out from an intellectual setting that was provided distinctly by the English-speaking debate about religion during the eighteenth century – the question raised by deism, and the use of the 'evidences' of religion to demonstrate that Christianity is really a revealed religion. The high authority accorded to reason in itself marks off the Princeton theology, like the fundamentalist doctrine that has followed it, from preceding doctrinal understandings in the same tradition.

3. *Textual variation*

Conservative evangelicals nowadays often admit that there are errors that have crept into the biblical text in the process of its copying through the centuries. A common formulation maintains that the Bible is inspired and infallible 'as originally given'. That is to say, the original autographs, the copies written by Moses, by St Paul or whoever it was, were totally without error, it was they that were fully inspired. Since there may have been errors in the transmission of manuscripts, a Bible of the present day may not exactly represent the original inspired text. Textual criticism is therefore justified, is indeed necessary, as an endeavour to ensure the purity of the text. 'It is one of the tasks of textual scholarship to trace back the text as near as is possible to the autograph copies bequeathed by the writers.'[28] Or, as it is sometimes said, 'lower criticism', the study of the history and variations of the text, is accepted by conservatives, while 'higher criticism', the reconstruction of sources and datings and different authorships, is not. What is to be thought about this? The subject will reveal some paradoxical relations.

To begin with, some people may feel that the claim for an inspired Bible makes no sense when inspiration belongs only to the words of the original autographs which will never be found. What is the use of an inspired Bible, they say, when no one knows exactly what is in it? This is a common criticism of the conservative position. It is not clear, however, that this argument is in itself conclusive. On the contrary, it can be argued that the conservative position is quite a sensible one. The claim is that the Bible is inspired, and that this inspiration extends to the very words themselves. It therefore becomes necessary to specify which set of words they are. They are not the words of the English Authorized Version, nor are they the words of any one or other Hebrew or Greek manuscript, and even the conservative reader accepts that there are variations in these respects. The only reasonable locus for inspiration lies in the original. It is true that the original will never be recovered, but this does not mean that it is a quite useless ideal. The conservative evangelical, as he sees it, simply wants to go along with the best that textual criticism can offer him. Since textual criticism can (he thinks) lead him back to within a fairly short space of time from the originals, this is adequate. In any case, it is said, no one seriously supposes that substantial doctrinal differences, affecting the centre of Christianity, are at issue in the variation between one text and another. Such an argument does something to make the conservative position about the original autographs seem a reasonable one.

But before we accept this we have to make a deeper analysis of the conservative position. Writers often give the impression that conservatives, in accepting textual criticism as a legitimate operation, are not as reactionary as they are supposed to be. At least in recent years, it is suggested, many of them have become more open-minded, and their acceptance of and welcome to textual criticism is a sign of this.[29] This view, pleasant as it sounds, rests upon a total misunderstanding of the role of textual variation in conservative thinking. The misconception, however, is an understandable one, for two different strata of conservative opinion have to be considered separately.

On the one hand, in much popular fundamentalism there was practically no awareness of an original text at all, much less of any variations within that original: what functioned as the inspired text was the English of the Authorized Version. Officially, no doubt, there was some awareness that the translation was not the original, but in practice this made little or no difference, since for all practical (i.e. all religious) purposes the English translation was a precise transcript of the will of God. This Authorized Version fundamentalism still continues in many quarters, but we have already seen that the more intellectual strata of conservative evangelicalism have recognized other translations, and therewith also by implication the presence of textual variation. In this respect it can be said that some limited liberalization has taken place.

In the intellectual stratum of fundamentalism, on the other hand, the position was always the reverse. Far from being a sign of softening of the doctrine of inspiration or of liberalization of the attitudes that went with it, the recognition of textual variation was from Warfield's time on an essential part of the most rigid conservative point of view. We have already briefly mentioned the part which the 'original autographs' argument took in Warfield's position.[30] That argument, far from being a concession to critical methods, was a very useful device for negating them entirely. For, in those many cases where there seemed to be a discrepancy between one biblical source and another, the theory of the original autographs permitted the argument that the discrepancy was a result of textual corruption and therefore had not been present in the original inspired texts. The argument from the original autographs was thus a substantial help to the hardest fundamentalist view of inspiration: far from being a sign of an open mind, it was a means of making it impossible for discrepancies to be demonstrated. Thus Warfield in his demand for 'proof' made absolute textual certainty his first condition: 'Let it (1) be proved that each alleged discrepant statement certainly occurred in the original autograph of the sacred book in which it is said to be found.'[31]

Now the full form of this argument is seldom set out in print nowadays, but it is easy to see the results it has or to find examples of biblical interpretation which exactly fulfil Warfield's wholly conservative intention. The figures for soldiers, or for men slain in battle, and the like, in Samuel/Kings, with the comparable numbers in Chronicles, are a happy hunting-ground for this sort of explanation. In II Sam. 10.18 David slew 700 chariot fighters of the Aramaeans; in I Chron. 19.18 he slew 7,000 in the same battle. Take then *The New Bible Commentary Revised*, where H. L. Ellison writes (p. 370b):

> One of the main problems in Chronicles is bound up with the numbers contained in it. Many are impossibly large, some disagree with Samuel and Kings, others are incompatible with the discoveries of archaeology. Yet there are other numbers that will not make sense of the usual suggestion that we are dealing with plain exaggeration, e.g. the 300 chariots in 2 Ch. 14.9 contrasted with the million footmen. The most obvious solution is that we are dealing with textual corruption either in the sources or in the transmission of Chronicles.

So also the ultra-conservative E. J. Young:

> In early times numbers were sometimes represented by letters of the alphabet. It is quite probable, therefore, that somewhere along the line these letters were misunderstood, and the numbers written out in full. This may account for some of the difficulties as far as the numbers are concerned. In such a case textual errors may very easily have been introduced . . . Even though we today are not in a position to explain satisfactorily precisely how the textual errors in the numerals may have arisen, it must be remembered that these numerals, since they are so isolated, cannot shake the general historical credibility of Chronicles . . .[32]

Who killed Goliath? The average Bible-reader will suppose that David did. The full story is in I Sam. 17. But II Sam. 21.19 says that Goliath was slain by one Elhanan. Worse still, I Chron. 20.5 says that Elhanan slew Lahmi the brother of Goliath. One might suppose that Elhanan was another name of David in the books of Samuel, or that there was a quite different story, which also got into these books, which ascribed the killing to a quite different man, Elhanan. If so, the writer of Chronicles, which is a rewrite of Samuel/Kings done at a much later date and under very different religious presuppositions, was puzzled by the statement in his source that Goliath had been killed by Elhanan. In order to remove the difficulty he supposed or invented a brother of Goliath, the name element Lahmi coming from a fragment of the word 'Bethlehemite'. This would mean, however, that Chronicles, or some source on which he drew, had been making up stories to get rid of difficulties. Conservative evangelical works prefer to say that the text in II Sam. 21.19 is wrong. Chronicles keeps the correct text. That is to say, from the beginning David killed Goliath and Elhanan killed Goliath's brother. To declare that the text at II Sam. 21.19 is corrupt is at least a favourite device of ensuring that no historical discrepancy between Samuel/Kings and Chronicles is found. There are, however, a variety of ways of doing this: another is to suppose that David was indeed Elhanan, so that David slew Goliath and Elhanan (=David) also slew the brother of Goliath. By this time we are coming close to Peter's warming himself at the fire four times, if not eight.[33]

In sum, then, the reader can be assured that the appeal to textual corruption is a frequent and basic resource of conservative interpretation. The examples cited above are only a small proportion of the whole.[34]

It is interesting to relate this use of textual variation to the philosophical principles we have just illustrated from Hodge. One can well understand how the fact of textual variation forced itself upon the intellectuals of the fundamentalist movement. Manuscripts physically exist which long antedate those used in the Authorized Version and differ from it in many details. Short of ignoring textual study altogether, or of taking the desperate step of affirming that the manuscripts of some particular tradition, for instance those used in the text translated by the Authorized Version, were the bearers of unique divine inspiration, there was nothing for it but to accept the validity of textual criticism and say that the inspiration attached to the original autographs, lost though they are. Philosophically all this could commend itself because it belonged to the realm of what counted for Hodge as 'fact'. A variant manuscript was a 'fact', a variant reading testified to by a multitude of manuscripts was also a 'fact'. The need for a text-critical approach could therefore be commended as an acknowledgment of 'facts'.

This is all very well in itself, but, as used in the train of the original autographs argument presented by Warfield, the procedure moves away from the realm of 'facts' and into the realm of what Hodge would have had to call 'theories'. The argument from a differing text is used not only where actual textual evidence exists but where it simply would be convenient if it did exist. In the vast majority of instances, where conservative interpreters appeal to the possibility of a corrupt text, there is in fact no evidence at all that the text is corrupt. The corruption of the text is commonly pure guesswork, entered upon in order to avoid the possibility that biblical reports are erroneous, or are legendary, or are discrepant with one another. This follows logically the procedure set out by Warfield: if there is a danger of a discrepancy, it must be proved that the text involving the discrepancy stood in the original autographs. In most cases where conservative evangelical works appeal to a corruption in the text, there is no textual evidence whatever to support the hypothesis: it is an attempt to get rid of a discrepancy by wishful thinking. In general, though textual criticism can be a study of hard facts, the actual use of it by conservative writers within this sector of problems has no factual status; it is pure hypothesis, motivated solely by the will to avoid acceptance of a discrepancy or error or legend in the biblical documents.

And this is not all. It is much to be doubted whether the average fundamentalist reader of the Bible finds it comforting when his scholarly leaders tell him that the biblical text contains numerous corruptions, and that its historical inerrancy can be understood only when these corruptions are taken into account. To him this sounds like bringing in Satan as an assistant to God. It leaves him, as a practical student of the Bible, very much in the dark. How can he tell when the text is reliable or not? How can he tell who slew Goliath and/or his brother? What use is it to him to read the books of Kings or Chronicles, and to be assured by conservative commentaries that they are historically trustworthy, if that historical trustworthiness depends on the theory that the words he is reading have at some stage been corrupted and are wrong in the form that he sees before him on the page?

In fact conservative writers spend a good deal of time minimizing the textual variations of the Bible. They continually tell their readership that one must allow for variations of text, but that the extent of these is extremely small and practically never such as to affect any point of substance for faith. No work has been preserved with such remarkable fidelity over so long a time as the Bible.[35]

Thus, to summarize the point, conservative evangelical leadership is putting before its people the sublime pair of propositions:
(a) The Bible is reliable because its text has been preserved free from corruptions;
(b) The Bible is reliable because its text contains numerous corruptions, the detection of which will enable readers to see how historically correct the narrative is.
In this, as in many other matters, the fundamentalist army is marching in both directions at once.

We now begin to see how the location of inspiration in the 'original autographs', while at first sight it seems in some degree justifiable, begins on deeper examination to break down into absurdities; and the farther we go towards the more marginal and the more difficult cases the more fully we land ourselves in absurdity. But before we see the full extent of this we have to look at some other aspects.

Meanwhile, however, one note: we remind readers that, while Warfield tied his inspiration doctrine to the original autographs, so conservative a theologian as Orr applied it not to the writing of the books but to 'the entire process by which the inspired record has been produced'.[36] And this might bring us back to the Westminster Confession, which had declared that the Old and New Testaments in Hebrew and Greek were not only 'immediately inspired by God' but also 'by his singular care and providence kept pure in all ages'. God had taken care of the scriptures, so that, though the church had woefully lapsed from the true faith, the scriptures themselves had been kept free from corruption. A Greek or Hebrew Bible of the seventeenth century was therefore for practical purposes as good as the original. The Confession goes on to concede that, since not all Christians know the original languages, it is necessary, proper and right that the Bible should be translated into modern vernaculars. The final appeal however is to the Hebrew and Greek texts.

4. *Jewish conservatism*

It will be convenient at this point to add a short note on conservative attitudes to the Bible within Jewish scholarship, because one of the chief points of difference is in the attitude to textual variation, which we have just been discussing. While many Christian conservatives, as we have just seen, make some concessions to textual variation and even exploit it extensively as a device to obviate discrepancies that would otherwise appear, Jewish conservatism shows a marked attachment to the Massoretic text and an extreme reluctance to admit that it may be corrupt or in error.[37] It is easy to understand why this should be so. The Massoretic text is the liturgical text read in the synagogue and hallowed by age-long loving devotion; its importance for religious practice is thus even higher than was the importance of the Authorized Version for the old-fashioned Christian fundamentalist. Even more significant, all sorts of central rulings of religious law and homiletic interpretation rested on precise details of this text. The Jewish community was thus working with a text in the original language, in a way that few Christian communities have experienced. Moreover, no really variant texts in Hebrew were generally known in Jewish culture. The Dead Sea Scrolls are a recent discovery; the Samaritan, though in Hebrew, was a matter of interest only to a few scholars and not to the general religious public; and the most important really deviant text, the septuagint, was in Greek and had come down through the ages in a Christian, not a Jewish, channel of transmission.[38] The very strong attachment to this text, and the corresponding reluctance to give sympathetic consideration to any other, is thus easy to understand.

Historical source-criticism of the J, E, D and P style is also often looked on with disfavour by conservative Jewish interpreters. Yet it is not probable that they are as bothered by it as Christian fundamentalists are. The fact is that the structure of the two religions is very different in certain respects that affect this. The linkage of the historical and literary data of the Bible with the 'claims' of Christ and the apostles, which is so essential for fundamentalism, has no real parallel in Judaism. Again, the primary function of the Bible in Judaism is its function as the basis for law, and this function is not nearly so deeply threatened by source criticism as is the Christian fundamentalist scheme, which is orientated towards historical accuracy. Again, and in parallel with this, the different sections of the Hebrew Bible receive markedly different ranks in the hierarchy of values within Judaism: by far the highest value is accorded to the Torah, and therefore there is great concern about the accuracy of its text. The historical books and the prophets are much less a matter of concern, and the Hagiographa still less. Thus it is most unlikely that even very conservative Jewish interpreters would be worried about the possibilities of discrepancies from exact history in Chronicles as Christian fundamentalists are. They would probably be content to accept that Chronicles belongs to the genre of *midrash* and thus contains imaginative creations of the interpretative fancy such as are familiar to Jewish readers from a multitude of sacred books.[39] And, finally, there is a major difference between the total structure of Jewish conservatism and Protestant Christian fundamentalism in the matter of tradition. Jewish conservatism is a tradition-affirming type of religion, and its affirmations about the sacredness of the Bible, especially of the Torah, lead on into affirmations of the sacredness of post-biblical tradition. Fundamentalism, though itself in many ways bound by tradition, does not recognize post-biblical writings and persons as a source of authority that could be set alongside scripture or given authority to declare its true meaning.

It remains true that modern biblical criticism grew up mainly on Christian Protestant soil, and it has taken some time for it to indigenize itself in Jewish life, as has been the case also in Roman Catholicism until quite recent years. It was possible to attack it as a theory constructed on the basis of Christian theological ideas, and this line has from time to time been argued by some Jewish scholars. It was also thought that some critical scholars erred in tending to depict the post-biblical Jewish religion as a degeneration from the more free and active life of the early tales. This criticism had some basis, and I have already suggested that this was a much more viable criticism of the traditional critical school than the criticism for Hegelianism and evolutionism so often advanced by Christian conservatives.[40] But, in so far as this criticism was at all valid, it was not at all specific to the critical approach: it derives rather from general structures within nineteenth-century Christianity and earlier, and was probably a more serious fault of conservative than of critical and liberal Christianity. Regrettable as this tendency was, there was never any proper justification for the deplorable remark 'Higher criticism – higher anti-Semitism', a remark which should never have been made by a great scholar,[41] and yet is still sometimes repeated.

In fact it is probable that the majority of Jewish scholars working in institutions of university level operate with some kind of historical-critical scheme, which in its total effects on the perception of biblical literature is similar to the situation generally found among Christian biblical scholars who follow the critical approach.

5. *Verbal inspiration*

Readers will perhaps be surprised that more has not as yet been said in this book about verbal inspiration, for it has commonly been taken that this phrase defines the boundary line between the critical and the fundamentalist views of the Bible. It is precisely for this reason that I have not made very much of verbal inspiration, and I do not intend to regard it as a very important issue. The point is simple: the idea of verbal inspiration, if properly defined and guarded, is not at all incompatible with critical scholarship and modern theology. Verbal inspiration is incompatible with critical scholarship and modern theology only if it is understood, as fundamentalists have understood it, to mean and entail necessarily the total infallibility and inerrancy of the Bible, not only in its doctrinal content, but also in historical details, dates, numbers of persons in battles, ascriptions of authorship, unity of books and such things.

In other words, I am suggesting that non-fundamentalist Christianity took a turn in the wrong direction when it reacted against the fundamentalist insistence on verbal inspiration. What one tended to say was that perhaps the ideas were inspired, or the general contents were inspired, or the people who wrote it were inspired, but the actual words were not inspired. The intention was quite right: it was to make it clear that the Bible was not historically perfect and that a critical examination of it, based upon an understanding through the human thought-processes of the writers, was totally justified and necessary. But this should perhaps have been expressed in another way. Instead of saying that the Bible is inspired, but not verbally inspired, it should have been said that the Bible is inspired, and even verbally inspired, but it remains fallible; it is not inerrant; and investigation of it has to proceed on the lines of examining the writers through normal human relations, and not as a book that shares in the perfections of God. 'Inspiration without inerrancy' was a theme of Roman Catholic discussion for a time, and it might have been better if Protestant thought also had gone along this line.[42]

In other words, the conservative argument that, if the Bible is to be considered as inspired at all, the inspiration must extend to the words, is not in itself an unreasonable position. It is not very convincing if one supposes that the writers were inspired, but not the sentences and books they wrote, or that the ideas were inspired, but not the verbal form in which they are expressed. Theological assertions about the status of the Bible can quite properly be assertions about its verbal or linguistic form. What we know about the authors, the ideas, the inner theology and so on is known ultimately from the verbal form (I would prefer to say, the linguistic form) of the Bible. As in any other linguistic work, the verbal form is its mode of communicating meaning. If the verbal form of the Bible were different, then its meaning would be different.[43]

But in putting it in this way I must make it clear that I approach the subject from a direction entirely different from that followed in conservative evangelical thought. Firstly, any such view of inspiration would have its main locus not in the writing down of the sacred books but in the formation of tradition in Israel and the early church. Only secondarily would it apply to the process of making this tradition into scripture, and only in an indirect and remote way would it refer to the actual writing down of the books. The doctrine of scripture would thus be a special part of the doctrine of the church; and the writing down of the texts, far from being the primary locus of inspiration, as it was with Warfield, would be only a minor, though not insignificant, manifestation of its working. Thus inspiration as a power influencing the writing down of the text, far from being the most important aspect, is a very unimportant one, though not therefore to be neglected. The real lively centre of the process is the fact that God was with his people in ancient Israel and in the early church.

Secondly, as already indicated, verbal inspiration would have to have nothing to do with inerrancy or infallibility, or with the idea that God had somehow himself provided exactly the right words in which the infallible doctrines were expressed. The words would be fully human and in every way explicable as words of men spoken in the situation of their own time and under the limitations of that situation; they would be subject not only to mistakes in historical and geographical matters, but also some of them might be legends and myths with no historical basis whatever. Moreover, they would be subject to the faults of human passions, defects and sins, and even taken as doctrine, where this is possible (for much of the Bible is not doctrine at all), they would not be final and infallible but would have to be considered and evaluated, respectfully but also critically, by the community of the church.

Such a doctrine would not begin from the idea of an antecedent 'revelation', the communication of which to the church would be the essential function of scripture. It would not, therefore, be the first and initiatory article in statements of Christian belief: in other words, authority, though not to be neglected, is not the first thing to be stated nor the thing from which all else has to be derived. The idea of the Bible would belong rather to the doctrine of the church. And the conception of inspiration, even of verbal inspiration, far from being antithetic to critical scholarship, would be founded upon that very understanding of the early stages of the church, in Israel and in early Christianity, which has been gained through historical and critical study.

It remains a question whether for such a view the term 'verbal inspiration' is very fitting, very characteristic or very helpful. Perhaps it is not worth the bother of working out. It does seem worth while, however, in so far as the limited valid insights used in the fundamentalist idea of verbal inspiration can in fact be restated in this other form, that one should do so. In any case it is essential that the fundamentalist concept of verbal inspiration should be totally dismantled, and what follows is a discussion of some aspects of this.

The central feature of the classical fundamentalist doctrine seems to be that the Bible is part of a movement of true doctrine from God to man. It does not emerge from the community; rather it is directed towards the community and transmitted to the community by people like prophets and apostles who are authoritative didactic functionaries. These people can, indeed, be understood historically as persons emerging from the situation of their time and community. But as writers of scripture they are not seen in this way. What they write as writers of scripture comes to them from God and they pass it on to the community. In this sense they are teachers of true doctrine to the community.

If this is right, there is surely a striking structural similarity between the fundamentalist doctrine of inspiration and the Roman Catholic doctrine of papal infallibility which was defined at about the same time. The Pope can quite properly be regarded as a product of the church and society of his time, emerging from it through normal historical development. But when he speaks *ex cathedra* about faith or morals, he is speaking with absolute infallibility and irreformability to the church: he tells them the final truth. So in fundamentalist doctrine the prophet or apostle can be understood as a product of his society; but as writer of scripture he is a vehicle of God's word addressed to the community.

In any case the Bible is truth communicated from God to man. In this connection fundamentalists are extraordinarily anxious to deny that the Bible is dictated by God or that any mechanical mode of inspiration is suggested. Their position, and here they seem to follow the Princeton theology, is that the effect of inspiration is known and is essential, but that the mode of inspiration is not known. Writers wax lyrical about this: 'How we would love to understand how this dual authorship worked! How was it that God overruled all that was written by the human authors, so that nothing was omitted that He wished to be there, and nothing included which was against His will? The Bible never explains this to us.'[44] They bitterly resent the allegation that they hold any mechanical view or hold that the Bible was dictated through the writers: 'We need not suppose that there was anything mechanical in God's inspiration of the sacred writers, as if they were God's secretaries to whom He dictated His letters!'[45] Packer, extremely irritated over this matter, claims that the 'dictation theory' is without substance: 'it is safe to say that no Protestant theologian, from the Reformation till now, has ever held it; and certainly modern Evangelicals do not hold it.'[46] It is true that many theologians of the sixteenth and seventeenth centuries spoke of scripture as 'dictated by the Holy Ghost'; but, according to Packer, 'all they meant was that the authors wrote word for word what God intended'.

I find it impossible to see what real difference is made by all this argumentation. A dictation theory would make much better sense than the sort of position that conservative apologists ask us to accept. Purely as a matter of history, it seems to me obvious that many theologians of Protestant scholasticism in the sixteenth and seventeenth centuries seriously intended divine dictation in the strict sense. According to J. K. S. Reid,[47] from whom I take these quotations, and who gives a helpful discussion of the doctrines of that period, Hutter held 'Holy Scripture is verbally dictated by the Holy Spirit, in such a way that no iota set down by the prophets and apostles in their books is not God-given.'

Quenstedt raised the question whether in scripture even the single words are inspired and dictated by the Holy Spirit. His answer is: 'The Holy Spirit not only inspired in the prophets and apostles the content and sense contained in scripture, or the meaning of the words, so that they might of their own free will clothe and furnish these thoughts with their own style and words, but the Holy Spirit actually supplied, inspired and dictated the very words and each and every term individually.'

A dictation theory about the mode of inspiration may be wrong, but it makes some kind of sense. What modern conservative apologists put before us does not make sense. I can understand it only in the following way.

First of all, people like Hodge and Warfield were impressed by the differences of literary style as between the various biblical writers. This is what would seem to them to be a 'fact' and would have to be taken very seriously. If the writers had contributed 'nothing but tongue and pen' (*nihil praeter linguam et calamum*), as Quenstedt maintained,[48] the stylistic differences would not have been explicable. It would be wrong therefore to say that the Holy Ghost did the whole thing except for the physical holding of the pen and moving it over the paper. Not at all, we are told, the writers were fully conscious and God did no violence to their individuality.

Secondly, the coyness of fundamentalists about the mode of inspiration seems to be analogous to what we have seen in the matter of miracles in general. First of all very strong assertions are made about the supernatural and how we must believe in it, but as soon as we come to practical cases we find that the impact of the supernatural is minimized as much as possible and something apologetically more 'reasonable' is put in its place. The very obvious annoyance of conservative writers at being thought to hold a dictation view is the annoyance of people who do not want to be saddled with a bigger miracle than they can help.

Thirdly, fundamentalists have probably moved quite a long distance towards the modern way of looking at historical figures like prophets and apostles. They do not, most of the time, think of them as persons who merely received an inspired message which was passed on to us as the Bible. They think of them to some extent as people with diverse consciousnesses and experiences, who worked out judgments and ideas out of their own experience in the life of their time. In this they are far removed from sixteenth- or seventeenth-century orthodoxy, to which this would have been entirely strange. The modern conservative tries to allow for all this in his doctrine of scriptural inspiration. Allegations of a dictation theory infuriate him because in this respect he belongs to the modern world. But the modern world suddenly cuts off the moment any critical implications might be suggested. What if the writer of the fourth gospel, a man of lively individual consciousness, had thought up out of that consciousness some of the terms and images in which he describes Jesus? What if the story of the virgin birth is a legend worked out by the early church? What if St John shifted the cleansing of the temple from one end of the gospel story to the other because it seemed to him to give better literary satisfaction that way? Any suggestions of this kind, and fundamentalists are back in a moment with an inspiration that excludes these ideas. They don't know how it works, but they know enough to know that it can't work in that way. The message comes from God to the biblical writers. Rigid conservative writers stress the passivity or receptivity of the biblical writers before the inspired message. Modern thought 'dislikes the proposition that the minds of the writers of the Bible were necessarily receptive ("passive") before the divine control and it questions knowledge which is said to have been imparted solely on the divine initiative'.[49] Against this modern thinking we must insist, along with Warfield, that 'the organs of revelation occupy a receptive attitude. The contents of their messages are not something thought out, inferred, hoped for or feared by them, but are something conveyed to them, often forced upon them, by the irresistible might of the revealing Spirit.'[50] Here once again, then, we find that the position of the fundamentalist is a vacillating one. He can look on the gospel of St Mark quite happily as the product of the conscious initiative of Mark, or on Romans as the result of personal human initiative of Paul; but whenever critical questions emerge he turns to doctrine, and his doctrinal refuge is in a position quite different in character: it belongs to an older world, where the Bible is a message sent from God to men.

Fourthly, many of the views on detailed questions which fundamentalists require us to take make no sense except on the assumption of dictation, or something as near dictation as no matter. According to fundamentalist opinion, Isaiah 40–66 was spoken or written by the original Isaiah himself. Living in the later eighth century BC, he foresaw the return of the exiles from Babylon after that city had been destroyed by the Persians about 538 BC. Critical scholars have thought that these chapters were actually written by a later prophet, who was in fact a contemporary of these events. Conservatives turn deep scorn upon this critical judgment: surely this is denying the supernatural, denying that prediction of the future can take place under the inspiration of God! Let us accept then that it was a prediction. Isaiah foretold the whole thing. But how was he able to produce (Isa. 45.1) the actual personal name of the Persian conqueror, Cyrus? Obviously, the Holy Ghost told him. Divine inspiration must have articulated the name or spelt it out to him. There was no other way by which he could have known.[51] The same applies to the man of God from Judah in I Kings 13 who knew, several centuries in advance, the name of Josiah, who was to destroy the altar of Bethel. God, or the Holy Spirit, must have told him the precise name. Why not? More or less all cases involving detailed long-term future prediction come effectively to the same thing as dictation. If Daniel (living, as fundamentalists believe, in the sixth century BC) was able to furnish a detailed plan and account of events, with some names of places, plus figures, plus family relationships, all for events which at the earliest took place in the second century BC (to say nothing of the possibility that they are still to come), it is a futile pretence to say that this was not done by dictation. It was, no doubt, the existence of these very phenomena, among others, that led older theologians, and, within their terms of reference, quite reasonably, to the dictation idea. Two brief notes on aspects of verbal inspiration may be added here. One is purely terminological. Many conservative writers use the term plenary inspiration rather than verbal inspiration. There is, however, no distinction in this. Hodge, for instance, who uses the term plenary, makes it entirely clear that inspiration extends to the words themselves. As he says succinctly, 'plenary is opposed to partial'. Inspiration does not refer to parts of the Bible, but to the whole; and it is not partially inspired, but totally inspired.[52] Plenary inspiration, in Protestant fundamentalism, is the same doctrine as verbal inspiration; but the name is taken from another part of the same doctrine.[53] It is probable that the term plenary has been preferred out of concern that verbal might suggest the theory of mechanical dictation. But there seems to be no real difference here.

Secondly, one sometimes comes upon formulae which taken in themselves suggest a sort of negative inspiration. Inspiration, if taken in this way, would not mean that God (or the Holy Spirit) supplied the matter or content to the biblical writer, but only that he preserved him from all error in his writing. Thus Hodge writes: 'The effect of inspiration was to preserve him [the recipient] from error in teaching.'[54] Theoretically, one might suppose that fundamentalists might go over more fully to such a negative approach (Hodge himself, of course, did not do so; all I say is that his words could be extended in such a direction). They would then admit that the biblical writers worked out their own ideas, doctrines, social comments and so on; but that inspiration prevented them, in so doing, from teaching error. It is quite probable that some conservatives really think in this way about some parts of the Bible, e.g. about the letters to the Romans and Galatians. But large areas of their belief would not be guaranteed by such a negative inspiration doctrine; it would not give good justification for their hostility to critical scholarship; and not surprisingly they mostly work with a positive inspiration doctrine, i.e. a belief that content, matter and even words were positively supplied by inspiration.

The other aspect of traditional conservative doctrine about verbal inspiration that is now most out of place is its strict attachment to the point of writing. This has already been implied in the importance attached to the original autographs. Inspiration ensured that the original autograph was without error. But what of what happened afterwards? And what of earlier drafts, previous editions, and of oral tradition from which reports were later taken to be written down? The tradition of people like Hodge and Warfield still looked on these matters in an unhistorical way; it seemed possible to separate the moment of origin of a biblical book from all its prehistory, and postulate a special divine intervention at this moment. But readers will remember the 'more dynamical' view of Orr, a view of inspiration which, rather than concentrating on the writing of the books, concerned 'the entire process by which the inspired record has been produced'.[55] There was in fact no single point at which the scriptural text was 'originally given', and if inspiration is to be talked of at all it must apply to the entirety of a long process of origin, often involving use of sources, multiple previous editions, changes of text, and additions of explanatory matter. Even in New Testament books and on a conservative basis, this process may last a generation or more; and in Old Testament books it may have lasted hundreds of years. On modern and historical modes of understanding the Bible, even as the most conservative scholars use them, it is no longer possible to fix upon a moment when scripture, or any one book of scripture, was 'originally given', a moment therefore to which inspiration could be uniquely attached. And this means, on the other hand, that there is no single unique form of words which could be counted as the one inspired text. If inspiration is to be thought of at all, it has to extend to sources used, to previous drafts, in some degree to variant texts, in some degree to books and sections of books which in the end have not been counted as within the canon of holy scripture, in some degree to translations of the original text, and in some degree to post-biblical tradition, since not only the preservation but also the very formation of the text is in considerable measure a work of post-biblical traditionists.

Any viable modern idea of inspiration, therefore, though it may indeed extend to the words themselves as conservatives have argued, cannot be localized at any particular point of original 'giving' or in the original autographs; on the contrary, it must be an aspect of the total tradition of Israel and of the church, a tradition that is known to us not through the Bible directly but through historical study of many sources, of which the Bible is only one. The position of the Westminster Confession, that the Hebrew and Greek texts were not only 'immediately inspired by God' but also 'by his singular care and providence kept pure in all ages', recognizes the historical realities better than the doctrine of Hodge, of Warfield, and of modern conservative statements. Why was this wider doctrine, which came not from modern liberals but from the Westminster Divines, not preserved by modern conservatives? There are probably two reasons: the first is the fact of textual variation; the second is fear of allowing church tradition to take a hand in the process.

Verbal inspiration, for conservatives like Warfield, had a strict, precise and quantitative character that for us today is difficult even to imagine. To say that God had inspired the scriptures verbally did not mean only that inspiration extended to the words, which as we have seen can be reasonably argued, but that God inspired one unique finite set of words, these and none other, namely the total string of words as set down in the original autographs. Textual criticism was therefore a vital matter. If a word had dropped out of a manuscript and been replaced by another word, that meant that an inspired word had dropped out and a non-inspired word had got in. From this point of view, since substantial variation of manuscripts was well known in the nineteenth century, it was clearly impossible to sustain the position taken by the Westminster Confession. It was the words as in the original autographs, and they alone, that were inspired. The general picture is somewhat similar to the doctrine of predestination, where one single unique finite set of persons had been destined for salvation and another single unique finite set of persons had been destined for reprobation. The way of looking at things is the same.

Though a modern doctrine of inspiration could admit that inspiration extends to the words, it could not possibly take the view that this meant that one word, i.e. the word of the original autograph, was uniquely inspired, while all textual variations were in principle non-inspired words and merely human intrusions. As inspiration would have to extend to varying sources and drafts before any final text was reached, it would have also to embrace the entire textual tradition in which the Bible has been preserved. One would no longer be dealing with absolutes. One could distinguish, within the total history of a portion of biblical text, elements that were more central, let us say the original words of a prophet, other elements that were less central, like the comments of an editor or glossator, and others that were still more peripheral, like attempts to improve the text centuries later. It would certainly not be possible to say that the words of any one stage, or the contribution of one person at any one stage, formed the unique and absolute locus of inspiration. It would be sufficient to recognize, somewhat with the Westminster Confession, that an adequate preservation of the text, for general religious purposes, has taken place; this both is in itself true and is supported by conservatives themselves in those passages where they get away from the idea of inspiration 'as originally given'.

Textual criticism therefore cannot possibly be thought of as the art of discovering which, out of the many sets of words furnished by the manuscript tradition, was the original and therefore the inspired set. Conservative scholars probably agree with this but do not make it plain, nor have they allowed the consequences of their own procedure to filter back into doctrinal formulation. Readers of the AV will remember the beloved words at I John 5.17: 'There are three that bear record in heaven, the Father, the Word and the Holy Ghost: and these three are one.' But these are not in old manuscripts, and an evangelical commentator like Leon Morris just ignores them: they are 'additional material', 'clearly a gloss', and 'rightly excluded by RSV even from its margins'.[56] In other words, they are not part of the Bible at all, and presumably are not inspired.

The story of the woman taken in adultery from John 8.1–11 fares a good deal better. Conservative evangelical commentaries agree that this did not belong to the original gospel of John.[57] But this does not mean that they ignore it. 'It is unquestionable,' says A. J. Macleod, 'that it forms part of the authentic tradition of the church.' It very early came to be 'accepted because of its antiquity and authority'. In its present context, however, 'it has no theological relevance'. Similarly Guthrie, agreeing that the section does not belong to this context in John, simply tells us that 'it has ancient attestation and there is no reason to suppose that it does not represent genuine tradition'. Well, well! Genuine tradition? Ancient? Authentic tradition? As true conservative evangelicals, readers must want to know one thing, and one thing only: is it inspired or not? What is the use of wasting time on ancient or genuine tradition unless the Holy Ghost inspired the original autograph, thereby insuring it against error? And here we find that conservative scholars, writing in a conservative work, simply give no thought to the question. This means, clearly, that they are in practice abandoning the criterion of verbal inspiration as conservative doctrine still holds it. Both writers say nothing about inspiration, and for the rest they take a compromise position. Because they think it is 'genuine tradition' they comment on it as if it was still a more or less valid portion of the Bible; on the other hand, because it does not have good manuscript authority, they seem to feel quite a lot freer in handling it than they would if it was an original part of the book. The Marcan ending is another case. It is uncertain if Mark 16.9–20 was part of the original autograph. But, C. E. Graham Swift assures us, 'all scholars agree that these verses are canonically authentic. They are part of the Canon of Holy Scripture.'[58] But how can we accept this? This only means that the church, knowing nothing of the history of the text, has included these possibly spurious verses in the copies of Mark it traditionally used. Either they were inspired or they were not. They cannot count as holy scripture, valid for the establishment of doctrine, unless they were inspired by the Holy Ghost. Swift not only shows himself unable to tell us whether they were inspired but does not even try to put the question. Here again conservative scholars in their practice demonstrate the inviability of the traditional verbal inspiration doctrine which conservative apologists still insist upon. In fact, when one comes down to detailed problems in exegesis and textual study, the absurdities generated by that doctrine are so many and so great that it is not surprising if conservative scholars in practice ignore it.

This has brought us back to the second reason why modern conservative evangelicals located inspiration in the text 'as originally given': they did this in order to exclude as far as possible any active role of church tradition in the formation and preservation of the scripture. But, as probably all scholars see it today, the processes of passing on oral tradition, converting it to a written medium, sometimes also translating it into another language, producing a final text, copying and preserving that text and adding exegetical comments at any or all of these stages, cannot be separated, but run into one another and form one total complex of tradition. From this point of view one does not need to say that verbal inspiration as conservative evangelicals apply it is wrong; it is more correct to say that it is totally irrelevant to work in the history and formation of texts as we now carry it out.

We may illustrate the matter from the rather amusing case of the Hebrew vowel points. Ancient Hebrew was written in a system in which only part of the phonetic structure of each word was registered in writing, and this was, very roughly speaking, the consonants plus some optional and ambiguous registration of the vowels.[59] Thus, for instance, a word pronounced as *kabbed* 'honour' (imperative), the first word of Ex. 20.12 'Honour your father and your mother', was actually written as *kbd*. Only in the period AD 600–900 did the Massoretes, through a system of additional points, add a specific registration of the vowels. The 'word' was thus written in two widely separated stages. If fundamentalists are to be believed, Moses himself wrote it, perhaps about 1200 BC, and the Massoretes put in the vowels about two thousand years later. Even if Moses did not write it, the gap is still almost as great.

In Calvinist and Lutheran orthodoxy, after it had already been defined that inspiration was verbal and extended to every detail of the words, the question was raised, whether the vowel points were inspired as the rest of the biblical text was. In much of orthodoxy an affirmative answer was given. Incidentally, this question makes sense only on the assumption that inspiration was understood as, or as including, dictation.[60] But that no longer concerns us. What concerns us now is the doctrine which supposes that a large portion of the written text of the Old Testament, a portion involving most of the vowels and some consonantal information also, was registered only about two millennia after the texts were composed; that this information now added had been preserved all this time in the form of tradition, and Jewish tradition at that; and that this component of the text was nevertheless an inspired element of the 'original' text.

The notion of the inspiration of the Hebrew vowel points is often put forward as the final *reductio ad absurdum* of verbal inspiration, and in a certain sense it is so. It strains to breaking point the theory that connects inspiration with the 'original autographs' or the original 'giving' of scripture. It strains to breaking point any theory that ties inspiration to the writing of the books. The older Protestant scholastics, on the other hand, had a certain amount of reason on their side. Firstly, they really thought, or tried to convince themselves, that the vowel points were ancient and went back to the historical origin of the books. Secondly, when their doctrine was so tightly connected with the exact verbal form of the biblical text, it would have been very peculiar if they had not regarded as inspired the vocalization, which is so essential for the determination of meaning. Thirdly, unlike fundamentalist doctrine since Warfield, their doctrine took care to provide for the authority of the Bible as it stood in their own time, and not only as it had been in its origins, and this could have made room for an activity of vocalization at a late date without too much doctrinal strain.

A modern view of inspiration, which saw inspiration as a part of the total movement of tradition out of which the Bible came, would not have difficulty in accommodating the vowel-points of the Hebrew text. These were preserved by tradition, and probably also altered in certain cases by tradition; but this was a tradition that was a valid extension of the movement of tradition that had taken place within the Old Testament itself. Thus tradition, even many centuries after the biblical text was 'written', is still contributing to that text not only secondary comments and interpretations, but a systemic element of the text itself. In a case like this inspiration does not guarantee inerrancy: but that would be true even of the original autographs themselves. The question will be carried a little farther in our remarks about semantics in the next section.

Enough has been said about verbal inspiration. I have tried to show how it could be asserted on a modern and critical basis. Inspiration in such an affirmation would be the church's affirmation that the Bible truly came out of the life and history of our God with Israel and with the early church: what came in the end to be written as 'scripture' is recognized as that people's intended expression of what had happened to them in that contact with God. Because that expression was a literary expression, it is not wrong to say that inspiration extended to the linguistic form, to the words. But inspiration, in this sense, is not the beginning of the church's thinking about the Bible, rather it is its ending; it is not the source from which authority is derived; it does not in the least guarantee accuracy in verbal form, much less in historical reporting, dating, attribution of authorships and so on: it affirms, rather than denies, the critical reconstruction of the history. Thus the fundamentalist apparatus of verbal inspiration has to be thoroughly dismantled. To do this, however, is not difficult. Though verbal inspiration remains the doctrinal affirmation insisted on by conservative evangelical leadership, conservative evangelical scholars working on actual biblical problems show themselves quite unable to solve problems by means of it. In the end verbal inspiration is not very important; and not too much sleep should be lost over it.

6. *Semantics*

Finally, a brief note about meaning. An inspired original text gives the impression of assuring certainty for the reader of the Bible. But an original text, however perfect in its accuracy as a series of signs upon paper, is useless for religious purposes unless one knows its meaning.

Conservative apologists are often very hostile to the emendation of the Hebrew text of the Old Testament, as practised in the critical scholarship of the subject. They want to assure their evangelical readership that the text is very sound. In this, as we have already seen, they are thoroughly contradicting another aspect of their own apologetic, which actually depends on corruption in the text as a

means of avoiding discrepancies in other regards.[61] But this can now
be left behind us. The text, then, is sound, and has been remarkably
well preserved. But what does it mean? Conservative writers
repeatedly assure us that new researches in the languages and
literatures of the ancient near east provide us with meanings that fit
ideally with the existing Hebrew text. Thus Kitchen:

> Until recent decades, Old Testament scholars were much too partial to
> emendation of the consonantal text of the Hebrew Bible . . . but nowa-
> days they show a much greater and commendable caution in this regard.
> The evidence of the Dead Sea Scrolls and the rich harvest of linguistic
> gains from Ugaritic or North Canaanite have repeatedly demonstrated
> the essential soundness of the consonantal Hebrew text at many points
> where obscurity had hitherto to tempted emendation.[62]

Let us take a simple example, from Kitchen's own discussion.[63]
At Jer. 49.4 the text, taken traditionally, might be understood as:

Why dost thou boast of the valley?
Thy valley flows away . . .

Kitchen tells us that the Hebrew word *'emeq* 'may now be taken
not as the word for "valley", but as a homonymous [i.e. identical in
form] word for "strength" '. This would give us the meaning:

Why dost thou boast of thy strength?
Thy strength has ebbed away . . .

Well, this may be so and may be not so. I am not in the slightest
concerned to dispute this suggestion. But it is nevertheless an
emendation. What I want to make clear is something that should be
obvious to any thinking person: in respect of reliability of the text,
there is no difference between a textual emendation, which supposes that the written signs were corrupt and should be restored,
and a suggestion that involves a new meaning, as proposed here by
Kitchen following Dahood. A Bible understood on the basis of a
few hundred or a few thousand new meanings, as here proposed, is
just as much a different Bible as one which depended on emendations of the text. The new proposal is a semantic emendation, just as
critical scholars have often offered emendations of the graphic text.
It is an illusion to suppose that, by protecting the written characters
of the text against the suspicion of corruption, one is indicating that
the Bible has somehow been right all the time. A Bible constructed
on semantic emendations is just as different a Bible as one slashed
about by textual emendations. If this is the way of showing that the

Bible is dependable, it actually shows that the Bible is not dependable at all. In respect of dependability, the procedure described is exactly as destructive of reliability as is textual emendation, with one difference: the belief that the actual signs on paper must be right, conjoined with the opinion that these signs should have semantic values other than those with which the text was transmitted, is a clearly superstitious attitude: the rightness of the signs creates the illusion of reliability, and the function of the signs, i.e. their meaning, is altered without concern. It is clear superstition to suppose that this preserves the reliability of scripture as a text.

I should perhaps, to avoid misunderstanding, make it plain that I am not in the slightest in favour of extensive emendation of the Old Testament text, and in respect of caution in this enterprise I am entirely in agreement with what Kitchen says. I merely observe that semantic emendations have, in respect of the effect of the Old Testament as a religious text, just as devastating an effect as textual emendations, usually in fact much greater. Textual emendations, while altering the written text, commonly produce meanings that are tame and normal; semantic emendations, though preserving the written text, often produce quite startling alterations of sense.[64] I would merely add to this that the assurance, often given by conservative writers, that the Dead Sea Scrolls have profoundly demonstrated the soundness of the Hebrew text seems entirely unwarranted. What possible reason is there to believe this? There is no reason to doubt that this is pure conservative wishful thinking.

But let us take the semantic question in a wider sense. Let us suppose with Warfield, and modern conservative doctrine in general, that God inspired the writers to write a text that was without error. But how did this work semantically? Signs on paper are not true or false. They have meaning only through their nexus with the semantics of the language in which they are written. We have to know what they mean before we can tell if they are true or false. By telling us that God inspired an inerrant text, therefore, the fathers of conservatism gave us a very useless piece of information. What we need to know is, in relation to what structure of meaning in natural language this text is to be understood. The answer is probably this: for conservatives the nexus between the inerrant text and the language was formed within the structure of meaning already existent in evangelical Christianity, a structure of meaning shaped by the theological priorities of that religion, sustained in practice by its 'comparing scripture with scripture', narrowed by its substantial neglect of extra-biblical and post-biblical areas of meaning, and emaciated finally most of all by the refusal to recognize the new stratifications of meaning which were formed by critical study.

Some examples we have studied above, for instance the attempt to show that 'all' does not mean 'all' when the flood covered 'all' the earth, because when Jesus told a woman 'all' she had done he could not really have told her everything, or the idea that 'day' does not mean day but might mean some far longer period,[65] are elementary semantic mistakes that are endemic to conservative interpretation and are to be explained in the way just stated. We are now doing no more than to say that these conservative interpretations are clearly wrong, but we are saying it in a different context. But it comes back to one thing: the inerrant text, given by divine inspiration, does not decide anything. To the conservative fathers this was sufficient and decisive because they assumed in any case the linkages between text and meaning that were already customary in evangelical Christianity. In other words, as was said at the beginning, the tradition of religion was always the key thing in the understanding of the Bible, and when eventually a method was evolved that at least to some extent got outside of this tradition of religion, conservative evangelicals repudiated it.

7. Conclusion

If one looks back over the doctrinal and associated questions surveyed in this chapter, one conclusion forces itself upon the mind: within the framework of inspiration as he conceived it, Warfield was entirely right. If inspiration means inerrancy, then one must go to the position that there is no error at all in scripture and that any actual error, whether proved or not, would destroy the entire structure. Little respect can be shown to those who maintain a doctrinal position like Warfield's but then cheerfully say that they are not tied to complete inerrancy. Such a position shows a pragmatic carelessness of what to Warfield, and rightly, was a strict doctrinal matter. For, supposing that there is an error in scripture, even a small one, how does one explain it doctrinally? To say that it is a small matter of a number of chariots or the like may work pragmatically and keep people from worrying, but how did the error get there at all? There are only two possibilities. Either the Holy Spirit inspired an erroneous statement, and if he did so once then he may have done so many times, for inspiration by the Holy Spirit is after all not a guarantee of truth. Or else the Holy Spirit did not inspire the portion of scripture in question; but if there is any part of the text that he did not inspire then there may be others, and so we cannot know that the entire scripture is inspired. So long as inspiration is understood as guarantee against error, if there is an error, it must be accounted for in one of these ways. Either the inspiration of the Holy Spirit does not guarantee truth, or there are passages or words of scripture where the inspiration for some reason was not working. Warfield was quite right in holding that either of these conditions would be destructive of the entire structure of biblical authority based upon inspiration. Fundamentalists must continue to bear this burden unless they make a drastic change, and not only a minor reservation, as against Warfield's doctrine. The problem is, if not removed, at least much alleviated, if it is thought that inspiration is not inerrancy and does not guard against error. But if that option is taken inspiration can no longer be used as an argument against biblical criticism.

As always, fundamentalism did not keep alive the understanding of the doctrine of its own masters, the Hodges and Warfield, in full. It retained only a skeleton, a simplified series of affirmations, that differed from the Princeton doctrine just as the fundamentalist credal statements, affirmations of 'aims and basis', lists of essential points and the like differed from the Westminster Confession. This was necessary for many reasons. Many fundamentalists did not sympathize with the complicated and systematic Calvinist position. Many were Arminians or millenarians. Many of them were not theologically trained and could not follow the type of intellectual argument that the Princeton theologians put forward. A common concern about biblical criticism, and an anxiety to form a common front against it, caused them to accept, but only in a skeleton form, the most rigid and powerful conservative position that could be found – probably, that will ever be found. It is extremely unlikely that fundamentalism will ever find a doctrinal position that will be stronger for its own purposes than that furnished by Warfield. As Warfield saw, qualifications to and reservations about his doctrine may ruin it entirely. Modern fundamentalists have to become aware of this risk; and the deeper they become aware of what Warfield really maintained, the more they have cause to worry about the integrity of their position and the chances of its future viability. The simple logical strength of Warfield's doctrine can avail little in the long run against the anomalies and unrealities into which it falls when applied to the detailed facts of biblical scholarship, as conservative scholarship itself is now showing.

10 · Mainly Personal Attitudes

1. Conservative literature again

No instance is a better test case for the historical-critical method than the proposed division of the book of Isaiah. As is well known, critical scholars mostly assign chapter 40–66 to one or more later prophets. On top of this, they do not hold that all of 1–39 go back to Isaiah either, and this means that some chapters in these books are also from a later time, probably even later than the date of 40–66. Against this critical position conservative polemicists have maintained a formidable barrage of hostility. This is exactly what is to be expected. Basically, they think that the Deutero-Isaiah theory is dogmatically forbidden for two reasons. Firstly, they think it is dependent on the assumption that prediction of the future cannot occur: as soon as you admit prediction, there is no difficulty in admitting that Isaiah wrote the whole book, more or less. Secondly, they say that all parts of the book were quoted in the New Testament 'as the word of the prophet Isaiah'. E. J. Young says that 'To every Christian believer this testimony of the New Testament should be decisive.'[1] Thus dogmatic theological reasons are sufficient reason to repudiate the critical proposal. Though other grounds are adduced by conservative writers, there is no reason to believe that they count for very much: the dogmatic argument is the one that counts in this case: it is sufficient, even if the others were not there. One subsidiary argument should be mentioned, however: a major objection to the separation of Deutero-Isaiah is that, having begun there, one cannot stop there. The critic has then to go on to posit a Trito-Isaiah, and on top of that, as already remarked, he has to divide up 1–39 into a series of yet other authors. All in all, then, the Deutero-Isaiah theory is a very bad thing, which conservative evangelicals should shun like the plague.

Surprisingly, when we turn to *The New Bible Dictionary*

(p. 573b), we find that things are quite a lot different. Professor N. H. Ridderbos tells us:

> The conclusion is that it is both unnecessary and open to objection to deny to Isaiah any share in the composition of chapters xl-lxvi. On the other hand, even those who desire to submit unconditionally to the testimony of scripture may come to the conclusion that the book of Isaiah contains some parts which are not of Isaiasnic origin. This is perhaps the situation already in chapters i-xxxix. And especially with regard to chapters xl-lxvi there are reasons for accepting this suggestion. In the opinion of the present writer it is acceptable to hold that chapters xl-lxvi contain an Isaianic core, upon which the prophet's disciples (men who felt themselves closely bound to him) later worked in the spirit of the original author. It is, however, impossible for us to assess how much belongs to the Isaianic core and how much to the later elaborations.

With this moderate and sensible summing-up of the situation Professor Ridderbos has surely embarrassed the conservative apologists. Are they to turn upon the respected Dutch professor the totally negative attacks that Harrison, for instance, turns upon critical scholars? But if they are not going to do so, what was the point of all these attacks in the first place? The fact is that the article of Ridderbos, though quite rightly pointing to the common elements that run through the entire book, and warning against the difficulties that the common critical analysis may have neglected, gives a qualified but definite assent to the legitimacy of the division of authorship. The exposition of the 'message of the book' that follows (pp. 574-7) separates three sections, 1–39, 40–55 and 56–66, clearly implying that these form three separate blocks in respect of content. The section on 40–55 begins with the sentence 'Jerusalem lies in ruins, Israel is in exile in Babylonia, and the Exile has lasted a long time' (p. 576a). The argument that, if you first separate off Deutero-Isaiah, then you cannot stop there but must also divide within 1–39, is accepted without difficulty as 'perhaps' the case in the statement already quoted above. As for the argument that critical scholars have reached their conclusion because they deny the possibility of prediction, this does not trouble Ridderbos at all. Prediction 'has not always been taken sufficiently into account by adherents of the Deutero-Isaiah theory' (p. 573a). But even if we accept prediction, it does not settle much. 'It is certainly inconceivable that Isaiah stood in the temple court, comforting his people in view of a calamity which was not to come upon them until more than a century had elapsed.' It is not clear that the prophet was predicting at all, and the strongest argument for the Deutero-Isaiah theory is the fact that the chapters from 40 on have the Babylonian Exile as their background, i.e. he is already living in that time. Moreover, Ridderbos raises an even more frightening spectre: 'if we credit Isaiah with these chapters, must we not assume that his inspiration took a very "mechanical" form, bearing no relation to the concepts existing in the prophet's conscious mind?'[2]

Now Ridderbos does not stop there, and he adds his own individual suggestions for the solution of the difficulty. But it cannot be questioned that Ridderbos, though clearly conservative in tendency, accepts it as an entirely tolerable scholarly position that Isaiah 40–66 should come from a time long after Isaiah was dead. As for the New Testament citations under the name 'Isaiah', which Young considered to be 'decisive' for every Christian believer, Ridderbos says nothing about them at all.

I do not wish to comment further on the specific problem of Isaiah; I cite the example simply to introduce some final thoughts about the modern scholarly literature published by and cherished in conservative evangelicalism. Conservatives look on this literature with pride and satisfaction, and are much reassured by the substantially higher intellectual level it reaches as compared with what they published or read thirty or forty years ago. But this must leave us with the question, how far conservatives themselves can tolerate the strains that must develop if all the tendencies in this literature are considered together. The average fundamentalist, though he believed all of the Bible to be inerrant, and thought this to be valid for details and the quite remote passages, has not generally had the responsibility of working out his position in detail. For practical purposes he worked with a gospel drawn from central New Testament passages, and he used much of the Bible devotionally. Though he believed everything to be true and inerrant, he probably did not give any active attention to the age of Methuselah, or to the numbers of chariots in various battles in Chronicles, or to the date of the Exodus. The more he is provided with detailed commentaries and dictionaries of reasonable intellectual level, the more he is faced with tendencies which seem to pull in three ways:

(*a*) Firstly, quite a lot of conservative literature now accepts as probable critical positions to which conservatives have been in the past bitterly opposed and on which they are often still directing volleys of hate. As we have just seen, Deutero-Isaiah and Trito-Isaiah are perhaps permitted, and also the separation of parts of Isaiah 1–39 from genuine Isaianic authorship. Marcan priority and Q in the gospels are not only permitted, they are put forward as the established and accepted positions. Even on II Peter conservatives in their scholarly works can often tell their readers no more than that it cannot be definitely shown that the letter was not by Peter.

(*b*) Secondly, and going in the opposite direction, conservative readers cannot help seeing in this literature the extent to which miraculous reports are de-miraculized and the supernatural reduced or eliminated.

(*c*) Thirdly, the more conservative readers study the remoter corners and problems of the Bible, the more evident will be made to them the degree to which meanings of words and passages are strained in order to obtain results that will fit with conservative views of inerrancy.

In other words, the literature already published is pulling its readers in three different directions. Believing in a true Bible is one thing, trying to work it out in detail over every chapter from Genesis to Revelation is another thing.

To this should be added two or three remarks about the general style and presentation of much conservative polemical literature. One is the quotation of non-conservative scholars within it. A piece of conservative polemic like Anderson's *A Lawyer among the Theologians* quotes a host of scholars and theologians, and many of them favourably. Pannenberg 'argues convincingly' (p. 36); Anthony Hanson's assessment is to be commended (p. 46 and elsewhere); C. H. Dodd 'speaks with caution and moderation' (p. 108). None of this work of citation makes any attempt to state the general position of the persons quoted. All of us, even the most radical, occasionally make statements that are more conservative than some statements made by someone else, or even by ourselves at some other time. A work like Anderson's simply picks out more conservative quotations in order to set them against less conservative (and therefore more deplorable) opinions. It does not observe that most of the persons quoted with so much favour, though apparently conservative in the context in which Anderson sets them in his own writing, would fully repudiate the position which Anderson himself is arguing.

This runs through a great deal of the conservative literature, wherever it tries to establish some contact with the world of general and non-conservative scholarship and theology. A popular guide like K. G. Howkins' *The Challenge of Religious Studies* (Tyndale Press 1972) is studded with quotations from T. F. Torrance, Alan Richardson, G. W. Anderson, S. C. Neill, H. H. Rowley and others. The book would look a great deal different if, after every case where one of these is quoted with approval, the annotation were added: *The scholar just quoted would, of course, totally repudiate the whole conservative position advocated in this book*. The point is a serious one. If these various scholars have, as Howkins clearly accepts, valuable insights to offer into the questions he is discussing, then the question has to be asked: how did they come to have these valuable insights when they fully reject the conservative evangelical position the author is trying to support? Or, to put it another way, since they have these valuable insights, is it not possible that the way to follow up these insights is to go in the way advocated by Torrance, Richardson, Anderson, Neill or Rowley, or whoever it may be? This is again part of the dilemma of conservative evangelical writing: having cut itself off, as in large measure it has done, from the world theological discussion, and insisted that no way other than the conservative evangelical has any right or justification in its favour, it now seeks to creep back in and borrow a few names of reputation. This it cannot honestly do. If it introduces names from the centre of theology or of biblical scholarship, it has to let them say what they themselves think, and it cannot rightly exploit their names just for the sake of getting hold of a quotation more conservative than some other. Or else let it remain fully polemical, which is probably its real honest position, and if so let it attack as it should the persons whom it now cites with favour, for as non-conservatives and questioners of biblical inerrancy they should surely be exposed for their radically wrong presuppositions in the same way as their slightly more liberal colleagues are exposed.

One other general point should be added here. There is another major circumstance which has not yet been mentioned and which has probably greatly favoured the survival and strength of fundamentalism. I refer to the now common preference for vagueness and generality about the Bible. Non-conservatives, as we have seen, reacted against conservative appeals to verbal inspiration by taking a more vague, distant or general view of the Bible. They did not want to spend time arguing about the number of chariots in a passage in Chronicles or the depth to which the flood covered the world. The result is that they have lost sensitivity to the detail of the Bible. Now it is very probable that many conservatives have in fact gone the same way. They are probably embarrassed by argumentation like that of Ramm about the problems of removing manure from Noah's Ark,[3] and similarly they do not want to be held to exact figures for the lifetime of Methuselah or the period during which the Israelites were in Egypt. But, though it is intelligible and permissible that non-conservatives should be vague about these things, because no doctrinal consequence for them hangs upon them, it is quite wrong that conservatives should be allowed to be vague about them. For they hold a doctrine which was expressly designed to maintain inerrancy, and if they hold that doctrine with sincerity they are bound to maintain it over the details of Noah's ark, or the depth of the flood, or the years of Methuselah, or the number of chariots in a Chronicles passage set against the account of the same incident in Samuel/Kings. The conservative should be forced either to maintain his position in face of the detailed biblical matter or else to alter his doctrine. He is responsible for the years of Methuselah and for the problem of manure in Noah's ark. He is responsible for the discrepancies in order between events in the various gospels. He has accepted a doctrine of scripture which makes him responsible for all these, and many more. He has no right to take refuge in vagueness, as the modern conservative evangelical literature increasingly does, while continuing to maintain the same doctrine of scripture which ties him to inerrancy in all these matters. Either he must bind himself to inerrancy in detail, or else if he is honest he must accept that his doctrinal position has been unjustified.

As I say, the common preference for vagueness has made it easier for fundamentalists. A hundred years ago this was not so. The average reader of the Bible was keenly aware of these detailed difficulties. Critics knew of them, as did conservatives also; both parties knew of them because in many cases ordinary Bible-readers had been agonizing over them for a long time. But these had not mattered too much as long as the doctrine of inerrancy was not drawn too tight. The more precisely it was formulated, the more serious these detailed evidences became. Critical scholars formulated their positions precisely because they were aware of the detailed problems in the texts, and they used these in their fight against the hardening fundamentalist position. Henry Preserved Smith, for instance, bombarded Warfield with detailed examples of this kind:[4]

	Samuel/Kings	Chronicles
taken by David	II Sam. 8.4: 1,700 horsemen, 20,000 foot	I Chr. 18.4: 1,000 chariots, 7,000 horsemen, 20,000 foot
mercenaries of Ammonites	II Sam. 10.6: 20,000 + 1,000 + 12,000 men	I Chr. 19.7: 32,000 chariots + army of king of Maacah

slain by David	II Sam. 10.18: 700 charioteers + 40,000 horsemen	I Chr. 19.18: 7,000 charioteers + 40,000 horsemen
census figures	II Sam. 24.9: Israel 800,000, Judah 500,000	I Chr. 21.5: Israel 1,100,000, Judah 470,000
price of threshing floor	II Sam. 24.24: 50 shekels	I Chr. 21.25: 600 shekels
stalls for chariot horses.	I Kings 4.26: 40,000	II Chr. 9.25: 4,000
capacity of the "sea"	I Kings 7.26: 2,000 baths	II Chr. 4.5: 3,000 baths

It seems to me only right that conservatives should be required to face facts of this kind. It is their doctrine, and not that of anyone else, that has made such sets of facts a problem. They have no right to say airily that they are not concerned about petty details. Unless these petty details can be explained they mean that one or another biblical source (or both) is in error about a matter of fact. As we have seen, conservatives hide behind the smokescreen of a (quite unevidenced) textual variation here: but even if the text had varied, it would still mean that the biblical text is at best conveying to us an infallibly correct copy of a set of errors. Do conservatives want to stick to that?

2. *Objectivity*

One of the amusing aspects of research into fundamentalism is that the official literature and statements of the movement do not give a full picture of what is believed or done. For example, though the belief that large numbers of Christians (in fact, most non-conservative evangelicals) are not 'true' Christians is basic to faith and life within fundamentalism, no statement to this effect is to be found within authoritative expressions such as *Evangelical Belief*. The same document coyly fails to mention the principle of non-co-operation with non-fundamentalist bodies, though that principle is perhaps more constitutive of the shape of a fundamentalist organization than any other. It does not make it fully explicit that negativity towards biblical criticism is an absolutely central principle of the movement concerned. As a result, even on infallibility, of all things, one can find remarkably soft assertions. According to

Evangelical Belief p. 21, the word infallible 'may be used in a transitive sense as equivalent to "not liable to fail or to deceive" '. Going on on this line, we are told, 'if the reader accepts the Bible on its own terms, remembers its primary purpose, and, where there seems to be obscurity, compares scripture with scripture, then it does not mislead the reader.' Does not mislead! Such a statement can be taken in quite a liberal sense. The reader can make highly critical judgments about the Bible without for a moment supposing that the Bible will 'mislead' him. Unquestionably, a document like *Evangelical Belief* understates the rigidity, the conservatism and the partisanship of the organization for which it is written.

Now in part this is done for the sake of the effect that would otherwise be made. It is probable that a good number of those who join the sort of organization represented by *Evangelical Belief* are able to do so precisely because of the occasional softness and vagueness of its language; or, conversely, if the newcomer were to be presented with a statement that set out in full the rigid conservatism of the organization, he would be much less likely to join it. But this is not the only reason.

The more profound reason lies not in the tactics of meeting the newcomer but deep in the mental structure of fundamentalist faith. Nothing is more marked in that structure than the sense of need for objectivity. Non-conservative theological arguments might be attractive, but in the last resort they are subjective, that is, they depend on the arguments of this man or that man, while some other man will have a different argument. Critical scholarship studying the Bible is also subjective: someone says that the J passages in Genesis are different from the P passages, but how can one be sure of this, especially when some other scholar will come along and make a different separation? How can one escape from this subjectivity? The only way is to make it clear that the centre of authority lies beyond the range of human opinion altogether. The inspiration of the Bible means that, though it is a product of identifiable human authors, it lies beyond the range of human subjectivity. It stands outside of man, as the sun stands outside of the revolutions of the planetary system. By accepting it as true and right one is accepting something that is objective, because it lies beyond the reach of one's own human subjectivity. To accept the Bible as true is objective and not subjective, because accepting it as true is not forming one's own view of the Bible, it is represented rather as accepting the Bible's own 'view' of itself. The fundamentalist thus thinks that he has a standard of absolute truth which stands entirely outside of himself and thus lends objectivity to his position as accepter of this standard.

This thought leads us to several valuable insights on our theme, but first its connection with conservative literature: conservative literature fails to give a clear or accurate account of what fundamentalists think or do, not because of any intention of concealing anything, but because the literature is not in fact focused on what fundamentalists think or do: it is focused on the external and objective principles which (as they believe) govern and control their faith and their acts. Literature therefore makes no attempt to describe what fundamentalists as people do or think: it concentrates on tracing the path from the external and objective authority to the things which must be believed or done. For this reason fundamentalist literature has produced no true social description, it has not even shown signs of attempting to do so. Only in the United States, where, as we have seen, conservatism is more self-critical and where also the pressure for social description is more advanced, do we find that something of the sort is attempted. All the British conservative evangelical literature surveyed by me is entirely authority-centred.

This leads us to state another way in which the difference between fundamentalists and other Christians could be stated: for many Christians and Christian groups, there is indeed an objective reality which is the authority standing over against them, but for them the objectivity is to be found in Christ as a person and not in the Bible; for fundamentalists the objectivity lies in the Bible. Faith in Christ cannot be considered grounded in objectivity unless the principle of biblical authority is fully conceded. This is one of the main features in the fundamentalist mind: the fact that a man says he believes in Christ does not seem objective to them, you can't trust that or rely on it, but if he believes in the Bible as infallible and inerrant then that seems to lend objectivity.

Objectivity thus comes to mean that the truth is not in people. Persons cannot be relied on. The only thing upon which you can rely is something objective in the sense that it stands beyond the realm of human personal life. The writers of scripture were of course persons but the fundamentalist does not trust in them as persons; he accepts them because of the inspiration of the book they wrote. Inspiration, infallibility and inerrancy are devices that withdraw the Bible from the field of human subjectivity and make it into an objective reality that stands over against human thoughts and opinions. Similarly, Christ is a person, but Christ as a person cannot be relied on except where objectivity is guaranteed by grounding, grounding not in scripture but in the inspiration and inerrancy of scripture. This determines the fundamentalist attitude to other Christians. The fact that they confess Christ and worship him is an uncertain factor: we don't know what they mean by that, it is all subjective, and only when it is conjoined with a clear statement about the doctrine of scripture is it made objective. The attitude to the churches, to church leaders and theologians, and to biblical scholars is guided by the same principle.

Thus, amusingly, fundamentalist faith, though concentrated on the Bible, would not have been possible during the biblical period itself. The biblical writers were only persons then. The objective written and external fixed authority that fundamentalists now revere did not then exist. The attempt of fundamentalist apologists to represent the situation during the life of Jesus, as if the Old Testament then had for Jesus and the apostles the total, final and objective place that the Bible has for fundamentalists today, can only be considered ludicrous. And for the time when the Old Testament was still in the making no such argument could even be attempted. The fundamentalist position depends entirely upon the finished and fixed body of canonical scripture. A fundamentalist, thrown back into the time of Isaiah or of St Paul, would have had to meet them as persons, 'subjectively', without the external objectified scripture that he now depends on.

This seems to me to be the centre and core of fundamentalism as a religious system: a search for objectivity leads to the reification of the Bible.[5] 'Reification is the apprehension of the products of human activity *as if* they were something else than human products – such as facts of nature, results of cosmic laws, or manifestations of divine will. Reification implies that man is capable of forgetting his own authorship of the human world . . . The objectivity of the social world means that it confronts man as something outside of himself.' These words, though not written (so far as I know) with fundamentalism in mind, seem to me to state very well the reality of that movement. Objectivity in religion means that man must have something 'that confronts him as something outside of himself'. God, or Christ, or the Holy Spirit, will not quite satisfy that need. They are not part of man's world, they do not guarantee objectivity, for they are not articulate and fixed entities; on the contrary, they are highly ambiguous entities, and indeed it is this fact that causes the dread of subjectivity: if we rely merely on God or on Christ, then we have no more to go on than what various people think about God or Christ. The Bible on the other hand is a fixed and articulate entity.

Is the objectivity attained by the reification of the Bible a real objectivity? The answer must be: no. What the conservative evangelical position about the Bible does is: it gives a sanction and protection to the collective ego, to the collective subjectivity, of the evangelical tradition in religion. It creates a world where there is no room for others. We can look at this first more philosophically, and then more personally.

It is often argued by theologians that modern man cannot understand Christianity except where it is re-expressed in a form that takes account of the major tendencies of modern thought. Fundamentalism shows clearly that this is not so. On the contrary, it is perfectly possible to form a version of Christianity which rejects or ignores large areas of modern thought and knowledge, but which works reasonably well for large numbers of people and is also reasonably stable. The decision between the two options is not at all a matter of inevitability: rather, it is a choice. One may choose to work out a reinterpretation in more modern terms, and if this is done it is not because that is the only possible way to go, but because it is the better way to go. Theologians are right, of course, in pointing out that it is not possible to ignore modern tendencies of thought and maintain consistency. This is true and, as we have seen, fundamentalist polemics and apologetics are in fact a mass of inconsistencies of all kinds. This fact however does not in the slightest affect the viability of fundamentalism as a creed to live by. This is, firstly, because the inconsistencies are not perceived as such by the people who live by this creed, and secondly because inconsistencies do not trouble people too much if they can be held together by some over-arching principle or symbol. In the case of fundamentalism that principle or symbol is the correctness of the Bible. Whether one is arguing for a miracle on the grounds of belief in the supernatural, or eliminating a miracle in order to obtain a non-supernatural but plausible account, the Bible is correct either way. All arguments are arguments for the correctness of the Bible, and they thus cohere or seem to cohere through their results even if their methods and premises are quite contradictory.

The idea that one cannot listen to the radio or use the telephone and at the same time believe in miracles like the talking of Balaam's ass or the journey of Jonah in the belly of the fish is quite erroneous: thousands of people combine both of these things without the slightest difficulty. The real and fatal cost of fundamentalist doctrine and ideology, as a system of life, is not its inner logical inconsistency, but rather its personal cost: it can be sustained as a viable way of life only at the cost of unchurching and rejecting, as persons, as thinkers or scholars, and as Christians, all those who question the validity of the conservative option. The presence of the questioner breaks down the unnatural symbiosis of conflicting elements which makes up the total ideology of fundamentalists. We can thus understand why 'liberals' and other non-conservative persons have not only to be disbelieved, discredited and overcome in argument; they have, still more, to be eliminated from the scene altogether. The fundamentalist policy is not to listen to the non-conservative arguments and then reject them: it is that the non-conservative argument should not be heard at all. Fundamentalism as an ideological option is profoundly threatened by the presence of people who do not believe in it, who do not share it, who question it.

It may perhaps be granted that fundamentalism combines many peculiar elements. It includes a philosophy of the eighteenth century, and a picture of what goes on in theology that is built and modelled upon the deist controversy. It can both affirm the unlimited potential of supernatural intervention and apply a rationalizing and naturalizing reduction to actual biblical miracle stories. It is bitterly hostile to liberalism, but this does not at all prevent it from including liberal interrelations, so long as the results or the general affirmations are conservative. It repudiates biblical criticism, and yet certain critical elements are quietly accepted. It argues simultaneously that the biblical text has been substantially corrupt and that it has been substantially kept free from corruption. Far from being a consistent conservatism, it is full of partial compromises with modern ways of thinking. It is a compromise religion through and through. The mixture of all these elements, however, does not render fundamentalism an unstable mixture. All the signs are that it has, perhaps fortuitously, achieved a highly stable state. It is the Bible itself that lends to the position that stability. For the believer all these different arguments hang together and cohere in one central affirmation: they are all arguments that join to support the inerrancy of the Bible. Because of this fact, though the arguments seem to outsiders to contradict one another, to fundamentalists they support one another. The fact that, let us say, the philosophy involved is an antiquated one does not trouble anyone. We have to accept that a constellation of elements of belief can come together in the way in which fundamentalism has formed itself, and can remain basically the same over a long period. It is perfectly possible that fundamentalism, in a form not much altered from what we now see, will remain with us for five hundred or a thousand years.

I have previously suggested that the fundamentalist use of scripture is best understood as a ritualistic procedure.[6] This is true not only of the use of scripture, but even more of the arguments used by fundamentalists against non-conservatives. These arguments have really changed very little in the last hundred years or so and there is little sign that they will change very much. Not only do they not succeed in making any contact with non-conservative Christianity, they do not at all seek to do so. The arguments are rehearsed again and again because they are deeply reassuring to the fundamentalist himself: it is for him that these arguments are formed, and also for such individuals, not yet fundamentalists, as may be willing to abandon everything and enter the circle of fundamentalist faith. None of the arguments are attempts at establishing communication with non-conservative faith and there is no reason to believe that that is intended or desired. The fact that they do not rest upon any real attempt to discover what non-conservative Christians think does not count as a disadvantage: indeed, the maintenance of the fundamentalist picture of what non-conservatives think is one of the necessary assuring functions of the fundamentalist myth as a whole. It keeps the actuality of the non-conservative Christian at a distance, and this fits in exactly with all I have been saying.

Accordingly, where it comes about that fundamentalists have the power, it must be expected that they will use that power to silence those of contrary opinion. They will seek to eliminate from structures of church and education persons who are not sufficiently conservative. The history of fundamentalism shows this clearly. Like other conservative movements, it has sought not merely the means to witness, to state its own position, but control, the power to silence or to remove from positions of responsibility any persons who did not conform. The rise of biblical criticism in the English-speaking churches was marked by a series of heresy trials and evictions from their professorships of persons who today would count as quite mild and moderate critics. In the major churches this has not in the long run worked: the major churches have repudiated their own conservatism, often much too late. But there is no reason to suppose that the motivation for it on the conservative side has in any way altered. Attempts to use church authority to depose professors holding critical views have continued in various parts of the world into the last few years. There seems to be nothing in the general doctrine or practice of fundamentalists that suggests any acceptance of a pluralist ideal, any willingness to concede that it might be good for one to hear a contrary view. The idea that it might be salutary and fruitful for the church to contain opposites and extremes within the one body is entirely absent from fundamentalism, except for the limited series of variations within fundamentalist faith itself. The church is not seen as a society embracing different theologies and held together by faith and trust: fundamentalism and its doctrine go back to that stage of the church, still not far behind us, in which it was considered a right and a duty to test the faith, especially of clergy and leaders, by question and answer according to strictly formulated credal documents. Naturally, there are many open-minded persons within fundamentalism who would regret the application of these methods; but there is no reason to suppose that their regret would make any difference.

3. *People and attitudes*

Readers may have noticed that I have made little or no use of the psychological arguments that are very frequently directed against the fundamentalist position. People say, for instance, that fundamentalism depends basically upon an attitude of fear, a sense of insecurity that demands something absolute and infallible to hold on to. This is said not only by critics of fundamentalism, but also by highly conservative people. Ramm himself, surely no liberal, says: 'Unfortunately the noble tradition which was in ascendancy in the closing years of the nineteenth century has not been the major tradition in evangelicalism in the twentieth century. A narrow bibliolatry, the product not of faith but of fear, buried the noble tradition.'[7] Thus the widespread feeling of non-conservatives, that much fundamentalist religion is dominated by fear, may have some justification. But, whether this is so or not, the position in this book does not depend upon it. I do not doubt that fundamentalism can be a reaction of fear, and that resistance to change can follow from fear of change. But I do not think that this is necessarily the case, and I do not see why fundamentalist convictions should not be found allied with a courageous and cheerful psychological constitution. The emphasis in this book falls not on the psychological states, but on the logical and methodological perceptions which go to form fundamentalism. This is surely a better approach, if only because it has a chance of doing some good; little is achieved by saying that such and such a religious trend is motivated by fear, except to irritate those concerned; the psychological argument is often paralysing and useless. It is my opinion that fundamentalism can and often does go with a quite stable and balanced personality, and this fits with the point I have already made about the stability of fundamentalist ideology. I do think that fundamentalism is a pathological condition of Christianity; but that does not mean that it is psychologically pathological, and I shall not pursue the psychological argument any farther except for limited points to be mentioned below.

The other argument of a personal kind most often directed against fundamentalists is the assertion that they are individualists. Doubtless this has some truth in it, but it seems far from easy to pin down what it can mean. In all evangelicalism there is an emphasis that each man must make up his own mind about Christ, but this, though individualist in a sense, is not clearly wrong; on the contrary, it seems quite right, and the most one could say in criticism would be that it has to be balanced with another emphasis that would complement it. What may be more harmfully individualist is the way in which the fundamentalist within any congregation or body of the church will often single out himself, and any who think like him, as the true Christian individuals: he does not identify himself with the body of the membership but pulls apart from them into his own world, his own Christianity. Even here, however, one should not go too far: many fundamentalists manage to co-exist in the life of their own parishes, remaining loyal to their contacts, friendships and duties within these, while at the same time belonging to and supporting an ideology that sees all others as 'nominal Christians' and finds the true form of the church in a fundamentalist organization. But, all in all, though one can see many ways in which fundamentalists can be described as individualists, it is not clear to me that this could be properly regarded as the key fault or weakness of the movement.

What is impressive about fundamentalists, much more than their individualism, is their intense group loyalty. Their organizations were formed, like those of the pietists before them, to a considerable extent because they longed for fellowship and did not find within existing churches and organizations a fellowship of shared interests and convictions such as they felt they needed. For many it is the life, the spirit and the dedication of the group, even more than the preaching or the arguments, indeed very much more than they, that lead them into a personal faith. This being so, the common convictions of the group come to dominate the individual, often very swiftly and to a frightening extent. Normal fundamentalists do not interpret the Bible individually: that is the last thing they do. Their normal biblical study and interpretation is a reiteration of the normal fundamentalist religious position, in different words and with varied individual emphases: it is a ritual repetition of what the group as a group believes, and this serves also as an initiation for newcomers. Faced with a problem in biblical study, they do not interpret individually: they go off to find someone with experience or authority, and they ask him what is the 'evangelical view' about this. They do not read individually the writings of theologians and try to decide individually whether these books are 'sound' or not; they get someone to assure them that this or that writer is 'sound' or 'liberal', as the case may be. A conservative student of theology, asked to consider the separation of Isaiah into various authors or the date of II Peter, does not in the slightest try to work out an answer through his own individual efforts and researches: he finds someone in a position of leadership who will tell him where to find the books and sources from which the 'evangelical view' can be found. Naturally, one cannot say that there is no individual biblical interpretation within fundamentalism. But much more characteristic of fundamentalism is the way in which the group stamps its norms and its claims upon the mind of the individual member. The very closeness and intensity of the fellowship puts it in a strong position to do this; and a still stronger factor is the doctrinal purity of the group.

In this respect, though we have not tried to *explain* fundamentalism from psychological causes, we cannot but observe that it may in certain situations have psychological *results*. Where the band of doctrinal purity is drawn tight enough, freedom and spontaneity can easily and quickly be lost. Lack of contact with non-conservative Christians produces a marked in-group mentality. Suspicion of unorthodox and non-evangelical tendencies becomes so strong as to inhibit thought. Instant defensiveness against anything that might seem to criticize the values of the group becomes marked. Free exchange of ideas with those outside the group comes to be lost, because all ideas are immediately measured according to whether they appear to favour the group's ideology or not. The problem of 'minority group attitudes' is noted by many of the conservative writers who have any degree of self-critical awareness.[8] It is, in fact, not surprising if an ideology so powerful and so exclusive as the fundamentalist one should have its effects on the personality. I do not suggest that this necessarily happens; but surely few with experience will doubt that it does sometimes happen.

In order to understand this more fully, some thought should be given to the way in which individuals pass into and out of fundamentalism. There are indeed certain people who remain earnest fundamentalist Christians, active and enthusiastic, all their lives. There are certain families in which this pattern of faith is passed on from generation to generation: the parents pray for the conversion of their children and in due course, perhaps at quite an early age, they come to be possessed of a full personal faith of fully fundamentalist type, which they retain throughout their lives and pass on to yet another generation. Anyone with experience in British evangelicalism will know of such families. But equally he will know that this is not the norm. Of those active in fundamentalist organizations at any one time, and especially in the student organizations, a large proportion will have become evangelicals quite recently, within the measure of a few years at most; and of these many will before long be moving into another sort of position, most commonly one within mainstream Christianity.

Now this kind of shifting constituency favours the unchanging rigidity of fundamentalist positions on faith, doctrine and biblical questions. Apart from those brought up in fundamentalist faith, newcomers into the group often have few well-formed religious convictions, and such as they have tend to represent 'liberal' positions widespread in our culture (worry about the deity of Christ, the inspiration of the Bible, the need to accept the Old Testament, and the moral faults of the God of the latter). It is for just these views that fundamentalism is geared. The clearly expressed and constantly reiterated fundamentalist positions, held with conviction and close unity by the entire group, along with all its welcoming and personally supporting presence, quickly establishes its views in the mind of the new Christian, especially since contrary opinions are as far as possible shut out.

Although in theory fundamentalism preaches a message that calls for nothing but decision for Christ, the dynamics of the group very quickly ensure that this is filled up with a content of distinctively conservative evangelical doctrine. The entry of new people into the group is used to sustain the stability of rigid fundamentalist positions. Within the group there is little interest in 'hearing the other side', in discussing the possible rights of some other position. Though discussions may be held, they are often sham discussions, intended in fact not to give an equal hearing to a variety of positions but to create opportunities for the rehearsal of the normal fundamentalist viewpoint. Again, people leave the fundamentalist group, because they lose interest or they move to a different position, perhaps a more 'liberal' or a more 'catholic' one. But this has little effect, for such people normally just fade out, they have gone somewhere else; they make little attempt to raise their change of mind as an issue within the group, the group has no mechanism for dealing with it sympathetically, and if they do raise the matter it is most unlikely that any change of direction in the group will result. Thus the social character of the group favours its continuance on its traditional lines. Its 'uncompromising stand' for the 'true gospel' and the authority of scripture is thus prized as the most valuable possession of the group.

Theologically assessed, the dynamics of the fundamentalist group must be considered as a betrayal of justification by faith. In spite of the general evangelical position that salvation comes through faith in Christ, fundamentalism will never allow that faith in Christ is enough. Its dynamics are quite similar to those of the opponents of St Paul who, having begun with faith, felt it necessary to add thereto a whole apparatus of the 'works of the law'.

As we have suggested, many of those who are fundamentalists at any one time, and especially in a mobile society like a university, are in fact on route to some other position. In ten years' time they will be something else. The stability of fundamentalism, to which I have referred, is thus the stability of the ideology and of the group as an abstract, and not of the individuals who belong to it. Many of them will change their ground.

It is probably as well for fundamentalism that it has a changing population of this kind. The impact of recent experience of faith in Christ is the most attractive aspect of the movement as a whole. When the recent is exchanged for the distant, the freshness and positiveness of this type of religion is greatly diminished. In 'culture fundamentalism', where conservative religion is the normal type within a whole society, one often sees a tired, moralistic, puritanical type of Christianity, still uttering the traditional evangelical sayings but not really very different from any other church. Where the opposition against 'liberalism' remains uppermost, people are often left with nothing but an empty negativism towards all non-conservative theology and biblical study: the evangelistic motives, which prompted the whole thing, disappear, and nothing is left but anti-liberalism. Much of the conservative polemical literature seems to come from this latter type.

One of the chief reasons, however, why many people move gradually out of fundamentalism is the one that has already been mentioned, that most of them have to live in a church that is not fundamentalist as a denomination. Sooner·or later they have to form a way of living that will get along with those who think differently. The position of clergy and ministers who hold fundamentalist views within a large and inclusive church like the Church of England is a good illustration. The position of no compromise that is normal in a fundamentalist student organization is hardly possible here. Brother clergy may be Anglo-Catholics or moderates of some kind. There are also the bishops to be thought of, and they too may fail to be conservative evangelicals. The fundamentalist clergyman cannot very well condemn and exclude the whole lot, as could easily be done in a student organization. He can perhaps, while being willing to co-operate, make it clear on every occasion that he takes a rigid partisan stance. It is rather more likely, however, that he will take up an uneasy position that goes now in one direction and now in the other. At one moment he will speak as if he spoke for the church as a whole, as if his minority position did not exist; at another he will take up a strictly partisan line, as if the position of the majority did not exist as far as his own views were concerned. While he thus faces the necessity of playing his part in a total church structure that is not conservative evangelical, he is likely to encourage young people to make their own home in a fundamentalist student or youth organization which will deny the possibility of doing what he himself cannot help doing. The difficulties of maintaining sincerity in this sort of position are obvious. One cannot help asking whether a strict sect solution, that is, separation as a strictly fundamentalist church, would not be a more honest and sincere position. The ambiguity is increased, moreover, by the fact that many conservative evangelical clergymen, though bitterly opposed to any overt liberalism in theology, have large liberal elements in their thinking and in their interpretation of the Bible, as is obvious to anyone who listens to sermons a lot. Finally, even within an inclusive denomination conservative evangelicals can act, and probable do act, by constituting a pressure group that seeks to press decisions of the church into a direction acceptable to conservative opinion.

This thought about the social structure of fundamentalism is important, because it enables us to avoid the impression, commonly held, that in order to be a fundamentalist a man must have a closed mind. This does not seem to me to be necessarily so. There are, first of all, probably many people who are quite open-minded towards some other forms of Christianity but who nevertheless for a variety of reasons adhere to a fundamentalist organization or attend a church with a fundamentalist sort of tradition. They may often have personal friends whose faith is of quite a different type, and they will entirely accept such friends as genuine fellow-Christians. They often have difficulty, however, in extending this beyond the limited range of personal acquaintance. Though they accept their own friends, they cannot bring themselves to think that all who think in the same way as their friends may also have to be accepted as genuine Christians. Moreover, their own open-mindedness, while fully valid for themselves, has great difficulty in making any corresponding impression on the group or organization.

Another point to be borne in mind is the following. At any one point of time fundamentalist positions are being supported and argued by a number of people who are not themselves committed, or are not yet committed, to the fundamentalist mentality as a whole. These are people who are under pressure from conservative argument and who in general sympathize with the direction that it takes. It would be quite wrong to suppose that they as persons have a committed and closed-mind attitude. They may be quite open and they may quite quickly veer away from their conservative sympathies. But the fact that individuals, and many individuals, who support fundamentalist arguments are not people of a closed mind does not alter the situation: these arguments come from a social and religious organism which does have a closed mind, and the evidence of this runs throughout its entire logical and doctrinal structure.

This leads us in turn to reconsider the matter of extremism within fundamentalist Christianity. As we have seen, the structure of the fundamentalist organization promotes and encourages a position of unchanging rigidity. Deeper investigation, however, shows that it is very hard to make clear, within fundamentalism, what exactly is meant by extremism. As with some other comparable social movements, there is always a position more extreme than the one you are talking with at any particular moment. A person whom an average mainstream Christian will regard as a rabid fundamentalist will often be found to consider himself rather moderate; beyond him there lie, it appears, whole tracts of belief that are much more intransigent and uncompromising. The fundamentalist polemicist thus puzzles people by assuming a pose of moderation. He affects to suppose, at least at times, that his is in fact a central position within Christianity. On the one side you have the severe distortions of Roman Catholicism, on the other you have the utter perversions of liberalism, and in the middle you have the sound, central and moderate position of his own conservative evangelicalism. There may indeed be persons who push the conservative evangelical position to unnecessary extremes, it is admitted, but the average sound conservative (i.e. the one you are talking to at the moment) occupies middle ground. It is thus not uncommon to find a person who holds absolutely all the tenets of fundamentalist belief, who believes that the Bible is in all respects infallible, inspired and inerrant, and that all non-conservative theology and all biblical criticism are absolutely wrong, but who nevertheless uses the term 'fundamentalist' not for himself but for some shadowy group of people who hold a yet more extreme position. This pretended moderation of the extremist is just one of the factors that have to be taken into account in all discussions. It is also an index of a real fact, namely that most fundamentalists who have any interest at all in discussing with people of different views come at once under pressure from the more intransigent.

This pretended moderation of fundamentalists, though noticeable, is not very important. The whole body of conservative evangelical opinion, and not only its extremes, far from occupying a central position in modern theology and biblical study, lies in at a remote extreme and hardly counts in the conversation at all, as the slightest knowledge of modern theology and biblical study will show. The pretence of moderateness is only a minor note in the complaint of fundamentalist faith: what is much more in evidence, and rightly, is its awareness of its own isolation.

Fundamentalism, as we have seen, is a constellation of differing positions, disposed around the centrality and inerrancy of the Bible. Sometimes people can be classified as moderate or extreme, but this does not make much difference to the understanding of fundamentalism as a whole. A person who is moderate by one parameter is often extreme by another. The term 'extreme' fundamentalism is often given to groups which are of the extreme political right, but these groups are not necessarily so concentrated in their polemic against academic theology and biblical study as are more 'moderate' groups. A person may have considerable openness to new trends of thought and still, in discussing a subject like faith in its relations to science, simply ignore all opinions not held by conservative evangelicals, not even according to them the dignity of being refuted. And even a 'moderate' fundamentalist group is unrelenting in its hostility to modern theology and biblical criticism, and in this regard is perhaps more extreme than 'extreme' groups are. All in all, the difference between moderate and extreme is at best a relative one.

Another relevant index in this respect is the extreme sensitivity of many fundamentalists to any criticism from without. The basis for this is to be seen in the very strong group loyalty of the movement. Though fundamentalism contains within itself deep conflicts and oppositions, these are forgotten when any criticism from without is met. The immediate defensive response of fundamentalists when faced with any sort of criticism is often a good indication that the appearance of moderation is only skin-deep. The fundamentalist wants to be the one who presents his own position; he does not want to hear it interpreted from without. This fits with the authority-centred character of his thinking, his speaking and his literature, already remarked upon above. Any critical appraisal from without, however carefully researched and documented, will be branded as a distortion and a caricature; this can be taken as automatic and discounted. The fundamentalist is avid for favourable notice of his position. In face of criticism he will often urge the remarkable progressiveness and open-mindedness of his movement: it is not at all as unfavourable critics have described it. This is one facet of the unwillingness to accept the classification as 'fundamentalists', which we remarked upon in our first chapter. But these are often only argumentative mechanisms: at the end of the day fundamentalist attitudes are there, just as rigid as they ever were.

The unbending and rigid position commonly taken by fundamentalist organizations is not in itself necessarily a sign of some kind of pathological psychology. Rather, it lies in the logic of this type of faith and doctrine, and in the function of the organization in relation to its membership. The idea that one must stick to an uncompromising position may well be logically determined by the nature of the position taken up. For it is in many cases true that any single atom of a critical approach to the Bible can form, for the individual in a year or two, as for the church in a century or so, the hole in the dyke through which the floods will swiftly come. Once one has got to thinking that the Book of Daniel might have been written in the second century BC and not in the sixth, once one has even given serious consideration to the possibility that this might be so, then the assurance of the fundamentalist position may have already potentially broken down. The assumption of an unbending and uncompromising position is well understandable.

Paradoxically, however, it remains possible that fundamentalism will shift its stand on a number of biblical questions. It seems to me perfectly possible that a number of critical positions which fundamentalists have in the past bitterly opposed will be absorbed within the fundamentalist system in the next few decades. We have seen that this has already been done in several regards. Evolution was once a line of absolute conflict, but conservatism, apart from some philosophical qualifications of little practical importance, has surrendered all along this line. The critical analysis of the synoptic gospels, as we have seen, is swallowed whole. Deutero-Isaiah, having had a qualified but definite sanction from Ridderbos, can hardly be ruled out. Maybe Daniel will move down to the second century after all. Possibly it will be accepted that the flood is legendary. On innumerable detailed issues conservative scholarly literature is taking up a position which in traditional conservative terms implies that the Bible is in error. In error! This is what would have been said, if these same adjustments had been made by critical scholars: it would have been said that these judgments implied that the Bible was wrong. Why then can conservatives make the same adjustments? The answer is simple: because they do not mention the implication. Conservatism is in process of shortening its lines for economy of force. It does not admit that it is changing its mind, and it makes no apology to the critical scholars whom it mercilessly lampooned in the past for taking the same positions that it now takes. The acceptance of a few critical possibilities will make it easier for conservative faith to defend itself in the modern world. Within conservatism it is possible to accept positions from critical scholarship without making any acknowledgment that this has been done; and it is possible to do it without having any great fear that one will thereby set off young conservatives on the critical path. If some movement is made over a limited range of biblical questions, such as Deutero-Isaiah and Daniel, this should not be construed as a liberalization. There is no liberalization unless freedom and encouragement are given to follow the critical mode of thought which led to modern positions about these books. It seems quite possible that a tacit adjustment over some biblical books will be made, but without any relaxation of the hostile polemic against critical method and modern theology generally.

In the tension about moderation and extremism within fundamentalism, an important argument is the Pauline argument about the weaker brother. St Paul (I Cor. 8) writes about meat that had been offered to idols. There were those who argued that, since an idol was a non-existent being, and since Christians have true knowledge of the one God, there can be no harm in eating meat that had been offered to idols. There were others, however, who did not feel themselves to have 'knowledge', and to whom the idol was a sort of reality. If you, who have the knowledge, eat meat offered to an idol, then it may do you no harm; but a weaker brother, seeing you do this, may be tempted to do the same, when for him it is a sinful act. 'Through thy knowledge shall the weak brother die, for whom Christ died?' (8.11). Therefore, Paul concludes, 'if meat make my brother to offend, I will eat no flesh while the world standeth, lest I make my brother to offend' (v. 13). In fundamentalism there are always people who are moderate about this or that question and who would personally be happy if there were some reduction in the movement's rejection of mainstream Christianity, mainstream theology and biblical criticism. They personally would welcome some adjustment; but they have to think of the others. What about the 'weaker brother' who could be brought into unbelief and sin through untimely concessions to dubious doctrine? The person who gains from this argument is not the weaker brother but the stronger: it is always an argument in favour of rigid and uncompromising policies. In fundamentalism the argument about the weaker brother is constantly used as a device to sustain extremism and to impede positive dialogue with other Christian points of view; it is a means by which the stronger, i.e. the more completely uncompromising, are able to maintain their control over the more flexible.

We may end this section by a brief discussion of two further 'personal' aspects of our question.

One is the relation between children and parents. It has been not uncommon for an adolescent to become converted to a fundamentalist faith and then begin to look on his own parents as 'nominal' or 'not real Christians', although they may have taken much trouble to bring him or her up in a good ethical and religious tradition, commonly in mainstream religion. The personal pain and suffering that this can bring about can easily be imagined. I mention it here, however, because it may be a valid psychological point: in cases of this sort, fundamentalist religion may share in the psychology of revolt against parents and in the establishment of teenage independence. And, while we are talking once again about the psychology of the matter, it may be relevant also to make some comparison with the world of secular and political 'fundamentalisms', now most marked in Marxism and most vividly illustrated not long ago by the Red Guards in China, with the little Red Book, the memorization of the words of the Chairman and the repeated chanting of these words and indoctrination through them. It is, therefore, perfectly possible that religious fundamentalism is a special religious manifestation of an approach to reality that runs across the spectrum of applications into politics and no doubt elsewhere. But I shall not follow this up.

One other 'psychological' argument that is often used is the suggestion that fundamentalists maintain pathologically censorious and puritanical attitudes towards such matters as sex and marriage, women's dress and so on. This may sometimes be so but it does not seem to be essential to fundamentalism and I do not think it should be stressed very heavily.[9] Some at least of these attitudes are very much culture-conditioned, that is to say, they derive from aspects of the general culture and not directly or distinctively from express fundamentalist belief or practice. In the matter of sexual relationships, the literature of central conservative groups gives little basis for the idea of a pathological prurience. My own criticism would be the opposite, that the material is childishly naive in a pre-1914 schoolboy-idealistic manner, culminating perhaps in the immortal piece of advice, 'To share a common interest in Sunday School work is not, in itself, a decisive indicator that you should get married.'[10] This was published in 1964! At least as far as one can judge from the published literature, the conservative evangelical view of sex and marriage, far from being haunted by sin and guilt, is light and superficial. What the conservative student gets from his reading matter is advice of a prudential kind about the unwisdom of playing with other people's affections, holding hands unless one is serious, kissing before becoming engaged and, most of all, getting married hastily on the basis of a common devotion to the work of the Lord. All these are indeed not matters without any importance: but as an ethical implication of the (supposedly earth-shaking) gospel they are just laughably negligible in comparison with the perception of ethical issues in theologians of mainstream theology. I suspect that relations between men and women in fundamentalist groups are commonly quite happy and wholesome, but for this no thanks are due to the mediocre guidance on ethical questions handed out by the group. More can be ascribed to the common sense of purpose and neglect of self in common devotion to the work of the Lord.

4. *Ecumenicity*

The antipathy of fundamentalists towards the ecumenical movement, often violent, is not easy to explain. It is not as if the frontiers drawn by fundamentalism were denominational frontiers, for they are not, and we have seen that evangelicals of different denominations maintain a good deal of understanding with each other. Sometimes it is said that ecumenism is suspected on the grounds that it must lead towards an approach for union with Rome; but this can hardly be considered an adequate explanation. Fundamentalists, though usually totally alienated from Rome, do not have for Rome, except in dominantly Catholic lands like Ireland, the burning antipathy they feel for modern theology and biblical criticism. In fact there is reason to believe that the ecumenical movement is felt as an issue by many fundamentalists: they are aware of the Lord's prayer that they all should be one, and they are anxious that evangelicals should not impede this unless there are very good reasons. From time to time they have to enquire of their own leadership whether there is adequate reason for hostility, or even for coolness, towards the ecumenical movement. We can suggest the following as probable reasons.

Firstly, the central ethos of the ecumenical movement, that one begins by accepting the essential Christianity of those who belong to a different doctrinal or ecclesiastical tradition, is anathema to fundamentalists, who proceed from exactly the opposite starting-point: though they are not so concerned about denominational affiliations, their whole separate existence and organization depends on not beginning by accepting the essential Christianity of those who think otherwise.[11]

Secondly, as we have seen, fundamentalists have not been able to gain or keep control of any of the major churches, and they have had to be content with this position. So long as things remain static this is all right. But as soon as the possibility of change in the direction or constitution of the churches comes to be thought of, things become different. Here is an opportunity to press for the basic conservative criteria. Change must not be thought of without attention to the doctrinal position, and that means in fact, change must not take place except as guided by pressure from conservative doctrinal views. The acceptance of the church situation by fundamentalists is put in question as soon as any move for substantial change is proposed.

Thirdly, it is probable that the long-term effect of fundamentalism is much more denominational than has been suggested so far in this book. Students and academics can concentrate on doctrinal and biblical questions, and it seems to them that denominational structures are not very important. But long-term existence in the church ties one down increasingly to the administrative structures and career prospects of this church or that. I would consider it probable that, of those whose background is in fundamentalism, and especially among the clergy and the leadership of churches, a substantial proportion end up much more more tied to the denominational structures within which they work than could have been predicted from their earlier conservative evangelical faith.

Fourthly, the entire evangelical movement arose and had its main history in a period during which the fragmentation of the church was largely taken for granted and by no means bemoaned as a bad thing. Conservative evangelicals do not on the whole feel that the work of the church has been discredited and damaged by its division into many denominations and sects. They do not find it a very bad thing that there should be Anglicans, Baptists and Methodists: the bad thing is that there should be liberals and biblical critics. The elimination of the latter is simply a far more essential task than the doing of anything about the former.

Fifthly, conservative evangelicalism is basically against change. The only change that would interest it would be an increase of support for conservative evangelicalism. It has grown and existed in the period since the eighteenth century, when there have been Methodists, Baptists and so on. Though there is much praise for the churches of the Reformation era, which are supposed to have held conservative evangelical doctrine, there is little nostalgia for them, little desire to go back to things as they were in the Geneva or the Scotland of the sixteenth and seventeenth centuries. But the situation since the eighteenth century counts as normality. It can and should be preserved. The position and the arguments of conservative evangelicals are all predicated upon this situation. If the situation were to be altered, everything might have to be rethought. How is one to know where this might take us?

But this means that the groupings and classifications into which people fall, and have fallen since the beginning of the modern era in the eighteenth century, should be allowed to remain. This applies to intellectual classifications, where as we have seen conservatives still understand the world of theology on an eighteenth-century model; it applies to national divisions; and it applies to ecclesiastical divisions.

And, sixthly, this is particularly evident wherever there is any influence of millenarianism, and in conservative evangelicalism this is probably never far away. In millenarianism any international or world-wide organization has a malevolent character. Anything trying to be universal or ecumenical, anything seeking to transcend the 'natural' divisions of man into nations and churches, is likely to be a force for evil. It was only to be expected that the church would fall into total apostasy and become an agent of the Antichrist; in this respect the growth of liberalism and biblical criticism gives that gloomy satisfaction of seeing that things have got worse, when one had foretold that they would do so. But the idea that this apostate Christianity is seeking to organize itself in international and inter-denominational form shows all the more clearly that it is part of the plans of the Antichrist, a new Babylon from which the saints have to keep themselves uncorrupted in every way.

The apocalyptic picture of the world, accepted and developed in millenarianism, takes national divisions as divinely-given and unchanging. The people referred to under a name in the Old Testament are the same people who today bear a similar name. Meshech and Tubal in Ezek. 38.2 are, according to the Scofield Bible, Moscow and Tobolsk. God split the totality of mankind into many groups, and these are to remain so until the second advent. 'This passage [the Tower of Babel story] shows that God's plan for the world until the Prince of Peace returns is not an international one-world government, but nationalism. This is the one way the world can keep from falling under a dictator who could virtually destroy mankind.'[12]

Obviously, we do not need to insist on much direct influence from millenarianism. The position of conservatives about ecumenicity is in line with their central eschatological position: the coming of the end is a totally supernatural intervention. It is not prepared by a progressive impact of God's will upon the affairs of the world. On the contrary, things will probably get worse. It is not our duty to make them worse or to rejoice if they do become worse, but they will in fact become worse. To press for the proximate realization of elements of God's will, by moving the churches towards a greater unity within the world as it now is, is not a desirable purpose. In particular, any scheme which would mean that conservatives actually sat round the table with non-conservatives and argued out their differences within a common framework would not be a step towards the realization of the kingdom of God. Ecumenical ventures which might involve such discussion are not to be encouraged.

5. *The conservatism of moderates*

In order to understand the position fully, we have to give some thought not only to the personal mentality of fundamentalists but also to the attitudes and opinions of others towards them. This immediately leads us to state a further reason why I have not in this book developed the 'psychological' sort of criticisms often made against fundamentalism: in so far as these criticisms are valid, they have to be levelled not only against fundamentalists but also against many other currents within Christianity. The idea that religious behaviour is motivated through fear rather than through love or faith is one that could be quite broadly spread, as a criticism of the most diverse Christian traditions; the accusation of individualism has also been made on all sides; and as for pathological attitudes about sex and other matters of life-style, the less said anywhere in Christianity the better. In so far as these are difficulties for fundamentalism, they are difficulties that it shares with a variety of currents, especially minority currents and extreme currents, within diverse segments of Christianity.

It is important that this should be noted, because conservatives react with resentment and hostility when they feel, as they often do, that they are being specially and uniquely picked on for criticism. Tired of being branded as closed-minded obscurantists and behind the times, they have in recent years come increasingly to pay back in the same coin. There was a time when some of them might have accepted that 'liberals' were more open-minded, but they would then have said that an open mind was not so great a virtue and that acceptance of the Word of God was a much greater virtue than any amount of open-mindedness. Now it is generally not so. The philosophical and cultural ideals of liberalism have been largely taken over by conservative polemicists and applied to their own partisans. A reading of modern conservative literature will quickly make one aware that all non-conservative theologians and biblical critics suffer from a closed mind, from narrow prejudice, from failure to pay attention to modern trends in discovery and science, and generally from ignorance and incompetence.

If scholars think that the pentateuch was made up from sources like J, D and P, or that Acts was a late document or that the gospels do not give a quite accurate transcript of the teaching of Jesus, this is not because they have looked at the facts, but because they have blindly followed the indoctrination poured into them by generations of teachers who were themselves totally dominated by wild philosophical theories and unbiblical speculations. Those who look at the subject with an open mind, without preconceived theories and on the basis of the evidence itself are, one discovers, the conservatives. Completely partisan writers like Harrison and Kitchen take this 'open-minded' stance all the time. Readers can judge for themselves on which side the right lies. I am concerned only to point out that the ideal upheld by conservative apologists, at least as an ideal, is the ideal of open-minded and unprejudiced investigation. It is not to be expected, however, that this fact will improve communications or discussion in any way; on the contrary, it shows that conservatives, having accepted that open-mindedness is an ideal of a sort, make immediate use of it by appropriating it to themselves. Its value is in any case much diminished by the numerous attacks made at the same time on any idea of an approach to the Bible made without religious presuppositions.

This brings us to one of the few points where conservative argument has something in its favour, and it is at first sight remarkable that so little use is made of this argument by controversialists. The point is that many people in the church, though rejecting fundamentalism, continue to treat some biblical passages, or some sections of the Bible, in a manner that seems to be close to the fundamentalist understanding. This is quite a serious matter. People do not think, with fundamentalists, that everything is accurate, and they consider some passages, perhaps in the Old Testament, to have no value for the church today or otherwise not to be the Word of God; but when they come to the passages that are important for them they use them as if they were a direct transcript of the actual words of Jesus, or as if they were in the fullest sense the Word of God. Is there not therefore something that might be called a selective fundamentalism in the mind of moderate Christians? And, if this is so, then is it not the only consistent course to adopt a universal fundamentalism and take all the Bible to be inerrant, historically accurate, and more or less a transcript of the will of God?

Now, though there is something of importance in this argument, we should not accept its validity too quickly, First of all, it is certainly true that many people who in other respects are not at all conservative think of sayings ascribed to Jesus in the gospels as actually spoken by him in this form, or they treat certain passages, let us say 'God is love', as being fully the Word of God when they do not give the same theological validity to many other passages. It is quite doubtful, however, whether the cachet 'selective fundamentalism' is deserved. If a person takes certain passages as the Word of God, while not including others in the same category, he may have reasons for doing so. Fundamentalism itself, as we have seen, does not really suppose that all texts of the Bible equally express the essence of God's being and works, so that it also has a grading of passages as more or less central. The difference is that in fundamentalism the grading is done by the evangelical tradition of religion, while in non-conservative Christianity people have the right to do some such grading for themselves. The attitudes involved are therefore in this respect entirely different from fundamentalist attitudes.

Nevertheless there is some cause for disquiet about this phenomenon. Within mainstream Christianity there continues to be a tendency to take sayings and narratives as historical, even though scholars do not count them as historical, and to take texts as a close transcript of divine reality, when any critical theology would count them only as approximations. We are dealing with what John Robinson calls 'the conservatism of the committed' as distinct from 'the fundamentalism of the fearful'.[13] People in the churches may know in a general way that the fourth gospel was probably not written by John the son of Zebedee and that Jesus in his actual life probably did not speak in the way that that gospel portrays him as speaking. They know that critics are uncertain of many of the sayings attributed to Jesus. But, though they know all this, they do not really adjust to it. They hope it will all somehow go away. They feel better if someone tells the story so that it happens just as the gospels narrate it. They feel that the critics have 'taken away' such a lot of what was to be known about Jesus, and they ask themselves dolefully what there is 'left'. These people are not in the slightest fundamentalists; they are not even very conservative, and often take a position of moderate churchmanship. They have no dogmatic feeling that all the stories must be true, and they do not feel this way about the Bible as a whole, but only about the gospel stories plus some other portions.

This means that, though they know and accept something of what has happened in modern biblical criticism, they have not found it easy to reorient their own basic faith to accommodate it, and therefore they feel much better if not too much is made of it. Among incidents and sayings narrated in the Bible, people just want so much to be told that at least this one really happened, that at least this one saying was really uttered by Jesus. Sometimes it is a more doctrinal element: people want so much to be assured that the doctrine of the Trinity, or of the Incarnation, is really deeply anchored within the biblical texts. They do not want to hear that stories are legends, or that they emerged from the consciousness of the primitive church.

This is not fundamentalism; but it is a sharing of the basic cultural structures upon which fundamentalism also developed. The idea that the final guarantees of faith rest upon accurate historical narrations, and upon doctrinal teaching (especially by Jesus), is deeply embedded in the Anglo-Saxon cultural heritage. It emerges in a drastic and violent form in fundamentalism; in the conservatism of the moderate it emerges in a mild, yet unmistakable, form.

Though the point is one of the arguments which fundamentalists might have pursued with some vigour and with some justification, it is also understandable why they have not done so. For the answer is also fairly obvious: though there is indeed a weakness in this respect in moderate Christianity, the answer lies not in a turn towards fundamentalism but in a more active turn away from it. The concepts and the results of critical study and critical theology have still to be more fully assimilated within the understanding of the church as a whole. There will now probably never be sayings of which we can say with certainty that Jesus of Nazareth actually spoke these words; and it is not only of the more developed theology of John, but also of the apparently simpler narratives of (say) Mark, that we shall always have to say: this is the interpretation of Jesus given by such and such a current within the early church. Or, at least, even those who personally take a more conservative line on these points will always do so in an atmosphere in which the positions just stated will still be present and active.

In this respect the clergy have been considerably to blame. They have represented incidents and sayings in the gospels as if they were real incidents and actual words of Jesus, not because they themselves firmly believed this, but because it was easier to do so. They have not sufficiently informed their people about critical approaches to the Bible and about the much deeper theological values that are to be obtained through them than through the supposition of narratives consisting in real incidents and actual words of Jesus. It is not very difficult to encourage the laity to develop for themselves an inner appreciation of the Bible that is not based on real incidents and authentic sayings, but the attempt has not sufficiently been made. Where there has been real difficulty felt about critical problems in the Bible, the minister has too often agonized over it alone in the privacy of his study and has condescendingly failed to share his problems, which are essential to his study and his faith, with his people.

More seriously still, this sort of craving for a Bible which at least in parts would be infallible and historically accurate means that the basis for fundamentalism is being laid within the moderate church. This is surely one of the most certain features of the situation. In many ways, if there is a fundamentalist problem, it is the middle-of-the-road, non-conservative church that is responsible for it. Liberal and moderate religion sows the seeds of fundamentalism. For a large number of those who go over to fundamentalism from mainstream Christianity, the way has already been prepared by their experience in the mainstream churches. These churches provide an acquaintance with the basic materials. They provide some knowledge of the Bible, but they take the Bible far too lightly, appreciating much too little the profundity and dynamic power of that which they are handling; at the same time they educate into an awareness of some religious and moral problems, but often without engendering a personal consciousness of faith deep and strong enough to deal with these. This religious and moral experience can turn into a sense of sin upon which the fundamentalist gospel plays; the far deeper concentration on the Bible in fundamentalism provides a widening and deepening of experience as against normal religious upbringing; and with a conversion to a more active faith within fundamentalism all these elements fall together in a different way. Thus fundamentalism is parasitic upon the mainstream church. It is in fact amusing and paradoxical that fundamentalism directs such violent polemic against liberalism in religion. Liberalism in religion is the best possible thing for the prosperity of fundamentalism, and sensible fundamentalists ought to encourage it rather than oppose it. It is in periods of theological liberalism that fundamentalism flourishes. The period of neo-orthodoxy in mainstream theology, when liberalism was in retreat (and indeed was thought by many to have disappeared for ever), was also a time when fundamentalism was on the defensive. With the rise of very radical theologies since 1960 or so, fundamentalism has been steadily gaining in influence. In general, the problems and difficulties of the churches with the Bible cannot be rolled away by putting the responsibility on to the fundamentalists.

For mainstream Christians conscious of the Bible fundamentalism is an extremely irritating phenomenon. It is active and vociferous, its arguments are solidly polemical in a way that argument within the churches in general has long ceased to be; its arguments are also stereotyped and unchanging and pay little attention to the actualities of modern church life and theology, and its destructive power is very considerable. But it should not on these grounds be isolated as if it were uniquely the enemy of peace and understanding in the church. This is certainly not the opinion with which this present book is written. To me, personally, the world of mainstream church and theology is not at all a rosy and happy world where everything is well: on the contrary, it is within that mainstream Christianity that the really serious problems and conflicts of our church life and theology lie. The problem of fundamentalism is not that it is the main foe of theology and critical biblical study; on the contrary, it does almost nothing to impede them. The problem is that it has peculiarly placed itself outside of the real task of theology and biblical study. This is the reason why it has to have special study devoted to it. Fundamentalism is connected with the main stream of theology and the main stream of church life in a peculiar skew relationship, different from that occupied by other theological options and different from that of any denominational structures. If fundamentalism has to be specially studied, it is not because it is uniquely damaging (though that can at times be so) but because of its peculiar alienated and cut-off character.

11 · Conclusion

For the church and theology as a whole, fundamentalism constitutes an ecumenical problem rather than an intellectual problem. Contrary to the impression given by many conservative writings, conservative apologetic arguments are having and are likely to have little or no effect on biblical scholars or on theologians. If, here and there, theology and biblical scholarship come around to views which are more conservative and are thus closer to those cherished by fundamentalists, this is quite accidental and has little or nothing to do with the reasons that fundamentalists advance. It is probable that the main trend in both theology and biblical study has long passed a point of no return, where arguments arising from traditional conservatism cease to have relevance or interest, much less have a chance of carrying conviction. Though much solid and valuable work is carried out by biblical scholars who are also conservatives, much or most of this is actually in conflict with the fundamentalist doctrinal principles and can be taken to support them only through misrepresentation or misunderstanding. It is of course perfectly possible that conservative evangelicals might produce a set of intellectual arguments that would seriously disturb mainstream theology and biblical study; but they would have to be arguments quite other than those which have now been standard for about a century.

The ecumenical problem is constituted by the frightening alienation of fundamentalism from the main stream of church life and theology. The basis of this alienation is religious. The root of it is the fact that fundamentalists deal with the real difficulties of differences in faith and life by deeming non-Christian the bodies and the persons who do not agree with them. At the root of the problem there lies therefore a judgment that is more religious and existential than doctrinal or biblical: the problem is formed by the absolute and overweening certainty possessed by fundamentalists that their form of religion is absolutely and uniquely right.

Yet the religion of evangelicals does not in itself necessarily entail this serious alienation. In the ecumenical community of the church the evangelical tradition is an honoured member. Though it is justifiably critical of some other forms of faith, it does not by any means entail complete alienation from other Christian traditions and forms. Its views of conversion, of personal salvation and so on constitute a source of riches; that they clash with some other views may be a difficulty, but not an insuperable or intolerable one. And, for those who stand within evangelicalism, their own emphasis on personal faith in Christ ought to carry with it, and normally does carry with it, a welcome and understanding for all others who share that personal faith.

It is when the evangelical faith is held to be necessarily linked with a certain kind of intellectual apologetic that the alienation between fundamentalism and the main stream of Christianity becomes nearly absolute. The nature of this intellectual structure is such as to render compromise with other currents of theology, and most of all biblical interpretation, almost impossible. Yet, as we have seen, this apologetic is not genuinely derived from the evangelical faith. On the contrary, the attempt to support that faith upon an intellectual apologetic is itself from the beginning a sign of abandonment of the inner core of that faith. Evangelical faith is betrayed by the fundamentalist apparatus of argument. For faith it substitutes dependence on rational use of evidence; and in place of the religious functioning of the Bible it takes, as primary guarantee of the authority of scripture, the absence of error, especially in its historical details. In pursuit of these principles it works out a whole apparatus of argument and interpretation, much of which is probably unknown to and unwelcome to the average evangelical believer. Contrary to fundamentalist argumentation, evangelicalism is a quite flexible form of religion, and it can easily bear the adjustments necessary to enable it to see much of the Bible in a way different from the ways traditional in the past. Criticism of fundamentalist doctrine and biblical interpretation is therefore not at all directed against the evangelical religious basis.

Nevertheless the examination of fundamentalism as a problem cannot but draw to our attention certain weaknesses which, though not necessarily present in evangelicalism, can easily occur there. The first is in the role of faith. It is striking that a religious form which places so much stress on personal faith in Christ is made dependent on a rationalist proof of the inerrancy of the Bible, in which the promises of God are not considered trustworthy unless they are enshrined in a book all statements of which are infallible and inerrant. Perhaps it is the fact itself that so much stress is laid upon faith that brings this about. Other religious securities tend to be lost: the church does not provide much, tradition practically none at all. Can faith really be relied on, quite alone? Perhaps doubts about this caused the doctrine of the infallible and inerrant scripture to be pushed more and more into the foreground.

The second such point is the place of others. Evangelical faith can seem to set one apart from one's own past within the church, and can lead to the idea that the essentials of the faith are unknown in other segments of its membership. Within certain limits this can have some justification. But when it is pressed farther and made into the central operating principle of one's relation to the church, it has gone too far. However justified the evangelical assurances are, they cannot provide a reason for exclusiveness and hostility towards other forms of Christian faith. The other in the church has to be accepted before he is rejected. In fundamentalism the endemic suspicion towards, and rejection of, non-conservative types of Christianity quickly erodes and corrupts the virtues of the evangelical faith with which one starts.

The third is the eschatology, the perception of movement towards the future as movement in which God does new things within this present age. The tendency in much evangelicalism has been to emphasize a totally new age, which at some moment, sooner or later, will be introduced; in its more drastic forms this means that nothing now happens, apart from individual conversion to Christ, that is a form of renewed impact of God's will upon man, and on the whole things get worse rather than better. Apart from a glorious future completely disconnected from the present world, the nearest to a realization of God's will lies in the past, in the Reformation or in the Evangelical Revivals. These last set up the form of religion that is as near final and perfect as man can achieve: all changes from that form are changes for the worse. As against this, it should be understood that change in this world does include elements of the realization of God's will. Such things as the rise of liberal theology or the rise of biblical criticism at the least may be positive elements in the movement of the world process towards its consummation.

Thus, to sum up this point, though I do not at all think that evangelical religion is in itself responsible for the fact of fundamentalism or that fundamentalism can be necessarily derived from it, these are elements in this tradition of Christianity that should be carefully guarded since they seem, more than any other, to be subject to harmful exaggeration in fundamentalistic expressions of that same religion.

The real problem of fundamentalism lies, however, in its intellectual structure; but this is not separable in the long run from the religion. As soon as people have to think about their faith and their understanding of the Bible they become involved in a process of reasoning. Within evangelicalism this does not at all have to be a fundamentalist process, but the fundamentalist intellectual system is very ready at hand and is quickly picked up unless one is ready with some other approach. It is very tempting because of its negative direction: it tries to define evangelical faith as against all others, and especially as against what is supposed to be 'liberalism'. And, once entered, the fundamentalist approach forms a tight circle from which it is not at all easy to break out. Yet, essential as this intellectual apologetic is for fundamentalism, it has been fortunate for fundamentalism that most of its adherents have not had to learn too much of this same intellectual approach. For, the more they learned of it, and the deeper they went into the peculiar corners of it, the more they would be likely to feel it strange to their own religious needs and convictions and alien to the approach of the simple reader of the Bible even within fundamentalism.

Fundamentalism is a highly self-enclosing ideology. The conservative apologist sees all the evidence as showing that the Bible is 'right'. He sees it this way, quite sincerely, and for one simple reason: that he has been a fundamentalist all along. The fundamentalist philosophical position, however, prevents him from recognizing this. On the other hand, the ideological character of fundamentalism calls in question one of its own most important functions, its evangelism. Does it really preach a gospel of salvation for men? Or does it use the gospel as a weapon in an ideological conquest of man? Carnell himself (op. cit., p.128) thought that the latter was often the case.

Our study of the intellectual apparatus of fundamentalism has shown us two things. Firstly, it has shown us that the conservative interpreter of the Bible actually goes by a route quite different from what one would gather from the vociferous conservative attacks on critical method. There is a large contradiction between standard fundamentalist doctrine and the practice of accepted conservative interpreters. Contrary to all that might be expected from polemic documents, conservatives often ignore the literal sense of the Bible, often minimize miracles and the supernatural, often postulate substantial corruptions in the text, and so on. Secondly, we have seen that conservative scholarship comprises different strata, one of which belongs almost entirely in sympathy to the polemic and doctrinal aspect of fundamentalism, while another, though somewhat conservative in approach, is reasonably at home with critical scholarship and noticeably refrains from all the attacks on it that are normal in doctrinal fundamentalism. This latter stratum has brought about the acceptance within the conservative constituency of some limited elements of critical scholarship which only one or two decades ago would have been bitterly resisted.

It is not to be expected, however, that these softenings and contradictions within fundamentalist studies of the Bible betoken any relaxation in the hostility of fundamentalism towards modern theology and the critical approach to the Bible. This hostility is an irreducible fact, and remains in existence independently of any particular instances of biblical interpretation or doctrinal conflict. Occasional fragments of critical approaches can be absorbed into fundamentalism without its making any difference to this basic hostility, especially if the absorption is carried out tacitly and without any public notice being given that this is an approximation to non-conservative thinking. The hostility is fundamental, and is based both on the religious and the intellectual levels: on the religious because non-evangelical religion seems to offer a quite different religious solution, which if valid would damage the exclusiveness claimed for the evangelical path to God, and on the intellectual because modern theology and biblical criticism offer a different organization of the biblical material from that which is basic to fundamentalism. And just here it is the link between the religious and the intellectual that is the ultimate value for fundamentalists: modern theology and biblical criticism, if valid, would break the intellectual link with the Bible which for fundamentalists provides them with the final assurance that their religious faith is true. Fundamentalists therefore fight hard because they are fighting for their own total perception of God and their own knowledge of salvation.

Fundamentalism, as we have seen, organizationally is not a sect; it is a position that overlaps into many churches and denominations. But intellectually it is a sect. Its doctrines, its literature, its biblical interpretation, its modes of speech, thought and friendship mark out a clearly identifiable social organism. The edges of the group are not at all clear and they shade uncertainly into other forms of Christian life; but the centre, the inner core, is easily recognizable and remains extremely stable. It is not at present to be expected that the doctrinal position of that centre will alter materially. Fundamentalists think that a rigid and uncompromising position suits their interests best. In the neo-orthodox period, when there was the nearest to an approach between fundamentalism and positions widespread in the church as a whole, no material concession was made, and it is less likely today, when more radical theologies have gained in influence in the church.

There is, however, one change. Fundamentalists today are no longer entirely content with their alienation; they are also craving recognition. They want their arguments to be taken notice of; they want their cultural achievements and their scholarship to be recognized. Especially in biblical scholarship they long for the recognition that there is a conservative 'side'. In this they very much misunderstand the situation. There is no conservative 'side' which can be set against the critical 'side'. There is critical scholarship, and within it there are many lines and opinions, but there is no 'critical side'. There is room in scholarship for the recognition of conservative opinions, but these can no longer in fact function within scholarship as a conservative 'side', and many or most of the conservative scholars do not wish them to do so.

The longing of the conservative for recognition on an intellectual and scholarly level is a revenge of the intellect upon decisions of the religion. His annoyance at being alienated from the scholarly world is a long-range spiritual and cultural effect of the decision of his religion to unchurch those who believed differently and to treat their theology and their biblical work as if it was an enemy of God. He cannot undo this by pretending that his scholarly arguments are totally objective thinking on the basis of the facts alone and without any preconceptions whatever – an argument put forward most strenuously by those whose results are most exactly in accord with traditional fundamentalist doctrine. If he wants to undo his alienation, without leaving the world in which he is now embedded, he has to go back to his own religious people – their leaders, their simple believers – and tell them something more positive about the world of scholarship and theology in which he himself partly or wholly moves.

For the churches, it is easy to be weakly welcoming and appeasing. The true situation is the reverse of what fundamentalists suppose. Far from it being true that the fundamentalists, sure of holding the true and ancient Christian faith, can sit in judgment on the rest of Christianity, the question for the churches is how far they can recognize fundamentalist attitudes, doctrines and interpretations as coming within the range that is acceptable in the church. The churches, on the other hand, have no ready means whereby to pass judgment on this matter. There is no formula which will tell us whether a person, or a church, that is fundamentalist is working positively for the church as a whole, or working negatively and destructively against it. That must depend on persons and groups, the content and expression of their faith, their understanding for others and their vision of God's work in the world.

Some may think that fundamentalism, in spite of its failings, deserves to have credit because it preserved something of importance that would otherwise have been lost by the church. Credit is certainly due for the great amount of sincere and devoted Christian work that has been done by persons who were also fundamentalists. It is not so clear that their fundamentalist ideology should receive the credit for this. Fundamentalism never sought or intended to preserve something which it would thus make available for the church as a whole: on the contrary, its distinctive and continual insistence was that the acceptance of the fundamentalist position was the one and exclusive way by which the essentials of Christian faith could be preserved. It never sought to provide an ancillary witness to a certain emphasis, for the sake of a wider church that thought differently. And what, after all, did fundamentalism really 'preserve'? It was the church which did not accept the fundamentalist option, and not the fundamentalist group, that preserved continuity with the older faith. It was the fundamentalist approach that thinned down and diluted the theological understanding of the Bible, replacing it with a jejune emphasis on authorships, dates and historical accuracy. But, most of all, whatever credit the church may wish to give to the fundamentalists for their achievements, it cannot and it must not give any unless it makes it clear that it at the same time gives credit and honour to those whom the fundamentalists most bitterly opposed. We do not have to be liberals: but we have to recognize that the liberal quest is in principle a fully legitimate form of Christian obedience within the church, and one that has deep roots within the older Christian theological tradition and even within the Bible itself. And those whom the fundamentalists attacked, and sometimes drove from their teaching positions, are and will remain honoured and accepted teachers of the church.

Notes

Chapter 1

1 For an example of recent discussion, see Martin E. Marty, *A Nation of Behavers*, Chicago University Press 1976, ch. 4 on 'Evangelicalism and Fundamentalism'. Some American writers use *fundamentalism* in a strictly historical sense, to designate a distinct past stage, with its centre more or less in the 1920s, the time of the controversy over evolution; see below, pp. 90ff.

2 Thus E. J. Carnell, *The Case for Orthodox Theology*, Marshall, Morgan & Scott 1961, p. 33, speaks of 'odious Biblicism', implying something a good deal worse than the qualities that in this book would be taken as normal fundamentalism.

Chapter 2

1 'Evangelical' has had a number of different senses; it is used here in the most common English sense, of a theological current 'which lays special stress on personal conversion and salvation by faith in the atoning death of Christ' (*Oxford Dictionary of the Christian Church*, OUP, 2nd ed. 1974, p. 486). The Revivals are movements in the eighteenth and nineteenth centuries; prominent leaders were Wesley and Whitefield in the eighteenth, D. L. Moody in the nineteenth. Billy Graham is much the best-known person continuing this line up to the present day. 'Evangelical' is sometimes used also: (*a*) to mean Protestant, in general, as against Roman Catholic; (*b*) especially in German usage, to mean Lutheran, as contrasted with Reformed or Calvinist. In continental usage 'Pietism' comes a little closer to what is meant by 'evangelicalism' in English usage; on this see further below, p. 189. Those 'Evangelicals' who left the deepest mark on social history through their reforming achievements, like William Wilberforce (1759–1833) and the seventh Earl of Shaftesbury (1801–85), fall in some ways into a special class, since their reformist activism is a feature that later conservative evangelicalism has largely abandoned; see below, p. 116.

2 For the doctrinal statement of The Inter-Varsity Fellowship, with a more or less official explanation of it, see *Evangelical Belief* (The Inter-Varsity Fellowship 1935 and many later reprints). The points listed are among the ten cited there, p. 9; but I have not reproduced the exact wording.

3 Marty, *A Nation of Behavers*, p. 103, citing a citation by Daniel Stevick of Carl Henry; I have not seen the original source.

4 Similarly, unless I am much mistaken, the campaign for prohibition in the United States was a social gospel phenomenon, rather than a conservative phenomenon.

5 On the question how far conservative evangelicals are actually orthodox in their picture of Jesus Christ, see below, pp. 169ff.

6 The term eschatology is very widely used in modern theology. In older theology it meant the doctrine of 'the last things', including the return of Christ to earth, the resurrection of the dead, the last judgment, heaven and hell. It is now used more generally for any kind of thinking that is dominated by the expectation of a coming 'end', or any ideas of ways in which God will bring to pass a better or ideal state for man and the world, this new state lying in the future.

7 I argue similarly in my *Old and New in Interpretation*, SCM Press 1966, p. 204.

Chapter 3

1 On this see already my *The Bible in the Modern World*, SCM Press 1973, pp. 168ff.

2 For a somewhat different approach, see D. Kidner, *Genesis*, IVP Tyndale Commentaries 1967, pp. 54–8.

3 For a simple survey, which requires however some minor adjustments, see A. Murtonen, 'The Chronology of the Old Testament', *Studia Theologica*, 8, 1954, pp. 133–7.

4 Thus K. A. Kitchen, *Ancient Orient and Old Testament*, IVP 1966, pp. 39ff.

5 Kevan, ibid., pp. 82f.; Kline, ibid., p. 87; cf. Kidner, op. cit., pp. 82f.; *New Bible Dictionary*, s.v. Methuselah, p. 819a.

6 On this see further below, pp. 191ff.

7 Not all conservative evangelicals support the gap theory as applied to creation; for a critical examination, from within a very conservative position, see B. Ramm, *The Christian View of Science and Scripture*, Paternoster Press 1955 (reissued 1964), pp. 134–44.

8 Kitchen, op. cit., pp. 54f. However, so extreme a conservative as E. J. Young still tells us that Amram was 'father of Moses', *New Bible Dictionary*, p. 33b.

9 Kitchen, op. cit., e.g. pp. 53–6, 57f., 72–5; LaSor in *The New Bible Commentary Revised*, p. 328b; H. L. Ellison in the earlier edition of the same, p. 307a, finds the chronological problem of I Kings 6.1 'at present insoluble'; cf. also *The New Bible Dictionary*, p. 216. On the procedure of LaSor, whereby he appeals to an error in the biblical text in order to save its historical accuracy, see further below, pp. 280ff.

10 J, E, D and P are the chief strands or sources within the pentateuch as discerned by the main current of scholarly criticism. D is now taken to be more or less the book of Deuteronomy. In the rest of the pentateuch one distinguishes older material, J or E (the letters come from the names of God, Yahweh, or in older spelling Jehovah, and Elohim) and the later material P, the Priestly source, usually supposed to have reached completion about the time of the Babylonian Exile, say 550–450 BC, about 400 years later than J and E.

11 Cf. Millard Erickson, *The New Evangelical Theology*, Marshall, Morgan & Scott 1969, p. 36.

12 Cf. J. S. Wright in *The New Bible Dictionary*, p. 94.

13 E.g. Alan Richardson in *The Cambridge History of the Bible*, iii, CUP 1963, p. 308: 'if the Bible is true, it must be literally true, since there is no other kind of truth than the literal'.

14 J. I. Packer, *'Fundamentalism' and the Word of God*, IVP 1958, p. 99.

15 See below, p. 263.

16 Michael Green, *The Authority of Scripture*, Falcon Books 1963, pp. 29f.

17 Green himself, after expressing the apparently flexible position, does nothing to admit any actual error and says that there is not, so far as he knows, any single discrepancy that it is quite impossible to reconcile. He then goes on with a series of examples intended to show that, in various places where the biblical text has been supposed to be in error, later discoveries showed that it had been precisely correct

(Green, op. cit., pp. 30f.). The reader is left with a clear message: though there could theoretically be errors or real discrepancies in scripture, we can continue to be sure that there are not any in fact. The theoretical flexibility causes no adjustment in the doctrinal position taken. But if there was a real error the doctrinal position would have to be altered.

18 In *The Cambridge History of the Bible*, iii, pp. 13–14. Sebastian Castellio (1515–63) was a Calvinist theologian and humanist, who later came into much disagreement with Calvin.

19 Cf. also the matter of Goliath and his 'brother', below, pp. 281f.

20 E. J. Young, *Thy Word is Truth*, Banner of Truth Trust 1963, pp. 130f.

21 E. J. Carnell, *The Case for Orthodox Theology*, states quite expressly that Romans and Galatians are and should be the centre: they are the 'highest-ranking sources in theology' (p. 66) and 'a denomination is not part of the church if its creed or confession is out of harmony with the system of theology taught in Romans and Galatians' (p. 134); cf. also pp. 58, 99. Not all conservative evangelicals will accept this as a ruling, but it is probable that it well represents the prevailing accent in practice, whether people will accept it in principle or not.

22 The symbol Q is used, roughly speaking, for a body of teaching not in Mark but used by both Matthew and Luke; it has generally been supposed to be a very early source, just as it has generally been held that Mark is the earliest of the three 'synoptic' Gospels (Matthew, Mark and Luke, because their common features can be conveniently seen in the form of a synopsis: John is built on a different plan).

23 See James T. Burtchaell, *Catholic Theories of Biblical Inspiration since 1810*, CUP 1969, pp. 164ff.

24 For instance, E. J. Young, *Thy Word is Truth*, pp. 131f., in one stage of his argument implies that the Bible cannot be trusted in major matters unless it is absolutely accurate in minor matters. 'If the evangelists were guilty of trifling errors and evidences of carelessness in so-called minor matters, we simply cannot escape the conclusion that they may have been just as careless in more important things. If the writers of the Gospels cannot even agree as to the number of those whose eyes were opened by the Lord, we may very rightly ask how we can know whether the eyes of any were opened? Since the accounts are so garbled, there may not have been any miracle performed at all.'

25 It seems impossible to omit a quotation of T. H. Huxley's words concerning the argument from the trustworthiness of Jesus Christ in such matters. After H. P. Liddon had used exactly this argument in a sermon in St Paul's Cathedral in 1889, Huxley wrote:

If the 'trustworthiness of our Lord Jesus Christ' is to stand or fall with belief in the sudden transformation of the chemical components of a woman's body into sodium chloride, or on the 'admitted reality' of Jonah's ejection, safe and sound, on the shores of the Levant, after three days' sea-journey in the stomach of a gigantic marine animal, what possible pretext can there be for even hinting a doubt as to the precise truth of the longevity attributed to the Patriarchs? Who that has swallowed the camel of Jonah's journey will be guilty of the affectation of straining at such a historical gnat – nay, midge – as the supposition that the mother of Moses was told the story of the Flood by Jacob; who had it straight from Shem; who was on friendly terms with Methuselah; who knew Adam quite well?

(for an account of the context see *The Cambridge History of the Bible*, iii, pp. 266ff.).

26 R. V. G. Tasker, *The Old Testament in the New Testament*, SCM Press 1954, p. 37; cited by J. I. Packer, op. cit., p. 61; J. Huxtable, *The Bible Says*, SCM Press 1962, pp. 69f.

27 *The New Bible Commentary*, p. 831; rev. ed., p. 877.

28 Huxtable, op. cit., p. 70.

29 See below, p. 267.

30 On the 'Bible teacher', and the 'Bible reading' as the term for his mode of exposition, see E. R. Sandeen, *The Roots of Fundamentalism*, Chicago University Press 1970, pp. 136–9. The 'teaching' terminology can be found also *passim* in *Evangelical Belief*: 'the Bible teaches', p. 31; 'the biblical teaching concerning sacrifice', p. 33; 'some Christian teachers', p. 17; 'our Lord's view of the Bible in His day', p. 15.

31 'Kerygmatic' is from Greek *kērugma*, 'proclamation', and it is used in much modern theology to express the atmosphere of New Testament preaching: a good illustration would be the early words of Jesus in Mark 1.15; 'The time is fulfilled and the kingdom of God is at hand; repent and believe the Gospel.'

32 E.g. *Evangelical Belief*, p. 22: 'the Bible's view of itself'.

33 It seems to me quite insincere when *Evangelical Belief*, p. 22, quotes Prof. W. Sanday as emphasizing the fundamental principle that 'a true conception of what the Bible is must be obtained from the Bible itself'; for the writers of that pamphlet must have known well that Sanday's actual opinion, and therefore the meaning of the words he used, was totally contrary to the use they make of them. Sanday (1843–1920) was perhaps the most influential single person in persuading the Church of England to abandon exactly the position which fundamentalists now seek to reinstate.

34 Wenham, op. cit., p. 109.

35 This approach is not peculiar to Wenham; the same argument is used by Charles Hodge himself in *Systematic Theology*, (3 vols, 1871–3), i, James Clarke 1960, p. 160: 'This proof bears specially, it is true, only on the writings of the Old Testament. But no Christian puts the inspiration of the Old Testament above that of the New. The tendency, and we may even say the evidence, is directly the other way.' In other words, it is admitted that only the Old Testament can be proved authoritative by direct scriptural proof. The extension of this to the New Testament depends on no scriptural proof, and rests on no more than an *a fortiori* argument from the opinions of modern Christians, and wrong opinions at that, since these are opinions that suggest that the Old Testament should, if anything, have less authority than the New.

36 Packer, op. cit., pp. 55f.; Wenham, op. cit., pp. 29–36.

37 Packer, op. cit., p. 55.

38 Wenham, op. cit., p. 68.

39 Wenham, op. cit., p. 71.

40 Ibid., p. 72. Wenham's interpretation rests upon a series of conservative scholars, notably J. M. Kik and R. T. France.

41 See above, pp. 74ff.

42 For instance, modern conservatives are increasingly pressing for an early date for St John's gospel, apparently supposing that an early date ensures a higher degree of reliability. To a truly dogmatic-supernaturalist approach this is irrelevant. That pillar of conservatism, the *Scofield Reference Bible* (OUP 1909), dates the gospel 'between AD 85 and 90', and 'probably the latter'. All the Johannine letters are also dated about 90. Revelation is dated exactly in AD 96. The Johannine literature, though believed to be by the apostle John himself, is thus the latest segment of the New Testament literature. If, like the Scofield Bible, you really depend on the supernatural, you have no reason to find pleasure in early datings.

43 This can be well illustrated from Calvin's attitude to the authorship of II Peter. Calvin knows that there has been doubt about the letter in the early church, and he himself thinks that the style is against attribution to Peter. 'Some, induced by a difference in the style, did not think that Peter was the author. For though some

affinity may be traced, yet I confess that there is that manifest difference which distinguishes different writers. There are also other probable conjectures by which we may conclude that it was written by another rather than by Peter. At the same time . . . it has nothing unworthy of Peter . . . If it be received as canonical, we must allow Peter to be the author, since it has his name inscribed, and he also testifies that he had lived with Christ' (See John Calvin, *Commentaries on the Catholic Epistles*, Calvin Translation Society, Edinburgh 1855, p. 363). As Calvin sees it, the stylistic evidence, and the history of ancient doubts, stand against Petrine authorship; but if the book is canonical, then it must be taken as by Peter (i.e. the dogmatic argument) on account of the presence of the name Peter, which must be true. But this leaves Calvin still rather undecided: '. . . to repudiate it is what I dread, though I do not here recognize the language of Peter. But since it is not quite evident as to the author, I shall allow myself the liberty of using the word Peter or Apostle indiscriminately' (Calvin, op. cit., p. 364).

44 As a contrast with Calvin we may mention E. M. B. Green, *2 Peter Reconsidered*, Tyndale Press 1961; in this paper the stylistic and other evidence against genuineness of II Peter is mentioned, but mentioned for the most part only to be refuted. Unlike the case of Calvin, the arguments against genuineness are not Green's own; they are forced upon him by critical scholars. He ends up by leaving the question open: 'It cannot be shown conclusively that Peter was the author; but it has yet to be shown convincingly that he was not' (p. 37). It should not be supposed that this is an open-minded position. What it means is that conservative people can feel free to continue believing that Peter was the author on dogmatic grounds, which is what they believed all the time, though this is not used as an argument within the paper. See also *The New Bible Dictionary*, pp. 977b–979b.

Chapter 4

1 I owe this point to John A. T. Robinson, who adds the question: 'are there fundamentalist sociologists or psychologists?' I do not know the answer. One work on psychology from an evangelical point of view is M. A. Jeeves, *Psychology and Christianity: the view both ways*, IVP 1976; but it is not clear that this work is deeply *conservative*.

2 It would be interesting to know the proportions of different fields and subjects among the students adhering to fundamentalist organizations at various times, for this could be an index of shifts in their total ethos and perspective. A group led by students of theology could be quite different from one in which medical students were the most active group, and so on.

3 *Encyclopaedia of the Social Sciences*, Macmillan 1931; article 'Fundamentalism', vi, pp. 526–7.

4 E. R. Sandeen, *The Roots of Fundamentalism, passim*.

5 As will be shown below, p. 93, the doctrinal position of British fundamentalism of the type studied here is in any case largely borrowed from the American conservative leadership, especially Warfield.

6 The most dramatic event in this story was the 'Monkey Trial' in Dayton, Tennessee in 1925. A school teacher, J. T. Scopes, was accused of teaching evolution contrary to a law of Tennessee, and the prominent lawyer and politician W. Jennings Bryan took part. It is generally held that the effect of the trial was to bring discredit on fundamentalism in the public mind.

7 Ramm, *The Christian View of Science and Scripture*, p. 204, and see his entire discussion, pp. 183–205.

8 See above, p. 45.

9 Hebert, *Fundamentalism and the Church of God*, SCM Press 1957, p. 87 etc.; Huxtable, *The Bible Says*, pp. 75f.; Richardson in *The Cambridge History of the Bible*, iii, pp. 307f.

10 See again below, pp. 272ff.

11 Ramm, op. cit., p. 159.

12 Ramm does insist on 'the biblical view of nature', pp. 55–65, and uses it in a sort of philosophical argument against people like Pascal, Kierkegaard, Barth and Kant; but it makes no difference to his treatment of the flood story.

13 Ibid., p. 164.

14 *The New Bible Commentary Revised*, p. 88a, allows both a local and a universal flood, without going into details; the older edition had a compromise formula, according to which the flood was universal in that it wiped out all mankind, but perhaps local in its geographical extent (p. 84). The writer, E. F. Kevan, thought that the ark could not possibly have taken in two of every species as we now know them. The *Dictionary*, pp. 427f., thinks that 'everything' was blotted out by the flood but that this is qualified by the statements of location, land, sky, etc., which would favour a local interpretation.

15 Wenham, *Christ and the Bible*, p. 74; the reference is to Psalm 110. Wenham thinks that 'those who deny the Davidic authorship are quite divided as to who wrote it and when'. We can therefore stick safely to the conservative attribution. The implication is that the conservative attribution is not one hypothesis among many. It is secure reality, only the others are theories or suppositions.

16 See, among many treatments, J. E. Barnhart, *The Billy Graham Religion*, Mowbray 1974, e.g. pp. 83–6. On Graham as a salesman: 'I'm selling the greatest product in the world. Why shouldn't it be promoted as well as soap?' (p. 84). Again, Barnhart says (p. 86), 'In that sense [i.e. in respect of salesmanship as a technique] the evangelist is definitely in the world and of the world'. But many of Mr Barnhart's racy judgments should be taken with a pinch of salt. He is amusing, and sometimes, as here, he hits the mark; but he is hardly a responsible theological analyst and does not pretend to be one.

17 H. F. R. Catherwood, *The Christian in Industrial Society*, Tyndale Press 1964, p. xi; on social-ethical questions see further below, pp. 112ff., where the idea of 'reformation by the social law' has to be allowed for.

18 Paul A. Carter, *The Decline and Revival of the Social Gospel*, Cornell University Press 1956, p. 12. Carter's interesting study suggests that the lines were often drawn differently in the nineteenth century from what is now familiar. Religiously 'liberal' churches were often socially conservative, and the social gospel often had an important place in conservative pulpits. Two other cases may be mentioned from my own reading. Firstly, the famous revivalist C. G. Finney (1792–1875) had a social emphasis in his evangelism. At Oberlin College, the centre of his movement, he and Asa Mahan 'trained professional evangelists and stimulated zeal for social reform, but their approach rested on faith in individual conversion as the key to social justice' (*The New International Dictionary of the Christian Church*, Paternoster Press 1974, p. 721a). According to Ahlstrom, in his survey 'From Puritanism to Evangelicalism', Finney did 'far more than [Billy] Graham has ever done to challenge the culture acceptances of his time and to lead his converts down a road to sanctification that required socially relevant activism': see D. F. Wells and J. D. Woodbridge, *The Evangelicals*, Abingdon Press, Nashville 1975, pp. 278f. Secondly, *The Fundamentals* themselves (xii. 108–19) included an article 'The Church and Socialism', by Professor Charles R. Erdman of Princeton Theological Seminary. This is distinguished by its moderation. Socialism, Erdman argues, is to be distinguished from communism, with which it is often confused. He is against the idea that Jesus Christ was a socialist or that socialism is merely the application of Christianity to economic

problems. The church 'leaves its members free to adopt or reject socialism as they may deem wise'. Erdman repels the socialist attacks on Christianity, which he regards as based on misunderstanding; but he admits that socialism is in any case 'a serious protest against the defects of the present economic system, against special privilege and entrenched injustice, against prevalent poverty and hunger and despair'. Though against any 'social gospel', Erdman insists on application of the 'social principles of Christianity'. The article displays an understanding of socialism quite different from the wild anti-socialism of much mid-twentieth century religious conservatism.

19 For a good study of these phenomena see Erling Jorstad, *The Politics of Doomsday: Fundamentalists of the Far Right*, Abingdon Press, Nashville 1970.

20 Martin E. Marty, *A Nation of Behavers*, p. 83.

21 Catherwood, op. cit., p. xi: 'The social gospeller's idea that society could be redeemed collectively through good works . . .'

22 This is the position taken by Catherwood in the work already cited; see pp. xi–xii, from which the following sentences are paraphrased.

23 This is not true, however, of Catherwood; see his *A Better Way: the Case for a Christian Social Order*, Tyndale Press 1975, p. 100.

24 See below, pp. 284ff.

25 On dispensationalism and the general problem of apocalyptic expectations among fundamentalists, see in detail below, pp. 191ff.

26 This, however, has not always been so, and may indeed be a quite modern development. Until quite recent times anti-Semitism was not uncommonly allied with extreme Christian conservatism in certain parts of the world; so, from a conservative evangelical source, 'Its deepest roots [i.e. of anti-Semitism] lie in Christian, especially fundamentalist, soil', H. H. Rowdon in *The New International Dictionary of the Christian Church*, p. 50.

Chapter 5

1 W. M. L. de Wette (1780–1849) and A. Kuenen (1828–91) were important theologians or biblical critics, associated with Julius Wellhausen (1844–1918) in the rise of the modern critical movement in biblical studies, especially in the Old Testament.

2 These are the names of various Old Testament scholars who took varying positions over source criticism, oral tradition and the general historical approach to the literature.

3 Michael Green, *The Authority of Scripture*, p. 3.

4 E. B. Pusey, *Daniel the Prophet*, OUP, 2nd ed. 1869, p. 9; the lectures were actually given in 1862–3. Pusey (1800–82), long Regius Professor of Hebrew in Oxford, was a leader of the Tractarian movement and one of the major figures of the Church of England in the nineteenth century. Though he knew much of German theology and biblical criticism from his early studies, he took an uncompromisingly conservative position on critical questions.

5 See below, pp. 140f.

6 Coptic, the language of the native Egyptians (as distinct from Greek-speakers) in early Christian times, is the language of important early translations of the Bible, and also of an extensive apocryphal literature.

7 Green, op. cit., p. 3.

8 Kitchen, op. cit., p. 115.

9 Ibid., p. 172.

10 John Dryden, *Religio Laici*, 146f.

11 See John Calvin, *Commentaries on the Psalms*, Calvin Translation Society, Edinburgh 1847, iii, pp. 159–60: Psalm 74 is 'not by David'; it is 'probable that many

Psalms were composed by different authors after the death of David'. It is not easy to determine what calamity is the occasion of Psalm 74. Either the Babylonian attack on Jerusalem, or the desecration of the Temple by Antiochus Epiphanes, could be considered. 'The conjecture will be more probable that their complaints belong to the time of Antiochus, for the Church of God was then without prophets.' Similarly on Psalm 79 (Calvin, op. cit., p. 281): 'This Psalm, like others, contains internal evidence that it was composed long after the death of David.' The probable occasion was either when the Temple was destroyed by the Assyrians (he means the Babylonians) 'or when the Temple was defiled by Antiochus'. 'Its subject agrees very well with either of these periods.' I am indebted to Prof. G. W. Anderson for information about this. He mentions also that Calvin never considers a late dating when the Psalm actually has the superscription 'of David'. This might suggest that he considers the superscription final and decisive in respect of the authorship question. Yet this cannot be applied to Psalms 74 and 79, for both of these have the superscription 'of Asaph', and Asaph is supposed to have been a contemporary of David.

12 *The World History of the Jewish People*, vol. ii, *Patriarchs*, W. H. Allen 1971, p. 166.

13 In this I follow Thomas L. Thompson, *The Historicity of the Patriarchal Narratives*, De Gruyter, Berlin 1974, pp. 234–48 and generally.

14 Speiser, *Genesis* (Anchor Bible), Doubleday, NY 1966, p. xl, cited by Thompson, p. 235.

15 See above, pp. 126ff.

16 'Proto-Luke' is the term given to a hypothetical previous stage of St Luke's gospel. The theory is that Luke put together the material from Q and material which he alone has, i.e. is not shared with Mark or Matthew (commonly marked as L), forming a 'Proto-Luke' (Q + L), which was later combined with Marcan material to form the extant gospel of St Luke.

17 Guthrie, op. cit., pp. 175–83.

18 *The New Bible Handbook*, IVP 1947, pp. 320ff.

19 D. Johnson, *The Christian and his Bible*, IVP 1953, pp. 119–22. The way of avoiding Q by supposing that both Matthew and Luke drew from oral tradition is, amusingly, considered as an 'extreme' by Guthrie, p. 156.

20 The Diatessaron of Tatian (2nd century AD) was a combination of the four gospels into one single document; it was widely used for several centuries in the Syriac-speaking church, but was finally replaced by the four separate gospels. It was also widely known in mediaeval Europe, but did not have general ecclesiastical authority.

21 See further below, pp. 304ff.

22 For examples, see Kitchen, op. cit., p. 18; Harrison, op. cit, pp. 21, 303, 381, 423. The Tübingen school, led by F. C. Baur (1792–1860), thought there were three stages in early Christianity: firstly a Petrine stage (Jewish Christians), then a Pauline (Gentile Christians), the two being synthesized in 'Catholicism' in the later second century. I do not think that Old Testament scholarship after Vatke has ever had a really 'Hegelian' phenomenon of this kind.

23 Kitchen, op. cit., p. 112.

24 Ramm, op. cit., p. 193.

25 For instance, Kitchen, op. cit., p. 18 n.5, quotes no evidence from Wellhausen; he cites a passage from Eissfeldt, which says the opposite of the case Kitchen is seeking to make; and he cites Perlitt (see below) whose book is a full-length disproof of the position taken by Kitchen.

26 R. Smend, in his introduction to J. Wellhausen, *Grundrisse zum Alten Testament*, Chr. Kaiser Verlag, Munich 1965, p. 7.

27 L. Perlitt, *Vatke und Wellhausen*, De Gruyter, Berlin 1965.

28 Harrison, op. cit., p.507: 'the flaws and weaknesses of the German national character ... that remarkable characteristic of the German mind which consists in the ability to arrive at definitive conclusions on the basis of only part of the total evidence ... the ability of the German mind to utilize the resultant hypothesis and its earlier supporting evidence as a means of refuting ... both the later evidence and the modifications of the original formulation that it demands.'

29 A. & C. Black, 2nd ed. 1960; SCM Press, 2nd ed. 1972.

30 Joyfully cited, for example, by J. N. D. Anderson, *A Lawyer among the Theologians*, Hodder 1973, pp. 60f.

31 It is distasteful to have to argue this; as a small instance I might cite my own study 'Philo of Byblos and his "Phoenician History"', *Bulletin of the John Rylands University Library*, vol. 57, Manchester 1974, pp. 17–68, which makes contact with a theme often discussed by Albright.

32 It is one of the few virtues of Harrison's *Introduction* that it correctly realizes that Albright and his school do *not* constitute a support for a conservative evangelical position; see pp. 513ff., etc.

33 The deists were influential in raising some of the problems about the Bible that led to early forms of biblical criticism; some deists argued against revelation and the supernatural, some that the deity had created the world but took no further interest in it thereafter. See the treatments in *The Cambridge History of the Bible*, iii, pp. 195f., 240–55.

34 For a conservative appreciation of form criticism see G. E. Ladd, *The New Testament and Criticism*, Hodder 1970, ch. 6; but Ladd is not representative of the average conservative evangelical apologists on a question like this.

35 Ibid., p. 11.

Chapter 6

1 On this see below, pp. 212ff.

2 An exception must be made in some degree for the 'new conservatives' in the United States, on whom see below, pp. 222ff. But I have found no echo in British conservative evangelical literature of the self-critical attitude seen among these Americans.

3 Colin Brown's *Karl Barth and the Christian Message*, Tyndale Press 1967, only proves the point, for it is no doubt the best (!) conservative evangelical monograph on a non-conservative theologian within the literature surveyed by me.

4 L. Loetscher, *The Broadening Church*, University of Pennsylvania Press 1957, p. 116. Machen (1881–1937) belonged to the tradition of the Princeton theology (see below, pp. 261ff.) and took an extreme conservative stand, finally leaving Princeton and becoming a principal founder of the very conservative Westminster Theological Seminary in Philadelphia. His book on *The Virgin Birth of Christ* (1930) is typical of strongly conservative apologetic. The book referred to by Loetscher in the quotation was his *Christianity and Liberalism* (1923), in which Machen maintained that liberalism is not a variety or deviation within Christianity but a totally different religion: 'modern liberalism not only is a different religion from Christianity but belongs in a totally different class of religions'.

5 Adolf Harnack (1851–1930) was a very distinguished German theologian, noted especially for his work on the history of doctrine in the early church. His work *What is Christianity?*, London 1901, emphasized the fatherhood of God, the claims of human brotherhood, the infinite value of the human soul, and the command to love; it stressed the moral much more than the doctrinal.

6 Michael Green, op. cit., pp. 4f.

7 J. I. Packer, *'Fundamentalism' and the Word of God*, pp. 83f.

8 *The Cambridge History of the Bible*, iii, p. 310.

9 I here follow E. A. Dowey, Jr., *The Knowledge of God in Calvin's Theology*, Columbia University Press, NY 1952.

10 Bainton in *The Cambridge History of the Bible*, iii, p. 14, with references in Luther's works.

11 Charles Hodge, *Systematic Theology*, i, p. 170. On Hodge and the Princeton theology see further below, pp. 261ff.

12 See Sandeen, *The Roots of Fundamentalism, passim.*

13 On this cf. below, pp. 272ff.

14 I simply, without going into the argument, point to G. Ebeling's essay, 'The Significance of the Critical Historical Method for Church and Theology in Protestantism', in his *Word and Faith*, SCM Press 1963, pp. 17–61. The thesis is that the acceptance of the critical method maintained and confirmed in the nineteenth century the basic decision of the Reformers in the sixteenth; this method has 'a deep inner connexion with the Reformers' doctrine of justification by faith' (p. 55).

15 For instance Harrison, op. cit., pp. 291ff.

16 For instance Kitchen, op. cit., pp. 172f.; and see above and below, pp. 306ff.

Chapter 7

1 Erickson, *The New Evangelical Theology*, p. 213 and 235n. 11, citing *Christianity Today*, x, no. 13, 1 April 1966 – source not seen by me. The reason was presumably Graham's willingness to co-operate with non-fundamentalist churches in his evangelistic work.

2 Erickson, op. cit., p. 194.

3 The original Arminius was a Dutch theologian (1560–1609), who protested against the extremely rigid Calvinism of his time. In the Netherlands, the church that has taken up his heritage is known as the Remonstrants.

4 For an interesting discussion, probing deeply into the social implications of Wesley's Arminianism, see Bernard Semmel, *The Methodist Revolution*, Heinemann 1974. George Whitefield (1714–1770) was the Calvinist among the two.

5 The great Princeton theologians, the Hodges and Warfield, who remain the basic theologians of fundamentalism, were however Calvinists; on this see p. 278.

6 Pietism is mainly a German term, not much used in English: it was a movement, mainly in the seventeenth century, for an emphasis on personal religion as against the stress on dogmatic orthodoxy. Through Count von Zinzendorf (1700–60) it exercised much influence on Wesley.

7 There is, confusingly, also the word millenarian, with one n because not derived from Latin annus 'year' but only from mille 'thousand'. It is often used as the general word for expectations that stress the thousand-year reign; one can also say chiliasm, from the Greek word, for more or less the same thing. In my usage millennial and millenarian are largely interchangeable.

8 In *The New Bible Commentary Revised*, pp. 698–700, E. J. Young explains the prophecy of the seventy weeks of years in Dan. 9.24–27. He expressly warns against the 'dispensationalist' interpretation, which makes the seventieth week commence with the return of Christ. He understands the figure, rather vaguely, as a symbolic number for the period down to the accomplishment of the Messianic salvation, i.e. down to the time of Christ. That is to say, the events 'prophesied' in Daniel lie in the past for the modern Christian, and not in the future. This kind of interpretation damps down millenarian fervour. In *The New Bible Dictionary* the section 'Millennialism' in the article 'Eschatology' (p. 390) is by G. E. Ladd; it is non-committal and certainly does not inspire fiery hopes of the millennium.

9 Sandeen, *The Roots of Fundamentalism*, p. 222; in what follows I largely follow Sandeen, pp. 62–70, and generally.

10 Sandeen, p. 67; he is actually talking of Darby here.

11 *Scofield Reference Bible*, notes on the four gospels.

12 Cited by G. E. Ladd, *Crucial Questions about the Kingdom of God*, Eerdmans, Grand Rapids 1952, pp. 102f., from A. C. Gaebelein, *The Gospel of Matthew*, Loizeaux, NY 1910, i, p. 64 (source not seen by me). Gaebelein was a well-known millenarian and a consulting editor of the Scofield Bible.

13 Cited by Ladd, op. cit., p. 105, from L. S. Chafer, *Systematic Theology*, Zondervan 1948, v, pp. 97f. Chafer (1871–1952) was founder, president and professor of the strongly dispensational Dallas Theological Seminary; his work in eight volumes is a major synthesis of dispensational doctrine.

14 Scofield, note on Luke 11.1–13.

15 *The New Bible Commentary Revised*, p. 700a.

16 G. E. Ladd, *Crucial Questions about the Kingdom of God*, ch. 5.

17 For example – if another example could be needed – at Acts 15.13–18, of which the Scofield note says that 'dispensationally, this is the most important passage in the NT.' After stating that God had visited the Gentiles 'to take out of them a people for his name' the speaker cites the words of Amos 9.11f.: 'After this I will return, and will build again the tabernacle of David . . . that the residue of men might seek after the Lord, and all the Gentiles . . .' This is important because it yields the exact sequence of the events of the end: 1. the formation of the church; 2. the return [of the Lord]; 3. the re-establishment of Davidic rule over Israel; 4. the Lord sought by the residue of men, i.e. Israelites (who will turn to Jesus as Messiah, see note on Rom. 11.5); 5. fulfilment for Gentiles also. This follows the sequence in which the elements appear in the text, and translates these into real sequential theological events; but it ignores that the quotation from Amos does not follow the original statement of Acts 15.14 but is an illustration of it – to say nothing of such other points as that the 'men' interpreted as Jews are Edomites in Amos, etc.

18 For instance, on the matter of the placing of the cleansing of the Temple by Jesus (see above, p. 56), the Scofield Bible does not discuss the matter at all, but simply places over the section John 2.13–25 the title 'first purification of the temple' and over Matt. 21.12–17 the title 'Jesus' second purification of the temple'. An uncritical reader will be likely to take it for granted from this that there were two such incidents; it will not occur to him that they might be one.

19 Sandeen, op. cit., p. 192.

20 Ibid., p. 204.

21 Scofield, notes on Ezek. 38.2, Rev. 19.17, 19.19.

22 Critical scholars commonly divide the book known as 'Isaiah' into several portions: Isa. 40–55 is commonly assigned to a 'Second Isaiah' or Deutero-Isaiah, living about the time of the Persian conquest of Babylon and the beginnings of return from exile. 56–66 are often assigned to a 'Trito-Isaiah'

23 This would leave, as the main intra-Old Testament example, the case of the man of God from Judah who in I Kings 13.2 names Josiah as the person who will, much later, defile the altar at Bethel (II Kings 23.15f.). This would be a time gap of about three centuries. But the story is a very peculiar one and I do not know that it has ever been much used in this connection. On prediction generally see again below, pp. 253ff.

24 G. T. Manley, *The Return of Jesus Christ*, IVP 1960, pp. 67–71.

25 Scofield tells us delightfully that 'in approaching the study of the Gospels the mind should be freed, so far as is possible, from mere theological concepts and presuppositions'. The point he has in mind is that it is essential to exclude the quite false (post-biblical and Romish, as he thinks) idea that the church is the true Israel. Israel according to his system always remains the Jewish people. See his notes, introduction to the four gospels.

26 On neo-orthodoxy and biblical theology, see below, pp. 213ff.

27 See O. T. Allis, *Prophecy and the Church*, Tyndale Press 1945, pp. 21ff. Allis was a doughty conservative controversialist and a bitter opponent of critical scholarship on such matters as the unity of the book of Isaiah.

28 Hal Lindsey, with C. C. Carlson, *The Late Great Planet Earth*, Zondervan, Michigan 1970, p. 111.

29 Or its aged parent, if we accept the theory that fundamentalism is descended from millenarianism rather than the reverse.

30 Lindsey, op. cit., pp. 42f.

31 Manley, op. cit., pp. 71–4.

32 Particularly attractive is the picture of the fourth kingdom of Daniel, which has to be a revived Roman Empire, as the European Economic Community (a ten-nation economic entity, corresponding with the ten horns of Dan. 7.24). See Lindsey, op cit., pp. 92–7. Readers must turn to the book itself in order to see what comes next; but they should remember, as Lindsey warns us (p. 113), that 'we must not indulge in speculation'.

33 I have not done any personal original research on this section. On Pentecostalism I have gained much from the fine work of W. J. Hollenweger, *The Pentecostals*, SCM Press 1972. On the position of scripture see especially pp. 291–310.

34 Hollenweger, op. cit., pp. 297ff.

35 Ibid., pp. 218–30.

36 Hollenweger, op. cit., p. 298: 'occasionally one still meets the primitive Pentecostal view that "the Word of God is not taught in his church to be discussed but to be obeyed", but it is increasingly giving place to a fundamentalist rationalism.'

37 F. F. Bruce, *The English Bible*, Lutterworth Press 1970, p. 196.

38 Bruce, op. cit., p. 200.

39 See below, p. 249.

40 See below, p. 243.

41 As we have seen just pointed out by Professor Bruce, every article of the historic faith of the church can be established from a modern translation as from an ancient one. This is entirely right. For fundamentalists, however, that is not the problem. The problem for them is not the establishment of articles of the historic faith, but the establishment of detailed interpretations of historical narratives, figures, etc., which will allow the conservative reader to continue supposing that the Bible is inerrant. The fundamentalist position is that one must have these interpretations if one is to preserve the historic faith. But not only do modern translations not establish these interpretations, older ones do not do so either.

42 Karl Barth (1886–1968) was a Swiss theologian. He taught in Germany until the Nazis came to power, and was long professor in Basle. His most revolutionary work was his commentary on the Epistle to the Romans, ET OUP 1933, which however does not fully represent his later position. His major opus was the bulky *Church Dogmatics*, ET T. & T. Clark, from 1936, in many volumes.

43 It is therefore well understandable that the argument of biblical theology from Hebrew or biblical ways of thinking was rejected by conservatives. The whole point of that argument was that Hebrew thought (or biblical thought) would lead to conclusions different from those that seemed obvious to natural (i.e. Western) reason. From the conservative point of view, this was subjective and could lead anywhere. The appeal of Hebrew thought and biblical thought continues to attract some conservatives, but only in so far as it can be used to support the traditional conservative positions, which were of course established long before any thought was given to Hebrew thought or biblical thought.

44 See my *Semantics of Biblical Language*, OUP 1961; *Biblical Words for Time*, SCM Press, rev. ed. 1969; recent surveys in 'Trends and Prospects in Biblical

Theology', *Journal of Theological Studies* 25, 1974, pp. 265–82; 'Story and History in Biblical Theology', *Journal of Religion* 56, 1976, pp. 1–17; article 'Biblical Theology' in *The Interpreter's Dictionary of the Bible*, supplementary volume, Abingdon/SCM Press 1977.
45 Kitchen, *Ancient Orient and Old Testament*, pp. 139–40.
46 W. Hordern, *New Directions in Theology Today: Volume One: Introduction to Theology*, Lutterworth Press 1968, p. 95, and see in general ch. 4, 'The New Face of Conservatism', pp. 74–95.
47 I regret that I have not been able to see a copy of this book.
48 See already above, pp. 162f.
49 I am not sure whether all the persons counted as new conservatives by Hordern really merit this; but there is a good deal of the literature that I have not been able to see for the present research.
50 Quoted from Ladd, 'The Search for Perspective', *Interpretation* 25, 1971, p. 47 (original source not seen by me). Ladd himself, speaking of 'evangelical scholars whose background is fundamentalism', here says that 'their major preoccupation has been to defend the inerrancy of the Bible in its most extreme form' and they 'have contributed little of creative thinking to the current debate'. Ladd's frank disclosure of his own background and standpoint is helpful.
51 E. J. Carnell, *The Case for Orthodox Theology*, p. 35; cf. above, pp. 74ff.
52 Ibid., p. 99.
53 Ibid., p. 109.
54 Ibid., p. 139.
55 Ibid., p. 33.
56 Ibid., p. 39.
57 See below, pp. 269ff. Carnell describes Warfield's attitude as one of 'complacency'; Carnell, op. cit., p. 104.
58 Ibid., pp. 102ff.; see again below, p. 281.
59 According to the conservative evangelical publication *The New International Dictionary of the Christian Church*, p. 910a, Smith was tried for heresy in 1892 and forced to give up his professorship. A factor in this was his support for the greater and better-known C. A. Briggs, one of the three editors of the standard Hebrew dictionary Brown-Driver-Briggs, professor in Union Theological Seminary, New York (1841–1913). Briggs was also tried for heresy and suspended from the ministry.
60 A well-known example is the late George Ernest Wright, for instance in his *God Who Acts*, SCM Press 1952, *passim*.
61 Charles Hodge, *Systematic Theology*, i, p.49. The passage comes under the heading 'Reason necessary for the reception of a revelation'.
62 See already my *Old and New in Interpretation*, pp. 201f.
63 See above, p. 221.
64 Packer, *'Fundamentalism'*, pp. 91ff.
65 Hodge conceived both revelation and inspiration in intellectualist manner: 'The effect of revelation was to render the recipient wiser. The effect of inspiration was to preserve him from error in teaching' (*Systematic Theology*, i, p. 155).
66 Ladd, 'The Search for Perspective', p. 62. The first quotation cited by Ladd is from E. J. Young, *Thy Word is Truth*.
67 Hordern, op. cit., p. 85.
68 Ibid., p. 89; the original source is K. S. Kantzer in *The Word for this Century* ed. M. C. Tenney, NY 1960, p. 38.
69 On this see my *Old and New in Interpretation* and *The Bible in the Modern World* ; D. H. Kelsey, *The Uses of Scripture in Recent Theology*, SCM Press 1975, pp. 209f. and generally.
70 G. E. Ladd, *New Testament and Criticism*, p. 10.
71 Ibid., p. 11.

72 G. E. Ladd, *A Theology of the New Testament*, Lutterworth Press 1974, pp. 602–7.
73 Ibid., pp. 222 and 215–222 generally.
74 Ibid., p. 221.
75 See already above, p. 196.
76 Ladd, *A Theology of the New Testament*, p. 221.
77 Hordern writes, apparently citing Carnell: 'Today most conservative writings bristle with references to non-conservative theologians, but one seldom finds any reference to the conservatives in the work of non-conservatives . . . Perhaps the time has come to ask which side has the "open mind" today'; Hordern, op. cit., p. 79.
78 See above, p. 223.

Chapter 8

1 R. Bultmann, *Existence and Faith*, Fontana Books 1964, p. 345; much cited in conservative writing, e.g. G. E. Ladd, *The New Testament and Criticism*, p. 183.
2 Bultmann, in H. Bartsch, *Kerygma and Myth*, SPCK 1953, i, p. 39; Ladd, op. cit., p. 184.
3 For a good general survey of the question of miracles, see E. and M.-L. Keller, *Miracles in Dispute*, SCM Press 1969.
4 H. L. Ellison in *The New Bible Commentary*, p. 320b, says 'No point would be served in enumerating various doubtful efforts to explain the miracle.' I take it that this means the miracle must be simply accepted, and alternative explanations are not worth bothering about. In the revised edition of the same work, however, W. S. LaSor frankly admits that the miracles in the Elisha cycle are different from other biblical miracles. Some of them violate the canon that a true miracle must have an ethical or moral purpose, while a spurious miracle has no purpose other than to cause amazement. 'Once we have admitted this for the Elisha miracles, we are free to defend almost all of the remaining miracles in the Bible according to the canon of moral purpose' (p. 349). It is dubious if this rather free and advanced position would have been accepted if it had come from a non-conservative scholar.
5 Kitchen in *The New Bible Dictionary*, p. 780, however, after giving several possible naturalistic explanations for the manna, concludes in the end that it remains 'ultimately in the realm of the miraculous'.
6 This citation from Kitchen, *Ancient Orient and Old Testament*, pp. 157f.; cited in full and taken as basis of interpretation in *The New Bible Commentary Revised*, p. 126 (Hywel R. Jones). Fuller statement by Kitchen in *The New Bible Dictionary*, pp. 1001–3. The interpretation goes back in its general outlines to an article by Greta Hort in *Zeitschrift für die alttestamentliche Wissenschaft* 69, 1957, pp. 84–103 and 70, 1958, pp. 48–59.
7 *The New Bible Dictionary*, p. 1003.
8 Blair, ibid., p. 244b.
9 Blair, ibid., p. 244a, after Kitchen, op. cit., p. 64 n. 27. Kitchen writes: 'The supposed standing still of the sun, or "long day", of Jos. 10:12–13 sometimes causes difficulty, but it may rest on nothing more than mistranslation. Possibly cease *shining* rather than cease *moving* should be understood.'
10 Ramm, *The Christian View of Science and Scripture*, pp. 108 and 107–12 in general.
11 Ramm, op. cit., pp. 113–15.
12 Ibid., pp. 207f.
13 I do not think anyone will question that the Hebrew word means 'appointed' (RSV) or the like: God assigned a particular fish (whale) to the task. The language will not bear the suggestion of a 'special creation'. For comparison, D. W. B. Robinson in *The New Bible Commentary Revised*, p. 749a, says that 'speculation as

to the nature of the *great fish* is needless'. He settles the issue with the common dogmatic argument from the reference of Jesus to the incident. He leaves it open whether the three days and nights are to be taken literally; even if Jonah himself supplied this information, it might be inexact, for Jonah, even if he was conscious the whole time, 'would hardly have had any means of marking the passage of time'. The reader should remember that this is a standard work, avidly read by conservative evangelical students at university level.

14 Cf. above, p. 212.

15 In a BBC Radio 3 discussion of John A. T. Robinson's *Redating the New Testament*, January 1977.

16 Harrison, *Introduction*, p. 775; cf. his general remarks on 'Prophecy and Prediction', ibid., pp. 757-9.

17 I would refer to the valuable study of E. Jenni on the 'political' predictions of the prophets: *Die politischen Voraussagen der Propheten*, Zurich 1956; the mere existence of this monograph is enough to show that prediction of the future by prophets is not ruled out by scholars.

18 This may perhaps be confirmed by the Greek text of II Chron. 36.8, which says that he was 'buried in the garden of Uzza with his fathers'.

19 See above, p. 236.

20 G. E. Ladd, *The New Testament and Criticism*, pp. 182f.

21 See above, p. 235.

Chapter 9

1 *The New Bible Commentary Revised*, p. 3; this is the first page of the article on 'The Authority of Scripture', obviously a key article in the work as a whole,

2 It is interesting and probably significant that *Evangelical Belief*, pp. 52f., in quoting the sections of the Westminster Confession that 'are the most relevant for the purpose of this present booklet', omits entirely the passage here quoted.

3 Charles Hodge, *Systematic Theology*, i, p. 153.

4 A. A. Hodge and B. B. Warfield, 'Inspiration', *Presbyterian Review*, ii, 1881, p. 245.

5 This was just the time when Anglo-Saxon Presbyterianism began to be most agitated by the rise of biblical criticism. The articles of W. Robertson Smith in the 9th edition of the *Encyclopaedia Britannica* had been appearing from about 1875 and had provoked severe criticism as undermining belief in the inspiration of the Bible. In 1881 he was removed from his chair in the Free Church of Scotland College in Aberdeen. This crisis caused much tension in the United States also; the two similar American cases, those of Briggs and of Preserved Smith, followed in the early 1890s.

6 B. B. Warfield, *The Inspiration and Authority of the Bible*, Marshall, Morgan & Scott 1951, p. 211.

7 A. A. Hodge and B. B. Warfield, art. cit., p. 242; cf. Sandeen, *The Roots of Fundamentalism*, p. 129f. On the importance of the argument from the original autographs see below, pp. 279ff.

8 James Orr, *Revelation and Inspiration*, Duckworth 1910, p. 199.

9 Ibid., p. 21.

10 Cf. Carnell, *The Case for Orthodox Theology*, p. 100f.; Orr, op. cit., p. 217.

11 Orr, op. cit., pp. 201ff., 217.

12 Orr, *The Fundamentals*, ix, p. 33: 'By all means, let criticism have its rights. Let purely literary questions about the Bible receive full and fair discussion. Let the structure of books be impartially examined. If a reverent science has light to throw on the composition or authority or age of these books, let its voice be heard. If this thing is of God we cannot overthrow it.'

13 For a typical popular presentation of this notion of liberal theology, absolutely without any evidence to show that liberal theology is really like this, see Michael Green, *The Authority of Scripture, passim.*
14 Charles Hodge, *Systematic Theology*, i, pp. 49–53.
15 Ibid., p. 53.
16 Ibid., p. 18.
17 Ibid., p. 57.
18 Ibid., p. 57.
19 Ibid., p. 56.
20 Sandeen, op. cit., pp. 116f.
21 Colin Brown, *Philosophy and the Christian Faith*, Tyndale Press 1969, p. 94.
22 Ibid., p. 166.
23 Ramm, op. cit., pp. 69ff.
24 Dooyeweerd, a Dutch scholar, has produced a massive work, *A New Critique of Theoretical Thought*, Amsterdam and Philadelphia 1953–8; Dutch original 1935–6. This turgid work seems to aim at a sort of 'philosophy' incorporating biblical and Reformational insights. See Brown, op. cit., p. 246 n., with references to conservative evangelical appreciations of it.
25 E. J. Young, *Thy Word is Truth*, p. 123, writes: 'The Bible, according to its own claim, is breathed forth from God. To maintain that there are flaws or errors in it is the same as declaring that there are flaws or errors in God Himself.'
26 Cf. already my *The Bible in the Modern World*, p. 179.
27 Cf. above, ch. 8.
28 *Evangelical Belief*, p. 27.
29 e.g. Alan Richardson in *The Cambridge History of the Bible*, iii, p. 308; W. Hordern, *New Directions in Theology Today*, p. 81.
30 See above, p. 268.
31 Hodge and Warfield, art. cit., p.242.
32 E. J. Young, *Introduction to the Old Testament*, Tyndale Press 1964, p. 397, and see pp. 396–7 generally.
33 See *The New Bible Dictionary*, pp. 212a, 361–2, 481a; *The New Bible Commentary Revised*, pp. 318f., etc. The problem is an old one: already the Authorized Version had inserted at II Samuel 21.19 the words *the brother of* (in italics, used by the AV to indicate that the words corresponded to nothing in the Hebrew or Greek), in order to harmonize with Chronicles and avoid the possible impression that Goliath had been slain by two persons.
34 Cf. also pp. 309ff.
35 E.g. Packer, *'Fundamentalism'*, pp. 90f.: 'the biblical text is excellently preserved' and 'no point of doctrine depends on any of the small number of cases in which the true reading remains doubtful'. We 'should not hesitate to believe that the text as we have it is substantially correct'. Cf. *Evangelical Belief*, p. 28. This contradicts the quite frequent appeal to textual corruption made, as we have seen, by conservative evangelical writers. Moreover, as we saw in the case of modern translations, while no point of doctrine may be affected, the conservative belief that the Bible is inerrant is very much affected.
36 See above, p. 269.
37 The 'Massoretic text' is the term given to the Hebrew text supervised and handed down through the activity of scholars known as the Massoretes. Their activity lay during the period about 600–900 AD. The Hebrew text of the Old Testament as thus handed down has a very high degree of uniformity, much greater than that found among the extant manuscripts of the Greek New Testament.
38 The 'septuagint' is the term used for the Greek translation of the Old Testament. It is generally held that the translation was made, mainly in Alexandria, in

various stages during the last three centuries or so BC; it was probably made by Greek-speaking Jews for the needs of their own community. When the Old Testament is quoted in the New, it is generally from the septuagint.

39 *Midrash* is the standard Hebrew term for a sort of homiletic and religious exposition of an already existing book, which may include all sorts of plays on words and the creation of somewhat fanciful tales as a means of explaining the text commented on; cf. the case of Goliath, above, p. 282.

40 Cf. above, p. 146f.

41 The remark comes from the title of a paper by the great rabbinic scholar Solomon Schechter (1847–1915). On the question generally see the recent discussion of R. Clements, *A Century of Old Testament Study*, Lutterworth Press 1976, pp. 142f.

42 Burtchaell, *Catholic Theories of Biblical Inspiration since 1810*, title of ch. 5.

43 This section follows what I have already written in *The Bible in the Modern World*, pp. 130–2, 178f. and generally.

44 Michael Green, op. cit., p. 26.

45 Ibid., pp. 25f. As a matter of fact the 'secretary' terminology was very common in traditional orthodoxy; cf. below.

46 Packer, op. cit., p. 79, cf. pp. 178–81. Hodge (*Systematic Theology*, i, p. 157) and Warfield (*Inspiration and Authority*, p. 421) had also taken this line.

47 J. K. S. Reid, *The Authority of Scripture*, Methuen 1957, p. 85, and see in general pp. 56–102. Hutter and Quenstedt are Lutheran theologians of the sixteenth to seventeenth centuries; for full information see R. Preus, *The Inspiration of Scripture: a Study of the Theology of the Seventeenth-Century Lutheran Dogmaticians*, Oliver & Boyd 1957. See also H. Heppe, *Reformed Dogmatics*, Allen & Unwin 1950 (German text 1861).

48 Cited by Reid, op. cit., p. 86.

49 D. Johnson, *The Christian and his Bible*, pp. 43f.

50 Ibid.

51 See again below, pp. 305f.

52 Hodge, op. cit., i, p. 165.

53 In Roman Catholic work, however, plenary inspiration sometimes means a more relative position, different from verbal inspiration; so Burtchaell, op. cit., p. 153.

54 Hodge, op. cit., i, p. 155.

55 See above, pp. 269f.

56 *The New Bible Commentary Revised*, p. 1269a.

57 *The New Bible Commentary*, pp. 880f.; *The New Bible Commentary Revised*, pp. 945f.

58 *The New Bible Commentary Revised*, pp. 885f.

59 For a simple explanation, requiring no knowledge of Hebrew, see my article 'Reading a script without vowels', in *Writing without Letters* ed. W. Haas, Manchester University Press 1976, pp. 71–100.

60 See above, p. 290.

61 See above, p. 281.

62 Kitchen, *Ancient Orient and Old Testament*, p. 140.

63 Ibid., pp. 163f.

64 On this see in general my *Comparative Philology and the Text of the Old Testament*, Clarendon Press 1968, and for the effect on Old Testament translations, *The Heythrop Journal*, 15, 1974, pp. 381–405.

65 Cf. above pp. 41f., 96.

Chapter 10

1 E. J. Young, *Introduction to the Old Testament*, p. 207. Young gives on p. 206 a table of quotations by name from Isaiah to support this argument.

2 On this see already above, p. 292.

3 See above, p. 95.

4 Cf. Carnell, *The Case for Orthodox Theology*, pp. 103f.

5 See Peter L. Berger and T. Luckmann, *The Social Construction of Reality*, Doubleday, NY 1967, p. 89.

6 In *Old and New in Interpretation*, p. 203; cf. favourable response by Hollenweger, *The Pentecostals*, pp. 299f., 486.

7 Ramm, *The Christian View of Science and Scripture*, p. 9.

8 Carnell, op. cit., p. 127.

9 See already above, p. 26.

10 *'A Time to Embrace'. . . Essays on the Christian view of Sex*, ed. O. R. Barclay, IVP 1964, p. 40.

11 For an example of a harsh and rigid opposition to any participation by conservative evangelicals in ecumenical meetings with non-conservatives, see D. Martyn Lloyd-Jones, *The Basis of Christian Unity: an Exposition of John 17 and Ephesians 4*, IVP 1962. People are not 'one' or in a state of unity if they disagree about fundamental matters like 'the historic fall' or 'the utter, absolute necessity, and sole sufficiency, of His [Christ's] substitutionary atoning work for sinners' (p. 61). There is to be no discussion about this. 'If men do not accept that, they are not brethren and we can have no dialogue with them. We are to preach to such and to evangelize them. Discussion takes place only amongst brethren who share the same life and subscribe to the same essential truth.' If people question and query the great cardinal truths, 'to regard them as brethren is to betray the truth'. 'They are to be regarded as unbelievers.' 'It is a sheer waste of time to discuss or debate the implications of Christianity with people who are not agreed as to what Christianity is' (pp. 62–3). Dr Lloyd-Jones, minister of Westminster Chapel, London, is a respected and central figure in conservative evangelicalism, and the above remarks cannot be dismissed as if they represented an extreme fringe opinion.

12 Lindsey, *The Late Great Planet Earth*, p. 118.

13 John A. T. Robinson, *Can we trust the New Testament?*, Mowbray 1977, pp. 25f. I am grateful to Dr Robinson for letting me see his observations on this point before publication.

Bibliography

The publication date given is that of the edition which I have used; I have not always been able to discover the date of publication in another edition, e.g. in the American edition of a work I have used in its British edition. In a few cases I have listed works known to me only indirectly and not seen by me. A few works which are mentioned in the footnotes but are only marginal to the topic of the book as a whole are not listed. A number of the works listed are brief booklets or mere pamphlets.

The Inter-Varsity Fellowship now publishes solely under the Inter-Varsity Press imprint. A few older titles bear the Tyndale Press imprint, which has now been discontinued.

1. Conservative evangelical works taken as basic in the research done

A. *Major works of reference*

Evangelical Belief, Inter-Varsity Fellowship 1935

The New Bible Handbook ed. G. T. Manley, Inter-Varsity Fellowship 1947

The New Bible Commentary ed. F. Davidson, Inter-Varsity Fellowship 1953

The New Bible Dictionary ed. J. D. Douglas, Inter-Varsity Fellowship 1962

The New Bible Commentary Revised ed. D. Guthrie and others, Inter-Varsity Press 1970

The New International Dictionary of the Christian Church ed. J. D. Douglas, Paternoster Press 1974

The Scofield Reference Bible, Oxford University Press 1909

Harrison, R. K., *Introduction to the Old Testament*, Inter-Varsity Press 1970

Guthrie, Donald, *New Testament Introduction,* Inter-Varsity Press 1970

B. *Lesser works*

Allis, O. T., *Prophecy and the Church*, Tyndale Press 1945

Anderson, Norman J. N. D., *The World's Religions*, (ed.) Inter-Varsity Fellowship 1950

    Law and Grace, Inter-Varsity Fellowship 1954

    A Lawyer among the Theologians, Hodder and Stoughton 1973

Barclay, Oliver, *The Christian's Approach to University Life*, Inter-Varsity Fellowship 1963
  'A Time to Embrace . . . ' Essays on the Christian view of sex, Inter-Varsity Fellowship 1964
Beegle, Dewey M., *Scripture, Tradition and Infallibility*, Eerdmans, Grand Rapids, Michigan 1973
Brown, Colin, *Karl Barth and the Christian Message*, Tyndale Press 1967
  Philosophy and the Christian Faith, Inter-Varsity Press 1969
Bruce, F. F., *The New Testament Documents*, Inter-Varsity Fellowship, rev. ed. 1960
Carnell, E. J., *The Case for Orthodox Theology*, Marshall, Morgan and Scott 1961
Catherwood, H. F. R., *The Christian in Industrial Society*, Tyndale Press 1964
  A Better Way, Inter-Varsity Press 1975
Chafer, L. S., *Systematic Theology*, Zondervan, Grand Rapids, Michigan 1947
De Wit, C., *The Date and Route of the Exodus*, Tyndale Press 1960
Ellison, H. L., *The Centrality of the Messianic Idea for the Old Testament,* Tyndale Press 1953
Fife, E. S., and Glasser, A. F., *Missions in Crisis*, Inter-Varsity Fellowship 1962
Gaebelein, A. C., *The Gospel of Matthew*, New York 1910
Green, Michael, *The Authority of Scripture*, Falcon Books 1963
Green, Michael (E.M.B.), *2 Peter Reconsidered*, Tyndale Press 1961
Griffiths, Michael, *Consistent Christianity,* Inter-Varsity Fellowship 1960
  Christian Assurance, Inter-Varsity Fellowship 1962
Guthrie, Donald, *The Pastoral Epistles and the Mind of Paul,* Tyndale Press 1956
Hallesby, O., *Prayer*, Inter-Varsity Fellowship 1948
  Why I am a Christian, Inter-Varsity Fellowship 1964
Hawthorne, J. N., *Questions of Science and Faith*, Inter-Varsity Fellowship 1960
Henry, Carl, *The Uneasy Conscience of Modern Fundamentalism*, 1947
Holmes, Arthur F., *Christianity and Philosophy*, Tyndale Press 1964
Hooykaas, R., *Christian Faith and the Freedom of Science*, Tyndale Press 1957
Howkins, Kenneth G., *The Challenge of Religious Studies*, Tyndale Press 1972
Jeeves, M. A., *Psychology and Christianity: the view both ways*, Inter-Varsity Press 1976
Johnson, Douglas, *The Christian and his Bible*, Inter-Varsity Fellowship 1953
Kidner, D., *Genesis*, Tyndale Press 1967
Kitchen, K. A., *Ancient Orient and Old Testament*, Tyndale Press 1966

Ladd, George E., *Crucial Questions about the Kingdom of God*, Eerdmans, Grand Rapids, Michigan 1952

The New Testament and Criticism, Hodder and Stoughton 1970

A Theology of the New Testament, Lutterworth 1974

'The Search for Perspective', *Interpretation* (Richmond, Virginia), 25 (1971), pp. 41–62

Lindsey, Hal, *The Late Great Planet Earth*, Zondervan, Grand Rapids, Michigan 1970

Lloyd-Jones, D. Martyn, *Authority*, Inter-Varsity Fellowship 1958

The Basis of Christian Unity, Inter-Varsity Fellowship 1962

Machen, J. Gresham, *Christianity and Liberalism* 1923

The Virgin Birth of Christ, 1930

Manley, G. T., *The Book of the Law: Studies in the Date of Deuteronomy*, Tyndale Press 1957

The Return of Jesus Christ, Inter-Varsity Fellowship 1960

Marshall, I. H., *Eschatology and the Parables*, Tyndale Press 1963

Martin, R. P., *An Early Christian Confession*, Tyndale Press 1960

Mickelsen, A. Berkeley, *Interpreting the Bible*, Eerdmans, Grand Rapids, Michigan 1963

Morris, Leon, *The Lord from Heaven*, Inter-Varsity Fellowship 1958

Spirit of the Living God, Inter-Varsity Fellowship 1960

Ministers of God, Inter-Varsity Fellowship 1964

The Abolition of Religion, Inter-Varsity Fellowship 1964

The New Testament and the Jewish Lectionaries, Tyndale Press 1964

Apocalyptic, Inter-Varsity Press 1972

Packer, J. I., *'Fundamentalism' and the Word of God*, Inter-Varsity Fellowship 1958

Evangelism and the Sovereignty of God, Inter-Varsity Fellowship 1961

Payne, D. F., *Genesis One Reconsidered*, Tyndale Press 1964

Ramm, Bernard, *The Christian View of Science and Scripture*, Paternoster Press 1955; reissued 1964

Rookmaaker, H. R., *Modern Art and the Death of a Culture*, Inter-Varsity Press 1970

Ruoff, P. O., *Personal Work*, Inter-Varsity Fellowship 1946

Schaeffer, Francis, *The God who is There*, Hodder and Stoughton 1970

Scorer, C. G., *The Bible and Sex Ethics Today*, Tyndale Press 1966

Short, A. Rendle, *Archaeology gives Evidence*, Inter-Varsity Fellowship 1951

Stibbs, A. M., *The Meaning of the Word 'Blood' in Scripture*, Tyndale Press 1948

God's Church, Inter-Varsity Fellowship 1959

Stott, J. R. W., *Personal Evangelism*, Inter-Varsity Fellowship 1949

Motives and Methods in Evangelism, Inter-Varsity Fellowship 1962

Tasker, R. V. G., *The Old Testament in the New Testament*, SCM Press, rev. ed. 1954

Torrance, J. B., and others, *Where Science and Faith Meet*, Inter-Varsity Fellowship 1953

van Til, Cornelius, *The New Modernism*, James Clarke 1947

Wenham, John W., *Our Lord's View of the Old Testament*, Inter-Varsity Fellowship 1964

  Christ and the Bible, Tyndale Press 1972

Wright, J. Stafford, *Interpreting the Bible*, Inter-Varsity Fellowship 1966

Young, E. J., *Daniel's Vision of the Son of Man*, Tyndale Press 1958

  An Introduction to the Old Testament, Tyndale Press 1964

  Thy Word is Truth, Banner of Truth Trust 1963

2. Other Works

Barnhart, J. E., *The Billy Graham Religion*, Mowbray 1974

Barr, James, *The Semantics of Biblical Language*, Oxford University Press 1961

  Biblical Words for Time, SCM Press, 2nd ed. 1969

  Comparative Philology and the Text of the Old Testament, The Clarendon Press 1968

  The Bible in the Modern World, SCM Press 1973

  Old and New in Interpretation, SCM Press 1966

  'Reading a Script without Vowels', in *Writing without Letters* ed. W. Haas, Manchester University Press 1976, pp. 71–100

Bartsch, H., *Kerygma and Myth*, SPCK 1953

Berger, P. L., and Luckmann, T., *The Social Construction of Reality*, Doubleday, NY 1967

Bruce, F. F., *The English Bible*, Lutterworth Press 1970

Bultmann, R., *Existence and Faith*, Fontana 1964

Burtchaell, J. T., *Catholic Theories of Biblical Inspiration since 1810*, Cambridge University Press 1969

Carter, Paul A., *The Decline and Revival of the Social Gospel*, Cornell University Press 1956

  The Cambridge History of the Bible, 3 vols, Cambridge University Press 1970, 1969, 1963

Clements, R., *A Century of Old Testament Study*, Lutterworth Press 1976

Dooyeweerd, H., *A New Critique of Theoretical Thought*, 4 vols, H. J. Paris, Amsterdam and Presbyterian & Reformed Publishing Co., Philadelphia 1953–8

Dowey, E. A., *The Knowledge of God in Calvin's Theology*, Columbia University Press, NY 1952

Erickson, Millard, *The New Evangelical Theology*, Marshall, Morgan and Scott 1969

Glock, C. Y., and Bellah, R. N., *The New Religious Consciousness*, University of California Press 1976

Hebert, Gabriel, *Fundamentalism and the Church of God*, SCM Press 1957

Heppe, H., *Reformed Dogmatics*, George Allen and Unwin 1950; German original 1861

Hodge, Charles, *Systematic Theology*, 3 vols, 1871–3; reissued James Clarke 1960

Hollenweger, W. J., *The Pentecostals*, SCM Press 1972

Hordern, W., *New Directions in Theology Today: Vol. I: Introduction to Theology*, Lutterworth Press 1968

Huxtable, John, *The Bible Says*, SCM Press 1962

Jorstad, Erling, *The Politics of Doomsday: Fundamentalists of the Far Right*, Abingdon Press, Nashville 1970

Keller, Ernst and Marie-Luise, *Miracles in Dispute*, SCM Press 1969

Keller, Werner, *The Bible as History*, Hodder and Stoughton 1956

Kelsey, D. H., *The Uses of Scripture in Recent Theology*, SCM Press 1975

Loetscher, L., *The Broadening Church: A study of theological issues in the Presbyterian Church since 1869*, University of Pennsylvania Press 1957

Orr, J., *Revelation and Inspiration*, Duckworth 1930

Marty, Martin E., *A Nation of Behavers*, University of Chicago Press 1976

Perlitt, L., *Vatke und Wellhausen*, Töpelmann, Berlin 1965

Preus, R., *The Inspiration of Scripture: a Study of the Theology of the Seventeenth-century Lutheran Dogmaticians*, Oliver and Boyd, 2nd ed. 1957

Reid, J. K. S., *The Authority of Scripture*, Methuen 1957

Richardson, Alan, *The Bible in the Age of Science,* SCM Press 1961

Robinson, John A. T., *Redating the New Testament*, SCM Press 1976
   Can we trust the New Testament?, Mowbray 1977

Sandeen, E. R., *The Roots of Fundamentalism*, Chicago University Press 1970

Semmel, Bernard, *The Methodist Revolution*, Heinemann 1974

Speiser, E. A. M., *Genesis* (The Anchor Bible Vol. 1), Doubleday, NY 1964

Thompson, Thomas L., *The Historicity of the Patriarchal Narratives*, De Gruyter, Berlin 1974

Turretin, F., *Institutio theologiae elencticae*, 3 vols, Utrecht and Amsterdam 1701

Warfield, B. B., *The Inspiration and Authority of the Bible*, Marshall, Morgan and Scott, 2nd ed. 1951

Wellhausen, J., *Grundrisse zum Alten Testament* ed. R. Smend, Chr. Kaiser Verlag, Munich 1965

Wells, D. F., and Woodbridge, J. D., *The Evangelicals: what they believe, who they are, where they are changing*, Abingdon Press, Nashville 1975

Wright, G. E., *God Who Acts*, SCM Press 1952.

Index of Subjects

'Aims and Basis', 24
Alcohol, 26
Allegory, 62, 181–83, 190, 195, 246
American church, see United States
Americanism, 109f.
Angels, 48
Anglicanism, 18, 20, 21, 31, 37, 167, 330
Antichrist, 330f.
Anti-clericalism, 101, 160f.
Anti-Semitism, 286, 351
Apocalyptic, 115, 118, 119, 195
Apocrypha, 79, 128, 239
Aramaic, 58f.
Archaeology, 128, 135, 150f.
Arminianism, 187–89, 303
Art, 122
Ascension, 48ff., 56f.
'Assured results', 'assured findings', 129, 141
Assyriology, 128, 130
Astronomy, 95
Atonement, 12, 16, 24, 25, 27f., 77, 112, 169, 177
Authorized Version, 37, 191, 209–13, 279f., 282, 285

Balfour declaration, 118
Baptism, 31
Baptists, 18, 31, 330f.
Bible as correlate of Christ, 36; as symbol, 36f.
Bible teachers, 42
Biblicism, 6, 102
Biblical theology, 128f., 162, 204, 213–33, 268f.

Calvinism, 18, 110, 113, 161, 175, 187–90, 204, 268, 278, 298, 303
Canon, 79, 296
Capitalism, 110, 111
Celibacy, 99
Charismatic movement, 207
Children and parents, 327
Christadelphians, 7
'Christian philosophy', 276
Christian Unions, 21
Christology, 168–73, 214, 223f.
Chronology, 42f., 44, 45f., 51f, 56, 98, 346
Church, fundamentalist view of, 18f., 30
Church of England, 3, 19, 30, 347, 351
Church of Scotland, 30
Civic religion, 100
'Claims', 60, 70f., 72, 77ff.
Common grace, 113
Communism, 109, 211
Confessions, 22f., 30; and see Westminster Confession
Congregationalists, 30
'Conservative' as term, 5; 'conservative evangelical' as term, 2f.
Conversion, 11f., 17, 28, 33, 35, 38, 320, 339, 340
Co-operation, 18, 310
Creeds, 22f., 30
Cross, 27f., 169
Culture fundamentalism, 103, 321

Daniel, Book of, 98, 158, 236, 238, 292, 325

David and Goliath, 281f., 283, 361
Days, of creation, 40f., 50
Dead Sea Scrolls, 285, 300, 301
Deists, deism, 153, 165f., 185, 241, 247, 253, 271, 278, 315, 353
Deity of Christ, 2, 28, 60, 77f., 169–73, 251, 320
Denominations, fundamentalism and, 18–22, 328ff.
Determinism, 205
Deutero-Isaiah, 158, 202, 236, 238, 292, 304–6, 319, 326, 355
Deuteronomy, 72, 78, 158
Diatessaron, 145
Dictation, 174, 289ff., 292, 298
Didactic emphasis, 76, 262, 289, 348
Dispensationalism, 191–207, 351, 354
'Doctrinal basis', 24
Drinking, *see* Alcohol

Economics, 99
Ecumenical movement, 20, 211, 213, 328–31, 338, 362
Edinburgh University, 220
Egyptology, 128, 130
Emendation of text, 299f.
Emotion, emotionalism, 17f.
Eschatology, 35, 83, 100, 114, 190–207, 330f., 340, 346
'Evangelicals' (in historical sense), 116
'Evangelicals' as term, 11
Evangelical Revivals, 11, 16, 34, 340
Evangelism, 12, 22, 24, 28, 33, 80, 101, 188, 205
Evolution, 90, 92f., 146, 150, 184, 286
Exclusiveness, 14, 318f.
Extremism, 323f., 327

Faith, 11f., 13, 15, 29 *et passim*
Faith healing, 7, 207
Fall of man, 115
Fear, 317, 332
Flood, 43, 94f., 308
Formalization, 175–79, 268f.

Form criticism, 140f., 154ff.
Free Church of Scotland, 18
Fundamentals, The, 2
Fundamentalist organizations, 349

'Gap' theory, 43, 45, 52
Genealogies, 42–47, 50f., 52f., 80
Germany, Germans, 116, 149
Gospel, 11–13, 20, 21, 25ff., 30
Greek Orthodoxy, 182
Group loyalty, 318f.

Harmonization, 46f., 55–71, 83, 198
Heaven, 35, 47f.
Hegelianism, 140–49, 184, 271, 276, 286
Hell, 35, 47f.
Heresy, 102, 169, 172, 182, 196ff., 316
Hermeneutics, 43f., 50f., 197
Historical Jesus, 155
Historical method, 97f.
History, 16
History of religions, 9
Holiness movement, 188
Holy Spirit, 163, 177, 207, 216, 261, 264, 269, 290, 291, 302, 313

Incarnation, 28, 169, 251, 334
Individualism, 318f.
Inerrancy, 1, 37, 40, 45f., 51–56, 57, 72–84, 97, 121, 125, 131, 138, 165, 172, 209, 262
Inspiration, 2, 14, 24, 40, 67, 78f., 84; *and see* Verbal Inspiration
Intellectualism, 18, 131
Intention of writers, 58
Inter-Varsity Fellowship, 21, 345
Isaiah, Book of, 9; *and see* Deutero-Isaiah
Islam, 7, 182
Israel, 192f., 206, 357; *and see* Jews

Jehovah's Witnesses, 7
Jewish conservatism, 284ff.
Jews, 118, 192f., 206f., 357
Jonah, Book of, 73, 75, 80, 81f., 98, 170f.

Judaism, 7, 182
Justification by faith, 321, 353

Kantianism, 272, 274, 275
Kerygma, 77, 348
Keswick Convention, 189
'Kingdom' in dispensationalism, 191–94, 198
King James Version, *see* Authorized Version

Laity, lay emphasis, 33, 35, 100f.
Liberalism, 12, 16, 20, 22, 28, 58, 66, 93, 103, 105, 160, 163, 164, 165, 185, 188, 197, 204, 211–14, 219, 241, 247, 277, 286, 295, 315, 320f., 329, 332, 336, 340f., 344, 349, 359
Literal, literalism, 40–55, 118, 341
Literature, conservative evangelical, 120ff., 304ff.
Lord's prayer, 194
Low church, 100
Lutheranism, 204, 298

Maccabaean date for Psalms, 85, 134ff., 173, 352
Marcan priority, 127, 141f., 306
Martyrdom, 117
Massoretic text, 285, 297
Materialism, 183
Maximal conservatism, 85, 98, 126, 127
Meanings of words, 51; *and see* Semantics
Medicine, 92, 99, 349
Methodism, 4, 18, 20, 30, 330
Military power, 110
Millenarianism, millennialism, 7, 190–207, 256, 330f.
Minority group attitudes, 319
Miracles, 123f., 165, 213, 234–59, 277f., 291, 314, 341, 347
Missions overseas, missionary societies, 21, 33, 34f.
Modernism, *see* Liberalism
Money, 34, 99
Morality, 25, 165f.

Nationalism, 110f., 286

Natural theology, 214f., 220, 271ff.
Negative inspiration, 293
Neo-orthodoxy, 162, 204, 213–33, 268ff., 271, 336, 343
New evangelicals, new conservatives, 222–34, 353
'Nominal' Christianity, 12ff., 16ff., 25, 30, 116, 318

Objectivity, 129, 131f., 310–17, 343
Occult, 206
Office-bearers, 24
Old Testament, authority of, 79ff.
critical use of by New Testament, 81–84
Oral tradition, 156, 294, 351
Ordained ministry, 19, 30
Organizations, fundamentalist, 21–25
Original autographs, 268, 279–84, 294, 295, 298
Orthodoxy, 7, 16, 21, 33, 166, 168f., 188f., 190f., 195, 197, 198, 223f., 291, 298, 345

Papacy, 289
Parables, 48, 50
Pentateuch, pentateuchal criticism, 46, 121, 133, 143–46, 157, 184, 195, 197, 346
Pentecostalism, 7, 207ff.
Perfection, perfectionalism, 189, 276f.
Philosophy, 10, 32f., 84f., 102, 122, 145, 148, 151, 182, 184, 209, 238, 264, 270–79, 315
Pietism, 11f., 188f., 318, 354
'Plain' meaning, 51f., 181
Plenary inspiration, 293
Pluralism, 316f.
Plymouth Brethren, 19, 30, 191
Polity, 19, 31
Prayer, 24, 29, 31ff., 92, 99, 188f., 207
Predestination, 168, 188, 214, 265, 294f.
Prediction, 28, 114, 118, 123f., 194, 234, 253–55, 292, 304, 305f.

Presbyterianism, 20f., 23, 263
Presuppositions, 141, 145, 230f., 234
Priesthood of all believers, 31
Princeton theology, 93f., 187, 224, 261–76, 289f., 303, 353, 354
Progress, 114f., 200
Prohibition, 345
Propaganda, 123, 126, 135

Q document, 66, 127, 141, 142, 154, 348, 352
Qumran, *and see* Dead Sea Scrolls, 135
Qur'an, 7

Rationalism, rationalization, 116, 185, 209, 217, 219, 239ff., 247, 271–74
Reason, rationality, 102, 116f., 130, 167, 177, 179, 220, 271–74, 339
Red Guards, 327
Redaction criticism, 140
Reformation, 16, 20, 57, 115, 168, 182, 290, 330, 340
Reification, 313f.
Religious studies, 122, 307f.
Resurrection, 28, 49, 56, 93, 124, 163, 169, 194, 247
Revelation, 166, 214, 216, 225–31, 273f., 288, 291, 353
Revivals, 17, 104, 161, 340; *and see* Evangelical Revivals
Ritual, ritualism, 37f., 116, 316
Roman Catholicism, 7, 20, 36, 105f., 182, 287, 328f.

Sabbatarianism, 53, 99
Sacraments, 19, 22, 31
Salesmanship, 99, 350
Salvation, 11f., 13, 27, 77, 80, 339
Sanctification, 29, 189
Scholarship, conservative, 31, 120–59
Science, 16, 40, 42f., 90–94, 272f.
Science fiction, 206f.
Scofield Reference Bible, 45, 191–207, 348, 355

Second Advent, 35, 48, 167, 177, 190, 192, 198f.
Sect, sectarianism, 2, 3, 29f., 102, 213, 322, 341f.
Secularism, 90f., 98f., 161, 206, 238
'Selective fundamentalism', 333f.
Semantics, 244, 249f., 298–302
Septuagint, 285, 360f.
Seventh Day Adventists, 7, 53
Sex, 26, 122, 328, 332
Sin, 12, 13, 24, 25, 27, 31, 104, 112f., 114, 164, 177–78, 189, 288, 328
Smoking, 26
Social ethics, 99f., 108–19, 122
Social gospel, 100, 112, 345
Social law, 113
Social studies, 10, 102, 349
Socialism, 108, 111, 350
Son of Man, 69, 83
Source criticism, 130, 140
State, relations of church with, 19, 168
Sunday, 53
Supernatural, 124, 127, 141, 152, 235–59, 277f., 291, 292, 314, 331, 341, 353
Synoptic Gospels, difference between, 58f., 141f., 306, 322

Teaching of Jesus, 28
Tennessee, 90–92
Terminology, American, 6
Textual variation and criticism, 45f., 128, 279–84, 295, 299, 309, 315, 341, 346
Theological education, 19, 102f.
Thirty-Nine Articles, 21, 168
Tongues, speaking with, 7, 207
Tractarians, 351
Tradition, 11, 24, 37, 183, 285
Translations of the Bible, 209–13
Trinity, 16, 24, 163, 166, 170–176, 214, 216, 334
'True Christians', 1, 13, 16ff., 25, 30, 310f.
Truth as correspondence to external reality, 49ff.

Tübingen School, 146, 352

Ugaritic, 128, 300
Unitarianism, 163, 176
United States, 21, 118, 345, 353
church history in, 10, 90f.
Universities and Colleges Christian
Fellowship, 21
Unworldliness, 99

Vagueness in interpretation, 43,
47f., 54, 58–60, 308ff.
Variety within fundamentalism, 23

Verbal inspiration, 286–303, 308
Virgin birth, 2, 28, 47f., 52, 81, 93,
124, 166f., 170, 176ff.
Virgin Mary, 36, 48
Vowel points, Hebrew, 297ff.

Weaker brother, 326f.
Westminster Confession, 21, 168,
261, 270, 284, 294f., 303
Word of God, 214f.

Zionism, 118

Index of Names

Aalders, G. C., 246
Ahlstrom, S., 350
Albright, W. F., 149ff., 353
Allis, O. T.., 356, 363
Anderson, G. W., 307f., 352
Anderson, J. N. D., 160, 257, 258f., 275, 307, 353, 363
Arminius, 188, 354
Athanasius, 16, 168, 169
Augustine, 168

Baillie, John, 218f.
Bainton, Roland, 57, 354
Barclay, O. R., 362, 364
Barnhart, J. E., 350, 366
Barr, James, 366
Barth, Karl, 214f., 218ff., 221, 270, 274, 275
Bartsch, H., 358, 366
Baur, F. C., 352
Beegle, Dewey M., 222, 229, 350, ·356, 364
Bellah, R. N., 366
Berger, Peter L., 362, 366
Blair, Hugh J., 239, 241, 243, 244, 249, 358
Blake, William, 195
Bonhoeffer, D., 117
Briggs, C. A., 357, 359
Bright, John, 150
Bromiley, G. W., 260
Brown, Colin, 275f., 353, 360, 364
Bruce, F. F., 141, 211, 356, 364, 366
Bryan, W. Jennings, 349

Bultmann, R., 104, 140, 164, 165, 219, 235ff., 257f., 358, 366
Burckhardt, Jakob, 149
Burtchaell, J. T., 347, 361

Calvin, John, 135, 173f., 278, 348f., 351
Carlson, C. C., 356
Carlyle, T., 149
Carnell, E. J., 222, 223ff., 345, 347, 357, 358, 359, 362, 364
Carter, Paul A., 350, 366
Castellio, Sebastian, 57, 347
Catherwood, H. R. F., 111, 116f., 120, 350, 351, 364
Chafer, L. S., 355, 364
Clements, R., 361, 366
Cullmann, O., 232

Dahood, M., 300
Darby, J. N., 191f., 195, 355
Davidson, F., 363
De Wit, C., 364
Dodd, C. H., 307
Dooyeweerd, Herman, 276, 360, 366
Douglas, J. D., 363
Dowey, E. A., 354, 366
Dryden, John, 131, 351

Ebeling, G., 354
Eissfeldt, O., 352
Ellison, H. L., 281, 346, 358, 364
Engnell, I., 125ff.
Erdman, Charles R., 350f.
Erickson, Millard, 187, 346, 354, 366

Fife, E. S., 364
Finney, C. G., 350
France, R. T., 348
Francis of Assisi, 16

Gaebelein, A. C., 355, 364
Glasser, A. F., 364
Glock, C. Y., 366
Graham, Billy, 48, 99, 109, 188, 345, 350
Green, Michael (E. M. B.), 126f., 129, 141, 142, 167, 346, 347, 351, 353, 360, 361, 364
Griffiths, Michael, 364
Gunner, R. A. H., 250
Guthrie, Donald, 140f., 142, 143, 352, 363, 364

Haas, W., 361, 366
Hallesby, O., 364
Hanson, Anthony, 307
Harnack, Adolf, 165, 353
Harrison, R. K., 131, 140f., 142, 145, 148, 149, 238, 253, 305, 332, 352, 353, 354, 359, 363
Hawthorne, J. N., 364
Hebert, Gabriel, 350, 366
Hegel, G. W. F., 148, 149, 184
Henry, Carl, 26, 222, 223, 345, 364
Heppe, H., 361, 366
Hodge, A. A., 93, 261, 271, 278, 303, 354, 359
Hodge, Charles, 93, 174, 226f., 228, 261ff., 271ff., 276, 278, 282, 290, 293, 294, 303, 348, 354, 357, 358, 359, 360, 361, 367
Hollenweger, W. J., 356, 362, 367
Holmes, Arthur F., 364
Hooykaas, R., 364
Hordern, W., 222, 279, 357, 360, 367
Hort, Greta, 358
Howkins, K. G., 307, 364
Hutter, Jacob, 290, 361
Huxley, T. H., 347
Huxtable, J., 73f., 347f., 350, 367

Jeeves, M. A., 349
Jenni, E., 359

Johnson, Douglas, 142, 352, 361, 364
Jones, Bob, 187
Jones, Hywel R., 239, 358
Jorstad, Erling, 351, 367

Kant, I., 275f., 350
Kantzer, K. S., 229, 357
Keller, Ernst and Marie-Luise, 358, 367
Keller, Werner, 139, 367
Kelsey, D. H. 357, 367
Kevan, E. F., 41, 42, 44, 346, 350
Kidner, D., 346, 364
Kierkegaard, S., 350
Kik, J. M., 348
Kitchen, K. A., 46, 130, 131f., 143, 145, 147, 148, 221, 241ff., 300, 301, 332, 346, 352, 354, 357, 358, 361, 364
Kline, Meredith G., 41, 44, 346
Kuenen, A., 122, 351

Ladd, G. E., 196, 222, 229ff., 258f., 353, 354, 357, 358, 359
LaSor, W. S., 46, 346, 358
Liddon, H. P., 347
Lindsey, Hal, 206, 356, 362, 365
Lloyd-Jones, D. Martyn, 362, 365
Loetscher, L., 165, 353, 367
Luckmann, T., 362, 366
Luther, Martin, 173, 354

Machen, J. Gresham, 165, 187, 353, 365
McIntyre, Carl, 187
Macleod, A. J., 296
Mahan, Asa, 350
Manley, G. T., 203, 206, 355, 356, 363, 365
Marshall, I. H., 57, 365
Martin, R. P., 365
Marty, Martin E., 345, 351, 367
Meignan, Guillaume, 68
Mickelsen, A. Berkeley, 222
Moody, D. L., 345
Morris, Leon, 296, 365
Murtonen, A., 346

Neill, S. C., 307f.
Newton, B. W., 191
Neibuhr, H. Richard, 90f.
Nixon, R. E., 245f., 248
Noth, Martin, 125f., 150

Oesterley, W. O. E., 146
Orr, James, 224, 269f., 284, 294, 359, 367
Origen, 181
Osiander, Andreas, 57

Packer, J. I., 82f., 171f., 226ff., 290, 346, 347, 348, 353, 357, 360, 361
Pannenberg, W., 307
Pascal, B., 350
Payne, D. F., 365
Pedersen, J., 125f.
Perlitt, Lothar, 149, 352, 367
Piper, Otto, 230, 232
Preus, R., 361, 367
Ptolemy, 173
Pusey, E. B., 127, 351

Quenstedt, J. A., 290, 361

Rad, G. von, 232
Ramm, Bernard, 92, 94ff., 244ff., 276, 308, 317, 346, 349, 350, 352, 358, 360, 362, 365
Reid, J. K. S., 290, 361, 367
Richardson, A., 173, 307f., 346, 350, 360ff., 367
Ridderbos, N. H., 305f., 326
Ritschl, A., 164
Robinson, D. W. B., 358
Robinson, John A. T., 157f., 334, 349, 359, 362, 367
Robinson, T. H., 146
Rookmaaker, H. R., 365
Rowdon, H. H., 351
Rowley, H. H., 307f.
Ruoff, P.O., 365

Sanday, W., 348
Sandeen, E. R., 91, 99, 274, 348, 349, 354f., 360, 366
Schaeffer, Francis, 276, 365
Schechter, S., 361

Schleiermacher, F. D. E., 164
Scofield, C. I., 45, 191f., 194f., 202, 348, 355
Scopes, J. T., 349
Scorer, C. G., 365
Semmel, Bernard, 354, 367
Shaftesbury, Earl of, 116
Short, A. Rendle, 365
Smend, Rudolf, 149, 352
Smith, Henry Preserved, 224f., 309, 357, 359
Smith, W. Robertson, 359
Speiser, E. A., 136, 137ff., 352, 367
Stevick, Daniel, 345
Stibbs, A. M., 365
Stott, J. R. W., 365
Swift, C. E. Graham, 56, 74, 141, 251, 297

Tasker, R. V. G., 365
Tatian, 352
Tenney, M. C., 357
Thompson, J. A., 41, 92, 235f., 250
Thompson, Thomas L., 352, 367
Til, Cornelius van, 220, 276, 365
Tillich, Paul, 164
Torrance, J. B., 365
Torrance, T. F., 307f.
Turretin, F., 175, 367

Ussher, Archbishop, 94

Vatke, Wilhelm, 146, 149, 352

Warfield, B. B., 93, 171f., 224, 261ff., 270, 271, 276, 278, 280f., 283f., 288, 290, 292, 294, 295, 298, 301, 302, 303, 309, 349, 354, 357, 359, 360, 361, 367
Wellhausen, J., 104, 121, 125f., 127, 140f., 145ff., 221, 271, 351, 352, 367
Wells, D. F., 350, 367
Wenham, J. W., 76, 79, 82f., 98, 348, 350
Wesley, John, 188, 345, 354
Wette, W. M. L. de, 121, 351
Whitefield, George, 188, 345, 354
Wilberforce, William, 116, 345

Woodbridge, J. D., 350, 367
Wright, G. E., 232, 357, 367
Wright, J. Stafford, 346, 366

Young, E. J., 59ff., 196, 238, 250,
   281, 304, 346, 354, 357, 360,
   362, 366

Zinzendorf, Count von, 354

Index of Biblical References

Genesis
1   45, 92
1.1   45
1.3   45
1.14–18   45
4.18   44
5   43, 52, 53
7.21–23   96
11.10–32   43
12.10–20   136
17.25   47, 56
20   136
21.14, 15   47, 56
26.6–16   136

Exodus
2   45
6.16ff.   45
12.40   45, 52
20.12   297

Numbers
1.46   212, 249
36.13   144

Deuteronomy
1.1   144
34   256

Joshua
3.13–17   239
10.12f.   213
10.12–15   243
10.13–14   243

I Samuel
17   281

II Samuel
8.4   309

10.6   309
10.18   281, 310
21.19   281, 282
24.9   310
24.24   310

I Kings
4.26   310
6.1   46, 52
7.26   310
13   292
13.2   355

II Kings
6.1–7   239
23.15f.   355
24.6   255

I Chronicles
18.4   309
19.7   309
19.18   281, 310
20.5   281
21.5   310
21.25   310

II Chronicles
4.5   310
9.25   310
14.9   281
36.8   359

Psalms
74   135
79   135
110   73, 74, 75,
            76, 85, 88,
            124, 170,
            171, 350

Isaiah
40–66   202, 292
45.1   292

Jeremiah
22.18–19   255
36.29–31   255
49.4   300

Ezekiel
26.7–14   255
29.17–20   255
38.2   331, 355
38–39   190, 201

Daniel
9   196
9.24–27   354
12.11   73

Amos
9.11   355

Jonah
2   247

II Maccabees
3.25–28   258

Matthew
3.2   195
3.5   96
5.17–20   83
6.33   195
12.40   73
13.11   194, 195
14.25   248
16.18   194
19.16ff.   58
21.10–17   56

21.12–17	355
24.14	36
24.15	73
24.29	83
24.34	83

Mark

1.15	348
5.39	251
10.17f.	58
11.15–19	56
12.35	73
12.35–37	74
12.30	83
16.9–20	297

Luke

11.1–13	355
18.18ff.	58
19.45–48	56
21.32	83
24.51	56

John

2.13–17	56
2.13–25	355

4.39	96
8.1–11	296
8.58	70

Acts

1	56
1.7	84, 199
5.39	270
15.13–18	355
15.14	355

Romans

1.4	70
11.5	355

I Corinthians

8	326
8.11	326
8.13	326
15.52	194

Galatians

2.11	178

Colossians

2.8	271

I Thessalonians

4.17	192

II Timothy

3.16	67, 78, 79, 85

Titus

2.13	170

Hebrews

8.8	194

II Peter

1.19–21	67
1.20	78, 79
1.20–21	85

I John

5.17	296

Revelation

19.17	355
19.19	355
20.8	190